27f

SCOTLAND'S
WINTER
MOUNTAINS

SCOTLAND'S WINTER MOUNTAINS

THE CHALLENGE AND THE SKILLS

MARTIN MORAN

DAVID & CHARLES

PREFACE

Though it is the middle of April, north and east winds have been blowing across the Highlands for almost a fortnight. Spring has arrived in the glens, but the hills are snowy and frosted above their lower slopes. I am soaking up the early morning sunshine on a wooded ridge above Torlundy, but across Glen Mor the north face of Ben Nevis stands detached in icy splendour, its summit rim shivering in an armour of rime ice. Sheer white streaks of ice can be spied tumbling from Hadrian's Wall and Point Five Gully, and the ski fields of Aonach Mor are once more whitened after a winter of rain and mist.

Up there yesterday on the summit plateau the snow was coated in feathery hoar crystals and the air was sharp and icy – and yet the sun shone with kindly warmth. In every direction the views were stunning, from the snaking trench of Loch Eil, round the massed ranks of the West Highland ridges, over the lonely plateau of the Monadhliath and Creag Meagaidh, through the forested gap of Laggan to the snow-sheathed Cairngorms and down across the sparkling lochs of Rannoch to the unmistakable cone of Schiehallion and a hazy backcloth of Perthshire hills. Once more I was converted. Few, if any, mountain expanses could rival these winter Highlands in spacious scale and lonely beauty, and surely no pastime could be finer than to roam across their icy ridges.

This revision of *Scotland's Winter Mountains* comes ten years after its first appearance. It has been a decade in which the climate has changed somewhat to the detriment of winter mountain sports, and we have often seen our winter climbing ambitions frustrated by fickle conditions. Much adverse publicity has also been devoted to the darker side of winter mountaineering: the accidents, the avalanches and the tragic loss of lives – to those of us who have climbed through it, the scene might well seem more sombre and less inspiring than once it was.

And yet, standing here in the cool morning air and seeing it all afresh, nothing has really changed at all. To innocent eyes the winter mountains are every bit as magnificent and entrancing as they have been to each new generation of climbers through the past century. They are a joy to behold and a thrill to climb. They stand as a yardstick of permanence to which we can reconcile our own transient lives and in which we can find our peace, whether young and ambitious or old and reflective.

If *Scotland's Winter Mountains* has established a rapport with the mountaineering readership, it is because it was written in celebration of these emotions and the deeds they inspire, as well as to inform and instruct. In this new edition I have retained the basic split in format between 'the challenge' and 'the skills'. The bare bones of some chapters remain unchanged, and a few anecdotes were too precious to replace, but I have added many new narratives, new points of view, new photographs and a thorough update on history and techniques. A new chapter devoted to 'avalanche awareness' is a recognition of the growing incidence of avalanche accidents and of the new research and monitoring of the avalanche phenomenon in Scotland.

I hope that the new edition will help to inspire and inform a whole new generation of winter mountaineers. Whatever the fickle whims of our climate, the sport continues to grow in appeal and popularity, and although moulded by a century of pioneering endeavour, the future of Scottish winter mountaineering is firmly in the hands of those who play the game today. Might this book keep the winter spirit burning into the new millennium.

MARTIN MORAN · April 1998

Page 2 *Spring gully climbing in Torridon: the exit of Access Gully, Fuar Tholl (Climber: Mike Arkley)*
Pages 6–7 *Traversing the upper section of the Forcan Ridge of The Saddle*

ACKNOWLEDGEMENTS

Without wide-ranging contributions, advice and reviews from many experts I should not have dared produce this new edition. To all who have helped I express my thanks. In particular I am indebted for the text contributions of Andy Nisbet (Chapter 12), Andy Cunningham, Jonathan Preston and Alan Hunt (Chapter 13) and Jim Barton (Appendix IV); and for the technical assistance, review and opinions of: Brian Davison and Richard Tabony (Chapter 1), Marjory Roy (Chapter 2), Blyth Wright (Chapters 3 and 8), Rab Anderson, Mark Garthwaite and Simon Richardson (Chapter 12). I also wish to record my thanks to all who have submitted the pictures for the book, in particular the assistance of Graeme Hunter with SMC archive photos. The photos tell as much as words just how splendid Scotland's mountains can be in winter. The contributions made by many others to the first edition provide an essential foundation to this revision, in particular Ric Singerton for his maps and diagrams, and Bob Barton, Bill Brooker, Helen Charlton, Sam Crymble, Gordon Davison, Mick Fowler, Eric Langmuir, Hamish MacInnes, Jimmy Marshall, the late Bill Murray, Clarrie Pashley, Derek Pyper, and Tom Weir.

A DAVID & CHARLES BOOK

First published in the UK in 1988
Second edition published 1992
Reprinted 1994
This completely revised and updated edition published 1998

Book design and typesetting by Les Dominey Design Company, Exeter
and printed in Italy by New Interlitho SpA for David & Charles
Brunel House   Newton Abbot   Devon

CONTENTS

Pages 10–11 *Coire Ardair and the Post Face of Creag Meagaidh*

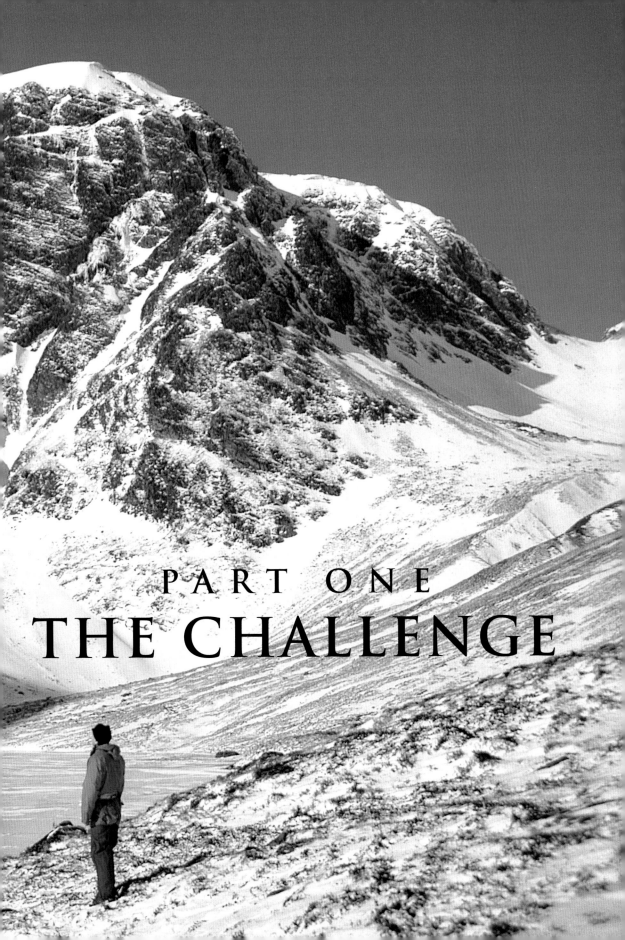

PART ONE
THE CHALLENGE

1: OUR WINTER MOUNTAIN CLIMATE

PAST HISTORY, PRESENT PATTERNS AND FUTURE TRENDS

THE GLACIAL HERITAGE

The Scottish mountain winter is unique in Britain's natural environment. The Highland winter harbours the last existing remnants of sub-arctic conditions in our temperate and maritime climatic regime: in their winter raiment of snow the mountains are projected in our imaginations a little closer to the glacial past, to the epochs when they were besieged by ice-cap and glacier.

To envisage the Highlands massif at the height of the last major ice advance just twenty thousand years ago is to dream of vast and silent snowfields spanning the high plateaux, with only the higher peaks of the Cairngorms poking through; to transform the western glens into ice-choked chasms tumbling off the heights in gigantic seracs and breaking into bergs over the Hebridean seas; to fill the eastern straths with the broad slicks of gently flowing glaciers; to stand in the sea-filled trenches of Lochs Nevis and Hourn and conceive of a 900m thickness of ice churning and grinding overhead; and to clasp the high corries in perpetual frost and a sheath of everlasting snow.

But of course the mountains were not simply smothered by the ice. Their present variety, complexity, and all the more dramatic features of their profiles were in the very process of being created as the moving ice carved and sculpted its pathways, and without its work, our modern scenic legacy would be much the poorer: the Highlands would comprise a series of plateaux, long-forgotten relics from the Caledonian era of mountain-building, their summits a rolling sweep of dip and swell, and their sides dissected gently and predictably into pleasing vales. So it is to the Ice Ages that we owe the thrill of the saw-toothed Cuillin peaks, the sudden brink of the Cairngorm corrie, the loch-strewn chaos of Fisherfield and the sheer, smoothed cliffs of Ben Nevis and Glencoe. And it is back towards the Ice Age that the winter experience entices the mountaineer.

From their peak, Scotland's glaciers ebbed and eventually disappeared. Geoff Dutton conjectured as to the time and place of their final demise:

'Our glaciers have gone. The last sulking remnants of the mighty Laggan-Spey glacier died out somewhere above the CIC Hut on a warm September afternoon 9,000 years ago. The half-hardy perennial drifts flowering occasionally since then are no substitute. Our corries are silent and empty; their meltwaters dried and vanished'.[1]

However, the retreat was by no means uninterrupted. There were two resurgences of ice before that fatal September afternoon on Ben Nevis, the second being the Lomond readvance of around ten thousand years ago (Fig 1.1). In this Lomond phase, the ice was largely confined to the corries, where it pulled and plucked the cliffs into their present delineation and scooped out their hollows and lips, which now hang high above the deeper glens; only in the major basins were there still confluent glacier systems. This was the period when great meltwater lakes such as those of Glen Roy were shored up inside valleys by more powerful main valley glaciers.

An overall rise in mean winter temperature of some 10–12 degrees C has accompanied Britain's emergence from the Ice Age. However, it is not correct to imagine that the climate has continued a progressive warming since the glaciers vanished. The post-glacial maximum of world temperature is thought to have been reached around six thousand years ago, when temperatures were 2–3 degrees C higher than those of today. Since then there has been an overall cooling, although several climatic cycles have been identified at intervals of 2,000, 200 and 100 years, with temperature amplitudes between 0.5 and 2.0 degrees C. For example, we know that a warmer world climate from the twelfth to the fourteenth centuries allowed the Vikings to colonise Greenland. Winter snow-cover has by no means been a permanent feature on Scotland's mountains since the Ice Age.

Longer-term climatic cycles have also been identified and correlated to fluctuations in the earth's orbit around the sun and to other gravitational pulls. Croatian meteorologist Milutin Milankovitch established cycles with 413-, 100-, 41-, 23- and 19-thousand year periodicity, which are strongly linked to the onset of Ice Ages. Projecting these astronomical theories forwards on a timespan of several millenia, the predicted future trend is one of renewed cooling towards another Ice Age, with the possibility of glacier revival in the Highlands 5,000 or 16,000 years from now.

Whilst such long-term conjectures are

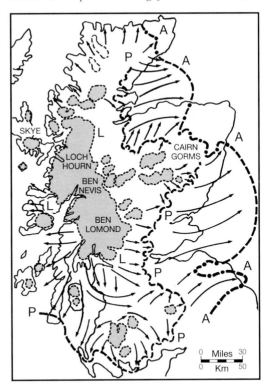

Fig 1.1 *Successive limits of the last ice sheet in Scotland, with probable dating (from Sissons 1967)*[2]

A – – – – A *Aberdeen–Lammermuir readvance (possibly equates to the maximal extent c20,000 years ago)*

P – – – – P *Perth readvance (c13,000 years ago)*

L ⌐ ⌐ ⌐ L *Lomond readvance (10,000–11,000 years ago)*

————→ *Direction of ice movement*

undoubtedly interesting, they dwarf the timescale of human interest and do not address our current concerns as to the health and longevity of snow and ice conditions on the Scottish mountains. Rather, it is upon the short-term patterns of climate and weather that the sport of winter mountaineering depends, on the cycles and shifts in temperature and the precipitation of a few years or decades in duration. Hence our particular interest in sunspot cycles, the positioning of the great ocean currents, and the reality of the greenhouse effect. Our sport is little over a century old – will it still be played a century from now?

THE LITTLE ICE AGE

The last mini-climatic recession in modern history was the 'Little Ice Age' between 1550 and 1850. At its height in the seventeenth century, observational evidence suggests that temperatures in Scotland might have been as much as 2 degrees C below their present level.

There were extensive permanent snow-fields on the mountains. In 1770, Thomas Pennant noted perennial snow on Ben Wyvis, north of Inverness, which at 1,046m is considerably lower in altitude than the higher haunts of the Cairngorm corries, which themselves were observed as holding sizeable summer snowfields by several eighteenth-century travellers. So perhaps there was less exaggeration than might be thought in the comment of an eighteenth-century English army officer quartered in the Highlands who wrote to a friend in London bemoaning that: 'as for the climate, there are nine months of winter, three months of spring and there is no summer at all.'

It is, however, open to debate whether these snows were sufficient to compact into ice and form glaciers. A 2 degrees C diminution in average temperature is theoretically sufficient to sustain glaciers in Scotland, and David Sugden's work on lichen-dating on the moraine debris in the Garbh Choire of Braeriach has suggested that a tiny ephemeral corrie glacier may have subsisted there as late as 1810. He also found similar evidence for six other glacier sites in the Cairngorms at around 1740. However, thermometer readings for central England for the seventeenth to eighteenth centuries averaged only 0.5–1.0 degrees C below today's levels; how, then, could Scotland's temperatures have been so much lower during these centuries? Certainly, Gordon Manley was sceptical that glaciers could have existed so recently: *'Undoubtedly there were groups of cool years in the 17th, 18th and early 19th centuries...but their duration appears insufficient to lead to revival in Scotland.'*[3]

Current climatic trends must be viewed in the context of the Little Ice Age. The present phase of global warming undoubtedly commenced as a natural cyclical rebound from the depressed temperatures of the seventeenth and eighteenth centuries. Although evidence for accelerated warming in recent years due to a 'greenhouse effect' induced by Man is now persuasive, we must see it as an enhancement of a natural warming trend rather than some sudden shift out of a stable climatic pattern.

THE LINGERING SNOWS

Today, Scotland harbours semi-permanent snowbeds in the highest nooks of the Cairngorms and Ben Nevis. These are best viewed as lingering relics of the Little Ice Age – although those of romantic disposition might like to imagine them as harbingers of the next glaciation. Certainly these dirty patches of near-perennial snow are conspicuous indicators of climatic change and thus have aroused a volume of research and emotion out of all proportion to their extent or scenic significance.

The existence of perennial snow is one of the defining characteristics of the sub-arctic climate which in Britain is now confined to Scotland's higher mountain summits, and particularly the Cairngorms whose altitude of 1,200m and inland location create a climatic environment as close to that of the tundra of northern Scandinavia as is found anywhere in Western Europe. The Cairngorm winter is the hardest and most prolonged of any region of the Highlands, and hence there is the greatest likelihood that snowfields will persist in the shaded recesses of their high corries. Since 1933 the snowfield at the head of Garbh Choire Mor on Braeriach (Plates 1.1 and 1.2) has disappeared in only three years: 1933,

Plates 1.1 and 1.2 *Haunt of the permanent snows – Garbh Choire Mor, Braeriach in winter (Brian Findlay), and on 1 October 1984 with sizeable perennial drifts (Andrew Nisbet)*

1959 and 1996; and the top 300m of Ben Nevis harbours the only comparable climate for snow-patch survival in Britain.

So what determines whether winter's snows will linger through the spring, summer and autumn seasons? Survival depends on the annual balance between the accumulation and melting (ablation) of snowpacks. Snowfall volume and low temperatures are obviously important, but do not by themselves guarantee persistence, and wind-packing and avalanche accumulation have an equal influence upon the depth and hardness of the snowpack that emerges from the winter season. Indeed, it is arguable that the beds in Observatory Gully of Ben Nevis are not true snowfields, being largely comprised of avalanche fallout, and that only the high open snows of the Cairngorms derive from pure snowfall.

The rate of snowpack lowering through the summer months on the Ben Macdui drifts was estimated by D. L. Champion as 1cm per day for each degree above freezing point of the day-time temperature. However, Gordon Manley's work on the Nevis beds concluded that there is no necessary relation between absolute temperature and snowpack persistence, the abnormally warm summers of both 1955 and 1960, for instance, failing to melt the snows; and the influences of air humidity, wind, the daily freeze-thaw cycle and the amount of direct sunlight must all be considered as well. But there is a general concurrence that two circumstances are crucial to the longevity of the snows: substantial fresh snowfalls are needed in March and April, any volumes during the early winter being of lesser significance; and the prevailing temperatures of September and October must be relatively cool to prevent rapid further shrinkage when the fields are already small in extent and vulnerable to both ground and air warmth.

Undoubtedly these tiny remnants of each past winter will continue to be watched with close interest; and meanwhile we may kindle the fond hope that, within our lifetime, they will suddenly burgeon in size to spawn the nascent glaciers of the future.

MOUNTAIN-TOP WEATHER STATIONS

Knowledge of the winter conditions on the Scottish summits derives partly from the personal experiences of mountaineers, but more importantly from the records of mountain meteorological stations. We are lucky in Scotland to have the legacy of twenty years of complete weather records from the Ben Nevis summit observatory which operated from October 1883 to October 1904. Given the great cost and the enormous physical difficulties of taking weather readings throughout the year at an altitude of 1,344m, the observatory was a remarkable accomplishment, a monument to Victorian philanthropy and scientific zeal, and its data forms the most comprehensive British record of all weather elements in such an environment.

The observatory scheme was instigated by the Scottish Meteorological Society, but its building cost of £5,000 was funded by public appeal, as was the larger part of its annual maintenance of £1,000. Constructed and operational within a year of its conception, the observatory was manned continuously, in winter its staff having to endure both isolation and privation as their quarters were pounded by the weather. This was Man's first-ever prolonged experience of the hostility of winter on the Scottish summits. One of the observers, W. T. Kilgour, remembered the storm of 22 November 1898 as the most gruelling of all, a wind of over 160kmph coupled with a driving blizzard. Despite barring every door and window '…fully a ton of snow sifted inside into

Fig 1.2 *Scotland's semi-permanent snowfields*

Details compiled for those locations which have been specifically studied or observed. Other semi-perennial sites are likely to exist in the high Cairngorms.

Location	Altitude	Aspect	Reliability
Ben Nevis Observatory Gully, below apex of Tower and Gardyloo Gullies	1,160m	NE	'Snow Book' in CIC Hut maintained from 1933 to 1970 reported its disappearance in 10 out of 38 years; the largest most persistent bed on Nevis.
Observatory Gully, under Observatory Buttress.	1,080m	NNE	Unlikely to survive after early September.
Observatory Gully, foot of Point Five Gully beside Rubicon Wall.	1,050m	NE	Unlikely to survive after early September.
Gullies Nos 2-5, Coire na Ciste	980–1,100m	NE	Persistence noted only in abnormally cool or snowy years.
Aonach Mor (Lochaber) Under summit on E cliffs	1,190m	E	Not closely observed, but occasional survival has been noted.
Braeriach (Cairngorms) Garbh Choire Mor, under Sphinx Ridge	1,075m	NE	'Never known to wholly disappear' – Seton Gordon, 1912. Between 1933 and 1997 it failed to survive in only three years – 1933, 1959 and 1996. The most likely spot in Britain for glacier regeneration.
Ben Macdui Garbh Uisge, ½ km NE of summit; known as the 'snowy corrie'	c1,150m	NNE	A true open snowfield rather than a gully bed and therefore exposed to summer sunshine. Not observed over a long period but known to survive through many years.
Feith Buidhe, 2km N of summit	1,080m	E	Easterly aspect and lower altitude makes survival less likely.
Cairn Gorm Ciste Mhearaidh, 1km NE of summit	1,080m	E	Open aspect; persists only in exceptional years.

the lobby and passages. The average indoor temperature fell to −3 degrees C, and just two metres away from the kitchen fire the thermometer could struggle no higher than −1 degrees C.'[4] The severity of the conditions outside can be left to the imagination.

Taking readings in bad weather exposed the staff to considerable danger as well as hardship, for the cliffs of Nevis's north face were only yards away. At the height of one February gale John Begg noted: 'At 4pm the notebook for the observation was torn in two and blown away. At 6, 7 and 8pm the observers went out at the tower door on a long rope, and had to be hauled back.'[5] The observatory was finally closed through lack of funds.

From 1905 to 1978 mountain-weather statistics are highly fragmentary, and such records as were obtained are owed to the dedicated work of a few individuals. Most notably, a small station was sited close to the summit of Ben Macdui by Pat Baird during 1956. Over 182kg of instruments and equipment were man-hauled to the site and erected during that most hostile period of late December and January. Thereafter, weekly visits, mostly by Baird himself, were made to recalibrate the graphs, rewind clocks, re-ink pens and measure snow-depth changes. In winter these stints were a prolonged battle against the cold. Baird remembered one particular occasion when '...*determined to have warm feet while standing for eight hours on site, I foolishly went up in felt-lined sealskin boots. On the gentle hard snowslope covering the Etchachan path I could get no grip, and while carrying a delicate instrument couldn't afford to slip. I was forced to cut steps with a snow shovel, but fortunately no other climber was around to witness this feat.*'[6]

On 23 March he found the anemometer encased in a solid pillar of ice 2.4m high, with a rime crystal nearly 1.2m in length growing out from the windward side of the screen. Truly, keeping a station running in these conditions required as strong a love for the mountains as for the cause of science.

Modern technology has overcome the need for such heroics. Since March 1977, an automatic weather station (AWS) has operated on the summit of Cairn Gorm at an altitude of 1,245m. Automatic operation is enabled by the housing of the sensors and instruments within a thermostatically heated unit, from which they are deployed outside at half-hourly intervals to sample the weather. This prevents icing up and avoids wind damage. Readings are broadcast direct via VHF transmission so that visits to the station are required only once every six weeks for routine maintenance. With on-line computer links, the current data from Cairn Gorm can be viewed on the internet (see Appendix V).

The Meteorological Office has two automatic mountain-weather stations which provide similar data, one at 1,150m on Aonach Mor at the head of the ski-lifts (Plate 1.3) and the other

on the summit of The Cairnwell at 933m above Glen Shee. The data from the Met Office stations is only available to authorised users.

However, the Cairn Gorm AWS has malfunctioned during several winter seasons, and even when running continuously, the reliability of some of its readings is questionable; furthermore, it measures only temperatures, windspeed and wind direction. The consistent recording of precipitation is not feasible in such a windy location and would require the continual exposure of instruments. Nevertheless, we now have a solid volume of summarised data for Cairn Gorm for the winters 1978–79 to 1987–88, and from 1990 to 1994–95. This, together with the Ben Nevis archives, offers an objective picture of winter mountain weather from day to day through the season, and of the general climate of the winter mountain tops.

THE WINTER MOUNTAIN CLIMATE

Temperatures

The November to March average and record minimum temperatures for the Ben Nevis and Cairn Gorm stations are as follows:

Ben Nevis (1884 to1903)
Average −3.8 degrees C
Record Minimum −17.4 degrees C,
6 Jan 1894

Cairn Gorm (1978–9 to 1986–7)
Average −3.0 degrees C
Record Minimum −16.5 degrees C,
12 Jan 1987

Cairn Gorm (1989/90 to 1994/5)*
Average −2.0 degrees C
Record Minimum −12.2 degrees C, 17 Jan 1994

* The 1989/90–1994/95 series is not complete: only twenty months out of twenty-eight with complete or >75 per cent readings are included.

Plate 1.3 *The automatic weather station on Aonach Mor in full winter garb (Jonathan Preston)*

While −3 degrees C is sufficiently low to present a risk of frostbite, and at −10 degrees C bare skin will stick to a metal surface, these figures are not inhuman by worldwide standards: for example, −20 degrees C is a normal winter temperature on the high Alps or the Scandinavian tundra plateaux.

Between 1978–9 and 1986–87 the average winter temperature on Cairn Gorm varied between −1.8 degrees C and −3.6 degrees C, a relatively small range. However, the coldest and warmest days recorded over this ten-year period were −15.9 degrees C and +9.7 degrees C respectively, a huge range of 25.6 degrees. Within what seems a consistent annual average there are massive swings from day to day and month to month.

Wind

The figures for summit windspeeds are considerably more impressive than those for temperature. For the Cairn Gorm AWS the average winter windspeeds (November–March) over two base periods have been:

1978–9 to 1987–8:	56kmph
1990–1994/5*	62kmph

* Only nineteen out of twenty-eight months with complete or >75 per cent readings are included.

Now, 56kmph is a healthy force 7 on the Beaufort scale, and this is 70 per cent higher than at an exposed coastal sea-level site such as Tiree where the average winter windspeed is 33kmph.

The windiest winter month in the Cairn Gorm series from 1978–9 to 1987–88 was January 1983, which sustained a remarkable average of 88kmph in an unbroken sequence of westerly gales; the wind only dropped below 40kmph for a few hours in the month, and gale-force winds (ie above 62kmph) occurred on every day. The second windiest day on Cairn Gorm in the period was 20 March 1986, with an incredible twenty-four-hour average of 145kmph; during that day the highest single gust was 275kmph. The all-time record gust to date on Cairn Gorm was a south-westerly blast of 282kmph which was recorded at 11.48hrs on 3 January 1993 – at which time my diary records that I was crawling up 494m Sgurr na Stri on Skye!

In every winter there are days with wind gusts in excess of 160kmph. Considering that mountaineers regard 120kmph as the threshold of windspeed where standing upright is no longer possible, these statistics indicate the remarkable severity of winter winds on the summits.

There is a temptation to focus only on the extremes of weather on the summits, and there are in fact many periods of settled weather when winds fall light. Nevertheless, these serve to emphasise the strength of the elements during a stormy phase of weather. In this regard it should be noted that there are on average about 100 days out of the 151-day November–March period on Cairn Gorm on which the wind reaches gale force 8 (62kmph) or above. And of course, when combined with air temperatures at or below freezing point, such winds create extreme conditions for the mountaineer, where success is measured only by survival.

Precipitation

The Ben Nevis data for precipitation (Fig 1.3) shows that the average monthly precipitation at the summit in the December to March winter period from 1885–1903 was 41.5cm, which is 22 per cent above the annual average of 34cm per month. By contrast, the average monthly precipitation over the same approximate period down in Fort William just 8km away was less than half of that on top of the Ben. December and January were the 'wettest' of the winter months over that period, and

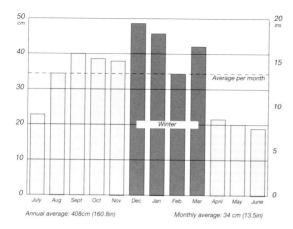

50 cm — 20 ins

Average per month

Winter

July Aug Sept Oct Nov Dec Jan Feb Mar April May June

Annual average: 408cm (160.8in) Monthly average: 34 cm (13.5in)

Fig 1.3 Ben Nevis summit (1,344m): average monthly precipitation totals 1885–1903
From the observatory records, Kilgour 1905

indeed were the wettest months of the year. February's precipitation was significantly lower, being close to the monthly average. This monthly distribution would not be so skewed were records available for the last ten years since 1988, when February and March precipitation totals have exceeded those for December and January.

What really interests the winter mountaineer is less the overall volume of winter precipitation, but rather the proportion of it which falls as snow. This was recorded by the observatory staff between 1895 and 1904, and is summarised in Fig 1.4. An average of 75 per cent of precipitation between December and March fell as snow. However, continuous wind action, coupled with periods of thaw and occasional rainfall, ensure that such a volume of snow does not accumulate at summit level.

To summarise, three features characterise the mountain-top winter climate:

1 Temperatures which average at or a little below freezing point, but which have an enormous range from arctic to mild temperate values.

2 Extreme windiness for mountains of such low altitude, with a prevalence of gales and

regular storms in excess of 100kmph.

3 High volumes of precipitation, with a high proportion of it – but by no means all – coming in the form of snow.

WHAT AND WHEN IS THE WINTER SEASON?

While the 'calendar winter' is strictly defined as falling between the 21 December solstice and the 21 March equinox, the 'mountain winter' falls into no convenient mould. To many hillgoers, winter is the period during which a snow- and ice-cover will be encountered during the greater part of a mountain excursion, and it is patently true that the calendar and mountain winters rarely coincide. Remarkable and frustrating mild spells can intervene at any time within the calendar span, as in February 1998 when virtually every scrap of snow was wiped off the hills by a week of torrential rain and temperatures in excess of 10 degrees C. Yet there is an equal probability that full snow and ice conditions will suddenly develop outside the calendar season. I have climbed Tower Ridge on Ben Nevis as a pristine flute of fresh-fallen snow

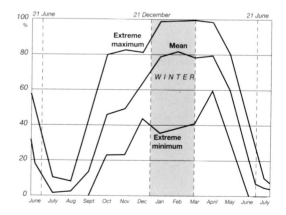

100 % 21 June   21 December   21 June

Extreme maximum   Mean

80

WINTER

60

40

Extreme minimum

20

0

June July Aug Sept Oct Nov Dec Jan Feb Mar April May June July

Fig 1.4 Ben Nevis summit (1,344m): percentage of precipitation falling as snow 1895–1904
From the observatory records as summarised by A.S. Thom, 1974 (Extreme maxima and minima are the individual months with the highest and lowest percentages within the nine-year period of observation)

metre long icicles. Although a true winter climb in September is but a freak, a sustained spell of snow and ice conditions can be anticipated with certainty at some stage between mid-October and early December. An examination of Fig 1.4 shows that while there is but minimal chance of a snowstorm in July and August, in any of the other ten months of the year an appreciable proportion of precipitation comes as snow. The 'extreme maximum' curve proves that the 'mountain winter' may begin as early as September and end as late as June, while the 'minimum' trace shows that it may all but disappear in a mild January when 60 per cent of precipitation can be rain even on Scotland's highest acre of ground.

Winter conditions are not only determined by snow falling, but also by the amount of snow lying on the tops. The accumulation of snow on the high summits tends to be progressive after mid-January, periods of thaw lowering the snow level only briefly before further falls pile up. Thus, the maximum depth of snow-cover lags considerably behind the big midwinter blizzards. The Ben Nevis Observatory recorded maximum snow depths on the summit between 1884 and 1903 (Fig 1.5). The greatest depths vary widely, from 1.37m in the leanest, to 3.60m in the snowiest years, and in only four of these twenty years was the maximum reached within the calendar season, a date in mid-April more usually marking the turning point when the rate of snow melt exceeds that of snow accumulation.

At lower altitudes, the snow-cover is increasingly transient. At a height of 450m the expected snow cover is just seventy days per year, compared to over 200 on the 1,220m summits. Further-more, the date of maximum depth usually occurs much earlier at lower levels, where melting is predominant from the start of March onwards. Thus in early spring,

from bottom to top, as late as 25 April. And in 1997, after an extremely lean winter season, a surprise blizzard on 4–5 May drifted fresh snow to a metre in depth over the western hills! In every year the summer visitor must remember that blizzards are regularly encountered on the high Cairngorms in May and June. Such spells may be relatively short-lived, but they instantly create winter weather and conditions on the mountains.

A premature freeze-up in the early autumn is no less likely. On an early ascent of the Tower Ridge in September 1896, W. Inglis Clark and J. A. Parker found the last 200m of the cliffs plastered with snow, and before commencing the climb were obliged to borrow an ice-axe from the then-staffed summit observatory whose doorway was found barred with

Fig 1.6 *Snow-cover and altitude:*
Observations of annual number of days snow lying at three Scottish mountain locations (from Manley 1971)

Altitude	457m (1,500ft)	610m (2,000ft)	762m (2,500ft)	914m (3,000ft)	1,066m (3,500ft)	1,220m (4,000ft)
Glen Lyon (Ben Lawers range) (24 seasons, 1946–7 to 1969–70	75	100	125	150	–	–
Ben Nevis (11 seasons, 1950–1 to 1960–1)	66	103	139	167	202	220
Ben Nevis (Summit Observatory) (1883–1904 approx)	–	–	–	–	–	230
Cairngorms (13 seasons, 1955–6 to 1967–8) (figures to end of May only)	79	116	153	178	191	200

conditions become strongly polarised to the higher slopes and the sheltered corries where the snows lie at their thickest, while the lower slopes are usually completely bare.

Therefore, a definition of 'winter' solely by snow-cover would include the first half of the calendar spring, but would ignore other factors intrinsic to the challenge of the mountains. The darkness of the December solstice, coupled with the potential storminess of those bleak harsh months on its either side, make strong claim on the mountaineer's conscience. One cannot pretend that to ski shirt-sleeved over the Cairngorm plateau in April, under the sun's full glare and with the assurance of its company for a full twelve hours, equates to the late-December battle with the oncoming storm and night, however much more snow there might be underfoot. If the probabilities of snow-cover, low temperatures, icing and blizzard are combined with the known allowances of daylight, then the four months of maximum elemental hostility are surely those from December to March, and within this period the real mountain winter might most likely be found and challenged.

WINTER AIRMASSES AND AIRFLOWS

The variability of the winter mountain climate is the direct result of the very different airmasses and airflows which can affect Britain's weather at any time during the season, and the fluctuating fortunes of our winter conditions are the result of Britain's temperate and maritime climate. In winter there are two main controlling dimensions to our weather (see Fig 1.7):

1 The North-South boundary between cold arctic airstreams and the warm sub-tropical air over the mid-Atlantic, known as the 'polar front'.

2 The East-West division between moist maritime air over the Atlantic Ocean and the dry, stable airmasses which are prevalent over the continental interiors of Europe and Asia.

Since Britain lies at the approximate meeting point of these two global boundaries, any slight shift in one or the other may cause a completely different airstream to cover the country. In any winter Britain stages what might be envisaged as a battle between these airmasses as they vie for control of our

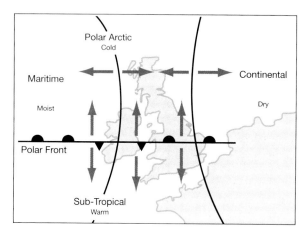

Fig 1.7 *The winter battleground*

weather. If the 'polar front' shifts its average position north of Scotland, our predominating weather influence will be from mild tropical airflows; whilst if it settles to the south of the country, polar air will predominate, bringing snow and ice to the hills. And if continental airmasses build out over Britain and the near-Atlantic, dry, settled and cold weather will set in; whereas a spell of moist and unsettled air is heralded if the maritime air masses make inroads across the country.

In all, six identifiable airstreams affect our

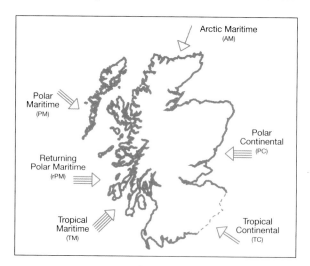

Fig 1.8 *Airmass influences on Scotland's winter weather (the average percentage frequency is indicated by the width of the arrow)*

winter weather, and these are detailed in Figs 1.8 and 1.9. Each airstream is in its character the product of its 'source region' – the area in which it originated – and the modifications which it undergoes during its passage towards this country. Britain is not itself a typical source region. Anticyclones (high-pressure centres) and cyclones (low-pressure centres) do sometimes develop directly over the country and persist for several days, but 75 per cent of our weather is determined by far-travelled and highly modified airflows.

The direction of the prevailing airstream is determined by the relative positions of high- and low-pressure centres around the country. Given the rule that in the northern hemisphere air flows clockwise around high-pressure systems and anticlockwise around low-pressure cells (see Appendix IV), the direction of airflow can be quickly ascertained from scanning a weather map.

The relative frequency with which each airstream has affected Scotland's weather over the eight winters from 1990/91 to 1997/98 is shown in Fig 1.10. Clearly the winter mountaineer must accept an appreciable probability that the prevailing airstream will be of the warm, moist TM variety or the cool and showery rPM, each producing unpleasant weather. Indeed, around 36 per cent of winter airflow over the mountains comes from the quarter from south to west. The relative absence of polar continental airflow in winter in the 1990s is remarkable. Prior to 1989, a winter windflow chart would have shown a frequency of easterlies of around 20 per cent.

It is the sequence and relative duration of airstreams that is all-important in relation to the development of good, stable snow and ice conditions on the hills. In this regard even the tropical maritime airflow has a role to play, because a short dose of warm, moist air within a general pattern of polar weather can temporarily

Fig 1.9 *Winter airflows and mountain weather*

Typical synoptic situation

Polar Maritime (PM) · *Generally north-west*

Source region:	Polar regions of North America – therefore very cold and dry.
Modification:	Gradual warming and rapid moistening during south-east track over North Atlantic.
Mountain weather:	Cold and unstable: −5 to 0°C on summits; warm moist lower air layers rising quickly over hills; heavy snow showers; strong blustery winds.
Typical occurrence:	Cold air-mass following cold front passage; low to north of country.

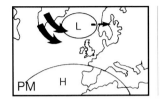

Returning Polar Maritime (rPM) · *Generally west*

Source region:	Same as PM.
Modification:	Forced into a more southerly track when a low lies to west of country; warmer and moister than PM, but slightly more stable.
Mountain weather:	Cool and showery: −2 to +2°C on tops; snow, hail or sleet; windy.

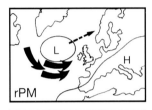

Arctic Maritime (AM) · *North to north-easterly*

Source region:	Arctic Sea; very cold.
Modification:	Slightly warmed but quickly moistened beyond saturation point during southward passage to Britain.
Mountain weather:	Very cold and snowy: −15 to −5°C on tops; heavy falls as air is uplifted over northern hills; winds bitingly cold.

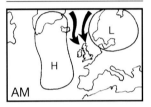

Polar Continental (PC) · *East to south-easterly*

Source region:	Scandinavian and Siberian continental interiors; very cold and dry.
Modification:	Brief warming and moistening as air passes over North Sea.
Mountain weather:	Very cold and stable: −15 to −5°C on tops; snow showers on east coasts and hills; clear and fine further west; any wind is bitter and persistent; gales over mountains if pressure gradient is high.

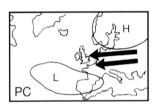

Tropical Continental (TC) · *South-east to southerly*

Source region:	Central and southern continental Europe; dry and can be warm.
Modification:	Cooled during passage over western Europe; moistened slightly by North Sea.
Mountain weather:	Rarely affects Scotland; weather is similar to PC but warmer; dry; wind speed depends on pressure patterns.

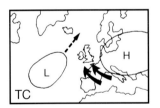

Tropical Maritime (TM) · *South to south-westerly*

Source region:	Mid-Atlantic, sub-equatorial; very warm and moist.
Modification:	Progressive cooling and stabilisation during north-east track towards Britain.
Mountain weather:	'Dreich' conditions; warm and moist; 0 to +8°C on tops; thick low cloud over mountains; light or steady drizzle; rapid thaw; wind may be strong if associated with a deep low.
Typical occurrence:	The warm air sector behind the warm front of an Atlantic low.

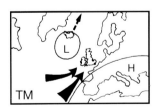

Key to maps:
H: High-pressure system (anti-cyclone); air-flow clockwise.
L: Low-pressure system (depression); air-flow anti-clockwise.
--▶: Likely direction of movement of depression.

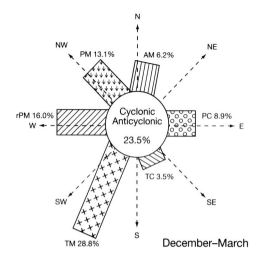

Fig 1.10 Winter airflows over the Scottish mountains 1990/1 to 1997/98

Source: Monthly weather summaries from the Meteorological Office published in The Scotsman

Key

TM – Tropical Maritime
Between South and West South West

rPM – Returning Polar Maritime
Between West South West and West North West

PM – Polar Maritime
Between West North West and North North West

AM – Arctic Maritime
Between North North West and North East

PC – Polar Continental
Between North East and South East

TC – Tropical Continental
Between South East and South

Cyclonic – Anticyclonic
Winds light or variable when low pressure or high pressure is centred over Scotland; no prevailing airstream. Such phases of weather are equally clear and cold or cloudy and mild.

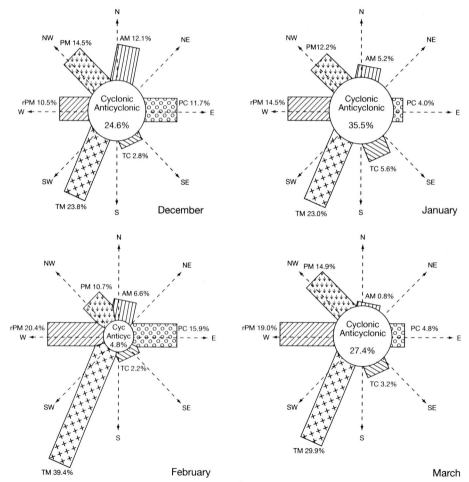

thaw the snow cover, and then the return of colder air will allow excellent freezing and bonding. Conversely, if the pattern is reversed and for every day of cool PM air there are two days of warm, rain-loaded TM, no substantial accumulations of snow can develop on the hills. However, there is no rhyme or reason in the duration and sequence of airstreams through the winter. The phasing of weather is determined by pressure patterns in the middle and upper layers of the troposphere. Large-scale ridges and troughs at an altitude of around 5km essentially control the sequence of weather types, but the mechanisms of change are highly complex and follow no predictable pattern. In truth, we climb entirely at the mercy of the weather in the Scottish winter.

A monthly breakdown of the frequency of each airstream between December and March is given in Fig 1.10. There are some significant variations. Most notably, the incidence of settled anticyclonic airmasses or polar continental (PC) airflow has been significantly higher in December and January than in February or March, and this overturns the traditional wisdom among winter hillgoers that wet and stormy conditions characterise the early season, with cold, settled weather spells predominating later in the winter. In fact, for those seeking frosts and calm, clear weather, the early season has been a much better bet during the 1990s. However, this base period is too short to conclude as to whether this is a persistent pattern or merely a temporary aberration.

This simple model of airmasses and airstreams explains the varying nature of the winter mountain climate without needing to invoke more complex aspects of meteorology such as depressions and frontal systems. If winter mountaineers have no more than this basic understanding of the types of weather associated with each airflow, they can predict and plan trips to the hills with better surety.

A quick check on the prevailing wind direction should be enough to estimate the likely weather on the mountains.

RECENT CLIMATIC CHANGE ON THE WINTER MOUNTAINS

'Is the winter climate changing, and will it continue to change in the next few years?'
This is the vexed question which is currently taxing all enthusiasts of winter mountain sports as well as meteorologists, the evidence being that the winter climate has shifted significantly towards warmer and wetter conditions in the ten years from 1989 to 1998. However, before we become preoccupied with current events or depressed as to the future prospects for winter mountaineering, let us be clear that the climate has never been static over the course of the last century: there have always been runs of warm years and clusters of cold or snowy seasons.

Fluctuating Fortunes: 1900–1960
In the period from 1900 to 1960, the Highland winters were, on average, warmer than during any comparable period since the early Middle Ages – yet these sixty years were an era of remarkable activity and advances in snow- and ice-climbing and skiing. However, reading between the lines of great winter deeds during the harder seasons of this period, one can find regular complaints of prevailing wet, warm and windy weather. Of a February visit to the Western Highlands in 1905, S. A. Gillon lamented: '... *The climate is becoming less continental and more maritime or insular, or whatever is the term for dampness, unseasonable mildness and more than feminine changeableness.*' [7]

Some winter months in the first half of this century deserve the term 'drenching' rather than 'dreich', especially on the west where the maritime Atlantic influence is so much stronger. The rain gauge near Kinlochquoich in the wildlands between Glen Garry and Knoydart collected 111cm in January 1916 and another 127cm in March 1938, which is approximately double the annual average rainfall for eastern England. Mild, snowless winters were also experienced further east in the Cairngorms. The naturalist Seton Gordon remembered the remarkable sight of stags grazing on the snow-free summit of Braeriach in mid-January. He also recalled the confusion that warm winters caused to the bird populations: miscalculating the seasons, they would make for their spring nesting haunts on the high moors, and the 'wild vibrating whistle' of the curlew, so evocative of spring, might be heard on the hills in the dark depths of January.

A Cooler Phase: 1960–1987

From the mid-1960s to the 1980s, winters in Scotland became progressively cooler, and were notable in producing more diverse extremes of weather than had been previously reported. Among the more notable phases of weather were these:

1978–9: The severest winter and lowest temperatures recorded in two hundred years over much of northern Europe.

1981–2, 4–14 January: A prolonged freeze. The temperature at Braemar plunged to a UK record minimum of −27.2 degrees C on the 10th, and sea lochs surrounding the Cuillin of Skye were partially iced up during this period.

1983–4: Winds of over 160 kmph and blizzards on **21 January** produced the worst Highland storm in living memory.

1986–7, 10–20 January: Another severe continental freeze, with temperatures in Eastern Europe falling to new record minima, and the lowest day-time temperatures of the century being recorded in England and Wales:

Cairngorm summit recorded −16.5 degrees C on the 12th, the lowest in ten years of automatic readings.

Interspersed with these seasons of prolonged refrigeration there were still some remarkably mild winters, notably in the early 1970s when the *Scottish Mountaineering Club Journal* of 1971 reported several sightings of the dreaded 'midge' on the Allt a'Mhulinn track to the cliffs of Ben Nevis during February.

A 'Step Change' in Rainfall: 1989–1993

Starting with 1989 there was a 'step change' in the winter climate towards significantly wetter and warmer seasons. The incidence and duration of arctic and continental airstreams reduced, allowing Atlantic weather systems to control more of the winter weather. The most remarkable change was the sudden rise in winter rainfall totals between 1989 and 1993. Examining the weather records for Fort William up to 1993 Richard Tabony of the Meteorological Office concluded:

'In the last five years an increased frequency of westerly winds has brought high rainfall to the Western Highlands and reduced snowfall throughout the whole of Scotland. Examination of the available record shows that the recent fluctuation in weather is without precedent.' [8]

For example, from 1861 to 1988 the highest January to March rainfall total for Fort William was 1,149mm recorded in 1920. Then 1989 weighed in with a total of 1,518mm, this only to be surpassed in 1990, which produced a record 1,754mm for the three months. As Fig 1.11 shows, these exceptional rains increased the decadal mean (ten-year average) for rainfall to an unprecedented level.

Such extreme seasonal totals have not been repeated since, although the tendency for exceptionally wet months has continued. The month of March has been particularly wet:

over Scotland as a whole, March 1994 was the wettest on record, followed by 1990 and then 1992. February has not lagged far behind: February 1997 was the wettest on record at many stations in western Scotland, only to be surpassed in 1998 when a non-stop deluge between 10 and 14 February gave Glenelg 337mm of rain.

The increase in rainfall has not been uniformly distributed across the whole of Scotland. The Western Highlands have soaked up most of the deluge, whilst over in the Eastern Grampians winter rainfall has been below its long-term average over the decade 1989–98. When westerly winds are in command the east of the country lies in a 'rain shadow', sheltered by the western ranges, and often remains dry though warm.

Winter Temperatures Rise: 1988–1998

Had the increase in precipitation mentioned above come largely in the form of snow, winter conditions on the mountains might have been greatly enhanced; but unfortunately this has not been the case, and much of the extra precipitation has come on a tropical maritime airstream from the south-west and has fallen as rain at all levels. Were the Scottish mountains 500m or 1,000m higher the story might have been very different. For instance, up at 1,700m on the Jostedalsbreen ice-cap of Norway, the increased precipitation from Atlantic weather systems since 1988 produced such a big increase in volumes of snow that its glaciers commenced a significant advance after 1990. In Scotland, 1994 was the only year when there was a dominance of polar maritime airflow from the west and north-west which gave continuous snow-cover on the hills from December to April.

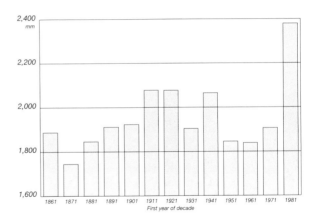

Fig 1.11 *Decadal rainfall at Fort William (ten-year average), 1861/71–1981/91 (from Tabony 1993)*

No part of Scotland has escaped the general rise in temperatures of the last ten years. The data from Cairn Gorm AWS show that the average winter temperature in the period 1990–95 was 1 degree C warmer than the average for 1979–1987, and temperatures in recent winters have only accentuated that trend. In February 1998, temperatures across north-east Scotland were a massive 5 degrees C above average, and across Scotland as a whole the month was 1.1 degrees C warmer than any previous February over a 130-year recording period. A 1 degree C rise in average winter temperatures in the 1990s does not sound significant, but it is three to four times as big as the long-term rise in temperature over the last 100 years. One must also realise that it would only take a 2-degree *fall* in average temperatures to cause a renewed glaciation of the Highland corries. A 1-degree rise, if sustained, would have a profound effect on our mountain environment, because it would reduce the duration of mountain snow-cover by some thirty days a year, spelling doom to many of our arctic-alpine

Pages 30–1 Plate 1.4 The Arrochar Alps; nearing the South Peak of the Cobbler in winter conditions (Rab Anderson)

plant communities, as well as killing off Scotland's fragile downhill skiing industry, and making winter mountaineering a rather more ephemeral pursuit than has been the case hitherto.

The rise in temperature is suspiciously consistent with the predictions of global warming due to the greenhouse effect, and we must turn to an explanation of the current trends if we are to forsee the likely future of the mountain winter.

GLOBAL WARMING AND SCOTLAND'S MOUNTAIN CLIMATE

There is now little doubt that the world's climate is currently warming at a rate beyond the predictions of natural cycles. Global mean temperatures rose by approximately 0.5 degrees C in the century to 1990: a warming phase occurred between 1900 and 1940, and then, after four decades of relatively static temperatures, a vigorous new warming commenced in the 1980s. The global mean temperature for the decade 1981–91 was approximately 0.25 degrees C above the average for the previous forty years, and warming has continued through the 1990s, with 1997 being the warmest recorded year.

The warming is consistent with the increased concentration of 'greenhouse gases' in the atmosphere. Although temperatures haven't risen by as much as was predicted by early models of global warming, the current forecast of the Intergovernmental Panel on Climatic Change is for further warming of around 1.5 degrees C in the next fifty years. Of course, the effects of global warming may not be evenly distributed across the world. So how will the maritime climate of Scotland be affected? There are two scenarios by which Scotland's winter climate will be altered:

1 The greenhouse effect raises the temperature of all airmasses by an even amount, so that winds from all directions become progressively warmer.

2 The greenhouse effect causes changes in atmospheric circulation patterns, altering the frequency with which winds blow from certain directions. In particular, the average winter position of the polar front will shift northwards, allowing an increased incidence of south-westerly (tropical maritime) airflow over Britain, and effectively shutting out the northerly and easterly airstreams.

From the evidence of the last decade, it is clear that the initial rise in winter temperatures was the result of a shift in airflow patterns: as Fig 1.10 shows, westerlies, and in particular the south-westerlies, have ruled the 1990s. When the north and easterly winds do take command of our weather there is no evidence that they are any warmer than before. This was evidenced by the big freeze-up over Christmas in 1995, when temperatures below –20 degrees C were recorded across much of the Highlands. The truth is that such spells of arctic weather have markedly diminished in frequency and duration by comparison to the previous twenty years. However, although all the climatic changes of the last decade are consistent with global warming theory, ten years is still too short a base period to be conclusive regarding a longer-term diminution of winter conditions on the mountains. Winter enthusiasts may take comfort and hope to know that natural cyclical phenomena are probably causing at least some of the current warming:

• Some meteorologists claim that the eleven-year sunspot cycles have an effect on climate, with periods of wet westerly weather predominating in the two years before the sunspot maximum, and dry settled weather at the minimum. A peak in sunspot activity is due in the year 2000.[9]

- There is also a regular two-yearly shift in wind direction over the equator in the stratosphere. When coupled with sunspot cycles, this shift gives a close fit to recent short-term climatic patterns. For example, periods when sunspot maxima coincide with a west phase of stratospheric wind correlate with a dominance of higher-than-normal pressure over America and lower-than-normal pressure over the Atlantic. In such phases we might expect wet and warm winters over Britain; the reverse occurs when the stratospheric wind is in the east phase.
- A regular oscillation of about ten years' duration has been identified in the strength and positioning of westerly airflow across the North Atlantic over a period of 125 years. In 1998, the northward shift of the oscillation was at a maximum, hence our recent mild moist winters. Whatever its cause, this North Atlantic oscillation is expected to decline in the next five to ten years.[10]
- Past phases of warm or snowless winters, such as the periods 1932–35 and 1971–76, might have led to similarly pessimistic predictions as to the future of winter conditions, yet the snows returned. Whatever the causes of short-term cycles in weather, whether sunspots or otherwise, past experience suggests that there will always be a swing back to cooler seasons, even if the underlying trend is one of slow warming.

Yet there are several opposing factors which give concern that the climate has significantly shifted and will not return to the patterns of the past century:

- In terms of Britain's temperatures we may only be seeing the start of the upward surge. Due to our maritime location, any temperature rises would lag behind those of the world's continental landmasses because of the *thermal lag* of the oceans. The seas have a higher *specific heat* than land, meaning that they will be slower to respond to the greenhouse effect.
- Once the sea temperatures around our shores start to rise, as they have done in 1997 and 1998, a positive feedback loop comes into operation, whereby approaching air masses receive additional warming, whether their source area is tropical or polar.

LOOKING TO THE FUTURE

The winter mountain climate of Scotland currently defies any simple definition. The mountain weather is turbulent in that it is typically characterised by high winds and stormy conditions, and equally it is unpredictable in its swings between temperate, polar and truly arctic conditions on the summits. For mountains of relatively small stature, Scotland's peaks continue to offer one of the most challenging climates to be found anywhere in the world in their winter season.

Whilst the trend in the 1990s has been towards a winter climate that is warmer and less stable, we cannot predict its future with any certainty. Global warming may now be an accepted reality, but how long will it last? Despite the ever-more detailed measurements of the atmosphere and ocean currents which are available, and the increasing power of computer models, there is no concensus among climatologists as to how the next century will unfold. The earth is too complex an environment to be confined to a unified computer model. It operates as a 'chaotic', rather than as a 'deterministic' system, whereby marginal changes in crucial variables can have long-term ramifications for climatic change. Therefore, climatic prediction is still open to individual interpretation. Two equally legitimate views of the future are:

1 Climatic records and geological evidence suggest that climatic change does not happen slowly and gradually, but occurs in short and dramatic shifts. The complex web of controls over the global heat balance may operate as a stable system for long periods, maintaining a relative equilibrium by checks and balances. Then, due to a new external factor such as greenhouse gas emissions or to a chance coincidence of natural factors, the thresholds of change are suddenly broken and the climate shifts into a new position. We could now be going through just such a phase, with world climate shifting into a warmer epoch for the twenty-first century – in which case it is goodbye to Scottish winters as we have known them.

2 Alternatively, global warming may trigger some environmental response which acts to check and reverse the warming trend. For example, the melting and break-up of the great ice-caps of Antarctica and Greenland could produce a cooling in ocean currents. At present, the North Atlantic Drift (NAD), an extension of the Gulf Stream ocean current, drives mild air from the tropics to northern Europe and guarantees Britain's temperate climate. If, however, the Atlantic becomes warmer due to global warming, the increased melting of Greenland's ice masses will release vast volumes of fresh water. Being less saline, this ice-melt will be less dense than the tropical ocean currents, and it could override and push the NAD southwards, checking and then reversing the current warming trend in maritime Europe.[11]

The wonderful conclusion is that we simply don't know for sure what will happen, any better than we can guess what next month's weather will bring. The very uncertainty of Scotland's current and future winter mountain climate is part of its fascination. We will watch the coming years with interest, but must revert to our dreams to project the Highland winter of future millenia.

Will the ice once more be chipping at the Cuillin pinnacles, tumbling the quartzite piles of the Torridon peaks into oblivion, and gouging the glens of the west still deeper? Or will the winter season be a brief release from stifling heat and subtropical humidity, the hills once more swathed in trees, the cliffs carpeted with moss and slime, never again to feel the pinch of frost or the peck of crampons and ice-axe? In the greater book of time, Scotland's present mountain winter is but the briefest clause.

2: STORMLASHED OR FROSTBOUND

WINTER MOUNTAIN WEATHER

(Note: Readers may wish to refer to Appendix IV for a basic explanation of meteorological theory and terms in conjunction with this chapter)

From booming tempests to wonderful days of silent frost, the Highlands' winter weather is a compendium of fear, fascination and utter delight to the mountaineer. Both the unpredictability and the variability of the winter weather give the Scottish mountains a singular stamp of quality, an infinite range of colours and moods, and a scenic impact out of all proportion to their modest height. Grim and cloud-swathed one day, gleaming and sparkling white the next, our hills have a lure and mystique that alpine ranges thrice the height cannot surpass. The mixture of weather conditions and their rapid changes pose both challenge and hazard to the winter hillgoer. The alpine and continental winter climate generally divides into prolonged spells when one type of weather is dominant, and the conditions, however severe, can be predicted with some accuracy. By contrast, a single mountain day in Scotland may start with a calm frost of –10 degrees C and a good forecast, yet end with a blizzard of wet sleet which catches the climber unprepared. Stable periods do occur in each season, but changeability is more the norm and rarely can our weather be wholly trusted. Furthermore, our maritime mountain climate frequently produces wet, windy and cool conditions that are more difficult to survive than the extreme dry cold typical of the greater ranges.

To know and understand the winter mountain weather we need first to examine its three main components: temperature, wind and precipitation. Then we must turn to the systematic causes of different types of weather in terms of air-pressure patterns and fronts. Finally, no winter mountaineer should venture far into the hills without being able to interpret weather forecasts or without an awareness of the visual signs of weather changes.

TEMPERATURE VARIATIONS

Of vital importance to the mountaineer in determining both snow conditions and personal comfort is the range and variability of temperature on the mountains over varying time-scales.

Diurnal (ie between night and day) The daily range is greatest in clear, stable weather when the day-time receipt of sunshine (insolation) and the night-time heat loss by radiational cooling are maximised. The diurnal range is much reduced in windy or overcast weather when radiational heat exchanges are small. For example, on 12 January 1987 when Cairn Gorm recorded its record minimum of –16.5 degrees C, the maximum temperature attained during the same twenty-four hours was just 1.5 degrees C higher at –15.0 degrees C, thanks to a continuous south-east wind and the cover of blowing snow on the summit. A diurnal movement across freezing point (0 deg C) produces a daily freeze/thaw cycle which consolidates the snow and ice into a safe enjoyable condition for walking and climbing.

Systematic (ie from day to day) Here the main control on temperature is the prevailing local weather system. The changeover from a settled cold phase to a stormy maritime spell of weather often produces a dramatic temperature change. For instance, over 27–28 January 1985, Braemar's thermometer rocketed from –17.9 degrees C to +5.7 degrees C as warm frontal systems advanced across the country. A day-to-day range around freezing point promotes consolidation of the existing snowpack. Least desirable is a sustained bout of tropical maritime air from the south-west which typically produces a day-to-day temperature range of +2 to +6 degrees C at 900m causing sustained thaws which will frustrate the climber's plans.

Periodic (ie weekly and longer) Settled anticyclonic airmasses produce sustained spells of low temperatures upon which only the diurnal range makes significant impact. These may last up to a month, but more normally in Scotland are displaced after a week or a fortnight at most. The longest continuous frost recorded on Cairn Gorm, when the temperature never rose above zero night or day, was thirty-six days between 27 January and 3 March in the superb winter of 1986, thanks to the dominance of a polar continental anticyclone over the country.

Seasonal (ie from month to month) The seasonal pattern of temperature is influenced by the annual heat budget of the earth's surface. While the receipt of sunshine reaches its minimum on the shortest day, the cooling of the earth lags behind so that the minimum temperatures at the surface are reached after 21 December. The delayed response is especially marked in our maritime climate because the sea has a greater heat-retention capacity (*specific heat*) than the continental land masses. Our sea temperatures generally continue to fall for two months after the December solstice, so that February should be our coldest month of the year. Thereafter, the re-emergent sun produces a progressive heating of land and sea back towards the summer. Although recent years have been anomalously warm in February, on a long-term average it is still the coldest month both on the summits and in the glens. Braemar's average daily minimum for February from 1951 to 1980 was –3.1 degrees C, and that on Cairn Gorm from 1978 to 1987 was –6 degrees C.

The Lapse Rate

The variation of temperature with altitude (the lapse rate) is of equal interest to the hillgoer. In normal conditions there is a steady drop in air temperature with altitude in the lower atmosphere. In unsaturated air the average lapse is 1.0 degrees C every 100m, but this falls to around 0.65 degrees C per 100m in air at saturation point. With these rates in mind, one can translate valley temperatures to those on the summits before commencing the day. The freezing level is all-important to the snow conditions. Suppose the sea-level temperature at Fort William is +6.5 degrees C and the summits are clouded, meaning that the air is saturated: applying the saturated lapse rate, the freezing level will be around 1,000m and one would be better advised to climb on Ben Nevis than to search for a frost on the lower hills of Glencoe, which would be futile. However, in certain conditions the normal lapse rates can be slowed or even reversed to give temperature inversions on the mountains where warmer air lies on top of colder:

1 **Warm air sectors:** When a warm air mass encroaches over the country it initially overrides the colder air which it is displacing (warm air being lighter and less dense than cold), and for a time, the temperatures on the hills may be equal to or warmer than those in the colder air at sea level. Once the warm front has pushed through, warm air will dominate at all levels, but the observed lapse rate may be very small due to the intense condensation of vapour over the hills, which releases heat into the atmosphere. Regularly when I go out in the wet misty conditions after a warm front has passed I will find that the air temperature hardly drops at all between valley and summit.

2 **Valley temperature inversions:** Cold, dense air will sink into localised valley floor 'reservoirs' at night during stable anticyclonic spells of weather when there is no wind to mix the air (see Fig 2.1), and it is notable that the extremes of summit temperatures do not match the depths of the frosts which are experienced in the adjacent glens when such inversion conditions are present. Thus, when Braemar experienced Britain's record known minimum temperature of –27.2 degrees C on 10 January 1982, Cairn Gorm's summit was 'basking' in a mere –12.6 degrees C.

3 **Anticyclonic inversions:** Anticyclones are vast areas of stable air which are subsiding. During phases of anticyclonic weather, low-level fog and cloud may form over a wide area at sea level due to night-time cooling of the land surface by radiational heat loss, or from sea mist which rolls inland. Such moist air is unable to rise and dissipate because it meets a warming, stable and sinking air mass above it. This creates a temperature inversion across the whole country coupled with a cloud inversion, which may on occasion lie below summit level. Such conditions are rare but precious. For instance, one moist and mild February we set out to climb Blaven on Skye in dank, chill air and miserable drizzle. At half height the air dried and a hazy sun began to filter through the mist, and then, a hundred metres from the top, we broke through the cloud into dry, warm air. Below us, 'brocken spectres' and 'glories' danced on the surface of the mist, and across to the west the whole of the Cuillin Ridge floated majestically on a sea of cloud (Plate 2.1).

Finally, there are two concepts which regularly cause confusion among mountaineers, and which should be clarified:

Wind chill: Having read the statement that our mountain temperatures are not particularly extreme, many will undoubtedly have exclaimed: 'But what about wind chill? Doesn't a strong wind reduce –10 degrees C to –30 degrees C?' In fact, the ambient temperature can never fall below the still-air thermometer reading; the wind merely serves to accelerate the rate at which the exposed body cools towards that level. Extra insulation is therefore

Fig 2.1 *The valley temperature inversion*

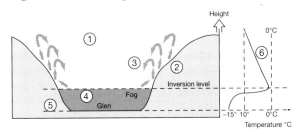

1 Calm, clear, stable upper atmosphere
2 Intense night-time cooling of mountain slopes by outward radiation from the snow surface
3 Cooled surface air layers are colder, denser and therefore more heavy than the outer atmosphere. Thus they tend to sink and displace any warmer valley air-pockets
4 Cold air reservoir formed glen bottoms often condensing into thick fog – temperature typically –15 degrees C
5 U-shape of glacial glens traps the cold air
6 Normal atmospheric lapse above the inversion to –10 degrees C at summits

Plate 2.1 *February cloud inversion on Blaven, looking across to the main Cuillin ridge*

an expensive and ultimately futile solution to the wind, and it is windproof garments that are required (see Chapter 7).

Air and ground temperature: The air temperature is used almost universally in meteorological recording, but the ground temperature (ie that of the snow surface) behaves rather differently, particularly in clear, calm weather when radiation is the dominant agent of heating and cooling. The earth's surface (and this includes snow) is far more responsive to radiational heating and cooling than the overlying air: therefore in sunshine the surface snow will absorb more heat and thus melt more rapidly than the air temperature might suggest; and conversely on a clear night, radiational heat loss from the surface may cause freezing and hardening even though the air temperature stays above zero. A prediction of the state of the snow should therefore not depend solely upon the forecast air temperature (see Chapter 3).

THE WIND AND THE WUTHERING

The mountain wind can on successive days be the mountaineer's foe and inspiration:

2 January 1892: the summit of Cairn Gorm:
    'Simultaneous with the discovery of the cairn came a terrific blast of wind before which we were glad to throw ourselves face downwards on the ground and remain in that position till its violence had subsided.'[1] (W. Brown)

3 January 1892: Ben Cruachan and Taynuilt Peak:
    'Two white peaks, soaring out of the mist appeared on either side in all their spotless sublimity; struck with a gleam of sunshine, throwing light and shade on their gleaming pinnacles, with wind-blasts howling round them like a legion of "storm fiends" shrieking their notes of wailing.'[2] (W. Douglas)

Fig 2.2 *Cairn Gorm summit: annual wind extremes, 1979–87* Wind speeds given in kmph (mph in brackets)										
Year	1979	1980	1981	1982	1983	1984	1985	1986	1987	1979–87
Maximum	55.8	72.7	73.2	64.5	88.3	62.7	57.6	68.8	56.6	88.3
Monthly Mean	(34.7)	(45.2)	(45.5)	(40.1)	(54.9)	(39.0)	(35.8)	(42.8)	(35.2)	(54.9)
Month	Nov	Dec	Jan	Nov	Jan	Dec	Feb	Nov	Mar	Jan 83
Maximum	93	109	112	122	135	143	128	145	146	146
Daily Mean	(58)	(68)	(70)	(76)	(84)	(89)	(80)	(90)	(91)	(91)
Average direction	SW	W	NW	W	W	SE	SE	SW	SE	SE
Date	4 Dec	18 Apr	6 Feb	19 Nov	5 Mar	23 Mar	9 Feb	20 Mar	7 Mar	7 Mar 87
Maximum	177	202	194	188	235	235	196	275	207	275
3-Second Gust	(110)	(126)	(121)	(117)	(146)	(146)	(122)	(171)	(129)	(171)
Direction	SW	W	S	SW	W	SE	W	SE	SE	SE
Date	4 Dec	29 Dec	13 Dec	12 Feb	25 Oct	24 Mar	31 Jan	20 Mar	7 Mar	20 Mar 86

Note total dominance of winter and late autumn dates even though these statistics are for the whole year.

Winter's Big Blow

The autumn and winter vie for supremacy as the windiest seasons in the Scottish mountains, but in terms of extreme gusts and severe individual storms, winter has the upper hand. In the nine years between 1979 and 1987 (Fig 2.2) the windiest month of the year at Cairn Gorm summit was always between November and March. Over the same period, the highest recorded single three-second gust came between December and March in eight out of the nine years. Fig 2.3 gives the rather disturbing information that a gale can be expected on Cairn Gorm summit for 30 per cent of the duration of the calendar winter, compared to only 9 per cent of the summer season.

Why, then, is the winter so much more windy? Windspeed is directly proportional to air-pressure differences across the lower atmosphere: the greater the pressure difference between two neighbouring airmasses, the stronger the winds between them, and in winter the pressure differences between the main airmasses in the northern hemisphere are more pronounced. The polar zone of cold air greatly intensifies and expands during the winter, whereas the temperature of airmasses nearer to the equator is little affected by the seasonal change. Thus, the boundary between the drier polar air and the maritime sub-tropical zone – the polar front – shifts south and becomes more pronounced in terms of both temperature and pressure difference. As a result it is less stable than in summer, breeding deeper and more active areas of low pressure (depressions) which generate higher winds. This is

Fig 2.3 *Seasonal frequency of gales on Cairn Gorm summit, 1979–82*

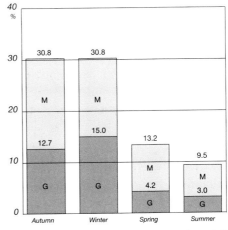

M   Percentage of hours in which a *mean* wind speed above gale force (61kmph) was recorded

G   Percentage of hours in which a *single gust* above storm force (109kmph) was recorded

due not only to the pressure gradient, but also to the uplift of air along the airmass boundaries (fronts).

The average winter position of the polar front lies east-west across Britain's latitudes. Therefore, our mountains lie directly in its storm-tracks, and as the first line of defence to the 4,000km expanse of the Atlantic Ocean, the Western Highlands receive the full blast of the roaring westerlies – many are the dark winter nights when the very ground itself reverberates with their power.

Furthermore, in winter there is a greater intensity and stability in anticyclones over continental Europe. As areas of low pressure, spawned out in the Atlantic, track eastwards, they frequently become blocked against these huge high-pressure masses over Europe which produce persistent and bitterly cold gales, typically from the south-east.

Topographic Effects

The mountains themselves produce further intensification of winter's vigorous airflows. Winds blow faster at higher altitudes due to the absence of surface friction; over Britain, the 'free air' windspeeds at 1,000m are 50 per cent higher than at sea level. Therefore, a 62kmph (force 8) gale in the valleys will blow at 90–95kmph on the higher summits. In addition to this, mountain topography creates remarkable local effects on both the wind's speed and its dynamic behaviour. For example on Goat Fell, Arran, an astounding wind phenomenon was observed and reported by W. Inglis Clark during the SMC's 1923 New Year meet:

'A series of wind vortices swept down the slopes, tossing members here and there. Owing to the slight sprinkling of snow the passage of these cyclones was made visible, each circle of wind raising a margin of snow like a wall some feet in height. Each large circle, revolving, say at 40 miles per hour, had on its margin five vortices, where the

velocity seemed more like 100mph, and at each of these a pyramid of snow was raised to a height of perhaps 30 feet. The whole circle with its satellites had a rapid movement down the mountain face when in the secondary vortex, the writer was thrown certainly more than 20 feet in a fraction of a second.'[3]

And yet, while such a gale can be devastating one side of a hill, perfect calm may reign over a brow just a few metres distant – it is as if the wind gods have chosen one small patch on which to vent their anger and left the rest unscathed.

It is not always the summits that are windiest. Tom Weir recalled a real howler of a south-easterly on Maoile Lunndaidh above Loch Monar in 1946. When he and his companion reached the dome-shaped summit plateau, they were suddenly gripped by the wind and forced onto hands and knees. Despite crawling and clinging to ice-axes, they felt powerless to prevent the wind sliding them inexorably across the ice-bound top towards the brink of the mountain's northern cliffs, and it was only with great effort that they managed to impose enough control over their direction to reach the summit cairn. Here, amazingly, they staggered into a near calm. In fact this could only have been the centre of the vortex of the storm which was sucking the air to either side of the topmost point.

There are three broad controls on windflow over mountains:

1   Shape of the mountains.
2   Direction of the wind in relation to the mountain relief.
3   General stability of atmospheric conditions.
Fig 2.4 illustrates the general effects of factors 1 and 2. If the wind blows perpendicularly to the alignment of relief as in (a), the air is forced upwards and over the summits, the uplift being accentuated where the windward slopes are uniform and concave in shape, so

that the maximum winds are experienced on the tops themselves. A convex windward slope tends to deflect the air sideways, until it finds a suitable gap through which to escape (b). This channelling effect produces extreme winds on the intervening bealachs between rounded and convex hills, while the summits themselves escape the worst blast. Where the wind blows parallel to the main mountain ranges (e), as a westerly may blow across the west-east alignments of the Western Highlands, a similar channelling will occur,

with a gale roaring through the glens like a high-speed express.

A particular feature of the wind in the mountains is its gustiness. On Cairn Gorm, single gusts are on average 25 per cent greater than the mean windspeed, although in winter, storm gusts can be double the average velocity. A gusting wind is the most difficult to handle on the hills because it is impossible to predict its timing and so take the appropriate defensive action. Nor is it just frustrating and exhausting when the wind 'plays with you' in

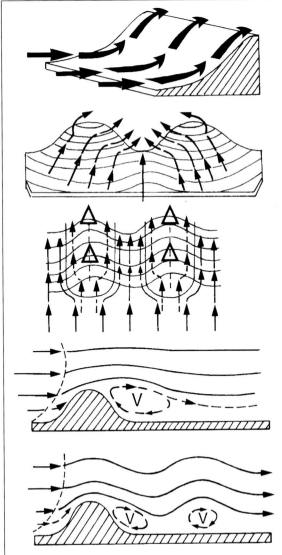

Fig 2.4 *Mountain effects on windflow*

a **Forced uplift and compression:**
   unbroken mountain barrier; concave windward slope; wind-flow perpendicular

b **Diversion and channelling:**
   linked rounded hills; convex windward slope; wind-flow perpendicular

c **Up-valley channelling:**
   wind-flow parallel to the main relief ridges

d **Lee slope turbulence – standing eddy:**
   moderate wind speeds; weak reverse flow and updraught

e **Lee slope turbulence – waves and rotors:**
   strong winds over 40kpmh; rotor vortex (v) in lee depression; standing rotor (v) under waves; turbulent reverse flow and updraught

Plate 2.2 *Travelling in high winds and spindrift: party close together to keep contact, and wearing helmets in case of being blown over (Martin Welch)*

this fashion: if caught on steep, icy ground the sudden gust can be deadly. In January 1994 I was guiding two clients off the summit of Fuar Tholl in a vicious north-westerly wind. In order to get off the exposed summit we headed downwind on slopes of hard névé snow, roped for security. However, this put the wind at our backs, and a sudden gust caught us teetering on our crampon points. I clung to my axe pick and pulled the rope tight. One of my team lost his grip and I held him at the limit of balance. Just as he regained his footing the wind tipped me five degrees further; my axe ripped out and I hurtled head first down a steepening slope. A solitary boulder stopped my slide just before my companions were plucked off too. Fortunately my shoulder rather than my head made impact, but the joint was dislocated by the blow. I then spent a painful and somewhat terrifying hour crawling off the upper mountain.

Gusting is a sure sign of turbulence in the airflows; Fig 2.4 (d) and (e) show how uplift and compression of the wind over a mountain massif creates an oscillating wave motion on the lee side. If the wind is strong, the release of pressure on the lee slopes and the associated downrush of air may create standing eddies or even a series of rotor vortices in which the airflow may be reversed or sent upwards. Violent updraughts are experienced regularly on the corrie headwalls by climbers, who then have to suffer a spindrift blast from below and above at the same time; in these circumstances they may reasonably complain of unfair treatment from the weather. Much of the gustiness in the hills is caused by these complex and ever-changing forms of turbulence.

The Cairngorm plateau and its northern corries provide a model example where all these orographic effects can act in devastating combination if there is a strong south-east airflow, particularly in association with a stable, subsiding upper atmosphere (Fig 2.5). The resultant windstorms can hold sway for many days during every winter, but are so highly localised that innocent observers enjoying sunshine and a light breeze down in Aviemore would not credit their severity. Similar local winds may be experienced in other areas of the Highlands when the juxtaposition of airflow and relief so favours.

There is no strongly prevailing wind direction in winter. The westerlies have had the upper hand during the 1990s, but the wind comes from all directions with substantial frequency. Severe gales are experienced from all directions, although more rarely from the north and north-east (see the maxima for the Cairn Gorm AWS on Fig 2.2); indeed, a gale can veer from south-east to north-west during the twenty-four-hour passage of a single depression over Scotland.

To be on the hills on a day of buffeting winds is an exhilarating, if exhausting experience. There can be no half measures: pitched into the teeth of a gale, one must give everything, or be beaten. The mountains are alive and bellowing with an unbridled and untameable strength. However, the limits between controlled excitement and terrifying danger are finely drawn. Beyond them one's life may be on the line, as we found on Fuar Tholl. Fig 2.6 gives a practical translation of the main wind-speed scales into the sphere of human experience. Careful reading of weather forecasts, prudent guesses as to the likely gust speeds, and sensible avoidance of exposed ground – all these can keep you on the right side of the margin; but it is unrealistic to think that you will never get caught on the wrong part of the mountain in a serious windstorm.

Surviving the Storm

When caught in a dangerous wind one's tactics are crucial to a successful extrication:

- Getting to the closest shelter may be vital, even if this means retreating. To push on with a route in the teeth of the storm is far more risky than a long walk home.

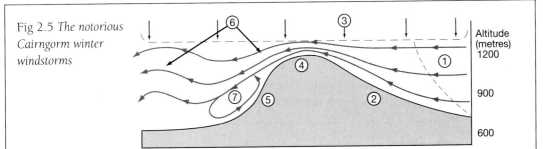

Fig 2.5 *The notorious Cairngorm winter windstorms*

Altitude (metres)
1200
900
600

1 Strong south-east airflow blowing perpendicularly to the massif
2 Smooth concave south-east slopes forcing uplift
3 Stable upper atmosphere at high pressure and therefore with a tendency to sink; restricts vertical lift
4 Severe compression and acceleration of wind at summit level (100–160kmph)
5 Steep corrie head walls on the north-west side cause a sudden release and down-rush into free air-space
6 Layer clouds often formed over plateau summit and in lee wave crests where saturation levels are reached
7 Vortex and eddies and corrie bowls: calm air-space, updraughts and random gusting

- If the dynamics of the wind can be roughly interpreted, then one can vary the route to get the best of available shelter, or avoid particularly turbulent spots. This might mean avoiding edges or gully exits where turbulence can be severe. The safest option is often to stay on easy-angled open ground where the wind is constant and the risk of injury in a fall is lessened.
- Removing all impedimentia minimises the risk of injury in the event of being blown over, and ski-sticks, all climbing hardware, ropes and spare axes should be stowed in the sack. The duel with the wind requires the simplest weapons: just you, your axe and crampons. A helmet should be worn if you have one, even on easy-angled terrain.
- Keeping the gale to headward, or to 45 degrees on either side, allows a greater measure of control even if the effort of progress is increased, because you can 'tack' into the wind in short, zig-zagging bursts. A tailwind is particularly dangerous when descending, and if forced into such a situation you should face into the slope and descend backwards so that the wind is kept to head.

Fig 2.6 *Wind speeds: a practical conversion guide*

Beaufort Scale		Kmph/Mph	Visual indicators	Travel problems on the hill
0	Calm	0		
1–3	Light	2–20 (1–12)	Surface drift of loose snow	
4	Moderate	21–29 (13–18)		
5	Fresh	30–39 (19–24)	Tree branches in motion	
6	Strong	40–50 (25–31)	Wavelets on loch surfaces	Severe windchill-rate of cooling at 0°C equivalent to –10°C.
7	Strong	51–61 (32–38)	Cairn Gorm's winter average; snow/rain falls 'horizontally'	Risk of frost-nip on exposed flesh if temperature is below zero (32°F).
8	Gale	62–74 (39–46)	Shroud of blowing snow on hills up to 50m thick	Leaning into wind – energy output doubled.
9	Severe gale	75–87 (47–54)	Streams blown back; large trees in motion	Trailing ropes will blow outwards horizontally.
10	Storm force	88–100 (55–63)	Raised whirlwinds of blowing snow on crests; plumes and streamers	Buckled against the wind; walking difficult – effort trebled.
11	Severe storm force	101–116 (64–72)	Storm shroud of suspended spindrift 100m thick	Extreme windchill (–20°C) exposed flesh freezes below 0°C.
12	Hurricane	over 117 (over 73)	Extensive structural damage	Crawling at 125kmph+; breathing difficult facing wind; humans can be blown off the ground for short distances at c160kmph.

Note: Wind speeds indicated at valley level should be increased by at least 50 per cent to give a prudent estimate of the wind on 900m summits.

Note: Knots and metres per second are also used to describe wind speeds in some sources. The unit conversions are: 1m per second = 3.6kmph (2.24mph); 1 knot = 1.85kmph (1.15mph).

- Crawling is a safer option than trying to stagger on your feet, even if it adds hours to the homeward journey.
- In a group the effort of fighting the wind can be reduced by keeping in tight formation and by taking turns in front, the leader shielding the rest of the party. Even when crawling there is benefit and safety in keeping in close contact.

The fundamental decision as to whether to escape or retreat may not be so easy if the wind is at your tail. As the great south-east gale of 21 January 1984 gathered force, three ski-tourers were heading north-west across the Monadhliath plateau, intending to stay overnight at the remote Findhorn bothy. On reaching the tops near Carn Balloch, they were blown over 'like skittles'. With the gale at their backs, it was tempting to have continued in search of the bothy. However, although such a decision might have served short-term convenience, it could have proved disastrous given the severity of the ensuing blizzard, which was the worst in over twenty years. Wisely, they turned back. After a desperate hour, they emerged on civilisation's side of the mountain and reached Newtonmore that night.[4]

The Cairn Gorm AWS data suggests that with the greater prevalence of westerlies in the 1990s the winds have become stronger. The winter mean for the period 1990–95 of 62kmph, although based on incomplete data, is 6kmph faster than the average between 1978/9–1986/7. This is consistent with the predictions of global warming, which have warned of a 30 per cent increase in the incidence of gales over the Highlands in the next fifty years.

RAIN, RIME AND SNOWFALL

For all the interest of temperature and wind, it is the complex behaviour of moisture in the atmosphere that gives mountain weather its greatest fascination. This is especially so in Scotland's maritime climate, and particularly in winter when the moisture translates into snowfall over the high ground. Snowfall exhibits an unfathomable complexity of form and process and, of course, produces a marvellously varied scenic effect. The wild grandeur of a blowing blizzard, the silent grace of drifting flakes, the delicate tracery of hoar from a long deep frost – these are some of nature's most wondrous sights and are all the more appreciated for their rarity of occurrence in Britain's temperate climate.

Rain and Cloud

However, before we let our imagination run away to a perfect world of unbroken snow-scapes, it is only realistic to remind ourselves that moisture means cloud, and of this the Scottish hills have more than their fair share in every season, while heavy winter rain is a well known and long-cursed phenomenon. In sheets and stair-rods, drizzle or deluge, it comes with appreciable frequency and intensity at all altitudes. As Figs 1.3 and 1.4 illustrate, the measurements on Ben Nevis in the late nineteenth century showed that the total precipitation of the winter months from December to March formed 41 per cent of the annual total at the summit, of which on average 25 per cent fell as rain. On lower summits the proportion of rain to snowfall is considerably higher, reaching 50 per cent at an altitude of 750m If prolonged, the rain simply washes away the lying snow, and because typically it falls at temperatures between +3 and +6 degrees C, it creates the wetting, chilly conditions that are so difficult to survive.

Records of cloud cover from the Nevis observatory concluded that in winter, on average only 10 per cent of the possible hours of sunshine were enjoyed, and the summit itself was clear of fog for only 21 per cent of the time between November and March. Ben Nevis is, of course, Scotland's highest ground. Independent observations from sea level over the winter of 1901–2 estimated the proportions of cloud cover as 67 per cent at the summit, 50 per cent at 1,000m and 20 per cent at 700m. You will obviously see a good deal more if you climb on the lower hills.

These averages ignore the happy fact that settled spells of anticyclonic weather break through the gloom of every winter to give an atmospheric clarity unequalled in other seasons. During such periods, remarkably low relative humidities of under 20 per cent were measured on Ben Nevis. In fact, 100 per cent is usual!

How Snow Crystals Form

Fig 2.7 classifies the main forms of precipitation experienced in Scotland in winter, the list being ordered in a decreasing sequence of air temperature. Much of our winter rainfall commences its life as snow crystals which melt during their descent, the crucial temperature threshold where snow turns to rain at ground level being +2 to +3 degrees C. The prevalence of ground temperatures on the mountains between –5 and +5 degrees C produces a greater variety of precipitation and frost deposits on our hills than might be encountered in a colder, less changeable climate. Attempts to recognise and identify these types both in the air and on the ground can add a new dimension of interest to a winter's day on the mountains.

Four main processes are at work in the production of winter's raindrops and snowflakes:

Supercooling Water droplets can exist in the atmosphere even though the temperature is below freezing point, and in this condition they are termed 'supercooled'. For droplets to freeze, there must be tiny impurities active in the air, called freezing nuclei, onto which the droplets freeze. As the temperature drops, the numbers of active nuclei increase, but only at –40 degrees C do all droplets in the atmosphere freeze spontaneously. Therefore, a parcel of saturated air at –15 degrees C will contain a mixture of supercooled liquid droplets and frozen ice particles. This is the usual state in Scotland where temperatures in the lower atmosphere are rarely lower than –20 degrees C.

Supersaturation The amount of water vapour present in the air decreases as it cools, any excess condensing into droplets at its saturation point to form clouds. In sub-zero temperatures, some of the droplets will freeze to form ice particles. As the temperature falls further – as, say, when an airmass is forced to rise over the mountains – the air becomes supersaturated and more vapour must be shed. However, the saturation point of vapour with respect to an ice surface is reached at a higher temperature than its saturation point with respect to a water surface. Therefore, there is a range of temperature where vapour is supersaturated over ice but as yet unsaturated over water, and the suspended ice particles will attract the vapour at the expense of the water droplets. Thus, a snow crystal is born.

Deposition and Vapour Transport (see Fig 2.8) The excess vapour is deposited directly onto the ice particles; it therefore passes from a gaseous to a solid state without going through the liquid phase. While this is happening, the water droplets may be evaporating because the vapour remains unsaturated relative to their water surface. This supplies further

Plate 2.3 *Rime ice cakes on the summit tors of Ben Avon, Cairngorms*

Fig 2.7 *The major forms of winter precipitation*

Type	Description	Size in mm (diameter)	Mode of formation
Rain	Aggregates of water droplets of variable size.	0.5–5	Winter rain is usually derived from ice crystals which melt and coalesce during descent.
Sleet	Partially melted snowflakes or a mix of rain/snow.	0.5–5	
Freezing rain (glazed frost) (silver thaw)	Rain deposited as ice on impact with frozen ground.	0.5–5	Air temperature: 2–5°C; ground temperature: below 0°C; raindrops coalesce, then freeze to form a sheet-ice surface.
Rime ice	Ice accumulations on windward sides of exposed objects; feathery fir-cone growths.		Cloud droplets freeze on contact with frozen ground; typically formed by uplift of warm moist air over frozen hills; best formed in fog and moderate wind.
Surface hoar (white frost)	Deposits of water vapour on ground surface; white feathery flakes with no cohesion.		Deposition from vapour to solid state on contact with colder ground; air and ground temperature will both be below 0°C for thick hoar to develop.
Snowflakes	Aggregates of snow crystals interlocked and of low density.	2–20	Coagulation of grains/pellets during descent; growth is promoted in moist warm air (temperature: –4–0°C); interlock of stellar crystals produces biggest size.
Ice pellets	Frozen raindrops or melted and refrozen snowflakes.	Less than 5	Formed in turbulent air where strong vertical updraught causes secondary uplift and recooling of raindrops; not easily differentiated from hail.
Small hail	Translucent, spherical; snow pellets encased in ice.	Less than 5	Originating as rimed pellets but coated with ice as water droplets collide, condense, coalesce and freeze during descent; will form when liquid content of air is high.
Large hail	Spherical ice-balls; usually showing layering of opaque and clear ice layers.	5–50	Forms as for small hail (ie, in moist air, temperature close to 0°C, but with turbulence causing repeated uplift and cooling, so causing aggregation.
Snow pellets (rimed crystals)	White opaque low-density ice growths showing roughly round, conical or irregular shape.	2–5	Formed by riming onto freezing nuclei (supercooled water droplets condensing onto ice particles): growth is gradual compared to hail; lower frequency and speed of impact; moist rising air.
Broken grains	Tiny granular grains of high density.	0.1–0.5	Pulverisation of crystals by wind; collision in air and on ground impact.
Snow grains (snow crystals)	Crystalline opaque ice grains (columns, plates, needles or stellar shapes); infinite variety of growths.	0.5–1	Deposition of water vapour onto freezing nuclei; form of growth depends on air temperature and degree of supersaturation of air with respect to an ice surface; growth maximised at air temperatures –12 to –16°C.

Note: Snow pellets and grains are not independent types; riming and crystalline growth can occur simultaneously or else grains are rimed during descent.

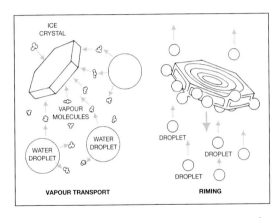

Fig 2.8 *The genesis of snow: vapour transport and riming (from* Avalanche Handbook, 1976*)*

vapour which is deposited onto the crystals. This process of vapour transport is therefore self-sustaining until the crystals grow to such a size that they fall out of the atmosphere as delicate *snow grains* or new snow.

Riming The ice particles may also grow by their collision with suspended water droplets which freeze on impact. This is riming (Fig 2.8), and it becomes predominant over deposition when the air is saturated with respect to both water and ice (so that vapour transport no longer occurs), or when crystals are falling down through moist air layers. In these situations, simpler *snow pellets* are formed.

Types of Snow Crystal

The varieties of pure grains and their modified rimed forms are literally infinite. Over six thousand different kinds of snow crystal were identified and photographed by an American, Wilson Bentley, in a life-long study between 1885 and 1931. Crystal development depends on two main controls: air temperature, which determines the direction of growth as between plate-like and columnar structures; and the degree of supersaturation to ice, which at high levels enables branching and elaboration into stellar forms. Fig 2.9 illustrates some basic

types of crystal, and shows how they might be modified by riming, temperature change and wind action.

In Scotland, atmospheric depositions of rime ice on the ground surface are of particular prominence, due to the regular influx and uplift of moist Atlantic air. Although created purely by the impact-freezing of cloud droplets onto exposed objects, the Ben Nevis observers witnessed the growth of rime at an incredible rate of 30cm per day. Surface hoaring may likewise be remarkably intense, producing aerated and cohesionless layers of crystals of ankle-, or even calf-depth in clear cold weather when the diurnal temperature range is large. Day-time heating/evaporation loads the surface air layers with moisture that is deposited as thick frost in the ensuing night.

Snowfall Volumes

Snowfall quantities are notoriously difficult to measure and compare because of their varying density. For example, a 10cm fall of light snow crystals may equate to 0.5cm of rain, whereas the same depth of heavy wet snowflakes might give a water equivalent of 2.5cm of rain. The volume of snow on the ground is therefore wholly misleading as an indicator of water quantity. The heaviest falls in water content indeed occur when the temperature is close to zero and the air is able to hold more moisture, which is carried up and over the hills where it is shed as snow.

While the winter weather of the Scottish mountains can indeed be wild and turbulent, never should it be regarded as uniformly hostile. It is vitally important that the mountaineer can predict with reasonable accuracy how, when and where the one extreme of weather or the other, or any of the shades between, will occur: it is for this reason that we now move into the realm of forecasting.

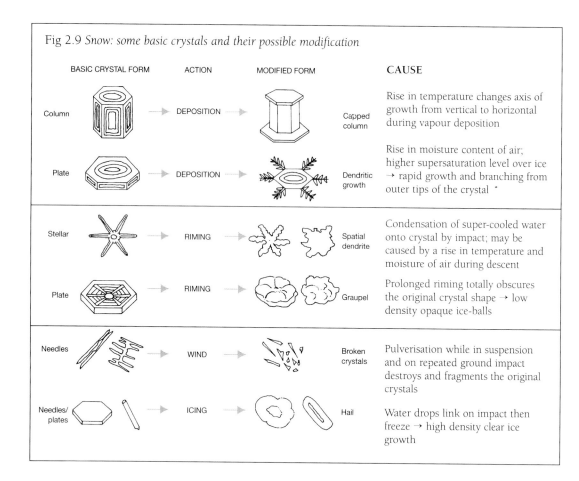

Fig 2.9 *Snow: some basic crystals and their possible modification*

BASIC CRYSTAL FORM	ACTION	MODIFIED FORM	CAUSE
Column	DEPOSITION	Capped column	Rise in temperature changes axis of growth from vertical to horizontal during vapour deposition
Plate	DEPOSITION	Dendritic growth	Rise in moisture content of air; higher supersaturation level over ice → rapid growth and branching from outer tips of the crystal
Stellar	RIMING	Spatial dendrite	Condensation of super-cooled water onto crystal by impact; may be caused by a rise in temperature and moisture of air during descent
Plate	RIMING	Graupel	Prolonged riming totally obscures the original crystal shape → low density opaque ice-balls
Needles	WIND	Broken crystals	Pulverisation while in suspension and on repeated ground impact destroys and fragments the original crystals
Needles/ plates	ICING	Hail	Water drops link on impact then freeze → high density clear ice growth

UNRAVELLING
THE WEATHER MAP

In Chapter 1 the basic idea of airmasses and airflows was introduced, together with the notion of the *polar front*. The daily weather map or *synoptic chart* reveals the detailed meteorological patterns prevailing on a particular day, including:

- the locations of areas of low pressure (depressions) and high pressure (anticyclones);
- the pattern of air pressure as shown by the *isobar* contour lines;
- the frontal boundaries between different airmasses which form around evolving depressions.

Most weather maps published in newspapers are projections for noon on the day of publication. To interpret a synoptic chart and assess the immediate weather prospects, look for four features on the map:

1. **The general airflow direction** as inferred from the relative positions of 'lows' and 'highs' – the temperature and moistness of the prevailing airstream can easily be guessed, as explained in Chapter 1.
2. **Frontal systems**: warm, cold or occluded. The presence of fronts indicates atmospheric instability along the boundaries between different airmasses; the uplift of air at fronts means cloud, precipitation and additional wind. Although all fronts give unsettled conditions, the exact nature of the weather is quite different between

warm, cold and occluded fronts.

3 **Pressure gradients**, as shown by the spacing of isobars, indicating general wind-speeds.

4 **Local wind directions**: these are shown symbolically on many weather charts, but can be easily inferred from the pressure pattern (in the Northern Hemisphere air flows clockwise with respect to 'highs', and anti-clockwise around 'lows').

Six Days in One Winter:

These features are best illustrated by looking at six weather maps taken from the 1997/98 winter season. I have deliberately chosen more pronounced or extreme weather situations because it is vital that the mountaineer can identify and avoid the most severe conditions from a reading of the synoptic chart, and equally can take advantage of the likelihood of fine weather. The selection also illustrates how strikingly different mountain weather can be according to airflows and pressure patterns. There are many days when the weather is less vigorous or less decided in nature – yet synoptic situations very similar to those selected will be encountered during any winter season. So be warned!

17 December 1997: A polar continental blast (Fig 2.10) No frontal complications to worry about on this map: the main feature is the strength of the continental anticyclone (1,048mb) which built out just north of Britain, and the tightly packed isobars where this abuts airmasses at considerably lower pressure (968mb) over the Atlantic. On the night of the 17th/18th the wind came screaming straight from central Europe, dry and cold to begin with, and picking up very little moisture or heat in its passage over the North Sea. Save for a few flurries of snow down the east coast this was a dry storm. The mountains stood frozen yet bare of

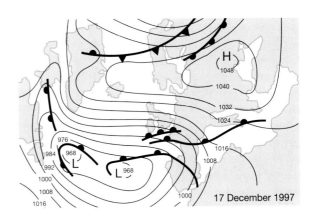

Fig 2.10 *A polar continental blast*

snow against this withering blast, with air temperatures at or just below freezing point, and south-easterly winds well in excess of 120kmph at summit level. Only late on the 18th did the anticyclone weaken sufficiently to allow a return to normality.

29–30 December 1997: Caught in the spider's web (Fig 2.11a–b) In the last days of the year a strong westerly airflow developed over northern Britain, with successive frontal depressions steaming in from the Atlantic to give wet and stormy conditions with a regular alternation of airmasses between tropical maritime, returning polar maritime and pure polar maritime as warm and cold fronts crossed the country. Such an entrenched westerly flow is sustained by 'jet-stream' winds in the middle and upper layers of the troposphere (above 7,000m in altitude), and can last for several weeks. On 29 December an active cell of low pressure developed in mid-Atlantic (1) along the approximate line of the polar front. Fuelled by the pressure and temperature differences between the polar and temperate airmasses to its north and south, and propelled into an eastward track with anticlockwise wind circulation by the earth's rotation, the centre of the low sped 1,000km north-east in twenty-four hours to become anchored near Iceland on the

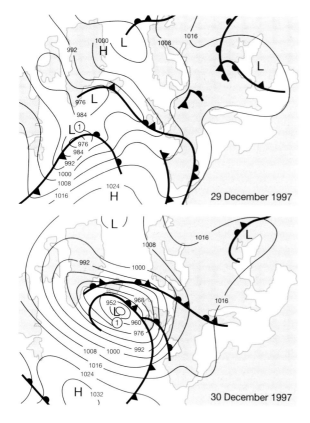

Fig 2.11a–b *Caught in the spider's web*

Faced with a weather map such as that for the 30th, plans for serious mountain expeditions might sensibly be modified or shelved.

12 February 1998: Tropical maritime in full flow (Fig 2.12) When depressions are passing just to the north of Britain in winter, climbers can expect a regular alternation between polar and tropical airflows; but if a strong anticyclone builds northwards from North Africa over southern Europe, depressions can be blocked and diverted northwards. As a result, the whole of the country gets stuck in a south to south-westerly airflow with associated warmth, thick cloud, and for the mountains of the western seaboard, prolonged heavy rain. This tropical maritime flow dominated February's weather, completely thawing all snow accumulations except for a few small fields in the Cairngorms and on Ben Nevis – a situation unprecedented in the previous twenty winters. The period from the 11th to 14th gave the heaviest rains, with an average of 7–10cm a day over the mountains. A scan of the weather map for the 12th gave no hope of an early end to the deluge, and indeed Glenelg received 219mm on the 11th and 12th. The anticyclone was drawing unseasonably warm Saharan air north to Britain, and its oceanic track ensured it was fully loaded with moisture.

30th. As it travelled, the depression sucked in moist unstable Atlantic air and deepened to a central pressure of 936mb. With such low central pressure, the surrounding winds were very strong, and Scotland was literally caught in the spider's web of isobars and fronts. On the 30th we were sandwiched between a weak occluded front and the vigorous warm front entrained by the depression, giving wild wet weather on the mountains. By evening the warm front had passed through, giving a brief twelve-hour spell of tropical maritime air before the advancing cold front brought polar air back across the country on the 31st. For the mountaineer, the alternation of different airstreams with precipitation switching from sleet to rain then back to snow, gave a difficult forty-eight hours with little respite from gales on the summits.

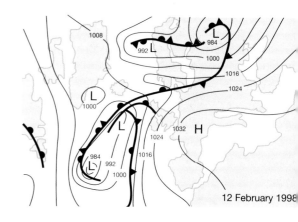

Fig 2.12 *Tropical maritime in full flow*

The sou'westers form a giant 'conveyor belt' from which there is no escape: weak fronts to the north-west of Scotland are slow-moving and themselves harbour air which is only slightly cooler than that which blights the Highlands. None of them pack the punch needed to break the mould of the weather, and the nearest pool of cold air is over 1,000km to the north. Unfortunately on this occasion there were thousands already committed to making the journey north because it was the start of the school half-term break, and therefore always one of the busiest winter weeks in the Highlands.

28 February 1998: Straight from the Arctic (Fig 2.13) An arctic maritime airflow can only be expected for a few days each winter, yet it can bring heavy snowfalls and severe temperatures. Northerly winds can set in when a depression pushes across Britain to become anchored over Scandinavia or the North Sea while simultaneously a ridge of high pressure builds in the Atlantic, so blocking the westerly flow of weather; then, the winds are drawn directly from the Arctic and flow down the west flank of the depression. The snowfall can be particularly heavy if the northerly flow is complicated by development of a 'polar low'. Such lows are small-scale, non-frontal features caused by the heating of arctic air as it flows over a relatively warm sea, and can be spotted as minor kinks or knolls in the general north-south alignment of the isobars. On 28 February a very strong arctic anticyclone over Greenland (1,040mb) had extended a ridge down across the mid-Alantic, breaking the eastwards run of depressions towards Europe. By contrast, a low of 960mb had become anchored over northern Scandinavia. The resultant northerly airflow brought blizzards to northern Scotland, with 30cm dry snow accumulating at sea level in a single afternoon fall of three hours' duration. After a month of

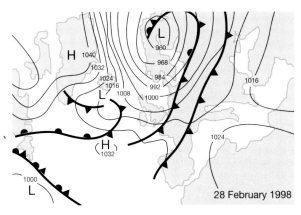

Fig 2.13 *Straight from the Arctic*

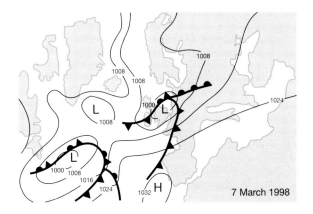

Fig 2.14 *Blizzard in the battlezone*

record-breaking warmth, the Highlands were suddenly plunged back into the depths of winter.

7 March 1998: Blizzard in the battlezone (Fig 2.14) After a week of real winter weather with alternating polar and arctic maritime air-masses, the hills were already well plastered with snow. Then during the 6th, a trough of low pressure with an associated occluded front pushed northwards from England. To the south lay mild air, and the trough marked the 'polar frontal' boundary. With moist mild air meeting such colder air to the north, the front became very active even though it was slow moving. Would it push the cold air away, or would it retreat back south? There could be either heavy rains or serious blizzards, depending on its position to within 100km. For weather forecasters the situation was too close to call. In the Highlands, the 6th was a bitterly cold day with dry east winds blowing hard as the trough edged in and deepened. Over the night of the 6th–7th the trough got stuck over the Central Highlands. Severe east gales were now loaded with moisture due to the uplift of the warmer airmass along the frontal boundary, yet the air temperatures remained close to freezing point. The ensuing blizzards were the worst of the season over the Northern Highlands, bringing havoc to the roads and major power cuts. When the storm receded on the 7th it left an unbroken snow-cover over the mountains and the best ski-touring conditions of the year.

The key feature of the weather map that warns of the blizzard is the marked contrast between the airstreams to the south and north of the front. The front itself does not show as the 'spider's web' of a fully fledged Atlantic depression, but nevertheless possesses the potential to deepen and strike.

8 March 1998: A glorious ridge (Fig 2.15) The polar airstream won the battle of the airmasses on the 6th and 7th. With the trough receding south-eastwards and weakening and a good ridge of high pressure building south-east-wards from Greenland, the cold air resumed control and gave a magical day of hard frost, unbroken sunshine and absolute clarity on the 8th. In some winters the mountaineer can enjoy many such days if a stable ridge or anti-cyclone becomes well established. In the troubled winter of 1998, this perfect day was an exception, but all the more to be enjoyed by the thousands who were out skiing or hill-walking.

Such a weather map is notable for its lack of isobars over northern Britain, and together with the gentle northerly drift of air, it ensured calm, cold and dry conditions.

Gauging the Outlook

To gauge the longer-term outlook from today's map is a great deal more difficult. Arrows are often used to indicate the likely movement of the major airmasses, so that the general trend of weather can be guessed. In predicting the outlook, there are three basic features to look for:

1 The positioning and relative strengths of anticyclones which may block or divert approaching weather systems. On any weather map look first for the big areas of high pressure: anticyclones such as that over southern Europe on 12 February are likely to dominate the weather over half the continent for the following week.

2 Boundary zones between distinctly differing airmass types: these will be sources of future instability, as so well illustrated by the frontal trough on 7 March.

3 Specific points of 'frontogenesis' (ie minor disturbances along frontal boundaries from which future depressions are likely to evolve). During phases of strong westerly flow, such as 29–30 December 1997, tomorrow's weather can usually be spotted halfway out across the Atlantic.

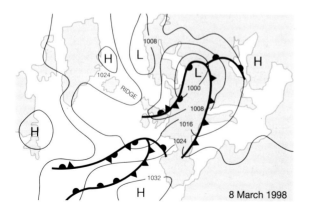

Fig 2.15 *A glorious ridge*

General Weather Forecasts

Given the wide availability of weather forecasts on all forms of communication media including the internet, there is no excuse for winter hill-goers not to obtain an up-to-date forecast before venturing out. However, one must also be aware that general weather forecasts sometimes lack local precision as regards the Highlands. How infuriating it is when weather forecasters at the Met Office merrily predict the West Highland weather to be 'a few spits and spots of rain', when the next day's reality is a non-stop deluge! Current sources of general weather forecasts can be summarised as follows:

National television The BBC gives the best detail, coupled with glimpses of the synoptic charts. Lunchtime forecasts, particularly the 'farming outlook' broadcast on Sunday, give a five-day outlook.

Regional television BBC Scotland currently gives a detailed weather report and four-day outlook on its evening news programme, and gives more attention to local variations across the Highlands. Many regional TV stations use different sources to their national counterparts and their predictions occasionally differ.

Radio Die-hard traditionalists can mentally construct the synoptic chart from the shipping forecast. Verbal forecasts on both national and local BBC radio are usually detailed for the forthcoming day but rarely give much attention to the outlook.

Newspapers Most broadsheets give a synoptic chart which can be studied at leisure, together with a regional split on the verbal forecast. However, input data is already twelve to sixteen hours old when the paper is read.

Internet Numerous forecasts and synoptic charts can be accessed by 'surfing' the net, and then viewed at leisure (see Appendix V), though none improve in detail on those available on other media.

The Translation Problem

Even armed with the best and latest weather information, winter enthusiasts must still apply the skill of translating a general weather forecast into the language of conditions up at 1,000m on the mountain tops. Thus a forecast intended for dwellers at valley or sea level needs to be translated in the following way:

- The appropriate lapse rate must be applied in order to work out summit temperatures and the likely freezing level.
- 50 per cent should be added to the forecast sea-level windspeeds in order to assess the free air winds at summit level.
- Allowance must be made for a wind-gust factor between 25 and 50 per cent higher than the free air windspeed at summit level due to topographical effects on the wind (this means that a 40kmph wind at sea level may be producing gusts in excess of 100kmph on the tops).
- The travel implications of the estimated summit winds must be considered, applying the sort of considerations listed in Fig 2.6.
- Likely cloudbases on the mountains must be considered; this requires interpretation of the prevailing airstream and any associated frontal systems. For example, lowering layers of stratiform cloud herald warm front passage while broken cells of cumuliform cloud form behind the cold front (see Fig 2.16).
- It is important to realise that any forecast precipitation will be more intense over the mountains due to the greater uplift and cooling of air, especially those peaks in the first line of defence to the prevailing airstream.
- Valley rain may be converted into mountain snowfall when temperatures and lapse rates so indicate.

Having made all these adjustments and translations, a vivid picture should be created in the

Fig 2.16 *A head in the clouds: weather omens*

CLOUD FORMS

LAYERED (STRATIFORM) Uniform layer above summits, eg fish-scale pattern		Stable air; usually an inversion lies above; quiet weather with anticyclonic conditions
Multi-layered; thickening and lowering in distance		Imminent approach of warm (or occluded) front; prolonged steady precipitation likely; accompanying warmth
HIGH LEVEL CIRRUS 'White mares' tails', wisps		Indication of moisture in upper atmosphere and an early sign of a frontal system 12–24 hours away
HALOES/ATMOSPHERIC HAZE Watery sky-haloed sun		General moisture in upper air; more reliable sign of the approach of fronts; layering sequence of cloud will follow
CUMULIFORM Vertical development; 'cotton wool'/'cauliflower' shapes		Instability and uplift in atmosphere; typical of a cold-front passage; air cooling; general weather likely to improve; snow showers
CUMULONIMBUS Towering cumulus forms; thunder clouds		Extreme instability; violent uplift and cooling; squalls of hail and ice; frequent in winter under strong NW air-flow
Anvil-shaped CuNimbus		The forward edge to the lee of the wind indicates a rapid rise of wind speed with height; gales on the tops
LENTICULAR/WAVE FORMS Regular waves or lens-shaped clouds in lee of summits		Uplift over mountains causing condensation; wave forms suggest an inversion against stable upper air; weather possibly windy but usually settled
Summit capping/shrouds		Often indicates severe wind on the tops, but not a reliable sign of a coming storm as is often thought
FOGS AND LOW-LEVEL INVERSIONS Smoke/mist rises vertically, then spreads at distinct level		Stable sinking air; anticyclonic conditions; light wind

CLOUD MOVEMENTS

DIRECTION Cloud layers veer with height often from SW-NW		Indicates the pattern of wind-shear typical of warm fronts
Cloud layers back with height often from NW-SW		Opposing wind directions indicate cold-front conditions
SPEED Judged against hill-sides		An obvious indication of wind speed, especially if clouds are individually distinct

mind as to what the weather will be on the summits. Such a picture may indeed be off-putting, but it is better to be realistic than fanciful when choosing a suitable route, and when packing necessary clothing for a winter's day in the mountains.

SPECIALISED MOUNTAIN FORECASTS

With the increasing popularity of skiing and winter mountaineering specialised mountain weather forecasts have been issued since the mid-1980s, solving the translation problem for those who struggle with lapse rates and their like. These are issued daily on recorded telephone or FAX message and are broadcast on Scottish radio and television at weekends.

One long-established mountain forecast is 'Climbline', which gives separate two-day predictions for the West and the East Highlands in the sort of detail that a general national forecast could never achieve. No longer do climbers have to make their own translations in order to uplift the general sea-level forecast: 'Climbline' gives the experts' prediction of the cloud base, also the freezing level and the summit mean windspeeds, and the wind direction, gust velocities and temperatures, as well as providing a general synopsis and further three-day outlook; it is updated twice daily (see Appendix V for details). 'Climbline' is prepared by Oceanroutes (UK) Ltd, a private meteorological company based in Aberdeen. Their local source data of air pressure, temperature and wind is derived from fifty or sixty low-level weather stations around the UK, together with automatic mountain stations, ships, oil-drilling platforms, aircraft and weather balloons. This is all fed into a numerical computer model developed by the National Meteorological Centre in the USA. Applying known equations of atmospheric physics, the model generates forecast synoptic charts for both surface and upper air levels, and with addition of global weather data these can be rolled forward to give a longer term outlook. The 'Climbline' forecast is channelled via the Ski Hotline media service and can be accessed by phone or fax.

Forecast accuracy is very high over a 24–36 hour period, but diminishes thereafter. Synoptic developments are extremely sensitive to minor local changes, as befits a 'chaotic' physical system. Moreover an unrecorded shift in weather variables in one locality can have a cumulative effect on the development of weather systems, so that after five days the actual weather situation may bear little resemblance to that which was originally forecast. Even so, while a degree of scepticism is sensible when interpreting longer-term forecasts, they do enable the winter mountaineer to plan ahead. Thus the feasibility of a weekend trip to the Highlands can be decided with reasonable confidence on the preceding Tuesday or Wednesday.

Weather forecasting in the mountains is a particularly tricky game. Lapse rates of temperature can be highly variable according to the prevailing airmasses and degree of cloud cover, meaning that the all-important freezing level is often hard to predict with accuracy. Windspeeds are subject to enormous local variation according to topography. Furthermore, a mountain massif as broad and as continuous as the Highlands may also deflect or retard approaching weather systems so that the expected weather is delayed or diverted. Realising this great complexity, one should forgive the mountain forecaster the occasional error of judgement.

AN EYE TO THE WEATHER

With regular trips into the hills, one develops an instinctive visual and sensual awareness of

Plate 2.4 *Winter cloudscapes: stratiform clouds lower over the mountains, killing the light and indicating an approaching warm front; heavy rain commenced 30 minutes after the photo was taken*

changes in the weather. Whatever the confidence and quality of the forecast, it is reassuring to be able to make an 'on-the-spot' prognosis of the coming weather, and if committed to a multi-day expedition in the hills, personal observation may be the sole means of prediction. However, although visual indicators of the coming weather are useful, they are by no means infallible and are sometimes ambiguous. Unquestioning obedience to distant atmospheric indications is not advised unless they equate consistently with a known forecast, or more than one indicative sign is present either together or in sequence. Many times I have curtailed an itinerary or hurried nervously through a day due to the sight of a

wall of cloud in the west, only for the expected front to falter or fail, or else to materialise as a harmless sea-haze rather than the imagined storm. Most visual forecasting focuses on adverse weather changes – partly because it is much harder to foresee an improvement in the weather when your vision is limited to twenty metres by the prevailing storm! Therefore, weather pessimists tend to make great play of the visual signs, because they can always offer the 'better safe than sorry' excuse if their prognoses prove groundless.

Cloud sequences and wind direction changes provide the best evidence of the pending weather, but there are other general signs: the sudden awareness of the temperature ris-

Plate 2.5 *Winter cloudscapes: cumulonimbus cloud cell bringing a squall of snow and hail in the wake of a cold front passage (Martin Welch)*

ing, and the flatness of the light as high pressure is displaced by an advancing low; or the drier chill in the air as an easterly breeze takes hold and repels the maritime weather. The interpretation of various cloud forms and wind patterns is summarised in Fig 2.16. It is particularly hard to estimate the timing and the intensity of bad weather from the sight of distant cloudbanks; however, with experience, a better discretion can be developed in interpreting them.

If confused by shifting winds, a useful ploy when trying to gauge the position of low-pressure areas is to establish the direction the wind is coming from in the following way: applying the law of anti-clockwise airflow, if you stand on a summit and position yourself so your back is to the wind, then the depression is on your left. Occasionally clouds can be spotted moving in different directions at different altitudes, indicating the approach of a front. With such information one can piece together the approximate synoptic pattern when on the hills.

The use of the altimeter as a barometer may be highly beneficial on multi-day mountain expeditions. Pressure changes in Scotland can be dramatic, with falls or rises of ten millibars or more over the course of a single night. A fall in pressure often precedes the onset of bad weather, and gives warning of the coming storm before the first clouds appear on the horizon. As a guideline, a change in apparent altitude of 10m equates approximately to one millibar of pressure change. Overnight changes in excess of 3mb are significant and should arouse interest. Bothy-goers who have imbibed too much whisky may forget that pressure varies inversely to altitude. In other words, an apparent rise in altitude indicates a fall in pressure, and vice-versa.

In all matters of personal interpretation of the weather, experience is the key. Regular climbers soon acquire a 'feel' for the weather; it is an integral part of a mountain education.

REGIONAL WEATHER VARIATIONS

The Highlands are some 325 by 240km in area and are bound to exhibit significant local variations of weather; this may crucially influence where one should choose to climb. For instance, regional contrasts are briefly manifested when a slow-moving depression crosses directly over Scotland, the differences lying in the timing rather than the substance of the associated weather: with practice, they can be effectively exploited. For example, if the depression or front has a northward track, it will bear easterly winds to its north and moist westerlies to its south; by keeping to the Northern Highlands, as much as twelve hours of cold, hard conditions can be snatched before the centre passes and the thaw sets in. So living near Torridon, I never abandon hope for the day if the depression is encroaching from the south. 'Beating the weather' is the most smugly satisfying of all mountain pastimes, and the pleasure of supping tea by the fireside with the rain drumming outside, yet having just enjoyed a hard, dry traverse of Liathach, is incomparable – but its achievement often demands an early start and a spurt of speed.

The mountains also exert a barrier effect on the weather, and this produces a more persistent regional effect, usually between east and west. Regularly and at any time of year Atlantic fronts cross the west coast, but expend their moisture before reaching the Eastern Highlands; thus the western hills are dreich and clouded, sweating in the tropical maritime air, while the east remains dry, clear and very warm due to the Föhn effect.

The greater dryness of the rain-shadowed east is, of course, generally known. Less widely appreciated is the winter phenomenon of the 'snow-shadowed' west, when the continental airflow brings cloud and snow off the North Sea over the Grampians and Cairngorms. Moreover west-coasters secretly enjoy long periods of winter sun that are denied elsewhere when the easterlies blow, and the further west the better.

So this is our winter mountain weather. It challenges, baffles and inspires, and it still remains far beyond our complete understanding. The hillgoer can gain immeasurable practical benefit from its study, but is never its master – and indeed, much of the particular fun of being in the Scottish hills in winter derives from planning in the face of its uncertainty. So we climb in the surety that the weather will continue to spring its surprises. Whatever our abilities, nature will on occasion assert an insuperable power and leave us humbled, yet strangely content…

AN IMPOSSIBLE STORM

20 March 1986 on the Cairngorm Plateau
(Fig 2.17a–b)
On the night of Wednesday 19 March, three groups from Glenmore Lodge occupied snow-holes at 1,050m in the valley of the Garbh Uisge Beag between Cairn Gorm and Ben

Macdui. Their leaders were Sam Crymble, Mark Diggins ('Digger') and Willie Todd, and the students were undergoing their Winter Mountain Leadership Assessment, which involved a two-night expedition with intensive navigation exercises.

While they lay sound and snug in the holes, insulated from the world outside, a depression and its associated fronts were tracking steadily eastwards over the Atlantic. At first the weathermen saw no particular evil in this approaching system, but as the night progressed it was squeezed into a north-east trajectory as a huge zone of high pressure built to its south. Then, quite suddenly, its further advance was barred by an equally strong anticyclone sitting over continental Europe (see Fig 2.17a). With nowhere to escape, the depression deepened fast. At half-past midnight, as its fronts occluded and swept into Britain, the anemometer on Cairn Gorm's summit recorded a southerly gale averaging 162kmph and rising to an incredible gust of 275kmph – Britain's highest-ever measured windspeed to that date. All hell was breaking loose.

Thursday morning's weather forecast was still a step behind the reality. When the groups radioed to the lodge at 9am they were told to expect 110kmph (100mph) winds gusting to 160kmph (150mph). Now, 100mph is difficult, and 150mph means crawling, but Lodge instructors are hardened to severe winds, and these speeds are by no means exceptional in winter on the high Cairngorms. Provided they were no worse, they could cope, and so at 9.30 the teams dug themselves out of the holes and separately embarked on a day of navigational tests. The wind had indeed dropped, and for a brief half-hour fell below gale force; but the storm was far from spent and in fact the depression centre was just crossing northwards over the Cairngorms massif, a vortex of calm within a tightening funnel of plunging

Fig 2.17a *An impossible storm*

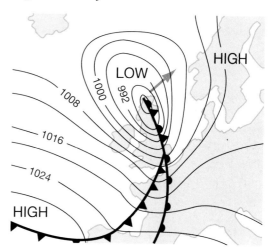

The forecast chart for 12 noon on 20 March 1986. Pressure in milibars

 Warm front
Cold front
Occluded front

pressure. Aviemore met. office staff had watched their barometer drop at the alarming rate of 10mb every three hours to a minimum of 974mb at the centre. Now the occluded front pushed through, causing the wind to veer sharply to the WNW and commence a rapid reacceleration – but by this time the parties were far from the holes.

Crymble took his group of three students north to Cairn Lochan, Todd went over to Loch Etchachan, and Diggins made his way further south on the upper slopes of Macdui. At 11.20 the wind was averaging 136kmph and was gusting 185, and by 12.50 it averaged 156kmph and was gusting to 227; thus the 100mph threshold of control was quickly exceeded, and with the frontal passage there came frequent blizzards to add to the furious clouds of spindrift. Diggins describes the havoc caused by the sudden rise of wind as his team were crossing a col south of Loch Etchachan:

'After 500m, the wind seemed to increase tenfold. The leading student was hardly able to

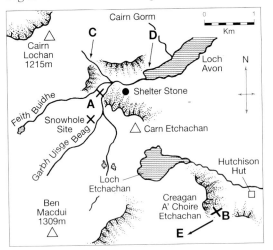

Fig 2.17b *The drama on the plateau*

A Crymble's avalanche
B Diggins' fall and avalanche
C Barton/Peter rescue route
D Fyffe/Walker rescue route
E Escape to Glen Derry/ Braemar – Diggins' team

stay on the ground at this point, being blown across the surface for 15–18m before braking with his axe. The wind would subside and we would slowly crawl to regroup, swinging our axes ahead of us and then hauling ourselves along with them. Sometimes the wind was so strong that we had great difficulty holding onto our axes while lying on the ground. Communication was also extremely difficult – it was largely done by gesticulating, for a shouted sentence could not be heard at more than two inches away from an ear.'

Any pretence at training was quickly abandoned, and it was obviously imperative that they reached some sort of shelter. For Diggins' party the Hutchison Hut in Coire Etchachan was the nearest sanctuary, and luckily their route lay with the wind; but it was snared by steep cliffs and bluffs at the corrie rim. Digger therefore took the lead – but as he neared the edge he was caught in an especially vicious squall and moments later he was airborne, precipitated straight over a cornice; he landed fifteen metres lower, minus axe but unhurt,

but with his party now stranded above. He tried vainly to climb back up, but the cornice edge was overhung – and as soon as he tried to descend, the whole slope avalanched. With a desperate scramble, he climbed up and off the moving slab and braked to a halt with fingers clawed in the underlying snow.

There was no choice but to descend to the hut, and hope against hope that his students had avoided the edge and could somehow find a route to safety. In the clearances he went out to search, but there was no sign of them. On one sortie the wind blew him right into the air, and he described a complete backward somersault before landing. Nor could he make any radio contact with the Lodge, and after a couple of hours he decided to attempt to crawl the 2km over to Loch Avon and thence regain the snow-holes.

Meanwhile Crymble had been close to the Feith Buidhe when the hurricane rose, and made straight back for the holes which were only a kilometre distant. He navigated solely by instinct and his intimate knowledge of the terrain, for compass-work was quite impossible. As he neared the site, he turned to check his team – and was horror-struck to discover that one man was missing: 'I could only assume that he had been blown away, onto and down the steep ground to the east.' With the remaining two students he sweep-searched the area but without success; they then crawled back to the holes, reaching them at 2.30pm, just as the gale built to its climax with a 180kmph mean and a 243kmph gust. No sooner had he radioed the loss of one team-member to the Lodge than his radio, like Digger's, packed up.

Down in Glenmore a major rescue operation was mounted: within an hour instructors Barton and Peter, and Fyffe and Walker were battling up onto the Cairngorm plateau in 160kmph crosswinds, and the police, the RAF and local rescue teams were all on alert.

On the mountain, despite the extreme weather and avalanche risk, Crymble's team had to face the fearful prospect of going back out to search for their man as soon as the wind had abated slightly – and it was indeed a trip fraught with danger. They were spread out five metres apart on the steepening ground north-east of the holes when the windslab released. All were carried off, but Crymble went the furthest: he was spat out of the avalanche minus axe and gloves in a pile of debris ninety metres lower, alive but with a suspected broken ankle. Rejoined by his students who were unhurt, it was to be a long slow crawl back to the holes.

At 17.20 just two hours of daylight remained. Still the wind gusted over 100mph, and in the north-west airflow the temperature had dropped to –5 degrees C. At the Lodge, the air was fraught with tension. There had been no radio contact with any of the teams, Todd's included, for nearly three hours. In desperation, the RAF were even asked whether they could raise a Nimrod jet to provide an airborne radio relay aerial above the plateau. There were eighteen people on the hill, one known to be missing and thirteen unaccounted for. Then, miraculously, things began to happen:

17.45: Braemar police ring to report Mark Diggins' four students safe. With great courage they had retraced their steps from the cornice edge and found an alternative route down to Glen Derry. In Digger's later words, it was 'a true display of their ability'. At base, however, anxieties for Diggins were immediately redoubled and one could only fear for the worst; but as the wind ebbed to 125kmph, some semblance of control could be regained by the men on the hill.
17.46: Barton and Peter radio to report they have reached the Garbh Uisge Beag and are searching for the holes.
17.47: Tim Walker radios; nothing heard except 'Digger!?'

18.11: Walker radios again from Shelter Stone. By pure chance they have found Diggins safe and well.
18.30: Crymble reaches the holes just before Barton and Peter arrive. To his incredible relief, the missing student is there. For nearly an hour he had remained where he had lost contact, and had then found his own way back to the holes, probably passing just metres away from Crymble's ill-fated search team. Using Bob Barton's radio, the good news is broadcast.
18.32: Walker, Fyffe and Diggins are climbing the avalanche-loaded slopes beneath the Garbh Uisge. Relaying messages via base, Barton guides them to the holes, using bearings and estimated distances from a boulder landmark.
18.50: The three reach the holes.

Of Willie Todd's group there had been neither sight nor sign. Then at 19.25, as if by magic, they walked through the front door of the Lodge, having evacuated by a 16km hike over the Saddle and down Strath Nethy when radio contact was lost at Loch Avon.

All were safe thanks to their own exceptional skill, resource and courage in the face of impossible conditions – though the element of luck cannot be denied. It was also just fortunate that none less experienced were on the high tops that day. A helicopter evacuation of the injured Crymble was arranged for the morning, and at the Garbh Uisge Beag, nine exhausted men recovered and repaired their wits.

No sooner was the drama over than the storm declined, almost in admission of its defeat. Having wreaked merciless fury for twenty-four hours and put those caught in its path to the ultimate survival test, the cyclone unwound, passing away north into oblivion somewhere over Scandinavia. By 10pm, Cairn Gorm's anemometer was spinning merrily at a mere 65kmph, just gale force 8 on the Beaufort scale and a playful breeze by the standards of the day.

3: EVER-CHANGING CONDITIONS

SNOW, ICE AND AVALANCHE

DIARY OF A WINTER'S DAY: 20 FEBRUARY 1997

From the moment we left the car we were assailed by a gale-force south-west wind. Driving wet sleet lashed into our faces. Less than half-way to the crag I was thoroughly soaked, chilled through and in the throes of agony from ice-cold hands. Why were we ploughing on through the slush? I suppose no one wanted to be the first to say 'Let's turn back', and there was a hope, albeit a fast-fading one, that the squall would end and we would reach a colder zone up near 900m.

Gaining height, the precipitation turned to thick wet snow, and then at the base of the cliff we hit the freezing level. At once the air was drier and the snow softer. Our clothes began to freeze solid and give us some genuine protection from the wind, and warmth returned. Above us, the face was a stucco of snow, rime and ice, plastered by the gale. The battlements of turf, so characteristic of the Western Highland cliffs, were completely smothered.

The first pitch was wholly iced, and the second was a delightful open-book corner with a foot-wide dribble of ice at its back. The tufted grooves of the upper slab were dependably frozen, and conditions had rarely been better for years. Over the summit the fresh snow lay like wet cement, sticky and stable.

We hardly noticed that the precipitation

had continued all day, but when we came down into the glen the rain was still pouring down in curtains. So, the expedition ended with a waist-deep crossing of the swollen River Cluanie, arm-in-arm, braced against the spate of the day. We drove home, bemused and weatherbeaten, but with an epic ripe for the telling!

No topic arouses more discussion in Highland bars and bothies on winter nights than the state of the snow and ice. Our obsession with the conditions is understandable, for they largely determine both the safety and enjoyment of all the winter mountain activities. Since they are dependent upon the weather regime, they exhibit its same capricious temperament. During a typical Scottish winter, the conditions can be eternally damned and immortally praised on successive days without our feeling the least inconsistency of opinion.

THE SUPPLY OF SNOW

'Conditions' are the product of what is laid down as precipitation and its subsequent alteration on the ground. The mechanics of snowfall have already been discussed in Chapter 2 (pages 46–50). There are four main weather situations when significant snowfall is produced over the mountains:

1 **Polar maritime (PM)** airflow in depressions gives frequent and often heavy showers of hail and rimed pellets (graupel),

usually accompanied by a strong north-westerly wind. The snowfall is widespread, but is most concentrated on the west and north-west coastal mountains. Graupel pellets form a distinctive and persistent layer in the snowpack, being resistant to alteration except by wholesale thaw. PM air returning from a westerly quarter tends to produce wetter, heavier snow turning to sleet or rain low down (ie snowflake aggregates). The duration and intensity is much increased by associated frontal activity.

2 **Polar continental (PC)** airflow over the North Sea gives snow showers, which are strongly localised on the east of the country. The snow is usually drier and exhibits less rime icing. If the easterly or south-easterly airflow is intensified by approaching depressions, the snowfall may spread inland as blizzards over the Cairngorms.

3 **Depression tracks** over southern Britain often produce winter's greatest blizzards, especially when a deep low moves north-eastwards across England and southern Scotland, entraining curling fronts which produce an easterly or south-easterly airstream over the Highlands. This is moister than the pure polar continental air, but is cooled sufficiently to give heavy, widespread snow at all levels.

4. **Northerly arctic maritime (AM)** airflow produces localised falls on exposed coastal hills, usually as showers, but occasionally intensifying into gentle steady snowfall of a dry crystalline type over the whole country. When a depression is sitting in the North Sea, the resultant northerly flow may bring particularly heavy snowfall over the Cairngorms and Northern Highlands. Low pressure cells are often embedded in a strong arctic airflow. One such 'polar low' produced the severe blizzards which swept the Northern and Western Isles on Christmas Eve in 1995.

CHANGES ON THE GROUND

Snow begins a process of alteration or *metamorphism* as soon as it reaches the ground, the initial characteristics of the snow crystals being quickly obscured; only graupel pellets and hard windslab tend to resist alteration for more than a couple of days after deposition. The changes in the snowpack may be slow or rapid, progressive or cyclical, superficial or hidden; moreover two or three processes may operate simultaneously in one place, yet quite separate ones may be at work on different sides of the same mountain. The sequence of these processes determines how conditions develop:

Settling: As fresh snow piles up, it becomes compressed by its own overlying weight, so that the new grains may be considerably deformed and the density of the snow cover increased. Typically, the air content of fresh snow which has fallen without wind is 90–95 per cent, but settling may on its own reduce this to 70 per cent in twenty-four hours.

Equitemperature metamorphism (ET met) (Fig 3.1): Simultaneous with settling there occurs a process of vapour transport within the

Fig 3.1 a–b *Equitemperature metamorphism*

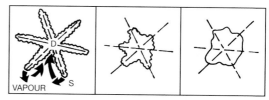

S Moisture sublimates from crystal tips into vapour
D Vapour deposited at centre of crystal

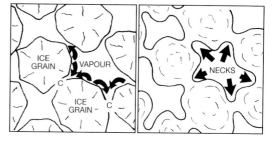

C Vapour deposited at contact points between the grains

lying snowpack which produces first, a rounding of grain shapes (Fig 3.1a), and then their joining together by the formation of necks at the contact points (Fig 3.1b). During the first stage there is a temporary loss of stability as the interlocked crystals are modified, but once bonding begins, the snowpack becomes progressively more stable.

The process occurs because the vapour saturation pressure of concave ice surfaces is lower than convex ones, so there is a progressive migration of vapour from the crystal tips to their concave interstices. ET met is accelerated at temperatures of just below zero, and has a more pronounced effect on elaborately branched snow crystals, whereas rounded pellets and hail may lie unaltered in loose piles for long periods. If uninterrupted it will, over many days, produce hard, stable 'firn' snow with about 35 per cent air content. The process does not involve any melting of the snow because it proceeds wholly at sub-zero temperatures. In the Scottish climate the gradual evolution of ET met rarely runs its course, usually being prematurely eclipsed either by wind action or a thaw in the snowpack.

Melt-freeze metamorphism (MF met): Thawing and refreezing within the pack is the more usual stabilising agent of Scottish snow, much of it melting immediately as it makes contact with a ground surface with a temperature above freezing point. Alternatively, a lying snow-cover will melt from its surface downwards during a thaw. Melting creates 'free water' within the snow which clings by surface tension to the larger remaining snow grains. On refreezing, whether due to night cooling or on arrival of a colder airstream, the grains are enlarged and bonded. A strong, uniform snowpack is produced with as little as 20 per cent air content, which British climbers refer to as 'névé'.

However, if MF met proceeds through many successive cycles, grain sizes enlarge to a point where free water can percolate down through the snow during the melt phase; no longer do the grains bond on refreezing, and loose granular snow is produced which is roundly cursed as 'sugar' or 'corn' by mountaineers, but more correctly termed 'spring snow'. Such granular grains are most frequently found at the bottom of the snowpack close to the ground surface.

Kinetic growth (also known as temperature gradient metamorphism or TG met): When fresh snow layers are not subject to any melting, a high vertical gradient of temperature can develop between very cold air at the snow surface and the ground which, due to retention of stored summer heat and the insulating effect of snow cover, may remain close to 0 degrees C. (Fig 3.2). In this situation vapour can migrate vertically through the snowpack, creating a destabilising process. Vapour sublimed from the warmer climes of the basal layers can be redeposited in the form of stepped, *faceted* crystals in the cold surface layers; these loose and fragile cup-shaped crystals (Fig 3.3) form a weak layer known as *depth hoar*. This process overrides the slow, equilibrating effect of ET met. Initially the faceting process was thought to require extreme cold (ie air temperatures continuously below −10 degrees C) and to take

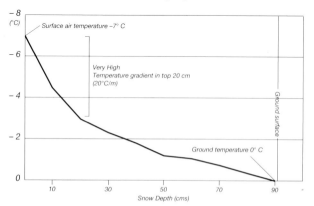

Fig 3.2 *Snow temperature profile: 0.00hr 27 February 1994, Coire Laogh Mor, Northern Cairngorms (from Power, Barton & Wright, 1995)*

Plate 3.1 *Wind transport in action: vicious spindrift on the ridge of A'Chralaig, Cluanie (Rab Anderson)*

one to two weeks to evolve, and so its relevance to Scottish conditions of fluctuating temperatures and regular wind-action was therefore discounted. However, recent research and snow observation findings have forced a rethink:

1 Temperature gradients in shallow snowpacks have been found to be extremely high. The threshold gradient for TG met to produce faceted crystals is approximately 10 degrees C per metre, and in a snowpack less

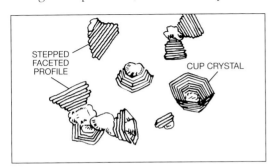

Fig 3.3 *Kinetic growth grains from temperature gradient metamorphism*

than half a metre deep this threshold will be passed when air temperatures are no lower than –5 degrees C, a regular occurrence in the Scottish mountains.

2 Monitoring of snowpack temperatures has also found that sudden and extreme changes in temperature occur at the borders between different layers, particularly where low density snow (fresh powder) lies on an old base hardened by MF met. Within these narrow interface zones temperature gradients as high as 60 to 70 degrees C per metre have been recorded by snow observers, and under such an extreme gradient it is thought that faceted crystals could develop within twenty-four hours.

Although they are not a regular feature of Scottish snowpacks, the striated translucent crystals produced by TG met have been identified on several occasions, and avalanches are known to have run on them.

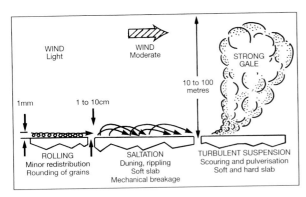

Fig 3.4 *Forms of wind action on snow*

Wind transport and alteration: At the higher altitudes, strong winds are the predominant agent of snow alteration at low temperatures. Wind action, either during or soon after a snowfall, lifts and pulverises the grains into tiny broken particles (typically a tenth of their original size) which are then packed into drifts in sheltered lee slopes. As Fig 3.4 shows, the mode and volume of transport varies with the windspeed. Wind-deposited snow may be three times denser than new loose snow, with an air content of about 35 per cent and a uniform grain size. It has a dull, chalky appearance because rounded grains are not reflective of light as is unaltered crystalline snow.

Water infiltration: This is highly significant in Scotland's warm climate and occurs by several means (Fig 3.5).

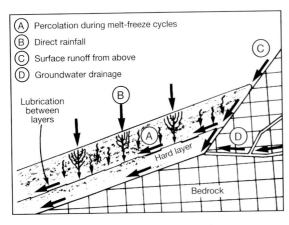

Fig 3.5 *Water action on the snowpack*

In its liquid form, external water lubricates and destabilises the snow, but if it freezes within the pack, it causes immediate bonding and hardening to produce an ideal climbing surface.

Surface crusting: Crusting at the surface is a very important stabilising force in a snowpack. Breakable crust is the bane of the winter mountaineer, whilst a supportive, crisp snow surface offers fast, exhilarating cramponned walking – and the difference between the two extremes might be only a couple of centimetres in thickness. Three agents of crusting are commonly operative:

1 A thaw is often confined to the surface layers during a temporary rise in air temperatures, and an icy top to the snowpack will be produced on refreezing. Even if the MF met cycle is restricted to the top 2 or 3cm of snow, a single night's freeze will produce a supportive crust.

2 'Sun-crusting' is produced by radiational melting of the surface by sunlight on days when air temperatures remain below zero. The surface refreezes at night, but the resultant crust is often wafer thin and will not support the weight of a human.

3 'Wind-riming' of the snow is a characteristic process on ridge crests and windward slopes. Rime ice is deposited on snow at the same time as it is on rocks, producing a ruffled texture to the surface which is flecked to windward.

Surface hoar: Surface hoar crystals form readily in sub-zero conditions, given a regime of daytime insolation (radiational heating by the sun) and night-time radiational cooling; this will occur in clear, settled weather when the flux of surface temperature is far greater than that of the overlying air. Unlike crusting, hoaring of the surface does not promote stability, and later may form a weak layer in the pack if buried by subsequent snowfalls.

Convection and evaporation: A dry wind of

an above-zero temperature rapidly accelerates the removal of snow, by evaporation of melted water on the surface and by direct sublimation of the snow grains into vapour. A block of snow may be reduced in volume by 20 per cent due to direct evaporation if exposed for just one hour to a dry wind of 30–35kmph. Accompanying this shrinkage is a disintegration of the bonds between the snow grains to produce a granular texture. Convection therefore accelerates the development of rotten spring snow (see Melt-freeze metamorphism, above). Conversely, when a fall in temperature to below zero is accompanied by a wind, freezing and hardening of a wet snow surface is almost instantaneous.

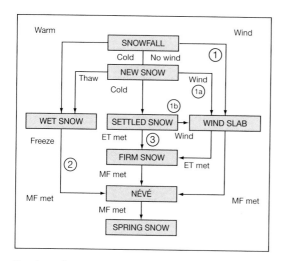

Fig 3.6 *Changes within the snowpack*

Disaggregation: On several occasions thin but dangerous air gaps have been identified between layers, in particular at the join between a surface slab of fresh snow and an old névé base layer. The development of such gaps suggests the operation of another form of vapour migration within the snowpack, leading to material loss at the interface and leaving dry granular crystals on the névé side. The instability created by such gaps has been linked to at least two recorded avalanches.

The main processes of alteration link into regular sequences of snow and ice development, which can be traced in Fig 3.6.

THE RESULTANT SNOWSCAPE

The layered profile: The progressive deposition and modification of snow during the season produces a multi-layered pack in the major accumulation areas, ie the corries, gullies and sheltered concavities. If a trench is dug to expose a multi-layered profile, a visual history of the snow is obtained and potential avalanche danger is often revealed in the form of weak layers, sharp discontinuities or water lubrication (see Chapter 8 for full details of snow-pit testing). Fig 3.7 examines four profiles that were encountered during the winter of 1997-98, each reflecting different weather history and snow metamorphism, and providing contrasting climbing and walking conditions.

Windslab: Most prominent and notorious of all layered forms of snow in Scotland is the windslab. Wind-blown snow is deposited as an independent layer of broken grains which has little or no physical anchorage with the larger grains and crystals of the underlying layers, yet is internally cohesive due to its uniformity of texture and packing. The texture of different slabs varies greatly. There are perhaps three wind factors which determine the location and the hardness of slabs:

1 *General windspeed* determines the degree of pulverisation of the snow crystals. In high winds snow grains are carried further and for longer, and are therefore broken into finer particles and laid as a denser and harder slab. In winds greater than 50 kmph slabs are nearly always built up on the lee sides of the mountains, windspeeds being too great to allow deposition on any slopes with windward aspect.

Fig 3.7 *Snow profile examples*

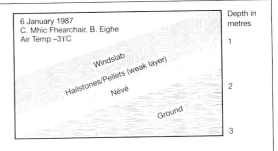

EARLY SEASON DANGER
Weather: turbulent polar airstream → hail, followed by northerly wind (strong at first) → slab
Conditions: in sheltered gullies and lee hollows wind-slab is deposited on loose hail, an unstable weak layer → avalanche risk

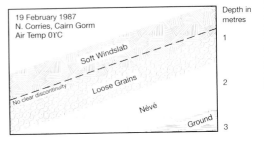

HEAVY ACCUMULATION
Weather: slow-moving front giving prolonged steady snowfall. Wind light, then rising to fresh → very soft slab laid on top of loose grains
Conditions: deep 'bottomless' snow in corries; danger of collapse due to overloading of loose snow and growing avalanche risk as wind-slabs thicken on top. Awful climbing conditions

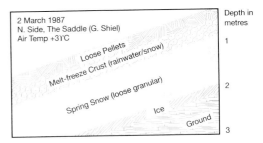

A QUICK FREEZE
Weather: heavy rain on the previous day; a cold-front passage bringing an overnight frost; light snow showers
Conditions: rainwater penetration of the top 30cm enabled a rapid freeze to give an excellent stable crust. Superb snow-climbing conditions were created overnight. No avalanche risk because water flowing through the profile has now refrozen and stabilised the layers

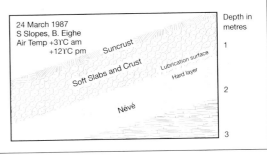

SPRING CONDITIONS
Weather: successive snowfalls over the last four days were separated by sunny spells; frost during the previous night
Conditions: four layers of moist slab and frozen crust were identified, directly reflecting the sequence of the weather. Surface sun-crust was supportive early in the day, but insolation quickly melted the top layers producing slush by early afternoon. Possible wet-slab avalanche risk due to water lubrication later in the day. Best to make an early start

2 *Surface windspeed* is critical in the deposition of blown snow. Any vertical wind profile shows a tailing-off in wind velocity towards the ground due to surface friction; for example, a free air speed of 56kmph is reduced to 11–13kmph at ground level (Fig 3.8). Wherever windspeed falls below a threshold level, airborne snow grains will adhere to the surface. This generally, but not always, occurs on lee slopes. Rough ground surfaces exert greater drag on the wind and are favoured sites for deposition.

2 *Local windflow* seems to play an equally crucial role as to whether snow is deposited as harmless loose drift or dangerous windslab. The importance of updraughts caused by rotational eddying of the wind has been observed repeatedly in the formation of slab. Such updraughts are typical on lee slopes where a wind vortex is created.

Plate 3.2 *Cornice on the Forcan Ridge of The Saddle with climbers taking a safe line well downslope of the crest (Martin Welch)*

However, they may also occur wherever local topography produces pockets of shelter, as for example in windward gullies, with the implication that slab avalanche risk is not solely confined to lee slopes.

For ease of classification a broad grouping of windslab into 'soft' and 'hard' is made according to whether the slab will support the human weight. The hardest slab can be impenetrable to any implement except the pick of an ice-axe.

By contrast, the very softest slab is produced in somewhat differing conditions to regular windslab and might be given a separate categorisation. 'Very soft' slab is laid when star-shaped (dendritic) snow crystals are deposited, carried on light surface winds; the resultant layer is of very low density and has a mousse-like consistency. Yet because the crystals have suffered little mechanical breakage, their tips interlock readily and quickly develop the potential to avalanche. Such slabs may develop on any slope aspect during a snowstorm when general winds are light to moderate (see Liathach narrative in Chapter 8).

The processes of windslab formation are closely allied to those controlling cornice development (Fig 3.8). They can remain only weakly anchored to the slope beneath until metamorphism creates some bonding. The stabilisation of slabs can be achieved by surface crusting or prolonged ET met, but in Scotland a melt-freeze cycle more normally intervenes, the melting destroying the definition of the slab and the refreezing bonding the snow into an amorphous profile.

Cornices: The tearing wind that blasts the wearied climber and lays down the hidden trap of the windslab is also responsible for creating the most elegant snow sculptures, of

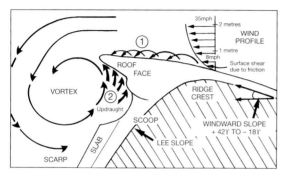

Fig 3.8 *Cornice and windslab – features and formation*

which the cornice is pre-eminent. Gerald Seligman described the contrast thus:

'Curling over the crest of a ridge, the shrieking storm whirls the snow grains with it, and deposits them with a gentle care fantastic for so wild an agent, gradually fashioning the most perfectly moulded cornice coverings to the ridge, every curve a delight to the eye – surely one of the most extraordinary paradoxes of beauty arising from evil.'[1]

The typical cornice shape and features are shown in Fig 3.8 and Plate 3.2. Fresh cornices regularly harbour windslabs in their lee scarp. The wind is the cause of both, but how exactly does it produce an overhang of snow? The dynamic action of wind-flow over ridge crests (as described in Chapter 2, pages 40–43) creates a standing vortex with associated updraught on the immediate lee side (Fig 3.8(2)). The updraught causes a steepening scarp to be built up at the lee edge which eventually becomes a slight overhang as snow grains hook on to the surface. Cornices develop within the windspeed range of 24–72kmph, above which they tend to be scoured and destroyed. Once established, the overhang intensifies the vortex on the lee side and is then rapidly enlarged by continuing updraught of spindrift. During a thaw, a wetted snowpack tends to sag and slump at a break of slope, producing a meringue-shaped roll over the edge.

The enormous size of some cornices deserves our respect. The Garbh Choire of Braeriach develops some of Scotland's biggest cornices due to its altitude and to the vast snow supply area of the Great Moss to its windward. Horizontal projections of over 6m are normal late in the season. Cornices harden and stabilise in the same ways as any other snow, and an alternating cycle of fresh snowfall and melt-freeze enables the progressive construction of these huge multi-layered features.

Other wind forms: In its more tender guise, the wind creates a variety of small-scale snow forms, each the product of differential rates of erosion and deposition, and which are closely akin to desert sand features. When in a dry loose state, snow behaves mechanically in similar fashion to sand. For example, dry snow of varying crystal content can be sieved and sorted by a light wind, then deposited as a series of laminates of equal grain size to produce a striated surface (Fig 3.9a) evocative of desert scenery. Likewise the scoops, dunes, ripples and barchans depicted in Fig 3.9 are all formed by surface drift under gentle wind action, a constant flow and sifting of grains close to the ground which produces a mesmeric and disorientating visual effect. Together they produce a winter landscape of distinctive beauty and symmetry on our high moors.

Sadly, light winds and low temperatures are rarely sustained for long in Scotland, and these delicate features will often be destroyed by a gale or will collapse during a thaw. More commonly encountered are *sastrugi*, erosion forms carved by stronger winds; typically these are initiated by the selective penetration of a surface crust which allows the wind to dig out pockets and troughs in the loose snow beneath. The resultant ridge-and-furrow pattern is a delight to behold but a bane to enjoyable skiing. The sight of *sastrugi* should also arouse the sneaking concern that the

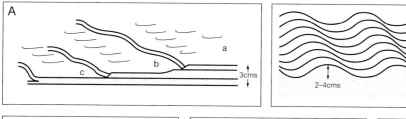

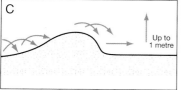

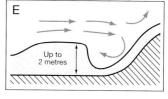

Fig 3.9 *Snow sculptures*

A Surface striations: a, b, c – laminae of different grain sizes sorted by wind (largest on bottom), then exposed by differential wind erosion

B Wind ripples: wind sorting in to ridge and furrows possibly by bombardment of surface gains (saltation). NB: wind-slabs are never rippled

C Wind ridges/dunes: continuous saltation of grains by light winds

D: Barchans: horseshoe dunes formed by eddy in lee of dune crests

E: Wind scoops: eddy action at base of obstacle

eroded snow is likely to have been deposited as windslab on the lee slopes.

The scoured summits: Wind is the predominant agent in the construction of Scotland's snowscapes, but its action also leaves the exposed parts of our mountains relatively bare for most of the season. Thus on windward convexities and summit plateaux it is rare for a snow profile to develop beyond a single layer plus surface crust; similarly the summits are regularly ice-glazed or coated with rime and hoar deposits to give a suitably wintry appearance, but they hold no lying snow as such.

SCOTTISH AVALANCHE TYPES

Five types of avalanche occur with regularity in Scotland:

Dry windslabs on open slopes: The slab may be 'hard' or 'soft' and threatens climbers, walkers and skiers alike. Slab avalanches run readily on frozen névé or on a weak layer of buried hoar crystals, graupel pellets or depth hoar. Wherever windslabs lie on such dubious base material, they hang by a hair-trigger, waiting for a false move.

Dry windslab in gullies, and fresh cornice collapse: These often occur together, owing to the typical formation of cornice plus wind-slabbed scarp on cliff headwalls overlying old névé (see Fig 3.8) – a cornice collapse will almost always trigger the slab beneath. Both cornice and slab are usually of the 'soft' variety, and the hazard can develop within an hour of the onset of a blizzard. These avalanches are as likely to be triggered naturally by overloading of the slab as by the weight of unwary climbers. However, the risk may persist for long after the cessation of wind action, and is often confined to the final metres of a gully climb with no prior warning signs lower on the slopes.

Overloading during snowfall: Loose slides are common on cliff-faces and in gullies during heavy, prolonged snowfall. They do not have great destructive power, but are quite sufficient to dislodge climbers.

Wet slab: During a thaw, liquid lubrication at

Plate 3.3 *Airborne powder-snow avalanche in Coire na Feola, Beinn Bhan*

the snowslab base (see Fig 3.5) may so weaken its anchorage as to trigger an avalanche. During spring, the drainage of running water at the base of the snowpack may cause a full-depth dislocation, especially over rock-slabs. The Great Slab of Coire an Lochain in the Cairngorms is a prime example of this type.

Wet-snow slides and cornice collapse: These may be associated with either a widespread thaw or localised insolation on sunny slopes. The snow-slide is quite different in nature from the slab, commencing at a single point and accumulating in width and volume as it travels downslope. Typically, a 'snowball' rolling off a sun-warmed rock-face will trigger the slide, which is slow-moving and usually small in scale. However, the spring cornice collapse may produce far greater slides which possess considerable destructive power. Wet-snow avalanches are more easily predicted than the dry-slab varieties. Given an intense thaw, there is no excuse for any climber wandering across threatened slopes or attempting gully climbs. Wet snow has a minimal air content, and a victim's chances of survival if buried are very slim.

There is also a sixth type of avalanche, the **airborne powder-snow avalanche** with destructive frontal winds: seen regularly in the greater mountain ranges of the world, it occurs only very rarely, in Scotland. Such climax avalanches require large snow volumes and big vertical drops. Whilst cornice collapses can give spectacular visual results if the debris falls out over a big cliff face (Plate 3.3), the development of pressure differentials sufficient to produce a frontal hurricane is unusual on our

Plate 3.4 *'Beauty rising from evil': snowsculpted ridge after the blizzard (Martin Welch)*

mountains and most of our avalanches are small-scale ground-running snow slides – although these are no less dangerous to the unwary mountaineer. The development of an avalanche awareness is therefore one of the most important skills which the aspiring winter mountaineer must develop; it is covered fully in Chapter 8.

THE SNOW TEMPERATURE PROFILE

When a freezing level is quoted in a weather or avalanche forecast, the figure refers to the *air temperature*, as opposed to the temperature of the snow or the ground surface. The effects on surface conditions of a change in air temperature across freezing point vary in timing and intensity:

- The **snow surface** responds very quickly, crusting or thawing within minutes of the change. However, at depths of more than 2 or 3cm in the pack, the snow temperature takes many hours to alter, and often remains wholly unresponsive to short-term fluctuations in air temperature.
- The **snow density** greatly affects how quickly the conditions respond. For instance, air temperature changes are conducted quickly through dry powder snow because of its high air content, and the

rapidity with which a pristine cover of powder snow is reduced to thin slush by a thaw is both surprising and depressing. By contrast, a hard-packed snow cover is immune from a short-term thaw.

- **Ice** has a much higher density than snow, with a specific gravity of between 85–90 per cent as opposed to 10–60 per cent for snow; therefore any thawing of ice lags behind that of the snow.
- The **ground temperature** exhibits its own specific cycles. If vegetation is thin and the soil is already in a saturated condition, exposed ground freezes quickly at the onset of cold weather. However, non-saturated soil protected by thicker grass or heather takes a few days to freeze solid, and the lag is especially long if the ground is blanketed by fresh snowfall, which acts to insulate the surface from very cold air temperatures. This can bring frustration to mixed climbers who see the buttresses well snowed up, yet find the ground beneath unbonded.

The ground temperature at the base of a snowpack remains at, or just below 0 degrees C throughout the winter. By contrast, exposed ground can freeze hard for several weeks in a cool winter, resisting temporary thaws and giving consistently hard walking and climbing conditions.

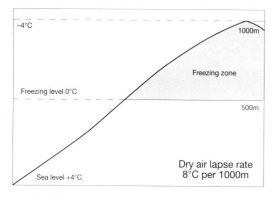

Fig 3.10 *Freezing level – dry air*

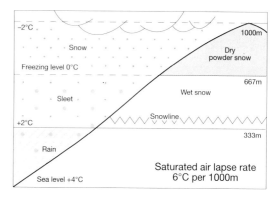

Fig 3.11 *Freezing level – saturated air*

The snow temperature profile from the Northern Cairngorms shown in Fig 3.2 is typical. In cold weather the snow temperature rises steadily with increasing depth. Whilst recreational mountaineers cannot sense or measure snow temperatures, the basic principles, as here outlined, do form a useful framework for understanding winter mountain conditions.

THE FREEZING LEVEL

The vertical gyrations of the air freezing level are as pronounced in the maritime climate of western Scotland as anywhere in the world. A change in windflow from north-easterly to south-westerly can occur with the passage of a single weather system and raise the freezing level from sea level to an altitude of 2,000m within thirty-six hours. The freezing level is crucial in determining the state of the climbing conditions.

The freezing level varies with three main factors:

a **Altitude:** The vertical lapse rate of temperature in the prevailing airmass gives the basic freezing level as quoted in forecasts. However, the lapse rate and the freezing level differ greatly between a dry, clear airmass and a saturated, cloud-filled airstream (see Figs 3.10 and 3.11). Inexperienced mountaineers often make the mistake of

assuming that anywhere above the freezing level will offer good conditions. In fact, fresh snow above the freezing line remains unconsolidated for several days, especially early in the season when there is little sunlight to produce radiational melting of the snow. Without any daytime thawing, the snow cover in the freezing zone stays dry and loose and potentially unstable.

During a spell of stable weather, the best climbing conditions develop within the zone of the **diurnal range** of the freezing level – that is, between night and day (Fig 3.12); within this range the daily melt-freeze cycle creates solid snow and promotes ice formation. Thus ideal conditions can be found early in the morning, although a slow afternoon thaw does not render conditions unduly dangerous, and releases some meltwater for the subsequent overnight freeze.

b **Aspect:** The diurnal range of the freezing level is considerably higher on south-facing slopes where insolation from the sun warms the surface air layers and is directly absorbed by the ground surface, creating 'hot-house' conditions during the day. By contrast the shaded northern slopes remain in sub-zero air and receive no insolation (see Fig 3.13). Over a period of several fine days this regime can strip the southern slopes bare, whilst good snow and ice conditions

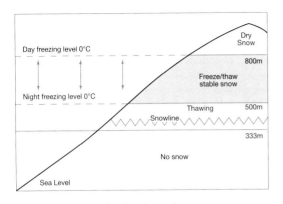

Fig 3.12 *Freezing level – diurnal range*

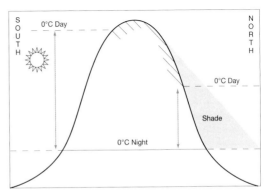

Fig 3.13 *Freezing level – effect of aspect*

Plate 3.7 *Full snow cover and superb anticyclonic weather: the peaks of Glencoe from Beinn a'Bheithir, with the Bidean nam Bian massif to left (Mike Arkley)*

are preserved on the northern cliffs. Thus ridgewalkers stroll along the crests in shorts at the same time as Gore-tex-clad, cramponned climbers emerge from icy gullies.

c **Period in season:** Later in the winter season as the potential hours of sunlight increase these effects of aspect become more pronounced. During a fine spell in March and early April, even the northern slopes get a substantial dose of insolation, and the zero degree isotherm can soar above summit level during the day, only to plunge back to valley level at night. It is vital that climbers make an 'alpine' start for the cliffs to match such alpine conditions, because the daytime thaw is intense and dangerous.

ICE FORMATION

A liberal smearing of ice on the hills adds a spectacular splendour to the winter scenery, whilst a satisfactory ice development is crucial to the climber's sport. All too often we are fooled by the ice conditions, or the lack of them, so it is worth trying to understand how, when and where ice forms. There are several sources of water from which ice can develop:

1 Direct rainfall: typically, freezing rain which ices on impact or percolates through the snow.

2 Ground-water drainage: the seepage of stored water from joint-lines in the rock.

3 Surface drainage in gullies and stream-lines.

4 Water circulation within the snowpack from melt-freeze cycles.

5 Meltwater draining out of the snowpack.

One or more of these water sources must be present in significant volume over a period of several days for substantial ice to form.

It is possible to differentiate several types of ice in Scotland, depending on their water source and the formation process:

White ice: The further hardening of névé snow by MF met and rainfall infiltration, increasing the ice content of the pack; absolutely stable and yielding; the climber's dream, but it rarely forms above 70 degrees in angle.

Blue ice: More dense and watery, therefore less reflective and so blue or even green in hue; it develops from water drainage combined with direct snowfall (or spindrift fall) which 'sticks' to the ice, augmenting its volume and giving it a plasticity of texture; it may thicken progressively to 50cm plus; forms at any angle; safe and dependable.

Water ice: Pure icicle development from external water flow with no crystalline content and therefore transparent; it lacks plasticity and so is hard and brittle; is often thin and hollow; may exhibit organ-pipe development or else is layered and 'dinner plates' on being struck; hard and scary to climb.

Verglas: Surface skin of water ice, firmly stuck on to ground surface; formed by impact freezing of rain (ice-glaze) or melt-freeze of surface trickles over rocks; tough and glue-like, less than 2cm thick, and a hazard to walkers and climbers alike.

Ice crust: Overlies loose snow; a film of ice may initially form by melt-freeze at the surface; it is developed by water trickling from above which freezes over the top of the initial film; highly brittle, with a false appearance of stability.

Eggshell ice: Bloated ice crust with air gap beneath, which may develop under daily sunshine cycle, the transparent surface film exerting a greenhouse effect on the underlying snow which is evaporated; highly disturbing when encountered on a climb.

The disappointment of failing to find ice on a chosen cliff after a lengthy approach march is intense. The day is sunk, and the agonising conjecture is inevitably raised that conditions might have been far better had you gone somewhere else. However, the opposite experience can occur...

CREAG MEAGAIDH: 21 MARCH 1997:

A ten-day thaw had left conditions lean and bare everywhere in Scotland. Only a few ice climbs above 1,000m were in condition on Ben Nevis, and we should have known better than to expect ice on Creag Meagaidh. The Coire Ardair headwall is 300m lower than the north-east face of the Ben, and facing broadly south-east, gets a goodly dose of daily sunshine in late March. We'd already walked 3km by the time the cliffs came into view, and despite the chill morning, there wasn't a scrap of ice left anywhere on the Post Face. Small wonder that no one else was walking in to the cliff! Nevertheless, we were now committed to make a day of it, and decided to go into the Inner Corrie to do The Sash or Cinderella, both grade II snow routes.

Two hours after setting out we puffed and sweated up from the corrie lochan towards the Window. The line of the Pumpkin was bare, and we even wondered whether grade IIs would be sufficiently banked with snow to be climbable. The main amphitheatre of the Inner Corrie swung slowly into view. High on the face, standing proud of the greys and dirty whites of the snow-streaked face, were two

Plate 3.8 *Icicles on the south face of Liathach*

magnificent cascades of ice, Diadem and The Wand. With their sheltered aspect and higher altitude they had somehow managed to survive the thaw.

Whilst the line of Diadem was broken in one place, the Wand was complete and we cramponned up hard névé in the approach gully to its base. The icefall was in weird and wonderful condition. Due to the erosion of running water of recent days, the ice shield was wholly detached from its gully bed, where a stream still cheerfully gurgled, yet the sides of the fall were well frozen to the bounding walls. The ice itself, watery and bubbly from the spray of the meltwater, was solid after the night's frost and a delight to climb. We weaved from the open left side of the fall to the big corner bounding it on the right, bridging across the hollow central section where necessary to avoid breaking through into the cavity. A sec-

ond and third pitch of steep ice and solid névé followed the main icefall.

This was the only ice climb in condition on the whole of Creag Meagaidh – or rather, the only climb on Creag Meagaidh with any ice on it at all! We just could not believe that it had been so good.

IDEAL CONDITIONS

Ideal conditions rarely exist at the same time for all branches of winter mountain sport. The thick fresh snow that delights the ski-tourer will be the bane of the walker: buttresses may be frozen, snowy and rimed to perfection, while gullies are bare of ice and full of dangerous powder snow. In Scotland's volatile climate it is the mountaineering all-rounder who prospers, by switching between walking, climbing and skiing according to the conditions prevailing, while the specialist becomes frustrated. This is illustrated by comparing the requirements of each winter activity:

Walking: A hard, fast surface – either bare frozen ground or névé snow; wind action clears the tops and improves the ridgewalking conditions; deep snow on approach marches is highly detrimental.

Snow-climbing: A good banking of stable snow – firn or névé or a melt-freeze crust; recent snowfall with wind action produces unfavourable soft drifts, cornices and windslabs.

Ice-climbing: A prolonged melt-freeze cycle is needed; a steady water supply and regular small snowfalls to build up blue or white ice. Sustained thaws are disastrous.

Mixed climbing: Melt-freeze to consolidate snow on the rocks, then a good frost to freeze vegetation; rime-icing from a moist, cool airstream is ideal; heavy fresh snowfall swamps the cliffs; good conditions can evolve within three days.

Ski-touring: Continuity of cover with a solid base is paramount; a consistent surface layer of powder or spring snow is better than hard névé; surface icing or crusting makes skiing very difficult; strong wind action is therefore highly detrimental.

Snow and ice conditions have certain seasonal tendencies which favour one activity over another. For instance, December and January may be excellent for walking or buttress climbing – they can give the hard frosts and light snow-cover ideal for either, but rarely develop the volume, continuity or stability of cover needed to give a good skiing surface, or to fill the gullies. Heavy snowfall early in the winter often remains unconsolidated.

Later in the season, progressive accumulation and regular melt-freeze cycles give the stability needed for snow-climbing, and there is a more continuous base for skiing. However,

by mid-March pure ice-climbing becomes highly vulnerable to the incidence of strong sunlight, and the sustained and intense insolation that can occur in the longer days of late season also produces wet slushy snow on the ridges and southern slopes which is inimical to pleasurable walking. Repeated MF met and wind-drying can render the gullies full of sugary 'spring snow' by April.

Through an average Scottish winter only the prolonged and unmitigated thaw will keep the all-rounder at bay – and even then there is bothying or river-crossing for amusement!

A BIG WINTER

Few winters pass without offering some spells of good conditions but it is only occasionally, that patterns of weather and snowfall contrive to create a prolonged season of good conditions for every mountain activity. In the twenty years from 1978 to 1998 we might identify seven such seasons: 1978, 1979, 1980, 1984, 1986, 1987 and 1994. Each offered a long, generally cool season, substantial volumes of snowfall and spells of cold fine weather.

There are several particular features of 'big winters' which can be picked out for future reference:

- A wet December does not indicate a poor coming season. The December of 1985 was a wash-out, yet the subsequent winter was possibly the 'best' of the last twenty years.

- A cold autumn, whether dry or snowy, is not helpful to the following winter. By the law of averages, a warm wet phase is likely to intervene and dominate the middle of the winter season. Long anti-cyclonic spells need to be reserved for later in the season when the snow is already on the ground.

- Heavy snowfall between Christmas and early January provides a solid starting base for snow and ice development.

Plate 3.9 *Cairngorm sunset; descending from Cairn Lochain looking across the Lairig Ghru (Jonathan Preston)*

- An early-season, prolonged spell of cool, changeable weather early in the season enables a progressive build-up and stabilisation of snow and ice.
- All 'big' winters have at least one long spell of settled easterly weather in mid- or late season. Once established, a polar continental airflow is hard to unseat. The five-week spell of February 1986 astonished even the natives.

Fig 3.14 (page 84) describes the evolution of the remarkably snowy winter of 1993/94. The sequence of cool weather spells, coupled with unusual volumes of snowfall, left the mountains well covered until the end of May. Much of the weather during the season was appalling, particularly in January and March, and the avalanche risk was generally high, but 1994 was in all respects a 'real' winter.

It is disturbing to see that in the last ten years I have identified only one 'big' winter, whereas in the previous decade I scored six! This is more proof that our winters have become less snowy and more volatile in their temperatures. If our winters are getting less reliable due to global warming then we must be prepared to be more opportunistic in our visits to the hills, and must savour the periods of good conditions for their rarity value.

WHERE TO CLIMB?
THE REGIONAL PATTERNS

The major areas each have their own regimes of temperature and snowfall, and may come into good condition at quite different times. By learning the specific qualities of each region, whether by advice or bitter experience, an aide-memoire is created in the prediction and planning of trips, and it is rare that there is

Plate 3.8 *Winter conditions on the Cuillin; on the East Ridge of Am Basteir looking towards Sgurr nan Gillean on Hogmanay 1996*

nowhere in the Highlands which cannot offer good winter sport. By keeping your arrangements flexible, and by developing a keen awareness of the likely conditions, usually both journey and effort can be profitable.

The Cairngorms and the Eastern Highlands: Owing to their greater average altitude and relative dryness there is a greater chance of finding snow cover on the eastern mountains than in any other area.

The Cairngorms and Grampians receive a greater volume of snowfall when an easterly polar continental airflow is predominant – although they lose out when nor'westers are bringing large snowfalls to the Western and Northern Highlands. With slightly lower average temperatures and less risk of rainwash, the Cairngorms maintain their accumulations for longer, often producing good conditions in late March and April. The greater continuity of snow-cover gives much the most reliable conditions for ski-touring in Scotland. Invariably a good spell of climbing conditions is enjoyed in late autumn in the Cairngorms when a local snowfall is followed by a freeze/thaw cycle, and undoubtedly the potential span of the winter season is greater than elsewhere in the Highlands.

However, the cold and relative dryness of the eastern hills can be disadvantageous both to consolidation of the snowpack and to the formation of ice, particularly early in the season when the sun is low and frosts are sustained at all levels; without some degree of water lubrication, hard stable conditions are very slow to develop.

The West – Argyll, Glencoe, Torridon: Here the maritime influence plays a decisive and often disruptive role. Conditions may be the mirror image of those in the east, developing very rapidly by melt-freeze and water percolation after a single initial snowfall, but disappearing overnight in a major thaw. The relatively low altitude of many of the cliffs and corries accentuates the volatility of the condi-

Fig 3.14 *1993/94: A big winter*	
DEC 4–JAN 14	After the driest autumn in Fort William since 1915, winter gets going early with a continuous series of Altantic depressions bringing polar maritime (PM) air across the country; there is a steady build-up of snow on the hills; temperatures are 1.5 deg C below normal in the Central Highlands
JAN 18–FEB 9	An alternation of tropical maritime and PM airstreams promotes freeze-thaw, and high winds augment snow accumulation and create high avalanche risk; there are winds of 160kmph+ on Cairngorm summit on several days (with a 219kmph gust on 29 Jan); precipitation is 50–100 per cent above normal throughout the Highlands
FEB 10–28	A polar continental airflow with bitter east winds; hard icing of all lying snow giving treacherous walking conditions but excellent ice climbing; only seven days without lying snow at the Cairngorm ski car park throughout the whole of December, January and February
MAR 1–APR 10	An alternation of TM, rPM and PM airflows gives the wettest March on record in Scotland, yet it is still cool enough to maintain snow volumes; Rannoch has 388mm of rain, five times its March average; there are ice routes in condition all over the country in early April after a prolonged freeze-thaw; 70cm of new snow at Cairngorm car park on 9 April, the last big fall; and there were ninety-six days with snow lying at Braemar during the winter season (sixty-four is the average)
EARLY MAY	10m drifts of snow lie in the northern corries of the Cuillin, and gully notches on Main Ridge are still choked with snow; there is continuous snow cover on mainland summits and plateaux

tions – indeed, the progressive accumulation of a solid snow base may not occur at all in a winter of widely fluctuating temperatures.

Ice formation is accelerated by humidity and moisture supply. Walkers can more often enjoy harder snow and ice conditions on the ridges in the west, and are usually spared the labour of trail-breaking in deep powder. However, for long periods of most seasons the western hills are all but bare of snow. Good conditions must be grabbed with the fullest embrace.

The Central Highlands – Perthshire, Ben Alder Forest, Creag Meagaidh, Easter Ross: These intermediate regions offer a mixture of both the east and west, and often avoid the unhelpful extremes of conditions found in the latter. They are ideal locations for those who like to 'hedge their bets' and are excellent fall-backs if a long drive to the north-west proves fruitless.

Ben Nevis: Offering an extra 300m of height over all other mountains of the western seaboard, the Ben produces heavy snowfall in a humid environment, and so develops the most reliable snow- and ice-climbing conditions of anywhere in Scotland, fully deserving its reputation as the king of the winter playgrounds. Indeed, the calibre of its ice conditions is unique. Blue and white ice can choke the gullies and, coupled with a good banking of snow, gives magnificent and relatively 'easy' climbing, while a thick ice-plating that is rarely seen elsewhere develops on the higher faces. However, like the Cairngorms, good conditions may be slow to evolve, and after heavy fresh snow, a high avalanche risk can persist long after the lower climbing venues have consolidated. Yet once established in mid-season, the conditions are hard to shift – an ice ascent of Orion Face Direct has been recorded as late as 1 May.

The Cuillin of Skye: Although hardly in the mainstream of Scottish winter mountaineering, the Cuillin deserve a separate niche because they epitomise a maritime environment and all its concomitant frustrations, and yet occasionally they present themselves as a necklace of white pearls without compare in the whole of the British Isles. Opinion among the experts has varied widely on the rarity of winter conditions on the ridge. Naismith was dismissive of the chance as long ago as 1890:

'Indeed, considering their sharpness and their exposure to wind and sun (to say nothing of the Gulf Stream) it is doubtful, I think, whether much snow is ever likely to be found on them.'[5]

And Tom Patey experienced an abortive attempt on the Main Ridge traverse, defeated because the wind had blown the crest completely bare of snow, which at sea level lay knee-deep and blocked the roads; he noted the irony and lamented:

'I doubt whether satisfactory conditions for the Main Ridge ever obtain. By the time new snow consolidates, the principal rock features should have lost their winter garb.'[6]

However, he caught his elusive bird in full winter plumage three years later in 1965, when the first traverse under full snow- and ice-cover was achieved.

Winter experiences on Skye are never likely to be mundane. I've known the Cuillin so icy that crampons have to be worn all the way from 300m in altitude to the summits, climbed Gillean's Pinnacle Ridge in every condition from knee-deep slush to half an inch of verglas, and ploughed over the Clach Glas traverse thigh-deep in pristine powder snow. Best of all, perhaps, was a day when we fought our way up the Fionn Coire against a south-easterly blizzard to emerge at Bruach na Frithe just as the skies cleared and the Cuillin peaks emerged from the boiling mists like shining castles of ice. Days of such peerless conditions come but rarely, yet they are never forgotten, and justify all the sweat, toil and tears of winter mountaineering.

PART TWO
THE SKILLS

4: BREAKING THE TRAIL

WINTER HILLWALKING – TRADITIONS AND TECHNIQUES

THE FIRST TIME

When you opened the bothy door you had never expected this. All yesterday you had struggled with yourself, slogging up Glen Luibeg after the overnight drive from the south, then climbing alone into thick cloud and mournful snowfall on Cairn Toul. It had been so much easier to ponder the comforts relinquished than any joys to come. After the slithering descent of the water-slabs below Lochan Uaine, the sight of the tiny Garbh Choire bothy was your only chink of light in the mid-December gloom. You had slunk inside, shut the door on a bleak world and consoled yourself with food and sleep. This winter adventure, so long imagined, so avidly awaited, now seemed a mistake.

Waking late you thought of no more than the plod back out and a numbing 400-mile drive back home. Then face up to another week in the city, fighting boredom, holding back frustration…

The door creaked open and a shower of frost crystals fell in; you blinked twice before you believed it. The sky was brilliant blue and the mountains thickly clad in new snow. You could hardly get that breakfast down quick enough. The sunlight was already casting across the southern slopes of Braeriach and the tops shone with a clarity you had never known. Not a minute was to be wasted. You ploughed and floundered in the powder up the Coire Bhrochain screes, but what recompense there was in the unfolding vista of snow-plastered corrie walls. Then on reaching the summit came an uninterrupted view west to Ben Nevis, which sailed on the horizon sixty miles away. The scene was just too fabulous to stand and stare: no place this for detached admiration, you were young and your senses reeled with excitement, and you couldn't express your happiness except by action, pushing on and on over the hills.

And there was definitely time to do Macdui, too. A snowy tumble down to the Pools of Dee and an hour's grind up to the summit; three o'clock and you were there, sharing the lengthening shadows with a group who had walked over from Cairn Gorm. Striding down the spur of Sron Riach, you glimpsed icy depths in Coire Sputan Dearg and watched the rosy alpenglow slowly deepen on the flank of Derry Cairngorm. Then the light vanished to leave the hills as shrouds of ghostly grey, and a deep frost fell in the glens. No fears now of the long drive home, no sense of despair at the daily grind to follow; the wind of elation would sustain the weeks to come.

For all you had hiked and climbed in sum-

Pages 86–7 Winter walking in the West Highlands, looking from Sgurr na Feartaig to Sgurr Choinnich and the Cannich Hills (Clarrie Pashley)

mer, nothing you'd ever seen in the hills had been quite so wonderful as this. In the joy of new-found conviction, the only worry was how soon you could get back. That first winter's day on the high hills, how many lives has it changed?

EARLY TRADITIONS

Winter hill-outings have been undertaken of necessity ever since man inhabited the Highlands. Prior to the clearances and accompanying migrations of the late eighteenth and nineteenth centuries, the high glens were densely peopled, in contrast to their desolation today. Cattle-droving, shepherding, hunting and soldiering involved movement across the hills in every season.

The hazards of the winter mountains were therefore well known and viewed with fear and mystical significance. A famous Cairngorm landmark is the Clach nan Taillear (Tailors' Stone) in the Lairig Ghru where three tailors are reputed to have succumbed to a Hogmanay blizzard; legend holds that the pretext for this excursion was a wager that they would dance a reel on the same night in both Rothie-murchus and Braemar. Then in January 1805, five privates of the Inverness militia perished in a snowstorm on the neighbouring Lairig an Laoigh route. And before that, on 4 January in 1800, Scotland's first fatal avalanche was recorded: the Gaick tragedy, when five hunters were overwhelmed as they slept in a small cottage near the present site of Gaick Lodge in the central Grampians. This freak incident remains the only occasion when a human habitation has been destroyed by avalanche in Scotland.

Understandably, winter was not 'appreciated' by the native Highlander in the manner of the mountaineer of today. The seeking of the hills for recreational challenge, even in summer, awaited the Victorian era of industrialisation and urbanisation, which spawned a disaffection with city life and, by the light of stark contrast, an awareness of the beauty of natural mountain scenery. However, while summer tourism and mountain exploration developed in popularity, the hills were largely left alone in winter until very late in the nineteenth century, being still regarded with awe and trepidation and as offering little by way of beauty or fine weather. The first recorded winter conquest of Ben Lomond, for example, inspired only a fearful respect for the wild natural elements. After his ascent on 12 November 1812, Colonel Hawker recounted:

'To get to the most elevated point of the shoulder we found impossible, as the last 50 yards was a solid sheet of ice, and indeed for the last half-mile we travelled in perfect misery and imminent danger. We were literally obliged to take knives and to cut footsteps in the frozen snow, and of course obliged to crawl all the way on our hands, knees and toes, all of which were benumbed with cold.'[1]

Indeed, an aesthetic response to the mountains in winter did not develop until small groups of professional gentlemen formed the Cairngorm Club (CC) and Scottish Mountaineering Club (SMC) in 1887 and 1889 respectively. At its inception, one of the avowed purposes of the SMC was the encouragement of winter ascents, and to these earliest pioneers the winter hills were something of a revelation, their enhanced scale under snow making it 'difficult to realise that the ordnance surveyors have not been mistaken by some few thousands of feet' (Sir Hugh Munro, 1891);[2] the clear mountain air 'like a draught of champagne, with no gout or headache at the bottom' (Hely Almond, 1893);[3] and the sheer enjoyment of winter walking on the tops 'after a big fall of snow, followed by a severe frost, I know of no excursion more pleasant' (A. I. McConnochie, 1890).[4]

The most remarkable feature of early winter rovings when viewed against the norms of a century later is the prodigious distances that were covered. Living in a generation when a 24km hillwalk in snowy conditions is considered exceptional, few would be eager to emulate Munro's three-day round in the Eastern Grampians in January 1890:

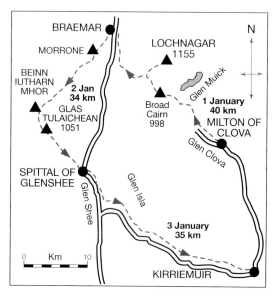

Fig 4.1 *A respectable winter round in 1890*

1 Jan: Milton of Clova; Broad Cairn; Lochnagar; Glen Callater; Braemar: 40km with 1,280m of ascent.

2 Jan: Morrone; Glen Ey; Beinn Iutharn Mhor; Glas Tulaichean; Glenshee: 34km with 1,370m of ascent.

3 Jan: Walked home to Lindertis near Kirriemuir; 35km on roads in 10cm of new snow.

Such a march must have required a military pace and discipline and displays fitness and fortitude that shame our modern standards. These performances were, of course, a product of the pre-motorised era when walking was the natural and traditional mode of country travel, especially in winter when snow

rendered roads impassable to horse and carriage and when mountain excursions perforce had to start and end at the railheads or widely spaced inns and hotels. Thus, Boat of Garten and Ballater became the starting points for trips into the Cairngorms from Speyside and Deeside respectively, necessitating 16km approach treks just to reach the base of the mountains.

Nevertheless, there was also a sporting spirit which stimulated these great treks. Although no rivalry is ever declared or implied, one can sense an element of competitive pride in the formal reports of early winter expeditions. Perhaps the epitome of such exploits was Naismith and Thomson's novel means of getting to the Easter meet of the SMC at Inveroran near Bridge of Orchy in 1892. Taking the night train to Dalwhinnie, they reached Bridge of Orchy via Loch Ericht, the summit of Ben Alder and the whole expanse of Rannoch Moor, a distance of 66km which took seventeen hours. Here was no deed of necessity, but a piece of pure mountain madness, and next day both were out on the hills with the rest of the gathered club. No doubt the trip gave Naismith a thorough test of his immortal rule for speed of travel in the mountains. Knowing Naismith's pedigree it is not surprising that many of today's hillwalkers struggle to keep up with his 3 miles per hour maxim!

A century later, winter hillwalking in Scotland is a sport pursued by many thousands; it is promoted annually by several outdoor magazines, has spawned a seasonal boom in equipment sales, supports dozens of instructors and mountain leaders, and attracts the glare of media attention whenever a major mishap occurs. And while the essential appeal of the pastime remains unaltered, the equipment and techniques have changed out of all recognition.

CHOOSING THE RIGHT GEAR

Boots

Winter walking boots are now classed as 'four-season boots' for sales purposes. The crucial feature which distinguishes them from summer trekking boots is the stiffness down the length of each midsole, this being a hidden component sandwiched between the sole and the upper of the boot. Traditionally a metal plate was used as the midsole, either half, three-quarters or else the full length of the sole, thereby providing differing degrees of stiffness for walking or climbing. Modern winter boots use moulded nylon or carbon fibres for their midsoles, these giving a lighter and warmer boot unit. This longitudinal stiffness in the boot is essential for winter walking, both to provide a secure fit for crampons and to give edge and toe grip when kicking steps in snow without crampons. However, a fully rigid boot sole, whilst great for steeper climbing, is less comfortable for long-distance walking than one which allows a limited degree of flex. Winter mountain walkers should look for a model which compromises the needs of both performance and comfort.

Winter hillgoers are today spoilt for choice of four-season boots, with dozens of makes available (see Plate 4.2). Leather boots are now firmly back in fashion instead of plastic-shelled models which were *de rigueur* for many walkers as well as most climbers in the 1980s. The latest leather mountain boots come complete with rubber toe protection rands and grooves to take step-in crampon bindings. These are more than a match in performance, and have superseded the relatively clumsy and inflexible character of 'plastics' for distance walking. Personal comfort is critical. There are still many who swear by plastic boots, but the majority of us groan at the thought of wearing them for many miles!

Leaving the 'leather vs plastic' argument

Plate 4.1 *Early pioneers on the winter hills, with long axe and alpenstocks (SMC Collection)*

aside, there are five key features in winter boot design:

- **Midsole stiffness and attachment:** A little longitudinal flex gives walking comfort. 'Blake' stitching of the midsole to the upper improves strength and enables resoling.
- **Sole grip and durability:** Vibram soles with deep tread and square-cut heels offer the best grip on snow and wear the longest.
- **Ankle support:** A high cut gives essential support for cramponning on steeper ground but must be well padded for comfort.
- **Width fitting:** Many models offer a choice of width size. Getting the right width fit is essential for comfort.
- **Crampon compatibility:** Winter boots are now categorised from B1 to B3 according to the types of crampon for which they are suited (see Fig 4.2).

Preventing snow and water getting in at the boot ankles is crucial to comfort and warmth, so gaiters are essential. The 'yeti'-style over-gaiter is ideal for use on snow, offering complete waterproofing and extra insulation; however, if it is not glued to the rand of the boot it has an irritating tendency to slip off the toe. Otherwise, cheaper knee-length alpine gaiters should be used.

The Ice-axe

This is an indispensable item in a winter mountaineer's kit, and it should therefore be of a quality and design which give the best security and lasting performance. A good walking axe will also be suitable for steeper mountaineering and lower grade climbing, so it is a false economy to buy a light and cheap model. Plate 4.3 shows a selection of suitable designs. Several features of ice-axes are important:

- **Length:** Shaft length should be in the range of 55–75cm, selected according to body height. Ground clearance from the bottom spike should be 15–25cm when holding the axe by the side. Axes in excess of 75cm in length will be found cumbersome on steeper slopes, are awkward to swing and are hard to control in a genuine axe arrest.
- **Head construction:** Drop-forged one-piece heads, countersunk and double-bolted to the shaft are the strongest and most durable, and are to be preferred to heads with welded construction.
- **Pick design:** A curved pick is essential to give traction if the axe is swung in steeper ground. Notched teeth on the underside of the pick much improve its hold in snow. Pick length should be at least 14cm and its width should be 4mm (measured 2cm from the tip) in order to give effective braking performance.
- **Adze design:** A wide adze with sharp corners assists stepcutting and excavation of snow.
- **Weight:** Axes with aluminium or zinc/magnesium shafts with total weights of less than 500g are available but do not give adequate performance on hard snow or ice, nor in stepcutting. A weight of around 700g for a 65cm axe is ideal. Alloy shafts are now universal on axes.
- **Hand grip:** A rubberised sleeve on the shaft much improves grip, and insulates the hand from bare metal.
- **Spike (or ferrule):** A sharp tapered spike is recommended for penetration when walking on ice; it should be protected with a rubber bung when not in use.

Crampons

Nothing is more wasteful of winter's precious hours of light, nor more infuriating, than an ill-fitting crampon which springs loose at every tricky juncture of a mountain day. The selection of crampons which are compatible to specific models of boot has been simplified by the

Fig 4.2 *The boot–crampon compatibility scale*

BOOTS

B0: Unsuitable for crampons (three-season use only). Too flexible in the midsole to hold crampons. The fabric of the uppers is soft and would compress easily under crampon straps, causing discomfort and cold feet. Should not be used for winter hillwalking.

B1: Suitable for the easiest snow and ice conditions found when hillwalking. They have a reasonably stiff flexing sole and the uppers provide enough ankle and foot support for traversing relatively steep snow slopes (up to 45 degrees).

B2: A stiff flex boot with the equivalent of three-quarter or full shank midsole, and a supportive upper made from high quality leather. These boots, designed for four-season mountaineering, can be used all day with crampons. Suitable for easy Scottish snow and ice climbs (grades I and II).

B3: A technical mountaineering or climbing boot, either plastic or 'top of the range' leather, regarded as rigid in both midsole and upper. Used for mountaineering and ice climbing.

CRAMPONS

C1: A flexible walking crampon attached with straps, with or without front points.

C2: Articulated multi-purpose crampon with front points. Attached with straps all round, or a ring strap at front and clip-on heel.

C3: Articulated climbing or fully rigid technical crampon attached by a full clip-on system of toe bar and heel clip.

Note: A B3 boot is ideal for a C3 crampon, but will also take C2 and C1 models

A B2 boot is ideal for a C2 crampon and will also take a C1 model

A B1 boot is only compatible to a C1 crampon

introduction of a grading system, C1 to C3 (Fig 4.2). Boots of grade B1 will only take simple C1 crampons, whilst fully stiff B3 boots are ideally suited to C3 crampons but could also be used with C2 or C1 designs. However, several other considerations should be made when choosing crampons besides basic boot compatibility:

- **Construction:** Strength is vital for durability: walkers put their crampons through an incredible amount of stress on mixed ground of rocks and snow. The strongest crampons are made from one-piece forged metal, typically NiCrMo steel.

- **Number of points:** A ten- or twelve-point crampon, including two front points, is essential for serious mountain walking: without front points the user is highly disadvantaged on slopes of more than 35 degrees, and without eight or ten points on the sole of the crampon, grip on icy ground is seriously reduced.

- **Hinging mechanism:** Any crampon intended for mountain walking must have a hinging mechanism so that the crampon will flex with the boot as the foot rolls. Suitable models have either a flexible sprung-steel plate or a hinge at the instep. Rigid crampons will not withstand the stress of prolonged walking.

- **Ease of adjustment:** The length adjustment of crampons should be simple and the adjustment mechanism should itself be strong and durable; thankfully the days of crampons which looked like Meccano kits when first unwrapped are over. If adjustment does depend on a screw or a bolt, a spare should always be carried.

- **Fit to the boot sole:** The crampon frame should be flat. Models with vertical frames give a clumsy feel when walking, akin to wearing high heels, and snow will ball up in them easily. The frame must fit tightly to the

Plate 4.2 *Winter walking boots and crampons: (left) semi-stiff boot (B1) with flexible walking crampon (C1); (centre) three-quarter stiff boot (B2) with strapped articulated crampon (C2); (right) fully stiff mountain boot (B2) with articulated crampon with clip-up heel binding*

boot sole, both at the toes and heels. Long retaining posts help ensure a good fit. The test of a well fitted crampon is that it cannot be shaken off the boot even when the straps are undone.

- **Strapping system:** Three attachment systems are currently available (see Plate 4.2): *Full straps* (either one long strap or else one for the toe and one for the ankle): these are fiddly and time-consuming to tie especially when wearing gloves; *step-in bindings* with a bail bar for the toe and heel clip: these are only compatible with stiffer boot models, but are gloriously quick and simple; and *step-in/strap-on combinations* with toe ring strap and heel clip: these are an excellent compromise and compatible to most four-season boots. As with the fit, the crampon strapping system should be tested to every specific boot, particularly small boot sizes.

All models of crampon are prone to 'balling up' with soft moist snow, and many manufacturers now produce plastic anti-balling plates which fit on the sole of the frame. Although such devices add bother in fitting and will not withstand prolonged use on rocky ground, they do help reduce the risk of a slide when descending. When not in use, crampons are best kept in canvas bags and carried inside the sack; those models which telescope down in size enable easy storage.

Trekking Poles

Though not an essential part of winter hardware, telescopic ski-sticks or trekking poles are now immensely popular. They lend support and balance when flogging through deep snow, and cushion the impact on knee joints when descending. They are far better used as a pair: for instance, on a long descent in deep snow the poles can be held wide, enabling the knees to be kept close together, much as in the style of skiing.

There is no doubt that poles can prolong the longevity of one's winter walking career, but there is one big proviso: on hard snow slopes they must not be used as a substitute for the ice-axe. There have been several accidents in Europe where a contributory factor was the fact that walkers relied on sticks for support on dangerously steep ground; as soon as serious terrain is encountered both poles should be strapped to the sack and the ice-axe used.

The Essential Skills

'The axe may be thrown in the air, caused to revolve a determined number of times and caught on the descent, in either hand, as a good step-cutter should be ambidextrous. This is done while running down a steep slope without stopping.'[5]

So suggested Harold Raeburn in his 1920 textbook, *Mountaineering Art*, on the need to develop balance and co-ordination in the use of an ice-axe. Notwithstanding the eccentricities of early exponents of the game, it is essential that winter hillgoers acquire basic proficiencies in the use of the axe and crampons, and develop personal skills far beyond the simplicities of a summer fell-walk, whatever the extent of their ambition.

Winter walking on the high tops is a serious game; indeed, it is often said that in winter, all hillwalking becomes mountaineering. Therein lies much of its appeal, but also its inherent danger. Safe enjoyment of the mountains in winter is not just dependent on having the right kit, but on knowing when and how to use it.

Ice-axe Basics

The value of the ice-axe was quickly learnt by the early pioneers, who initially relied on the alpenstock, which was merely a form of spiked walking-stick something over a metre in length.

Alexander McConnochie was a rapid convert to the use of the ice-axe, learning that without it, a mountaineer has no effective brake. On a traverse of Ben Macdui in 1889, he slipped several hundred feet down the Loch Avon headwall, probably in the vicinity of the Feith Buidhe. With the greatest of difficulty he stopped himself with his alpenstock, and was only able to quit the slope by facing in and clawing his finger ends into the hard snow surface. Even more alarmingly his companion, who was watching from above, thought his hurried descent was voluntary and an easy way of getting down. So with total abandon he, too, plunged into the fray, coming to rest 60m lower. Both were extremely lucky to escape injury.

So the first rule is to take your ice-axe whenever there is snow on the hills, whether this be in December or May, and no matter whether you are walking on the jagged western ridges or the rolling Grampians. The second rule is to have the axe in the hand as soon as the snowline is crossed. When crossing patchy snow terrain it can be lodged temporarily when not required, then retrieved as

Plate 4.3 *Winter mountain axes: note the extra curve on the pick of the left-hand model for better traction in steep ground, wrist loops to be attached through hole at centre of the heads*

soon as it is needed, for example by pushing it diagonally down the back between the shoulders and under one sack strap.

In order of priority the uses of the axe are to assist progress, prevent a slip and arrest a slide.

Far too much attention is given to the last resort and not nearly enough to the first two needs, where the adoption of a few simple techniques can prevent all the theatrics of a full-blooded arrest. Plate 4.4 illustrates the essential axe grip and positioning.

The axe should be held in a vertical position close to and parallel to the leg so that the shaft or pick can be immediately plunged into the snow to stop a slip.

The pick must point to the rear to enable immediate arrest in a slide. The only exception to the 'pick back' rule is when surmounting or descending a steep section in excess of a 45 degrees angle, when the pick should be turned forwards and jabbed into the snow to give extra support.

Plate 4.4 *Ice-axe grip and stance: axe held on uphill side close to body; hand held over the head with fingers and thumb twisted round top of shaft and with the pick pointing back; body in sideways stance to slope; boots edging on hard snow surface*

By plunging the shaft into the snow with some force on every step one obtains a firm anchorage. Many walkers plant their axe limply, if at all. Frozen terrain demands vigorous use of the axe above all else.

Many axes come supplied with a wrist-loop, and most walkers use one for security against dropping the axe and occasionally for wrist support when swinging the axe in step-cutting or steeper climbing. There are drawbacks in using a loop, however; first there is the nuisance and delay of continuously having to change the loop from hand to hand when zig-zagging, and more worryingly, there is the risk of a swinging axe causing serious injury in a slide if the hand loses its grip but the loop remains attached. However, I have several grey hairs from witnessing serious slides on snow where the victims have not been using a loop and have let go of the axe completely, leaving

their fate to the luck of the landing.

Of these, the most memorable occurred while guiding a couple from Aberdeen, Bill and his wife Angela, who was several weeks pregnant at the time. On the first day's descent we were ploughing down fresh but wet snow. I was going ahead with Angela, and we had just descended the brow of a steepening, leaving Bill out of sight some way behind. Then, as so often happens in soft snow, Angela's foot suddenly plunged into a cavity, pitching her head first down the slope. In the shock of tripping she promptly let go of her axe, rendering the hour we had just spent in axe arrest practice somewhat irrelevant. I could only spectate as she gradually picked up speed, shot over a final snowbank and landed in some seriously bouldery terrain 40m below me. After a tactical glance upslope to check that Bill hadn't seen the fall, I hurried down, praying that she had avoided serious injury and pondering the potential for a miscarriage! By the time I reached the bottom she was picking herself up, and save for a few bruises, declared herself unscathed. I guess that Bill was concentrating too much on his own descent to see the prone body down below, or notice the skid-marks on the slope; when he arrived he merely looked surprised that we had got down so quickly! I was relieved to meet them at a lecture a few months later and see a healthy baby cradled in Angela's arms.

Had she been using a wrist-loop she might have gained control of the axe and saved herself; not surprisingly, I am of the opinion that beginners are best to use a loop on steep ground. Nevertheless, of all basic axe skills, the most important is the instinctive reaction to keep a tight grip on the axe in the event of a slip. By plunging the shaft down if the snow is soft, or jabbing the pick in by one's side if it is hard (Plates 4.5 and 4.6), a slip can be stopped instantly and prevented from becoming a slide.

For all the instructional emphasis on ice-axe arrest, nobody should have any illusions as to the chances of a successful arrest from an accelerating slide on hard snow. Prevention is much more sure than the cure...

Ice-Axe Arrest

The prospect of deliberately hurling oneself down a steep snowslope with nought but an axe for security is daunting for most and terrifying for some, but without prior training the chances of arresting a real fall are slim. Practice in axe arrest is also very important in building one's general confidence in walking on snow and ice. If you know you can control a slip, your movements on icy slopes will lose their inhibition, your techniques and balance will improve, and your winter mountain days will become much more enjoyable as well as safer. A high proportion of beginners now attend an instructional course to learn and practise the basics, but there is nothing to stop individuals from learning the techniques provided they apply themselves and choose suitable training slopes.

Practice areas must have a smooth, safe runout at the bottom so that a failure to arrest will not be catastrophic; concave slopes are therefore to be chosen rather than convex ones. The snowpack should be thick enough that rocks close to the surface do not present a hidden danger, and ideally the snow should be firm or frozen. Ice patches should be avoided though equally, little is gained from trying to practise in deep, unconsolidated snow. The angle of the slope should be sufficient to attain a reasonable speed, but not dangerously steep; for instance on hard névé a 30-degree angle is quite enough to achieve a satisfactory acceleration.

Crampons should never be worn in practice sessions. The wearing of helmets is advisable if they are possessed, and old clothing is recommended – repeated arrest practice does no favours to Gore-tex garments! However, the wearing of overtrousers is suggested to give

Plate 4.5 *The side brake with pick in snow*

Plate 4.6 *The side brake with shaft in snow*

Plate 4.8 *The self-arrest position: body flat on snow, legs apart for stability with heels raised, chest and shoulders pushing down on axe*

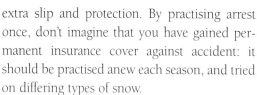

Plate 4.7 *The axe held in the braking position across the chest, lower hand gripping bottom of shaft*

extra slip and protection. By practising arrest once, don't imagine that you have gained permanent insurance cover against accident: it should be practised anew each season, and tried on differing types of snow.

The 'across the body' method of arrest is standard for all British mountaineers, adopted as much to avoid self-inflicted injuries by keeping the axe away from the face as for its braking effect. To achieve it, the axe should be held with the pick pointing back and the other hand must grasp the bottom of the shaft as soon as a slide begins, no matter whether falling head or feet first. Without control of the axe nothing can happen. The aim is then to achieve the braking position with the axe diagonally across the chest, as in Plates 4.7 and 4.8. The simplest practice routine is to start by sitting on the snow with the feet down the slope, and to slide with the axe already held firmly across the chest. Then roll the body towards the hand which is holding the head of the axe; only half a roll is needed to achieve the braking position. Even those who are terrorstruck and flatly refuse to try the more flamboyant head-first arrests should be able to do this basic routine.

It is during descent that there is a greater likelihood of tripping and falling into a head-first position. Common causes of a head-first fall are one leg plunging into a hidden cavity and pitching the body forwards, a crampon catching on gaiters, overtrousers or the straps of the other crampon, or a sudden gust of wind from behind.

The routines for head-first arrest (Plates 4.9 and 4.10) must be executed quickly. First, it is vital to pivot the body into the feet-first position in order to avoid head injuries on impact. Second, very often you may achieve a pivot only to find you are still sliding with the axe pick above the head, and unless the pick is replanted under the chest the necessary braking force will not be achieved and the pick may simply slice through the snow.

Whilst the basic motions of arrest are the same in different snow conditions, the style does need to be varied. For instance, on soft snow the pick must be planted firmly for maximum penetration but the same action on rock-hard névé might result in one's shoulder being wrenched out of its socket! The pick should be placed at an angle against an icy

Plate 4.9 *Ice axe arrest: falling head first on chest; axe planted horizontally to the side to allow body to pivot into feet-first position*

Plate 4.10 *Ice axe arrest: falling head first on back; axe planted at hip level; pull up on the shaft and simultaneously roll towards the axe; this enables the body to pivot and roll into the upright face-in position*

snow surface to create enough friction to allow the necessary pivot or to gradually slow the slide.

It is instructive to try axe arrest wearing a rucksack in replication of a real situation. Coming off Sgurr nan Clach Geala in the Fannichs one January during a two-day trip with a group of students, I tried to demonstrate this and got quite a shock. Finding a patch of névé on an otherwise rocky slope, I flung myself forwards head first and immediately the heavy sack rode up over my head, trapping my shoulders and preventing my planting the axe out to the side. By the time I'd extricated my arms I'd hit the rocks. My students were not convinced!

The most common mistakes made by beginners are:

- Instinctively rolling to one's natural side (usually the right) instead of to the side which is holding the axe; this involves whipping the axe-head close to the face and doing a full 360-degree roll; when witnessed in others the mistake is obvious.
- Delayed reactions caused by the shock of sliding, allowing dangerous acceleration;

repeated practice enables slow thinkers to speed up their reaction time.

- Failing to plant the axe firmly in soft snow; without some braking friction from the axe nothing will happen.
- Instinctively kicking the toes into the slope as soon as one rolls over; this could cause somersaulting if wearing crampons on hard snow.
- Pushing the body up as soon as the braking position is reached, which immediately reduces the braking force; knees, hips and shoulders should be flat against the snow until the slide is stopped.
- Planting the axe in front of the head instead of out to the side in a head-first front fall; this is disastrous at speed, causing somersaulting.
- Adopting a *rigor mortis* position in a head-first slide on the back; if nerves get the better of you and your body 'freezes', nothing will happen when the axe is planted; the body must stay supple and roll towards the axe to allow the crucial 'pivot and roll'.

In view of the regularity with which people lose their grip on their axe in a fall, it is sensible to practise self-arrest without an axe, although this is only advised in soft snow. From a horizontal starting position, roll down the slope. As the body rolls, the legs being heavier will begin to pivot the body into an upright position. On coming out of the second or third roll, at the point where the chest is against the snow, throw the arms and legs out into a star shape (but keep the heels raised); this eliminates the roll and stabilises an upright position, and the knees and elbows can then be used to slow and even to stop the slide. Note that on névé the same actions may achieve an upright position, but will not stop the slide.

In all considerations of ice-axe arrest it must be remembered that this is a 'life-saving' technique, and an attitude of bare-nailed vigour rather than relaxed expectancy is essential if it is to work.

Glissading

'Within the letters of this word are contained some of the most subtle and fascinating joys of the snow climber.'[6]

Yes, it's that man Harold Raeburn again, extolling the virtues of a snow technique which is today regarded as potentially dangerous and which has resulted in many accidents over the years. Yet the fun and speed of descending by glissade cannot be denied. Like Raeburn, most mountaineers were great enthusiasts. In early writings we read of a 'terrific glissade of 2,100 feet on Cairn Toul', and even a claim to a record continuous descent of 762m on Ben More by Crianlarich in 1898. In 1928, an average velocity of 40kmph was calculated for a descent off the east end of Beinn Eighe. There are two methods of glissade, and in both the ability to slow or arrest the slide with the axe is paramount to safety.

- **The standing glissade:** (Plate 4.12, page 102) This may be compared to skiing without skis. Propulsion is effected by pointing the toes down the slope so that the boot soles are flat on the snow, and the speed is controlled by digging in the heels of the boots. The body's weight is taken wholly through the knees which are slightly bent and held together. Turns can be made by little jumps. Standing glissades require good balance, deft technique and strong thighs. They are best achieved on firm but granular 'spring' snow, which gives the necessary grip and support. A continuous 150m descent off the Cadha Goblach col after a traverse of An Teallach was my longest standing glissade, but even in short bursts the technique has enlivened many a mountain day.

- **The sitting glissade:** (Plate 4.11) Although inelegant, wetting and unkind to new Goretex shellsuits, the sitting glissade or 'bum-slide' is much more popular. The ice-axe is held across the body and the spike can be applied to the snow as a rudder and temporary brake. Glissaders must at all times be confident of their ability to make a full axe arrest if necessary. Legs must not be allowed to dip under the snow surface where they could get trapped. Bum-slides are fine in sloppy wet snow or in sugary 'spring' snow, but they must *never* be chanced if there is névé, ice or boulders around. Hidden rocks are also a danger. One is always safer to glissade slopes one knows from climbing earlier in the day, and a glissade should never be started on a convex slope where the full runout is not visible.

In dismal thawing weather when all the snow is like sugar, a good sitting glissade can redeem the day. One soggy March day I was out on Sgurr an Lochain, Glen Shiel, with a local rescue team practising snowcraft skills. Due to hangovers the lads had needed a liberal supply of Coca-Cola and cigarettes to get up the hill, and we had ploughed through all the safety drills until thoroughly soaked. Having reached the summit I pointed out the possibility of a 300m glissade back into the corrie, and the mood changed from one of duty to elation as we swooped down 40-degree slopes, creating a *luge* run in the slush. Without that surge of excitement the day would have been eminently forgettable.

Stepcutting

Prior to the advent of crampons in the 1950s, stepcutting was perhaps the most essential function of the ice-axe. Now the need for cutting arises only occasionally:

- to get across short, frozen sections of ground and save the bother of putting on crampons;
- to make a resting step or ledge to give some relief when walking over long frozen slopes.

Cutting steps requires wrist strength and subtle swing. To make a horizontal 'slash' step the adze must strike the snow close to the limit of its arc, so that it not only penetrates but also comes back out on the return; the wrist should give a little twist at the point of impact to aid its extraction. The axe is best held in the downhill hand when stepcutting in order to give full freedom of swing, although most people will use their stronger natural hand whichever way they are facing. Three or four swings of the axe should be sufficient to fashion an adequate horizontal edge in névé snow, where the frozen crust is rarely more than 2 or 3cm thick, though up to two dozen may be needed in water ice. By cutting away from you with successive swings the snow or ice is easily excavated into the initial cavity. The resultant step should give a real feeling of security. Steps which are too shallow or sloping, or which are too far apart are simply not doing their job, particularly if you are making them for a following party. All winter walkers should never

Plate 4.11 *A late Victorian sitting glissade (SMC Collection)*

Plate 4.12 *Standing glissade with axe shaft used as rudder and brake*

forget that however icy and delicate a slope becomes, the situation can always be relieved simply by hewing out a platform in the snow.

Footwork

When walking on snow without crampons, *stepkicking* and *edging* are the key words for footwork. The best grip is achieved if the boot is kicked firmly into the snow and held in a horizontal position (with assistance from the stiff sole) (Plate 4.4). In soft snow, steps are easily kicked with the toe, but on a firm snow surface they should be kicked obliquely so that the side of the boot gets a good edge; this gives a greater surface area of grip and is much less tiring than toe-kicking. In descent the heel must be stamped vigorously into the snow and the boot held level in order to gain a sure grip. 'Jackbooting' is the best description of a good descending technique without crampons. Whether ascending or descending, and whether on hard or soft snow, the boot will tend to slip as soon as it is flexed down the slope. A consistent discipline must therefore be maintained in footwork.

So why not wear crampons all the time if they are simpler and safer? Well, crampons do slow progress, adding perhaps 10 per cent to the effort of walking due to their grip. Secondly, there are some snow types where crampons are more dangerous, such as soft damp snow in which they 'ball up'. Finally, crampons themselves are a potential hazard, easily catching on gaiters or overtrousers and so causing a trip.

With growing experience winter mountaineers learn exactly where and when crampons are needed. The limits to stepkicking soon become apparent as the slope angle and surface icing increase. Simultaneously they develop good footwork so beginners can handle safely soft fresh snow, granular spring snow and low inclines without them. They should follow the dictum 'if in doubt, stick them on', but they should be equally willing to try taking them off again if softening snow conditions or easing slope angles suggest. With sub-zero temperatures and hard surface crusting, crampons may be a necessity on every slope above 20 degrees in angle; yet an overnight thaw can render the same route perfectly safe without them. The greatest skill in winter hillwalking is dealing appropriately with such fluctuating conditions.

Crampon Techniques

- **Basic walking:** Though it may seem unnatural to novices, safe walking in crampons requires the feet to be kept further apart than normal, and demands the knees to be raised and the boot planted with a positive deliberate force. Such advice leads to a walking style which, although it at first feels exaggerated and awkward, prevents the points catching and ensures a proper grip on an icy surface.

- **Flatfooting:** *Flatfooting* and *flexing* are the key techniques of cramponning on hard snow indeed, these are quite the opposite of the edging and kicking methods of footwork used without crampons. By

flatfooting, the sole of the boot is planted flat (perpendicular) on the snow surface; on slopes this requires the ankle to be flexed, which can cause some strain on untrained ligaments. Plates 4.13 and 4.14 show the application of this principle on easy angle ascents and on descents. By planting the full sole on the surface, all the points on the base of the crampon get a grip, and the effort of progress is reduced by comparison to balancing up on the toes alone. The consequence of failing to flex the boot on steeper slopes is that only one side of the crampon is presented to the snow and it can skid off instead of penetrating the surface. Wearers of plastic boots should be aware that the required ankle flexions are more difficult or painful to achieve because the plastic is relatively unyielding; however, by keeping the lacing loose at the ankle, the worst of discomfort and ankle bruising can be avoided. The flatfooting techniques should cope comfortably with slopes up to 35 degrees in angle.

- **'Pied à trois':** Above a 35-degree angle it becomes uncomfortable and precarious to keep both feet sideways and the ankles flexed. But instead of changing straight to

Plate 4.13 *Flatfooting: feet sideways to slope and both flexed outwards to give full sole grip on hard snow surface*

Plate 4.14 *Descending direct: both toes pointing downslope to give sole grip*

Plate 4.15 *'Pied à trois': uphill foot frontpointing; downhill foot sideways and should be flexed outwards to give better sole grip with all crampon points*

Plate 4.16 *Descending diagonally: downhill foot flexed down-slope; uphill foot planted sideways and flexed outwards*

frontpointing with both toes which is both strenuous and insecure, a hybrid technique should be adopted which French alpinists have christened *pied à trois*; in this the downhill foot remains horizontal and flexed perpendicular to the slope angle, whilst the uphill foot frontpoints with the boot held horizontal (Plate 4.15). With good co-ordination of axe and feet, a good rhythm of movement can be achieved in *pied à trois* which allows a rapid diagonal ascent of steeper ground up to 45–50 degrees in angle. By zig-zagging, strain and fatigue are shared equally by both sides of the body.

The diagonal line of progress is equally well adopted on descents at angles of up to 40 degrees (Plate 4.16). A diagonal stance enables the axe to be firmly planted and is more secure than facing fully outwards when the angle steepens.

- **Frontpointing:** On walking ascents it should rarely be necessary to use the full frontpointing method with both toes kicked into the snow, save for the occasional short icy step; those who find themselves frontpointing by habit on medium-angle slopes need to rethink their techniques. However, on steeper descents it is advisable to face in and frontpoint down the exposed section *as soon* as a sense of insecurity is felt when facing out from the slope. By facing in, the axe can be used to give real support and the psychological insecurity of teetering solely on the feet is removed. The prevalence of accidents during descent puts safety rather than style as the priority.

Problems of conditions and terrain
- **'Balling up' on wet snow:** This is the greatest single problem with crampons, occurring whenever there is a surface layer of soft snow

and the air temperature is above zero. A clod of moist snow attaches itself to the metal crampon frame, covering the points and eliminating their grip. 'Balling up' can occur so quickly that one may be wholly unaware of it until sliding downslope! In such conditions there are three options: 1 – take the crampons off; 2 – tap the side of the boots every few paces with the axe to remove the clinging snow; or 3 – face in and kick steps down the slope. The option of removing the crampons may not be available when the wet snow is lying on an icy base.

- **Crusted snow:** Crampons add to weight and penetration at the snow surface, making it easier to break through a thin crust. They are best removed provided the surface is not too icy.

- **Water ice:** During a prolonged cold spell, all drainage lines, including long sections of approach paths, develop floes of hard, clear water ice. Alternatively, a sudden freeze after a wet or thawing spell can turn the plateaux into sheets of verglas. Crampons then become essential even on horizontal ground, and a positive stamping action is needed to get a grip on the surface. Attempts to negotiate frozen ice floes without crampons will prove either frustrating or painful, or both. Coming down from Sgurr na Ciche to Sourlies bothy after dark on a January evening, I was too lazy to get my crampons out when I encountered sheet ice in the valley of the Allt Coire na Ciche. After half an hour of dangerous skating punctuated by several bone-crunching falls I realised that I *should* have bothered!

- **Frozen ground and iced rocks:** Even though there might be little or no snow on the ground, a severe freeze can leave steep grass slopes very slippery and build a coat of rime ice on the rocks. Crampons will be of help on such frozen ground, giving an especially good hold on turf. When walking on rocky ground in crampons one must develop a neat style, taking the weight on the front or heel of the crampon but not on the instep, where the hinge bar would be prone to breakage.

BIG ROUNDS ON THE WINTER MUNROS

This detailed examination of tools and techniques for winter hillwalking should not obscure their eventual purpose, for they are merely the means to break a trail quickly and safely over the snowy tops. Adopt and use them competently and a host of great mountain days awaits. A winter trail in the snow is one that leaves no mark or blemish on the mountain. Perhaps it is in the accessible Southern Highlands that the sense of wilderness regained is best felt in winter. The ranges of Perthshire and Argyll, now so trammelled in summer, offer many great winter rounds, big days that will live long in the memory if the conditions are right. By a 'big' winter round I mean one that starts at or before dawn, covers 20 to 30km in distance, includes several Munros, and battles to finish before nightfall. Climbing all the Munros in a single winter in 1984/85 gave me the opportunity to enjoy several of them during a New Year anticyclone:

The Forest of Mamlorn Hills
Beinn Heasgarnich–Creag Mhor–Ben Challum–Meall Glas–Sgiath Chuil from the roadhead at Kenknock, a circuit of upper Glen Lochay: 32km, 2,750m ascent.

For some reason this round really fired my imagination: was it the remoteness of upper Glen Lochay, the historical romance of Mamlorn and Breadalbane, a boyhood glimpse of Challum so far away at the head of the glen, or simply the grand scale of the undertaking?

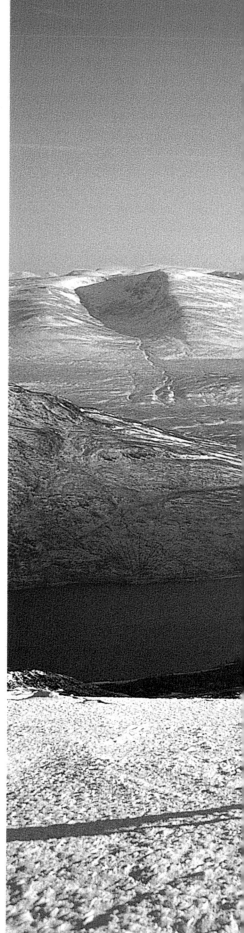

Plate 4.17 'Breaking the trail': hard labour on the North Glen Shiel Ridge

Plate 4.18 Winter walking in the Central Highlands: Beinn a'Chlachair and the Aonach Beag range from Creag Meagaidh

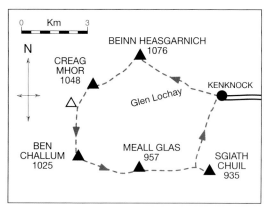

The Forest of Mamlorn

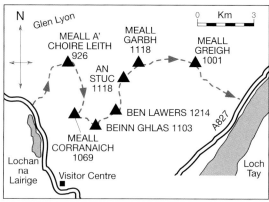

The Ben Lawers range

The reality did not disappoint: a pre-dawn slog up endless braes and into thick mist on the crest of Heasgarnich; the sudden view of the north-east face of Creag Mhor shining icily like some Alpine giant as the fog parted; the kind brush of the sun as we rested by the summit cross of Ben Challum, chasing our lengthening shadows on the frosted trek over Meall Glas with the sky at our backs glowing like hot coals; and inevitably, the weary but contented slog in the dark down the icy track to the van: these were highlights in a 10-hour day. The height separations between the peaks are considerable, nowhere less than 300m. There is a great temptation to shortcut the day after Ben Challum, especially since the last two are comparatively dull hills, and the valley crossings are long and may feel tedious. Yet the face of Creag Mhor is steep enough to challenge, Challum is truly a noble hill and to circuit the glen in a January day is a real achievement of stamina and good planning.

The Ben Lawers Range

From Lochan na Lairige to Lawers village over Meall a'Choire Leith–Meall Corranaich–Beinn Ghlas–Ben Lawers–An Stuc–Meall Garbh– Meall Greigh: 21km, 1,650m ascent.

A traverse of a range gives a special satisfaction, and save for the initial detour to Meall a'Choire Leith, this route held the twin attractions of natural logic and completeness. And why not be honest and admit that to cover all the Munros of a range in a single day gives a special satisfaction? This one gave me six, which henceforth is seven thanks to the questionable promotion of the An Stuc carbuncle to fully-fledged Munro status. Lawers is the ideal range for a ski traverse, but don't be waiting for ever. We had a thin icy snow cover and a memorable day on foot. Shifting mists above the summits were periodically pierced by sunlight which made delicate spectra dance on the cloudbanks; then all would clear to reveal the icy ridge ahead. An Stuc and the cliffs above Lochan na Cat gave a welcome jolt of exposure and we wore crampons for the scramble. This excitement over, we sloped gently down towards the still waters of Loch Tay with a sense of regret. Why had we rushed such a perfect day?

The Blackmount Range

From Loch Tulla to White Corries over Stob a'Choire Odhair–Stob Ghabhar–Creise–Meall a'Bhuiridh: 20.5km, 1,850m ascent.

A wild, remote tangle of ridges and summits, the shifting aspects of the range lend inspiration to the drive over Rannoch Moor. A clear cool morning, deer at play on the lower moors

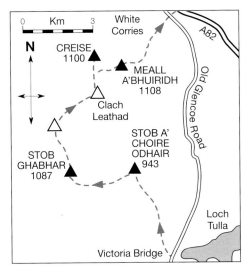

The Blackmount range

and a coating of overnight snow on the hills lent me wings for the initial climb, but once on the tops a succession of squalls blew in, fuelling a near-continuous snowfall and obliterating all distant views. Little cornices were forming on the edges as I walked them, and the day became one of windblasted struggle and tricky navigation of discordant ridgelines. What little was seen was enough to sense the raw quality of these hills. As usual, satisfaction was proportionate to effort, and there is plenty of both on the Blackmount in winter.

Beinn Dorain and the Bridge of Orchy Hills

Beinn Dorain–Beinn an Dothaidh–Beinn Mhanach –Beinn a'Chreachain–Beinn Achaladair: 26km, 2,275m ascent.

Another natural set of hills, formed like a clenched fist with Mhanach as the thumb knuckle, they form an obvious winter challenge for the Munro-chaser who likes to tidy a range with one sweep. There are no illusions about the climb of Dorain but for the chill airs of a frosted morning we might have complained of a grim slog. The traverse over Beinn a'Dothaidh holds little excitement, yet in the rising gossamers of mist we found both

enchantment and promise. And why bother with Beinn Mhanach, a sore thumb at the head of Loch Lyon? For completeness, for a look into some very lonely country, and as a psychological crux imposed to discipline the day, there was just enough to justify. And thanks to the detouring tramp through tussocks and powder snow, our return to the rim of the fist at Beinn a'Chreachain was exalting to the highest: its crowning beacon stood at the brink of Rannoch Moor, where every lochan reflected in unison the last of the day's sun, and beyond the moor, the twilit ranges of the Mamores and Nevis rose in clustered splendour. We filled our chests deep with cold air and scanned every feature of the scene, yet struggled in vain to comprehend the whole. One sublime hour traversing the ridge to Beinn Achaladair with the sunset dead ahead over Cruachan, and then our eyes were brought back to our feet for the dark and icy descent to Achaladair farm…

Days so special as these are, I contend, reserved for winter conditions, for it is then that the act of hillwalking acquires a combined challenge of strategy, technique, physique and attitude, and it is only then that the Scottish mountains assume their full grandeur.

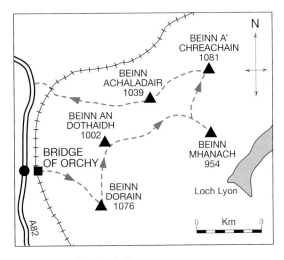

The Bridge of Orchy hills

5: ON THE EDGES

THE CLASSIC WINTER RIDGE TRAVERSES

An arrow-headed crest suspended in an ice-blue sky: Liathach in winter's clutch is the possessor of a true majesty. Screes and grasses, tracks and terraces, that coarse-grained spread of summer shades – all are whitewashed crystal clean. A brilliant gloss gleams in the midday sun down the southern flank, while a muted chalky mat hushes the shadowed northern cirques. These two sides soar to meet in the glittering apex of the summit ridge. Only the sheer cliff bands of ancient sand break the icy glare, thrusting bold and black against the hazy western seas.

To straddle this winter crest is to perch atop a cathedral roof whose polished eaves plunge down both left and right to unseen voids. Here is natural geometry and symmetry of stunning simplicity, drawing eye and mind into grand designs and here, too, is found a mountaineering which combines classical purity with technical intrigue.

The great Scottish ridges! They fire the passions of those whose sights are drawn to the snowy tops. Liathach is but one – albeit one of the finest – of a score of scything edges which chequer the Highland mountain scene. All are pleasing, if modest summer scrambles with a spice of exposure and a wealth of views – but all are quite transformed by snow and ice, and to embark on their winter traverse is to engage in a graded climbing expedition of I or II in standard, and some are harder in the worst conditions. The exposures are real rather than perceived; they can menace as well as delight; and our gentle rocky clamber requires varied and even devious climbing on every conceivable type of winter terrain, where speed is of the essence and no elaboration of modern gear can by itself ensure safe passage.

So, while the winter lustre of an Aonach Eagach or an An Teallach must surely entice the dedicated walker, there is seemingly a quantum jump of skill and experience needed for the task.

Unfortunately the techniques and ropework for such undertakings are not readily to be found in either instructional textbooks, or indeed practical teaching, both of which have tended to draw a convenient barrier between the walker and the technical climber. The crucial intermediate ground is left unturned – though perhaps this is understandable, because the roped ridge traverse cannot be reduced to a set of unvarying rules and procedures: there is rarely a single means of solving any particular problem en route, and no two problems are ever quite the same.

However, one should not, and need not be deterred from the challenge of the ridges for want of knowledge. The skills to be sought are largely those of traditional alpinism whose natural simplicity is the very antithesis of the modern climbing technicality. Equipment needs are not onerous. Good fitness, steady balance and technique, a clear knowledge of the purpose and effective application of basic ropework when moving together, coupled with a keen instinct (or failing this a proper patience) in route-finding: with these alone the winter ridges may be tackled in a flowing, joyous rhythm and they are then accessible to those who have no ambitions in the domain of technical climbing.

Plate 5.1 *Liathach: 'An arrow-headed crest suspended in an ice-blue sky': looking west to the main summit, Spidean a'Choire Leith, from Stuc a'Choire Duibh Bhig*

THE SCOPE AND THE PLEASURE

It is an invidious task either to specify exactly the relative quality and difficulty of Scotland's great ridge traverses, or to compile a comprehensive gazetteer of the routes. Their charm and challenge depend crucially on the uncertainty and variability of their winter condition, while a spirit of adventure can still prevail in seeking out obscure or hitherto unknown gems on the far-flung hills.

Fig 5.1 attempts no more than to list the most famous, together with a selection of lesser known expeditions. Whatever their summer character, they attain a difficulty of at least grade I in average winter conditions, but are also recognised summer scrambles up or over the major summits. The upper ceiling is drawn at grade III in technical difficulties, where pitched climbing will usually be needed for long stretches. Classic grade III ridges such as Tower Ridge, Ben Nevis and Pinnacle Ridge on Sgurr nan Gillean are the preserve of the more experienced climber.

The greatest ridge of all, the Black Cuillin, cannot be omitted, but those sections listed on Skye are distinctly more serious than the mainland routes, and require ideal conditions with well banked, stable snow on the crests. The complete traverse *integrale* demands a wholly separate niche, for it is a sustained grade III/IV expedition of super-alpine length.

Fig 5.1 *The winter ridge traverses: a selection*

SOUTHERN HIGHLANDS	Technical Difficulties
The Cobbler Traverse: Arrochar Traverse of all three summits, ideally started with an ascent of Great Gully (II) direct to North Peak; traverse Central Peak; descent by abseil from South Peak Summit.	Grade II, but escapable with short, difficult sections; a grand 'wee' day when in condition.

GLENCOE AND LOCHABER

Aonach Eagach: N side Glencoe Usually done E–W, Scotland's most popular winter ridge; compact and magnificently positioned. Rapid access from glen but inescapable to S once started. Final descent tricky (Clachaig Gully the main trap).	Grade II in full conditions; intricate weaving on pinnacled crest with steep pitches both up and down.
Sron na Lairig–Beinn Fhada: S side Glencoe A fine route, less intimidating than A Eagach and rarely as crowded. Quick access up Lairig Eilde; the Sron is easily quitted at top to the SE, but continuation over S. C. Sgreamhach and B. Fhada recommended.	Grade I/II; steep initial buttress, then exposed knife-edge and snow head-wall to finish.
Curved Ridge: Buachaille Etive Mor, Glencoe Ridge and face route exploring superb cliff scenery. Fast approach but inescapable once engaged; descent from Buachaille down Coire na Tulaich is treacherous and hard to locate in severe conditions.	Lower ridge is hard grade II if taken direct, otherwise grade I; varied climbing, interesting route-finding.
Ring of Steall: Mamores Forest Airy circuit of five Munros. Best start is via Nevis gorge to An Gearanach. Escapable at cols but Steall Fall bars lower exit of Coire a'Mhail.	Devil's Ridge and An Garbhanach arêtes rate mild grade I.
Carn Mor Dearg Arête: Ben Nevis Finest approach to the Ben with stupendous views of NE face; very popular but a hard round from lower Glen Nevis in heavy snow. Arête escapable at its end (easily to S but steeply to N into Coire Leis). Now approachable from Aonach Mor ski station.	Exposed rock edge; grade I usually but problematic given verglas, thick powder, or high wind.

WESTERN HIGHLANDS

Ladhar Bheinn, Round of Coire Dhorrcail: Knoydart Ascent via Stob a'Choire Odhair, descent over Stob a'Chearcaill.A great round and very remote (base at Barrisdale bothy).	Grade I; S. C. Odhair a knife-edge with a steep snow exit; full conditions rare.
Forcan Ridge: The Saddle, Glen Shiel Direct access from Glen Shiel on good path. As fine an arête as any on the mainland. Fast descent from summit to SE, but the W ridge makes a grand (though easier) continuation, finishing at Shiel Bridge.	Grade II; rocky buttress to Sgurr na Forcan, tricky descent, then an exposed razor-edge and easier slopes to summit.
Mullach Fraoch-Choire, S. Ridge: Cluanie–Glen Affric A fine gendarmed ridge. Remotely situated with a long approach over A'Chralaig, but difficulties are short. Descent via N ridge to Affric.	Grade I; broken rocks, winding descents and traverses; dangerous in soft snow.

Fig 5.1 *The winter ridge traverses: a selection* [CONTINUED]

NORTH-WEST HIGHLANDS	Technical Difficulties
Beinn Alligin Traverse: Torridon Best done E-W starting with the Horns. Fast tracked access from Coire Mhic Nobuil. Not escapable from 1st Horn to main summit; thereafter down W flanks. Scenically magnificent and not technically demanding.	Grade I; difficulties concentrated on Horns (exposed rocky drops off 1st and 3rd); avoiding traverses not advised.
Liathach, Main Ridge Traverse: Torridon The mainland's most serious peak in winter; a worthy challenge. Short but brutally steep access from Glen Torridon. No escapes on pinnacles and retreat from main summit complex. . Normally done E-W	Pinnacles are sustained and grade II if taken direct; avoiding traverses often too dangerous in loose or soft snow.
The Black Carls of Beinn Eighe: Torridon The first link in the B. Eighe traverse. Approach from Kinlochewe. Exciting but short and escapable at either end.	Mild grade I; weaving route around the carls with one steep pitch to finish.
An Teallach Traverse: Dundonnell-Fisherfield Forests The queen of the ridges usually done W-E with a long arduous approach over the main summits. Pinnacled section escapable only to S and with difficulty. Easiest descent at end down SE ridge of Sail Liath.	Grade II but less serious than Liathach, all types of terrain and exposed; crux is finding best way off Corrag Bhuidhe.
Stac Polly: Coigach Intricate and exhilarating little route when in its rare winter state. Quick approach. Escapable via steep gullies between the pinnacles.	Grade II; rock gendarmes and arêtes; hard moves at short steep steps.
ISLE OF SKYE	
Bruach na Frithe–Am Basteir: Northern Cuillin Approach up NW ridge of B. na Frithe, descent over Sgurr a'Bhasteir. Basteir Tooth avoided by descent on N side and Am Basteir climbed up E ridge with one short, smooth step (grade II).	Sensational knife-edges, grade I/II; firm snow conditions essential; Sgurr a'Fionn Choire gives a taste of mixed climbing.
Sgurr Nan Gillean Traverse: Northern Cuillin Up W Ridge, down SE Ridge (Tourist Route). A good mixed outing which added to that above gives a magnificent long day. Route-finding on descent will be problematic in mist and thick snow.	Chimney pitch on W Ridge is a steep grade II; otherwise sustained at grade I and exposed throughout.
Mhadaidh–Ghreadaidh–Banachdich: Central Cuillin Approach from Glen Brittle over Sgurr Thuilm. A sustained and demanding expedition. Only easy escape is at An Dorus, but final descent down W ridge of Banachdich is easy. Good snow is rare but essential.	Sustained at grade II with razor crests, long descents and steep pitches.
Clach Glas–Blaven Traverse: Eastern Cuillin A step up in technical difficulty but a tremendous route when in condition. Start from Loch Slapin over Sgurr nan Each. Escapable at Blaven – C. Glas col. Highly scenic.	Grade II/III with the descent of Clach Glas the crux (weaving line); sustained and varied mixed climbing.
Coire Lagan Round: (excluding In Pinn and An Stac buttress) The technical limit of the classic mountain traverses. Start up W ridge of Sgurr Dearg; descent by Great Stone Shoot of Sgurr Alasdair. Inescapable between Mhic Choinnich and Thearlaich; needs stable snow on crest.	Grade II/III; crux is descent of Sgurr Mhic Choinnich – King's Chimney (long abseil) or Collie's Ledge (sensational).

To illustrate the calibre of the routes at the lower and upper end of the scale I can draw on two personal memories:

THE RING OF STEALL

The Ring of Steall around the heart of the Mamores Forest exemplifies the quality of the longer, easier circuits, and enhanced by an approach via the Nevis gorge, is an expedition as fine as any on the mainland. I took a party there one February day when the clouds were rolling back from a two-day snowfall. As we drove into Glen Nevis, the pinks of dawn were flush and a brilliant day was soon to flower; a trace of frost hugged the shady chasm of the Nevis, but the waters of Steall still flowed and spouted down to the glen. Aloft, the new snow thickly daubed the massive shanks of An Gearanach and Sgurr a'Mhaim, the sentinels of

the Ring. Hard work lay ahead, but our spirits were at last awake and in that ascendant mood when all things can be done.

And, as so often after a windless snowfall, all things had to be done to reach the heights. First I led a breathless battle up the vertical birchwood to escape the gorge, squirming in seeping grooves, hauling over heathered ribs, grasping snapping twigs and boughs, and clawing the snow with sore, bare hands. Freedom was tasted 400 metres up on the north-east spur of Sgurr a'Mhaim; but from here to the top, thick powder showed no mercy. At least we were five, and trail-breaking could be shared on the knobbled ridge; but as we flogged and flailed up collapsing steps, team morale was at that crucial stretch where the legs quiver and convictions waver.

But a magic crest was gained at last, wrapped in a silken mist and suffused with a golden midday sun whose rays shone close

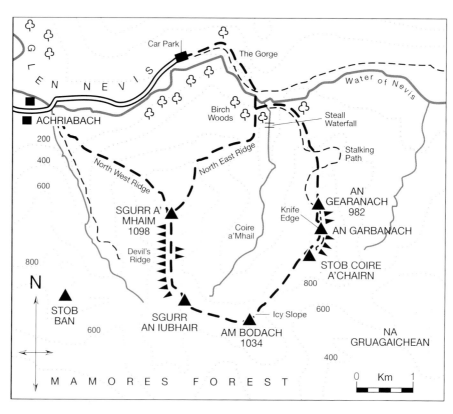

Plate 5.2 *On the Clach Glas traverse, Skye; looking across to the northern end of the main Cuillin Ridge* (Jonathan Preston)

above. Now wearing crampons, we picked up speed and strength on a burnished edge which some slight breeze had feathered clean, and all but floated along the Devil's Ridge. No rope was needed because the footing was good both on the crisp névé and in the light dry drifts that clung in the hollows. We forged our tracks around the ring in certain anticipation that the mist would clear. From Iubhair to Am Bodach the ridge was a broad-backed stroll, but then the onward link was barred by an icy face which slips, then swoops in deceiving convexity for 300 metres to either side. The descent might be innocuous and simple in soft or floury snow, but today's fields of polished névé motioned great caution. A slip here might have had serious consequences, and yet, without belays, a rope of five would feel equally vulnerable moving together with only the assurance of the leader's grip on the rope had

anyone slipped. We wore helmets and I kept the rope coiled round my shoulders ready to tie on if anyone looked nervous, but the team had steady heads and trusted to their personal abilities. With precise crampon style, a secure sideways stance and the ultimate insurance of the ice-axe brake, we were soon down the 40-degree slope.

The sun had slowly burnt through the summit mists, but now the colder valley air boiled skywards in towering cumulus masses which framed the silvery pate of Bodach. Yet through this spectacle of atmospheric convolution, not the softest breath of wind had stirred to deflect our gaze.

The new-born clarity of the afternoon distilled the pleasure of the final link over An Gearanach, the trickiest section of the Ring in technical terms, with exposures both on left and right that can bite deep into one's composure. We roped up four or five metres apart, and edged and balanced along the bare-boned spine, using the crenellations of the ridge to provide natural belays. Group safety was actually enhanced by having a large party on this section, for the rope weaved reassuringly from side to side of the ridge. At the highest point its defences parted and a sweep of open slopes unfolded to offer a romping descent to Steall.

After just a few hours of filtered winter sun the lower snows were wholly altered, now slumped and heavy, balling on our crampons and cloying our patience in contrast to their fine-grained aeration of morning.

We forded the Nevis in the valley twilight, while the summits above still proudly burned in the glory of the waning day.

While the Ring of Steall is a route where the main technical judgement is whether or not to use the rope at all, ridges at the upper end of the scale require continuous ropework and devious route-finding:

CLACH GLAS

Late in January 1995 the snows were lying thick and low, but would they have consolidated sufficiently to allow us to traverse a bit of the Skye Cuillin? In the morning Jas and I climbed a big ramp on the East Face of Clach Glas, an entertaining romp with a couple of short pitches. We emerged in deepening powder snow well to the right of the summit tower known as The Impostor (Fig 5.3). Our hope was to traverse the summit of Clach Glas towards Blaven, but I was dubious whether the final face of the tower could be climbed by its normal summer route up the west face. This is a slabby and exposed Difficult pitch. Such sections can become all but impossible in thick dry snow, and I knew that there were few if any belays in its thirty metres.

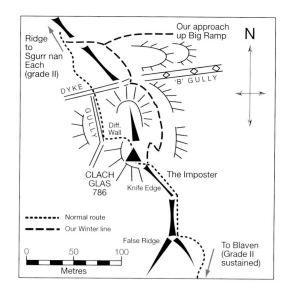

However, looking across the top of the East Face I noticed a horizontal terrace traversing The Impostor. Although it was steeply banked with snow and disappeared from view before its conclusion, I felt we might have discovered a feasible way to reach the summit. With the thrill of stepping into the unknown we commenced ploughing across the gangways and ramps of the traverse. I kept about five or six metres of rope between us, which I guessed would be enough to allow us to climb any short steps one at a time and to clip into running belays when they were available. Equally, five metres was short enough to give a fair chance of stopping each other had one of us slipped when moving together without belays.

We tested the stability of the snow at regular intervals but found that the snow was well attached to the rock beneath.

As we crept round the tower, the exposures down into 'A' Gully were at times profound and sudden. During such passages I tried to keep a running belay between us, but on occasions there were none. So I simply stamped a firm stance in the snow, took the rope round my waist and brought Jas across.

We continued traversing until a little beyond the top where easier ramps zig-zagged up towards the skyline. Now able to climb more directly upwards, I could take off my spare coils and use the full forty metres of the rope to lead a full pitch. Combined techniques of daggering my axe at waist height and punching my mittened hand deep into the snow, I got up most of the ramps, although on a couple of moves had to swing the axe into turf or rock cracks in order to surmount chockstones. Jas joined me and together we moved into the glare of the afternoon sun on the summit. We felt unusually isolated, besieged by the snow on all flanks. Our weaving line of steps to the top was our only lifeline. Despite fantastic views of the main Cuillin Ridge we did not stay more than ten minutes, during which time I discounted the option of continuing along the Ridge towards Blaven. With the snow making such laborious going and several tricky sections en route we would be hard pressed to get down to the col in daylight.

Our only choice was to reverse our ascent. With our tracks to follow and a knowledge of the available belays we took only forty minutes to get back to the base of The Impostor. Now relaxing and enjoying the wonderful conditions, we followed the crest of the ridge northwards to the col before Sgurr nan Each, where we plunged back into the shade and gathering frost of evening.

Ropework on the Ridges

Rope technique on the ridges is beset by the eternal paradox of trying to ensure speed as well as security of progress. Taken to their extremes, one is the diametric opposite of the other. To tackle the length of the Aonach Eagach by a series of fixed belays with only one person moving at a time invites a certain bivouac. Yet for a novice to do it unroped courts disaster unless you have near-perfect snow or the temperament of a budding Patey. The solution is an ever-varying compromise between the two, and the key to success lies in choosing the best compromise at each junction of a route.

When to Rope Up?

This is the critical decision of the day. Put the rope on too early and the consequent delays may lead to a late finish; put it on too late, and one risks a serious accident should anyone slip. Party members may also become increasingly tense without exhibiting undue nerves, yet no one dares suggest putting the rope on in case they are seen to appear weak. Even as a guide I have sometimes misjudged the timing of roping up. For instance, on a traverse of Liathach I considered it 'normal' not to rope up on the first section of the traverse over the eastern tops and main summit (see route map on page 125). However, in the variable conditions of the winter ridges there should be no such norms. So one very icy March day my party followed me over Spidean a'Choire Leith, cramponning on hard névé snow. The descent from the summit was similarly icy, but my group looked to be coping well. Yet when I did stop to rope up at the beginning of the Pinnacles, one of the party sat down complaining of breathlessness; when I looked closely at him I realised that he was in fact very anxious and was hyperventilating. We had no option but to get off the ridge as quickly as possible. Having already committed ourselves to the Pinnacles this meant we had to make a direct descent of the south slopes towards Glen Torridon, a route riven by gullies and crags which is highly inadvisable except in emergencies. Using my experience in route-finding, we managed to get down unscathed and he quickly recovered. But nonetheless we had lost our chance of the traverse, and all for the sake

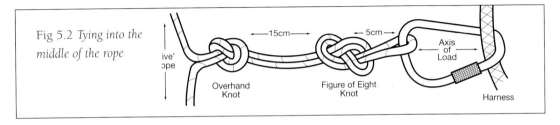

Fig 5.2 *Tying into the middle of the rope*

ive'
ope

←—15cm—→   ←5cm→

Overhand Knot

Figure of Eight Knot

Axis of Load

Harness

of the security and confidence which a rope can give.

There is no disgrace in asking for the rope, whether climbing with a guide or as a group of mates. Indeed, the person with the courage to speak up may bring relief to others in the party who are either too lazy or too proud to make the suggestion themselves. Every party should, however, be dressed ready to rope up as soon as tricky ground is encountered. If harnesses and helmets are worn from the outset and the leader has the rope coiled round the shoulder, the process of *encordement* can be achieved within a couple of minutes when the decision is eventually made.

Moving Together

The idea of moving together on a rope is distrusted by the majority of novices who see its inevitable result as 'one off – all off'. Nor is this scepticism easily dispelled, since first attempts to use the rope usually cause irritation and disharmony in an untried party.

Individuals must adjust their pace to that of the whole team. It is of no effect for a quick leader to drag the party to exhaustion, and it is dangerous that a fit tail-ender should be continually catching up, for this creates slack in the rope and thus the potential to accelerate in the event of a slip. Meanwhile, those in the middle are always getting the rope twisted around their backs each time the party changes direction, unaware that, by stepping over the rope behind at each turn, such tangles can

easily be avoided. The end result is a dishevelled, ill-tempered group; the rope is a hindrance and even a danger, and everybody yearns for that moment of freedom when the accursed thing can be taken off.

Nevertheless, once tried and practised, moving together on the rope helps develop a great sense of teamwork and interdependence: the fitter members learn to master their tendency to draw far ahead of the team, and those who are slower usually put in an extra effort when irrevocably linked to their companions. When it does become necessary to belay, the leader can quickly place an anchor and lengthen the available rope, and the switch to pitched climbing is thus smooth and simple. On the crest of a rocky ridge the weaving rope creates natural belays between team members, and on a snow arête the slip that might be fatal to the solo climber can easily be stopped by the others jumping down to the opposite side of the ridge. Moving together does, however, require certain disciplines if it is to be effective:

- The rope must be kept short and taut when climbing or traversing open slopes; guides use the term 'short-roping' to describe this method.

- Whoever leads the rope must feel a degree of confidence in their ability to stop a slip. In this regard, practice beforehand on training slopes in how to hold a slip is of immeasurable value. Sceptics are usually surprised at how effectively a slip can be stopped even in a rope of three or four climbers.

Plate 5.3 *Moving together in deep snow on the Forcan Ridge of The Saddle (Martin Welch)*

Fig 5.3a *Tying off the spare coils by an overhand at the chest*

Fig 5.3b *Tying off the spare coils by a stopper knot plus figure-of-eight to the waist*

- Those in the middle of the rope should tie in with a bight of about 20cm in length, and should keep the rope on their downhill side (Fig 5.2). With such a bight, a pull from behind can actually by-pass those in the middle, giving the leader first chance to stop the slip.

There are situations where a party may be better to climb unroped. For example, when crossing avalanche-prone slopes a closely roped party will all be swept away should a windslab be triggered. The rope can also offer little security when the whole party has to traverse exposed narrow ledges without belays, as can be encountered on some of the Torridonian traverses. Better here perhaps to let each member go unroped than to risk the whole party being plucked off should anyone slip.

The chances of a roped party stopping itself once it is tumbling are slim – even if one member arrests successfully, the momentum of the others will inevitably pull him or her off.

Moreover, the consequences of a big fall will always be more serious if the party is roped. When moving together it is critical to stop a slip before it becomes a fall. Dropping down onto the axe-shaft or pick and digging the feet into the slope the rope goes taut.

Shortening the Rope

When roping up, the party must gauge how much rope is needed between the climbers for each section of the route. This varies considerably according to the terrain, and indeed, the party may need to adjust its spacing on the rope several times during the course of a traverse. First and last members on the rope should always tie the rope ends in direct to their harness with a figure-of-eight knot or bowline; those in the middle can then tie in as in Fig 5.2.

Having tied in to the end, the leader should then coil any surplus rope around the shoulders, and tie the dead coils off at the waist. This spare is an accessible reserve should the live lengths have been misjudged, or should an emergency

Fig 5.4 *Tackling the winter ridges: ropework guidelines*

Assume a party of three. Gear carried: One 45 or 50m single rope, 10 or 11mm diameter, harnesses and screw-gate karabiners, minimum of 4 long and 2 short slings, 6–8 wired nuts and 2 larger hexentric chocks or 'Friends', 6–8 karabiners, 2 prusik cords per person, spare abseil tape, figure-of-eight for abseils.

Terrain	Example	Method	Pros and *Cons*
A Open Slope Ascent, descent and traverse.	Liathach, traverse round the south side of pinnacles.	Short tight rope; 2m maximum spacing; no belays; continuous moving together.	Fast travel over long sections. *Security highly dependent on immediate arrest of a slip.*
B Level Arête Rock or Snow	Carn Mor Dearg arête; Forcan Ridge, Saddle.	5–10m spacing; continuous moving together; hand coils optional.	Fast travel. *Counterweight arrest is sole security (jumping to other side).*
C Gendarmed Ridge (Grade I) Undulating and twisting	Sgurr nan Gillean, Tourist Route.	5–10m spacing; rope threaded over natural belays (ie, spikes, flakes) and woven side to side; continuous movement at same rate (no slack).	Fast rhythm of progress. Good security on broken rocky ground (friction and counterweight). *Rope abrasion (11mm better) and risk of jamming.*
D Gendarmed Ridge (Grade II) and **Steep Traverses** Exposed	Aonach Eagach pinnacles.	5–15m spacing; rope clipped into placed runners; last on the rope collects gear; always at least 1 runner on rope; continuous movement as in C.	Smoother running than C. Placed anchors more reliable. *Party must regroup to exchange gear. Delays for placing/removing runners. Rope abrasion (11mm better).*
E Short Steep Steps Easy Pitches up to 5m	The Horns of Beinn Alligin.	5–8m spacing; party moves one at a time from ledge to ledge; leader gives body belays at each stance; rock anchors used only if quickly accessible.	Delays for belaying are minimised. Seconds get a tight top rope. *Leader has no protection, and must not fall. Stances must be good and rope kept taut.*
F Steep Pitches 10–15m	Sron na Lairig, lower section.	Both leader and seconds belayed and anchored; Italian hitch belay used, direct on anchor by leader, indirect waist belay by seconds; seconds climb together 2m apart.	Fastest method of belaying. Anchors must be solid if direct belay used. *Italian hitch jams on frozen rope. Potential double load on top belay.*
		As above but seconds tie in 15m apart and climb one at a time.	More secure, seconds can't pull each other off, *but much slower.*
		As above, but leader ties on middle of rope; seconds tie one on each end and climb together for speed.	Leader has double rope protection. *Problem of belaying two ropes at once (belay plate needed). Party has to retie if reverting to any other method.*

arise. There are two methods of tying off the coils. The normal alpine method (Fig 5.3a) uses a simple overhand knot at the chest and clips the bight into a karabiner on the waist. This means that any load will be applied at the chest, which might be fine when dangling in an alpine crevasse, but is, to my mind, most undesirable if trying to stop a slip on steep ground in the Scottish winter. The alternative method, as shown in Fig 5.3b), ties off the coils with a double stopper knot, then ties a figure-of-eight knot into a screwgate karabiner at the waist so that any load is applied at the body's centre of gravity and pulls the leader down onto his feet. A few trials at holding slips using both methods will soon confirm which is to be preferred. Whenever a longer or steeper pitch is encountered on the route, the leader should always take off all the spare coils and rely on the knot at the rope end which is directly tied in to the harness.

Fig 5.5 *Tackling the winter ridges*

A SHORT ROPE MOVING TOGETHER

Open slopes and gullies up to 50° with no natural protection.

Spare coils tied off to figure of 8 knot on screwgate krab on waistbelt

Knotted hand loop (releasable) enables leader to take an initial pull on the arm

Axe in uphill hand plunged in under load: body straight and lies in to slope: feet kicked in

20-30cm bight allows a load from behind to bypass the middleman

2.3m

Screwgate krab on waistbelt

Figure of 8 knot on bight

Rope round downhill side of middleman

Rope taut (ie off the ground) at all times 2-3m spacing

NOTES No handcoils carried – if party is pulled off by a fall everyone goes for the classic axe arrest

D RUNNING BELAYS MOVING TOGETHER

Irregular mixed or ridge terrain with rock anchors

Fall arrested by runners and/or counterweight

Leaders tie-in as in 'A'

11mm rope advised due to abrasion

Running belay anchors

Tie-in as in 'A'

5-15m spacing depending on the terrain. No slack in rope

Last man collects runners

Rope weaved side to side on ridge. Hand coils not carried except on easy ground

F TOP-ROPING ON DIRECT BELAY

Short steep pitches up to 15 metres height.

Leader tied to anchor on separate sling and karabiner, faces in to the belay

Reliable anchors

Belay sling

Pear shaped (klettersteig) screwgate krab

Italian hitch on live rope tied direct onto belay sling

Seconds climb together

2m

Seconds would use waist belays to belay the leader

Seconds can climb one at a time either by using a double rope method or tying in 15m apart

Runners and Belays

Figs 5.4 and 5.5 offer some guidance as to the various modes of roped travel: continuous movement without belays on open slopes, the use of both natural and inserted running belays, and fixed belaying on more technical or steeper sections; this gives the range of speed-versus-security compromises that a party may encounter on a climb. It is to be recommended that climbers have a day or two of practice or instruction on rock outcrops to gain a basic confidence in belaying, abseiling and placement of rock anchors before these methods are applied on a high ridge.

The relative positions and stances of the party members need constant attention and adjustment. For instance, if all are perched precariously on a pinnacle crest, or should all be insecurely placed on the same side of the ridge, then there should be some running belays between them. And on steeper, exposed rocks the leader should always have a solid stance, and the party should move in short pitches, placing belays whenever available.

The leader's role in the system is especially crucial here. Confident leaders climbing well within their margins of safety may happily climb short pitches without needing a belay from the seconds, thus enabling their parties to climb with much greater speed. However, on the steepest pitches (eg the 'gendarme' pitch on Sgurr nan Gillean's West Ridge) the leader will usually want to tie the seconds into a fixed anchor at the foot of the pitch, arrange a belay from them, and then place sufficient runners to avert a serious fall. The chosen belay may be a waist belay (fast to arrange and quick to feed) or else the standard type of belay plate from the harness. A party of equal ability can share the leading in order to spread the mental strain

Plate 5.4 *Direct belaying off an Italian hitch on good rock anchors*

of going ahead; the leader has to select and organise the roping system, as well as find the route, and of course is the ultimate backstop to a fall anywhere down the rope.

Having surmounted a steeper pitch, the leader must then decide how to bring up the rest of the party. If there is a dependable anchor available such as a big rock spike, block or chockstone, the quickest method is to use a direct belay with an Italian hitch, as shown in Plate 5.4. If anchors are less reliable and more than one anchor is needed the leader will use the normal indirect belay from the waist or a belay plate on the harness.

Only with experience will a party make all the right choices as to rope spacing and belaying on a traverse. And until that level of judgement is attained, patience is needed as repeated adjustments are made in order to achieve the safest rope system.

Hand Coils

Most people's idea of moving together derives from old pictures of alpine arêtes where the climbers strike a dramatic pose with an indeterminate length of slack between them, and a long loose bunch of coils in one person's hands. Modern thinking strongly disfavours such practice, however, for the following reasons: if hand coils are held by the person falling, they are usually dropped in the panic, creating the very slack that invites disaster; while if coils are held by the leader, they tighten like a vice around the wrist under the strain, completely immobilising the holding arm and so preventing further efforts to arrest.

Hand coils are a positive aid to safety only on a snow arête where belays are wholly absent and the human counterweight method must be applied in the event of a fall: if the terror-struck 'counterweight' has a few spare coils to cast away on witnessing the fall, he or she creates another vital second for the leap down the other side of the ridge which will stop the plunge. Hand coils might only otherwise be gathered as an aid to speed on ground of uneven difficulty, where rearguard members can pick up the coils on easy ground and catch up the leader who might be momentarily delayed on a tricky step.

When spare rope is carried in the hand it is preferable to carry it 'lap-coiled' – in loops laid backwards and forwards across the lap of the palm; this prevents the coils from tightening round the wrist when loaded, and allows the spare rope to be released smoothly and without kinks.

Descents

The most problematic parts of every ridge traverse are the descents (Fig 5.6) – the chimney pitch of Am Bodach on the Aonach Eagach, the eastern face of the Corrag Bhuidhe pinnacles on An Teallach and the weaving descent of Clach Glas en route to Blaven on Skye are three notorious obstacles. Even the simplest line of route is hard to spot from above; the exposure

Fig 5.6 *Ropework guidelines for steep descents*		
Method	Typical Example	Pros and *Cons*
Down-Climbing Moving together as in Fig 5.4 (D) placing running belays.	The Saddle, descending the step direct from Sgurr na Forcan.	Fast, with reliable placed anchors. *Leader easily pulled off if second slips.*
Top-Roping Seconds climb down on direct belay placing runners to protect leader and fixing belay at bottom of pitch, ie the reverse of Fig 5.5 (F).	Aonach Eagach, descent of chimney off Am Bodach.	Much more secure especially for leader. *Time-consuming. Relies on seconds being able to fix good protection and belay anchors.*
Lowering As for Top-roping except seconds are lowered on direct belay with an Italian hitch one at a time.		Quick and smooth unless ropes frozen. Saves energies of seconds. *More difficult for seconds to clear and prepare route for leader. Italian hitch badly kinks the rope under load.*
Abseiling Using a figure-of-eight, karabiner brake or Italian hitch on rope, back-up anchor at top for first people down; safety prusiks advised (ie, sliding autoblock on abseil rope tied to harness).	Major dyke lines cutting the Cuillin Ridge, eg tops of Bidean Druim nan Ramh; mainland ridge descents in bad conditions.	Only possible method on snowed-up vertical ground. Leader relieved of strain of down-climbs. *Rope retrieval/anchor strength critical. Rope has to be doubled, so 20-25m is maximum drop for each abseil. Much slower in a big party.*

is more acutely felt when facing out and scanning the space beneath one's feet, and blind downward moves require a deft balance and a measure of faith in the footing below. The greatest cause of trouble is in failing to allow the extra time and spare mental energy necessary to make a safe descent. The leader, coming last down the steep ground without protection, is particularly vulnerable. On short downward steps such as the 3m notch on Am Basteir's East Ridge the leader might lower the rest of the team one by one, but must then either negotiate a tricky downclimb, or make a short abseil.

Decisive ropework is bedevilled by the uncertainties of descent, and at every potential impasse, parties may hesitate and confer. Unless the seconds on the rope can place reliable anchors for the leader while descending and can then set up a good belay from below, abseiling is to be preferred. Even this must be compromised, however, because although abseiling relieves the tension of downclimbing, it invariably takes longer in a big party, and the consequences of a rope jam during retrieval are

serious. If there is a possibility that abseils will feature in a traverse it is wise to have a good length of spare tape for anchors stowed in the sack. Note, too, that on some routes there are simply no satisfactory anchors for abseils. The descent off Clach Glas towards Blaven is a good example, where parties must seek out a couple of devious dykes on the left of the ridge crest in order to get round vertical steps.

For those who still mistrust the rope techniques proposed above, a story from Liathach – now eleven years old but still vividly remembered – should convince the sceptics that these are not just fanciful designs. They do work!

LIATHACH: JANUARY 1987

We were couched on the main summit just before noon on a clear, fine day, with ample time to traverse the Fasarinen pinnacles to Mullach an Rathain (see route map opposte). My team of four were fit and well drilled from five days out on every sort of grade I and II terrain. The conditions on that day seemed

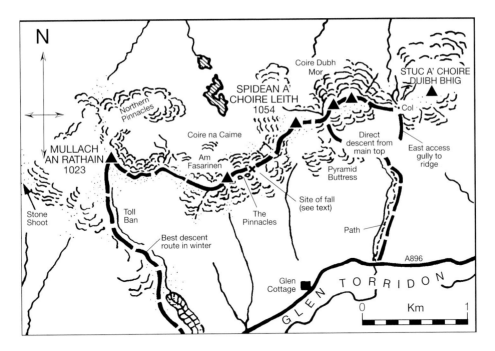

generally good but fresh drifts might pose problems on the steeper ground.

As soon as we had roped up at the first notch before the pinnacles, this difficulty became apparent. Moistened by the sun, the fresh snow was distinctly slabby and sufficiently liquid to cling tenaciously to our crampons. Furthermore, it was a virgin cover: there were no lines of tracks to guide our passage, and so we would have to take the crest direct. I went ahead as a rope of three, with Glaswegian brothers Peter and Paul following close behind on a separate rope, but using and collecting any runners which I had placed up front. The system paid due respect to the brothers' ability, for they had shown care and craft throughout the week.

Five-metre gaps between each man enabled us to weave a secure thread over the initial gendarmes where one is suddenly exposed to the sensational drop over Coire na Caime to the north. Few would deny a quiver of tension on these first delicate edges, but after a kilometre of the same, most are revelling in the 'crow's nest' situations and are only sad that the pinnacles end so soon!

Now the ridge drops steeply for over a hundred metres to its lowest col, and we were forced onto the soggy snows of its southern flank, descending a shallow chimney facing in, then turning out and shuffling rightwards along the base of the buttress. Not until ten metres beyond the chimney was I able to place a sling for a running belay. The unprotected traverse was unfortunate but unavoidable, so on I went, trusting the lads behind to take extra care as they bridged the gap.

But a yelp and then a piercing shriek indicated otherwise. Peter was in front down and along the traverse, but Paul, just turning out at the bottom of the chimney, had tripped and shot off downwards.

'Brake!' I yelled instinctively, but Paul was completely out of control from the moment he slipped. Below him lay a gully starting at 40 degrees and steepening down left and out of sight to I knew not where. The bump of a rock outcrop turned him upside down, and he was accelerating beyond the speed where self-arrest is of any avail. My eyeballs bulged with horror, riveted to his fall.

Then in an instant, he swung in an arc on a tautening rope and came to a stop. Looking straight back up, there was Peter rolled over his axe, in the classic braking pose and absolutely still. He had made a magnificent arrest, digging his pick mightily into the underlying turf and no doubt saying a momentary prayer before the rope came tight. To stop a five-metre fall from above and to the side without any belay was testimony not just to Peter's skill but equally to the crucial worth of the linking rope.

Paul picked himself up with no worse than a bruised knee and a shell-shocked gaze. They joined our rope forthwith and I pressed ahead before the impact of the fall sunk home, keeping moving without a pause for an hour and a half until the pinnacles were behind. Tensions eventually mellowed, however, on the sweeping slopes that curve up towards Mullach an Rathain: 'Practise your ice-axe brakes somewhere else next time, lads,' I quipped, knowing full well how close they had been to disaster.

Tactical Ploys

Size of Group

Easier ridges such as The Ring of Steall, Carn Mor Dearg Arête or Beinn Alligin, where roped sections are short, can reasonably be tackled by a party of four, five, or even six. However, large numbers become a liability on more sustained ridges, delaying progress and reducing security during traversing manoeuvres. For An Teallach, Liathach or the Aonach Eagach, four would be a maximum on the rope, while three is probably the ideal number, enabling the use of natural belays on the crests and allowing a continuous rhythm of progress. On sections of the Cuillin Ridge, where there is much pitching and occasional abseils, a rope of two is the most efficient.

Direction of Travel

Most ridges have an accepted direction of travel: for example, Liathach and the Aonach Eagach are rarely traversed any other way than from east to west. The reasons for such habit may be practical, in starting the traverse from a higher roadhead; or they may be emotional, such as the desire to keep the best views ahead. On An Teallach most folk do the circuit anticlockwise so that the two Munros are bagged before the pinnacles are chanced. Parties should, however, consider going the opposite way in two circumstances:

- in order to keep the prevailing wind at one's back: when a squally westerly is blowing both Liathach and the Aonach Eagach are a lot more enjoyable done west to east;
- and in order to tackle the hardest bits of the ridge in ascent, as this undoubtedly makes route-finding more straightforward. This logic should certainly be considered on An Teallach, where the east end of Corrag Bhuidhe is far more easily negotiated when approached from below.

Escapes

The seriousness of a ridge is as much determined by how easy it is to get off it, as by its technical difficulty, and escape options need to be carefully considered before embarking. Both the Aonach Eagach and Liathach have sustained pinnacled sections where there is no way down, and which are sandwiched between higher summits at each end. This lends a considerable commitment to the crux sections. By contrast, the Forcan Ridge of The Saddle has several points where a safe descent can be made down its south flank.

Use of Crampons

Very often the snow on the ridges is soft and moist due to exposure to the sun, or the rocky outcrops are bare of ice; moreover on popular routes there may be a well worn trail of foot-prints. In these situations there is every temptation to dispense with crampons. My personal *credo* is always to wear crampons unless they are balling up badly with snow and thus putting you at serious risk of slipping. If conditions are only marginally wintry, I still prefer to put crampons on but in this regard, many of the famous ridges are now becoming appallingly scratched by the passage of legions of clumsy cramponners. Good crampon tech-nique on the ridges is neat and precise, with minimal scraping and scrattling. Admittedly it is often very hard to keep to that standard when breaking through deep snow in order to get a grip on the rocks beneath; nonetheless, it is a standard to which one should aspire!

Route-Finding

Winter traverses on the ridges are often con-fusing because the trods and paths of summer are obliterated by the snow – indeed in many cases the summer route descriptions, so well described in guidebooks, are no longer applic-able. For example on Liathach, the summer option of traversing round the south side of the pinnacles is not feasible when the ledges are banked with snow to a 50-degree angle; it is safer to go over the pinnacles where there are belays.

Faced with these problems the winter tra-verser must be prepared to search for the route, reconnoitring different options before committing the party to any one line. And if there are no footsteps to follow it is often nec-essary to use your intuition to work out the right lines.

When in serious doubt of the route, the best option is nearly always to get back onto the very crest, where it is possible to view both flanks and to orient one's position; from this vantage point the best possible decision as to the route can be made.

Respecting the Weather

Whilst winter climbers can find shelter in their gullies, and walkers can afford to be blown about a bit on broad open slopes, the ridge tra-verser has no protection whatsoever from the weather, and no margin of error if the wind is threatening to dislodge his footing. The great traverses must therefore be reserved for days with a reasonable forecast: if summit winds are likely to exceed 60kmph, the crest of the Aonach Eagach is not the best place to be. Whilst I have enjoyed many days fighting buf-feting winds and hail squalls up on the Torridon ridges, the threshold of control on the edges is lower, and this must always be respected.

Snow Conditions

One of the foremost attractions of our great ridges is their unpredictability of condition. My most regular winter traverse, that of Liathach, is rarely the same twice, and it is never boring despite many repetitions. I have been on the mountain when the greatest chal-lenge was to wade through thick snow to get to the Pinnacles, which themselves were so smothered in soft snow as to raise barely a breath of exposure. Yet equally I have been over them when they were so steeply banked with hard, frozen snow that their traverse felt close to the upper ceiling of grade II in techni-cal difficulty, and somewhere in the region of grade V in psychological duress.

So take heed those who have had an easy time on a couple of traverses thanks to 'friendly' snow: they should beware of compla-cency, because the day will come when everything is very different! And while the ridges may be disappointing in a thaw, there will also be occasions when a brief dose of wintry weather produces amazing conditions out of nothing, up on the highest crests, as evi-denced overleaf:

An Teallach: January 1997

A decidedly lean period for snow-cover had been redeemed by pleasant, settled weather which inspired the idea of a camp on An Teallach. Having set up our tents close to the outflow of the Toll an Lochain at 9pm we all sat on rocks outside the tents, brewing tea and cooking supper in still, mild air. We held little hope of traversing An Teallach in anything other than summer conditions on the morrow, where only the tattered remnants of New Year's snow lay high in the deeper gullies. Despite packing a duvet jacket in mistake for my sleeping bag, I got a fair sleep, broken only by rain drumming on the tent roof late in the night.

On our emergence at 7am we were surprised to see a dusting of fresh but wet-looking snow up on the Corrag Bhuidhe face, and this gave us cause to hope for something slushy on the Pinnacles. Constabulary Couloir (I/II) was one of the few gullies holding substantial snow; it exits just below the terminal buttress of Corrag Bhuidhe, so it offered an ideal way of approaching the crest. I always put on crampons for a gully climb even if the snow is wet, but in fact we were soon glad of them because the snow turned increasingly crisp and frozen towards the top. Having had some 150 metres of decent snow in the gully we might have been reasonably satisfied with the day's offering – but on gaining the crest we were astounded to see the sandstone battlements of the Pinnacles plastered with rime ice. At 1,000 metres the overnight rain had been transformed into a wintry blast.

At our point of exit from the gully the traversing path sets off leftwards round the west flank of Corrag Bhuidhe and completely avoids the exciting sections. We were not tempted in the least, however, as this was a morning to savour every crenellation of the crest. We climbed a fifteen metre pitch up a step on the ridge to another belvedere. From here, a steep direct route might be attempted up the final buttress – but it is pretty exposed in nature, and under that morning's verglassed conditions looked as though it might have been grade III in technical difficulty. So instead we went twenty metres round to the left on another traversing path, but this petered out towards a gully. Now on the west flank of the ridge we spied a series of short grooves which led up to the crest between the Central and Southern Tops of Corrag Buidhe. We took these one by one, using nut and sling anchors on each intervening ledge. The grooves were lined with ice which actually bore the weight of our crampon points.

The atmosphere and exposure up on the crest were those of full winter conditions, and yet a hundred metres below us there was no snow at all. The day was bright and chill, and with the security of the rope we could enjoy posing on the brink of the Toll an Lochain cliffs. In forty minutes of happy scrambling we surmounted each turret in turn, adding Lord Berkeley's Seat for good measure. On reaching Sgurr Fiona the warmth of the sun was starting to melt the sheath of ice from the rocks, but we kept crampons on over Bidein a'Ghlas Thuill to maintain the spirit of the traverse. Our winter's day ended halfway down the ridge from Bidein to Glas Mheall Liath. Off came all the winter gear and half our clothing, and we loped down dry, sunny slopes to retrieve our tents from the lochan.

I have done An Teallach's traverse when there is snow down to sea level, and yet I could not say the conditions on the crest then were any more exhilarating than those we enjoyed on that day.

Plate 5.5 An Teallach rises from the mist – Lord Berkeley's Seat and Sgurr Fiona from Corrag Bhuidhe

▲ SGURR FIONA
1059

Lord's Gully

Lord Berkeley's Seat

N

Steep slopes
to Loch na Sealga

Toll an Lochain

▲ CORRAG
BHUIDHE
1020

Banded outcrops

Grade II
grooves

Terminal
Buttress

Constabulary Couloir

Traverse line
on ledge 90m
below crest

Rock
step

Possible descent

Route described

Route avoiding the pinnacles

Direct route up
Corrag Bhuidhe (II/III)

Grade I access gulley

COL
823

CADHA
GOBHLACH
960

0   250

Metres

To Sail Liath
and easy
descent

6: NAVIGATIONAL NIGHTMARES

THE PROBLEMS OF WINTER ROUTE-FINDING

'231 degrees grid for 150m, then hold dead steady to 281 grid for just over 1km until broad slopes sweep safely down and into the realm of vision.'

This must be the most often used piece of navigation in every Scottish winter, and for many climbers it is the only piece they will ever remember: the crucial bearings to locate the Red Burn track from the summit of Ben Nevis (Fig 6.1). How simple they sound, yet within these figures lurk the countless ghosts of navigational nightmares past and present; of hours creeping on the corniced brink of the north-east face, or dicing with fate in the exit chutes of the Glen Nevis gullies. A thousand or more ice-plated, heart-stopping battles in the storm and dark have been fought

on Britain's highest and most hallowed mountain top, tales that would be worth the telling but are rarely put to print.

Those whose sole experience of Ben Nevis is of following the cairns and candy floss of the Tourist Path in summer beware! The contrast between summer and winter navigation is astonishing. In summer, the ground is always visible to guide the route – even in the thickest fog there is a boulder or a clump of grass to give scale to the scene and fix the line of travel, while the general rise and fall of the land can always be judged. Compare the winter white-out, when cloud and snow form a blank monotone blotting out every nearby landmark: then one's sense of scale, direction and slope is not just distorted, but on occasion can be wholly eliminated. Most of the extra techniques and ploys in winter navigation are attempts to compensate for the visual loss of the terrain. Winter conditions also throw up other, more specific route-finding challenges: the avoidance of corniced edges, avalanche hazard, the threat and arrival of darkness, and the particular severity of blizzard conditions when wind and snow are unleashed together.

Above all, winter navigation is an intensely personal skill. Map and compass methods, well learnt and practised in summer climes, must be played with greater patience, precision and discipline on the winter hills. And in winter, however many are the days that

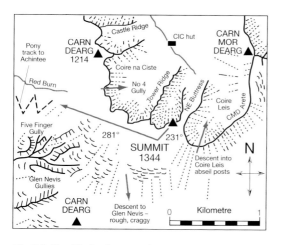

Fig 6.1 *Ben Nevis: the summit area*

pass without major incident, there will at some time come that hour of dire need on some remote and hostile top, when the odds are stacked and the clouds are down. Then it is one's human worth that bears the test: the ability to hold to a course with absolute conviction, a self-belief in each decision and calculation, unrelenting logic even though the mind is befuddled by cold and fatigue, and of course the strength and will to see the issue through and get home safely.

PLANNING THE ROUTE

Good route-planning can save many a navigational crisis late in the day – and route-planning necessarily invites a discussion of the desirability of making out route-cards. For the less experienced, or if one is venturing into new country, the preparation of a detailed card for personal use can be invaluable. Each main section can then be measured and timed to give a yardstick of progress according to which you can decide either to prolong, or to abort the expedition (Fig 6.2). The route-card can be inserted into the map case on the reverse side to the map, and is instantly accessible whenever a timing, distance or bearing is required in the heat of battle. This saves the fumbling needed to set a flapping compass against plastic-coated map in the storm, and ensures accuracy in the estimated bearings.

Stage	Grid Ref	Distance (km)	Ascent (m)	Descent (m)	Stage Time	Cumulative Time	Bearings
GLEN NEVIS YOUTH HOSTEL	128718	–	–	–	–	08.00	–
PATH JUNCTION LOCHAN M-ANTS.	148724	2.5	580	–	1.30	09.30	FOLLOW PATH
CIC HUT	167723	3	70	40	0.55 +5HALTS	10.30	10° FOR 500m · 60° FOR 500m THEN 120° DOWN TO ALLT A' MHUILINN
CARN MOR DEARG	177722	1.5	560	–	1.20 +10HALTS	12.00	74° TO RIDGE THEN 158° TO SUMMIT
BEN NEVIS – SUMMIT	167713	2	290	170	1.30 +20HALTS	13.50	184° ON RIDGE FOR 600m 242° FOR 55Dm · 260° FOR 25Dm THEN 314° TO SUMMIT
PATH JUNCTION LOCHAN M-ANTS.	148724	3	–	740			
GLEN NEVIS YOUTH HOSTEL	128718						

Fig 6.2 A route-card in the making

In addition to the route stages, distances, height gains and bearings, a route-plan must allow for escape or curtailment, with alternatives evaluated and assessed, and 'points of no return' identified. In making a route-card you must necessarily study the terrain and feasibility of the route in great detail: you consider all the options, all the pitfalls – literally, you live through the route before setting foot on it, and the intimacy of knowledge so gained could be vital in the storm. Nevertheless, I do not consider that there is any obligation for private parties to deposit detailed route-cards with police or in car windows. Some reliable person should know your approximate route and likely time of return, preferably someone who will not be panicked into making a premature rescue call if the party is only a couple of hours late.

TIMES, HEIGHTS AND GAINS

When planning a winter route, a realistic estimation of the time that will be taken for each section is vital in order to check the overall feasibility of the expedition within the available hours of daylight. Yet it is notoriously difficult to gauge a party's likely speed of travel.

Tailoring the Rule

Naismith's Rule of 5kmph plus an additional ten minutes per 100m of ascent works well on tracks, but 5kmph is a spanking pace in rough, pathless country and rather optimistic for most people's fitness levels; apply it to real winter days when there is thick snow-cover, and you will soon be enjoying your first unplanned bivouac! A more realistic pace in rough country, summer or winter, is 4kmph; 3kmph is reasonable on the high tops in snowy conditions, and 2kmph is not unusual in conditions of deep, unconsolidated snow, white-out or high winds. Timing estimates must be tailored to the pre-

Plate 6.1 *The summit of Ben Nevis – scene of many a navigational nightmare*

vailing weather and snow conditions as well as the party's general fitness.

Adding in the Descents

Adding ten minutes for every 100m of ascent generally works well unless you are wading in the snow, but extra time will be needed for steep descents, and very often the descent from the last summit of the day is sorely underestimated. Slopes steeper than 20 degrees take much longer than the map would suggest: you walk in endless zigzags, the slope adds to the map distance, and the stress on the knees and thigh muscles inevitably slows most people. By adding five minutes for every 100m of steep descent on top of Naismith's formula, more realistic time estimates will be obtained.

Winter Stoppages

Having worked out a walking time, extra provision for halts must be made in assessing an overall route duration. In winter, stops tend to be more numerous and prolonged than in summer. Adding ten to fifteen minutes for halts per hour of walking is reasonable for most parties.

The total time estimate for a route can be matched against the length of daylight. Then the length of the expedition can if necessary be trimmed to fit, otherwise a pre-dawn start fixed in order to give a safe margin of error at the end of the day.

GAUGING PROGRESS

In summer it is possible – though it is not to be recommended – to navigate solely on good bearings without any consideration of the distance being travelled. Features such as summit cairns are obvious when reached, and hazards such as cliff edges are equally clear when met on the ground. However, beware such compla-

Fig 6.3 *Memory cards for timing or pacing the map distance travelled*
(my personal guidelines are noted in the left-hand columns)

a Timings based on varying speeds of travel (in minutes)

Speed (kmph) and terrain	Distance travelled (metres)											
	100	200	300	400	500	600	700	800	900	1,000	2,000	3,000
2 Deep snowdrifts, severe head-wind	3	6	9	12	15	18	21	24	27	30	60	90
3 Soft snow, strong head-wind	2	4	6	8	10	12	14	16	18	20	40	60
4 Variable rough terrain	1½	3	4½	6	7½	9	10½	12	13½	15	30	45
5 Hard level surface	1.2	2.4	3.6	4.8	6	7.2	8.4	9.6	10.8	12	24	36

Add: 10 minutes for every 100m of ascent
           5 minutes for every 100m of steep descent

b Total numbers of double paces based on varying lengths of stride

Terrain	Distance travelled (metres)									
	100	200	300	400	500	600	700	800	900	1,000
Hard surface, level or gentle descent	50	100	150	200	250	300	350	400	450	500
Average on a firm surface	60	120	180	240	300	360	420	480	540	600
Rough undulating ground	70	140	210	280	350	420	490	560	630	700
Steep climbs, heavy drifts	80	160	240	320	400	480	560	640	720	800

cency in winter! Either features are masked by snow, or visibility is so bad that you have no inkling of your arrival. Cairns, tracks, streams, even lochans – all can be buried by snow, and corniced cliff-edges may be indecipherable in white-out conditions. Without an accurate awareness of distance in winter, a party will soon be seriously lost, and may find themselves treading on the brink of disaster.

Each section of winter navigation on open, featureless terrain must be timed or paced in order to judge the distance travelled. Both pacing and timing should be used in tandem, the one acting as a check on the other – but which is the most reliable?

Timing

To time a short section of navigation one needs a fairly close estimate of speed of travel, which can vary from 2 to 6kmph according to terrain and conditions. Close navigation by compass tends to induce dawdling progress and con-stant halts while bearings are checked, and the party's overall speed will therefore be slower than normally estimated. Timing works best for longer legs of navigation – upwards of 1km – where temporary fluctuations in speed will tend to balance out.

Pace-Counting

Just like timing, pacing sounds simple at first. You mark off a 100m section of your street and walk it, counting the paces (double paces are to be preferred over singles). Note the answer, and next time you are up on Ben Macdui heading for Cairn Lochan all you have to do is measure the map distance, mutiply it by the test-count, and away you go – not forgetting, of course, to start counting. This is easy for the metronomic, but disastrous for those whose attention span lasts about thirty-three paces! In short, pace-counting is more accurate than timing, but it is not as simple as at first it seems. Several adjustments are needed:

- An average pace-length on tarmac does not equate with that on the rough hill. To estimate your genuine stride on the mountains it is necessary to do several trials on varying types of terrain, and then calculate the average.
- Most people vary their length of stride quite markedly according to the roughness or angle of terrain. The range of paces may not be as great as that of their speed of travel, but it can vary from fifty paces per 100m on smooth, hard snow, to eighty per 100m in deep soft snow and undulating terrain. I try to regulate my own pace-count to my average of seventy.
- When counting, sideways or backwards paces must not be included. This can be a nuisance when the terrain dictates little detours from the line of travel.
- Keeping a tally of hundreds of paces can be difficult, and there must be no distractions. Whatever counting aids might be used, it is unreasonable to expect to keep an accurate count when the total goes much beyond 500, and it is for this reason that pacing is best applied on navigation legs of less than 1km in length.

Many walkers find the computation of times and paces difficult. Try converting millimetres on the map into hundreds of metres on the ground, then multiply the result by seventy to get the pace count, when chilled and buffeted by a blizzard. Similar arithmetical acrobatics must then be applied to get a time estimate. The chances of making a mistake are appreciable, which is a good reason for working it all out on a piece of paper before setting off from the car. Alternatively, a memory card such as that shown on Fig 6.3 could be carried tucked in the map case. Provided you can work out the ground distance from the map, remembering to apply the correct map scale, the paces or timings can simply be read off from the table against the particular terrain or snow conditions for the section.

USING WINTER LANDMARKS

In deciding the detailed line of a winter route, one must try to link those few features which can be identified with reasonable certainty in any conditions. This may mean extending or deviating from the shortest line of travel in order to visit specific landmarks which can prove one's position with certainty. The intervening featureless sections can only be bridged by techniques of distance estimation and assumed positioning. To navigate in bad visibility for long distances without any help from the terrain requires great self-confidence and rigorous accuracy in calculations and assumptions; a minor initial error can compound beyond recall over a long stretch. For instance, a 10-degree error in calculating a compass bearing produces a 50m deviation over a 300m section, but this multiplies to 500m if the leg is 3km in length. Therefore the length of each link in the overall route is best kept under 2km.

Two of the most vital landmarks, summit cairns and bothy doors, are pinpoints in the wilderness that will be missed if there is any error in the line of attack during a white-out. Well defined summits are found easily, simply by climbing the fall-line directly uphill; but the level plateaux of the Eastern Highlands pose major problems to the summit-bagger. Their cairns usually stand proud of the snow when the wind has been working, but they are fiendishly difficult to find in white-out. Most Munros have big summit piles, but a few, such as Aonach Beag (1,236m) in Lochaber, have tiny cairns which are quickly masked by rime and wind-crust in the winter. Many lower or subsidiary tops do not possess any marker.

Wherever possible, one should try to navigate to linear features that will forgive a reasonable margin of error in the line of approach. Fences are the only safe linear features that might be encountered on the tops, but they are not marked on the OS 1:50000 maps. Suitable linear features are forest edges, longitudinally shaped lochs and pronounced stream channels, and these are difficult to miss as long as a transverse – ie approximately perpendicular – line of attack is taken. One should always employ the 'aiming off' technique of bearing towards the centre of a linear feature, rather than to its edges.

If one is searching for a pinpoint feature such as a top or a bothy, then a nearby linear feature can be used to attain an 'attack point' – an identifiable position in its vicinity (Fig 6.4); there is then little chance of significant error in navigating the remaining distance to the destination. However, attack points are unfortunately few and far between on the high tops in winter, and should be grasped with gratitude when they are encountered.

The placing of marker poles to aid navigation at critical points, such as on the summit plateau of Ben Nevis, has become something of a *cause célèbre* in recent years, rescue teams and some mountain guides arguing for them on safety grounds, whilst purists and environmentalists fiercely denounce any such sullying

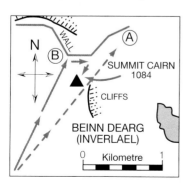

Fig 6.4 *Use of an attack point to find a summit: Beinn Dearg, Inverlael*

of the wild places. Such markers as do presently exist – for example, the abseil posts at the head of Coire Leis, and the metal wand at the head of No 4 Gully – are often an invaluable help and have undoubtedly saved accidents. However, leaving aside any ethical argument, such markers are pinpoint features and they can easily be missed. Moreover climbers could become over-reliant on finding them, and might then neglect the improvisational skills so vital in winter. Whether or not there are markers on a mountain, the fundamental rule of winter navigation remains – that one should be able to find one's way off the tops safely in the absence of any landmarks.

CHOOSING THE BEST MAP

The standard 1:50000 Ordnance Survey (OS) maps are used by the majority of winter hillgoers in most areas. However, they do not give a comprehensive detail of topography, and they are particularly selective in their delineation of cliffs and outcrops. In plotting the detail of a winter route, the smaller scale 1:25000 maps are much to be preferred. Special OS Outdoor Leisure 1:25000 sheets are, of course, available for the main climbing areas, such as the Cuillin Ridge, Torridon hills, Cairngorms, Ben Nevis and Glencoe. Harveys 1:40000 maps have been published for many popular areas. Some include special small-scale enlargements for vital navigational areas such as the 1:10000 enlargement of the top of Ben Nevis on the Outdoor Leisure map, which names the main gullies and buttresses. Even for areas where such special maps are not available, it is recommended to use the standard 1:25000 OS maps, which are found in good bookshops and outdoor stores; although the crowded symbols and faint contours on these maps can be difficult to read, and it may be necessary to carry two, or even three sheets to cover the route of the day's walk, their advantages are several:

- Screes, outcrops, cliffs, lochans and stream courses are drawn in complete detail.
- The crag detail enables major gully and buttress lines to be located, helping climbers to locate the bottom of snow and ice routes and then pinpoint the position where they emerge from their route before navigating across a summit plateau.
- Fences are shown on the 1:25000 scale maps, and these may be the only linear features on vast tracts of moorland over the Grampians, Monadhliath and much of the Southern Highlands. However, one must beware that fences can quickly become derelict, and that only the odd post of a fence-line may remain.

HAZARD AVOIDANCE: CLIFFS AND CORNICES

Because of their cornice hazard, the most obvious mountain-top features of all, the cliff edges, are out of bounds as an aid to positioning: paradoxically, one must do one's utmost to steer away from the very places that might tell you where you are. Thus W. Naismith's 'method' of finding the summit of Ben Nevis in 1880 should certainly not be taken literally:

'With appalling suddenness we found ourselves upon the brink of a yawning gulf, and walking straight for it. The black rocks were capped by heavy folds of snow many feet thick which overhung the abyss in a grand cornice festooned with colossal icicles. This episode enabled us to rectify our bearings, and thence to the top no difficulty was experienced.'[1]

Naismith clearly had the canny ability to convey his misadventures in a most kindly light. The plot of a route for bad visibility should ideally avoid any close contact with cliffs, especially a direct approach. The theory is admirable but cannot always be followed – for example, the return journey from the head of Loch Avon over the Cairn Lochan–Cairn Gorm plateau to Coire Cas inevitably involves passing close to the headwall of Coire an t-Sneachda.

One means of reducing cliff-top danger is to rope up, which works provided the winds are not severe. A winter walking-party should carry a safety rope of 7 or 8mm in diameter for the high tops. By roping up, cornice fears can be greatly reduced, at least for the rear members of the party who will tie close together on one end of the rope, while the unfortunate leader ties to the other and runs out its length towards the suspected edge. With a spacing of around 30m of rope, there is minimal chance of the rest of the party being dragged over should the leader fall over the lip.

Even so, it is the wise climber who abandons any ideas of finding the No 4 Gully descent on Ben Nevis in bad visibility and heads for the safety of the Tourist Path.

For a graphic illustration of the dangers of dicing with a cliff edge, witness the fearful

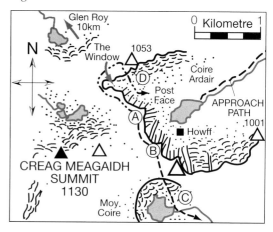

Fig 6.5 *Creag Meagaidh: two navigational nightmares*

A Geddes's exit from North Post

B Top of Easy Gully

C Escape into Moy Corrie

D Bonington's descent route

minutes spent by the late Mick Geddes on the notorious brink of the Post Face on Creag Meagaidh in 1971 (Fig 6.5). As if a solo ascent of the grade V North Post was not sufficient adventure, he emerged onto a misted plateau at nightfall with the realisation that he had forgotten a torch. Instead of chancing the longer route over towards the Window notch, he took the bigger gamble of skirting the cliff edge in the hope of quickly finding the Easy Gully descent into Coire Ardair; failing which, a southward march would take him down the less fearsome slopes of Moy Corrie and off the mountain, albeit with a 13km trek back to his base at the corrie's howff:

'Soon the white-out, or blackout, became complete. My feet were lost from view and the angle of the ground became difficult to judge. I thought I felt the short steepening before the bowl of the gully top, and the timing seemed about right, so I turned left; but after a few yards I lost my balance as the ground steepened alarmingly. The feeling of total disorientation was harrowing. I groped back until I was on the plateau again (perhaps), followed the bearing a bit more, and turned off left again. This time I backed down on all fours so that, with luck, I could follow the steepening over the crest and into an uncorniced Easy Gully. Then my feet went from under me again, leaving me clinging to my axe and hammer.

That was enough. You'd better stop fooling about, I told myself, and cramponned up the way. I headed south, thankful for the fluorescent dots on my compass.'[2]

The Moy Corrie route took him below the cloud, leaving a long but safe march home.

Plate 6.2 *On the approach to Coire Ardair, Creag Meagaidh. The Post Face is in the centre of the headwall, with the diagonal Easy Gully to its left and the Window notch on the right of the cliffs. It all looks so beguilingly simple on a perfect clear morning!*

Avalanche Risk

Avalanche risk goes hand in hand with cornice danger, as was amply illustrated by my own navigational indiscretion on Ben Wyvis during the winter Munros round of 1984–5. Losing the line of our bearing, we fell through a small cornice and triggered a massive windslab fracture on the slope beneath.

This experience was a forcible reminder that a lethal combination of cornice and windslab can form on grass slopes no steeper than 35 degrees – the vertical cliffs are not the only places of which to be wary in the winter storm. Cornices regularly form at a break in angle of a downward slope, and one must always be prepared for their likely existence in such locations.

A winter route-plan should take account of any prevailing avalanche danger, assessing the aspect and location of loaded slopes and steering well clear of such high-risk areas. Taking the example of the route from the Cairn Gorm ski car-park to Ben Macdui, such an evaluation will often counsel a high-level route up the Fiacaill a' Choire Chais and over the plateau, rather than the more sheltered and direct approach via Coire an t-Sneachda and the avalanche-prone Goat Track headwall.

The plotting of a safe winter route for bad visibility is therefore as much a matter of deciding which areas to avoid, as of linking those few features which can be identified. The resultant route-line may therefore look very different from that of summer.

ADAPTING TO THE TERRAIN

Quite apart from the need to avoid hazard zones, good winter navigation is highly responsive to the subtleties and nuances of geology and relief, both in one's instinctive awareness of terrain, and in the methods used.

Scotland's mountain scenery is infinitely varied, from Grampian moorland to the jagged Cuillin (Fig 6.6), and these differences are accentuated in winter.

Those who enjoy map-reading as they would enjoy reading a book develop an invaluable ability to interpret the map symbols into the ground terrain they depict. At just a glance of previously unseen map-sheets of the Western Highlands, the experienced map-reader will differentiate the roughs of Knoydart from the sweeps of Affric and the plateaux of Easter Ross. With such an awareness, the navigational problems of each type of land can be assessed and predicted, and this 'feel' for the terrain is an enormous help to one's confidence in the hills.

Of all the terrain types, the glacially discordant territory of the Cairngorm and Central Highland plateau is perhaps the most difficult and certainly the most nerve-racking to navigate, and it is surely epitomised by the summit zone of Creag Meagaidh (see Fig 6.5). The land is high and barren, and so is cruelly exposed to the wind; the corries have eaten great random chunks out of the plateau, disrupting the pre-existing drainage network, their cliffs immense and rambling. Meltwater channels cut the main ridge, obscuring the line of the true watershed, while to the north, the plateau sweeps for 6km away into the featureless outback of the Monadhliath.

For the walker or skier traversing the plateau eastwards, the location of the Window notch, a typical overflow channel, can be extremely difficult; it is deeply incised and rimmed with crags to the east, yet its definition is completely lost once the plateau is reached. Not only is it a crucial turning point on the traverse, it is also the sole escape route from the 3km stretch of the top.

The problem of discovering the Window in a January blizzard in 1965 made a deep

Terrain type	Route-finding problems	Methods and adaptations
Moorland Cairn Mairg Glen Tilt-Shee hills Drumochter hills Monadhliath	1 Absence of features; long sections without landmarks. 2 Prone to heavy drifting; slow and arduous progress. 3 Slope definition poor and difficult to judge. 4 Long traverses along contour lines often necessary.	1 Use of channelling relief (ie, stream valleys, passes) aids terrain awareness; fences often indispensable. 2 Vary route to seek firm ground (ie, névé on windward slopes rather than powder drifts on lee sides). 3 Distance travelled must be accurately known, so pacing and timing crucial. 4 Bearings difficult to follow; 'lining-up' methods must be applied.
Glaciated Plateaux Cairngorms Ben Alder Creag Meagaidh Beinn Dearg (Inverlael)	1 Featureless tundra terrain. 2 Remote, high and exposed. 3 Major cliffs, cornice risk. 4 Discordant drainage (eg, river capture, overflow channels).	1 Pacing accuracy paramount; long improvised sections. 2 Safe margins needed in route time and/or confidence in night navigation. 3 Roping up in vicinity of edges; 'aim-off' away from cliffs; avoid descents through cliffed terrain. 4 Terrain instinct confused; total trust in compass and ignore conflicting impulses – it is never wrong.
Regular Ridges Mamores Forest South Glencoe Glen Shiel/Affric	1 Main danger is complacency on well-defined terrain. 2 Ridge definition is sometimes lost in broad convexities. 3 Distance hard to gauge on steep ridge ground. 4 Cornice risk on crests.	1 Errors at ridge junctions (and three-way cols) are critical; compass checks, close map-reading, keep on crests. 2 Prime example is gaining the CMD arête from Ben Nevis; compass check essential; risk of complacency. 3 Pacing inaccurate; timing works on ascents but allow extra on steep descents; count ups and downs. 4 Roping up in white-out (provided wind is not severe).
Contorted Ridges Knoydart, Sgurr na Ciche Fisherfield Forest Black Cuillin Ridge	1 Irregular twists not shown on map (ie, as geology changes); ridge junctions confused; direction constantly changing. 2 Detours and delays at obstacles. 3 Escape is often difficult.	1 Terrain awareness and close map-reading essential; prior guide-book scrutiny helpful; judgement of height important, altimeter useful; counting ups and downs or tops and cols. 2 Allow extra time; keep direction of party lined to course; keeping to crests helps. 3 Careful route-planning; 'points of no return' and all escapes clearly noted.

Fig 6.6 *Terrain influences on winter navigation*

impression upon Chris Bonington. Tom Patey's irrepressible enthusiasm had persuaded him and four other experts into an impulsive and woefully late assault on Meagaidh's cliffs. Topping out from their gully at nightfall, Bonington's rope of four found that Patey, the local expert on whom they relied for route-finding, had deserted them, having climbed the route in front. His footprints had been quickly covered over, and the team was thrown back on its own resources – and a check on the equipment revealed that these resources were rather scanty: in fact they had no maps and only one compass. Yet, in Bonington's words:

'It was a strange, elating feeling – the situ-

Plate 6.3 *Stick grimly to the bearing and trust to the instinct of the terrain. White out conditions with a SE gale gusting to 120kmph on The Great Moss above Glen Feshie*

ation was undoubtedly serious, for a bitterly cold and gusting wind was playing across the surface of the plateau. We had no bivouac equipment, very little food and only one torch which we couldn't expect to last for more than a couple of hours' continuous use.'[3]

Bonington recounted the ensuing epic as on a par with any of those he had had during his expeditions to the Alps or the Himalayas. The Window's location proved elusive, and only when they were certain that they had overshot its exit and were therefore clear of major cliffs, was a blind southwards descent attempted. More by luck than design they landed back in Coire Ardair at midnight, their respect for Meagaidh immeasurably increased. The hardened winter climber is often the most culpable of blithely ignoring the basic rules and equipment for navigation.

Organising the Kit

Effective winter navigation requires quick and easy access to both map and compass. By threading or clipping the compass cord to a jacket zipper, the instrument cannot be dropped but is immediately to hand. The map should be folded to its correct panel and stowed in the map case before the weather gets rough; by securing the case with a neck cord the security of the map is guaranteed. However, it is not advisable to leave the case outside the jacket because moisture will eventually seep in; also you risk being garrotted as the case whirls round in high winds. Some mountaineers who visit an area regularly cut out the relevant part of a map, cover it with adhesive Fablon and carry it in their pockets. Specialist map sheets can be bought already laminated with a waterproof coating. The problem with plastic map coatings is their tendency to slip out of gloved hands; the loss of two maps in high winds on the Cairngorm plateau within minutes of each other during my winter guides assessment is my personal testimony of this. When preparing to navigate on the tops be sure that your watch, and your altimeter if carried, are placed where you can get a sight of them easily. Foresight is the key when organising navigating kit – once the storm hits it is too late.

HOLDING THE LINE

We tend to imagine that walking in a straight line is a natural instinct, yet when denied our field of vision we soon start making circles. Add in the effects of a strong crosswind or downslope gradient across the line of travel and it becomes nigh on impossible for a party to hold a straight course in a white out.

So how can the line of a bearing be held in featureless winter terrain? The answer is to use other members of the party by walking in line. There are several variations of this theme, as illustrated in Fig 6.7:

Moving together (Fig 6.7a): The leader goes forwards, and at regular intervals – say, 50m – turns and checks the line of the group; those following use shouts, hand signals or torch flashes to keep the leader on line. Although this method enables the party to maintain its speed, it also entails the risk that all might unwittingly and progressively veer off course, as in Fig 6.7b, particularly given a crosswind or if traversing a slope. Long contouring sections are therefore to be avoided if possible on a winter route. A much clearer awareness of terrain is maintained by tackling slopes directly up or down their fall-lines.

Leapfrogging (Fig 6.7c): This method involves keeping one member of the party stationary as a fixed point of reference, thus

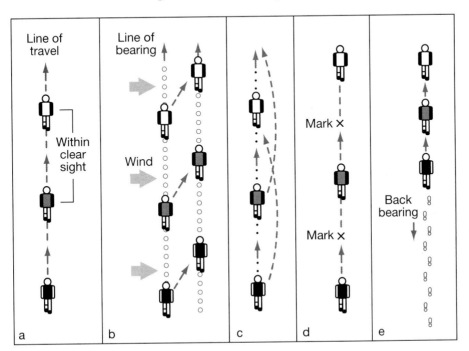

Fig 6.7 *Holding the course on snow-covered terrain*

reducing the risk of veering. It is slow, however, and should be reserved for serious conditions where accuracy is critical.

Marking the snow (Fig 6.7d): This could be a clever way of keeping in line without the delays of leapfrogging. If the snow is soft the leader simply marks a big 'X' in the surface with the ice-axe every time the party checks its line. The following team follows the line of 'X's and can keep moving.

Backbearings down your tracks (Fig 6.7e): This could be the salvation of the solo walker, provided the snow is soft enough to leave a visible trail of footprints. Even in what seems to be a total white-out, your sunken steps may leave distinct shadows. If so, check the backbearing down the prints by swinging the whole compass round so that the needle points south instead of north. Your forward bearing should now point back along the tracks and prove your course.

In a textbook it is easy to draw up a technique of travel that seems to cater for every type of condition, but the reality of staggering off the tops in a genuine storm can throw a party into complete disarray. Lining up and trying to operate some sort of smart semaphore system will be impossible if the party is reduced to crawling, and navigation has had to be reduced to its simplest components, as is the case in extreme weather. Nevertheless, one or other of the above methods will be applicable on most winter days.

THE DOG'S HIND LEG

Without landmarks, much of winter navigation on the high tops must be improvised insofar as one has to follow successive compass bearings without hitting any identifiable fea-

ture. The circuit from Braeriach to Cairn Toul in the Cairngorms is a good example (Fig 6.8), in that if there is a continuous snow-cover one might encounter no obvious features apart from slight changes of incline until Angel's Peak is reached. In summer, pools in the first dip (I), the springs of the Wells of Dee (II), the cairns at points 1,237m and 1,265m (III) and (IV), and the cliff edge of the Garbh Choire Mor (V) might all be used as guiding features. In winter, however, (I) to (IV) may be buried by snow, and (V) cannot be approached because it may be sporting a 5m cornice. Instead you must navigate the whole way by a series of doglegs, using timings and pace-counts to gauge the distance of each.

So you take a deep breath and walk 1km at 250 degrees, 1km at 223 degrees, 650m at 180 degrees, 750m at 149 degrees and 750m at 94 degrees. Then at last you sense the steeper slope rising to Angel's Peak and you can climb to the first clear-cut summit of the round. By then you will have spent nearly 1½ hours covering 5km without any certain orientation to the terrain.

Whilst the Braeriach–Cairn Toul circuit might be an extreme case of its *genre*, and would not

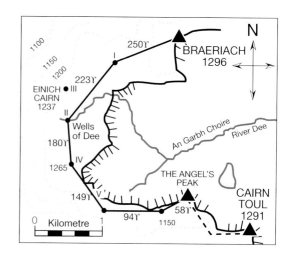

Fig 6.8 *Braeriach to Cairn Toul*

be advisable in really bad conditions, 'doglegging' is required with great regularity in winter, nowhere more so than when negotiating the tops of Beinn a'Chaorainn in the Creag Meagaidh range. Many people have fallen foul of the indented cornice between the south and central tops of the peak, but the flow of traffic on 3 April 1994 was unprecedented: within the space of an hour, two walkers and a Border Collie from different parties had separately stepped over the brink, coming to rest in close proximity 140m lower. Thanks to soft snow, none was seriously injured. The problem with Beinn a'Chaorainn is that the map cartography does not show a pronounced curve in the cliff edge, and tempts parties to take a direct line between the tops when a dogleg would be prudent.

Dogleg manoeuvres require a clear head and a confidence born of practice and self-reliance. But successful completion of such sections is a final proof of navigational skill, and will bring a rich satisfaction.

KEEPING TOGETHER

I have frequently speculated how easy it must be to lose a member of a party in a winter storm, and this thought was uppermost in my mind when instructing a group of nine hill-walkers for Glenmore Lodge one winter. I spent my greater energies each day in counting numbers every time we stopped. 'Don't you ever lose stragglers?' I asked Bob Barton, then one of the senior instructors at the Lodge. 'No; the folk seem to know how important it is to keep together, and they don't lag behind,' he replied. I was not convinced, and then two years later the unthinkable happened: I lost one of my groups.

The circumstances were slightly bizarre. We had climbed the south-east ridge of Beinn Damh in Torridon in dense mist, and I'd been checking that my party of four were behind me every minute. On emerging on the stony summit I looked to the right, spotted the cairn fifteen metres away and walked straight to it with thoughts of a cup of coffee uppermost in my mind. Due to a stiff westerly breeze I seated myself on the far side of the cairn and tucked into my lunch box. After a minute the singular thought struck me that no one else had arrived!

I wandered back to the top of the ridge. No sign of them. I descended the ridge for twenty metres to a point where I knew for sure that we had been together. By the time I returned five minutes had elapsed.

Logic told me to stay put on the top. The whole group must have walked straight over the top without seeing the cairn, and surely when they found themselves descending steadily, they would realise that they had overshot the summit and retrace their steps. So I decided to wait for ten minutes more. In fact the group's logic had told them that I must have continued beyond the summit without stopping, and so they had simply ploughed on, as they thought in pursuit; not having maps they were more than a little keen to catch me. In this urgency they failed to stop and communicate with each other, and very soon my group had become four individuals, each thinking only of getting down and catching their elusive guide.

With mounting concern I left the summit when my ten minutes were up. Beinn Damh has a broad stony top without a clear path, and major crags on either flank. I found several recent footprints in the snow patches, and just after the first dip I found one member. 'Where are the others?' I asked. 'I've lost them,' he replied. We hurried on, my thoughts a mixture of utter shame at the prospect of calling out a rescue in such circumstances, and real fear that some serious mishap might have befallen the others. At 650 metres we came out of the cloud, and there below us, bang on the correct path, were two more wanderers. But where on earth was number four?

With only a couple of hours of daylight left I decided that we would drive round to the west side of the mountain by Loch Damh and check the slopes ourselves. Loaded with spare clothes, bivouac bag and torches we hurried along the loch side scanning the slopes above. To our great relief we spied a lone figure ambling down in shirtsleeves. We had found our man, who seemed quite unconcerned by the events of the afternoon.

The incident serves to show how easily a party can become split, and how a badly organised team can compound an initial error. The observance of a few basic rules would have saved this unfortunate experience altogether:

- As many members of a party as possible should carry a map.
- In the event of becoming split, both 'splinters' should stop, and shout or whistle.

- If this fails there must be a clear understanding among all members either to continue, or to retrace the route to the nearest identifiable landmark, and to wait there for a further 15–20 minutes.
- At this point the groups should either abort, or proceed with the expedition to reach the eventual destination or starting point, whichever is the shortest or safest route.

FINDING THE DESTINATION

Having navigated into the vicinity of a landmark using pace-counts and timings to estimate position, the destination may not be visible, and set procedures should then be adopted for locating the desired point:

Deliberate overshooting and backtracking: This is only feasible if there is some clear terrain indication that the point has been passed – for instance the downward break of slope beyond a top (though not a cliff), a loch or river

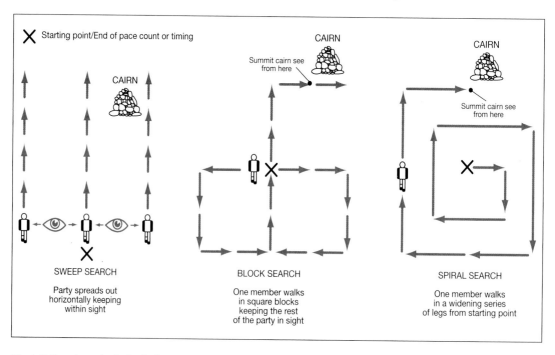

Fig 6.9 *Search methods for finding a point*

beyond a bothy, or a fence or wall beyond the summit. However, overshooting is hardly practicable on featureless moorland expanses, for example the heights to the east of Drumochter where you could walk a kilometre past the cairn without an inkling of downward incline.

Search methods (Fig 6.9): On featureless ground a formal search should be mounted from the point of presumed location. Sweep searches can cover a wide area of ground quickly; however, they require good team co-ordination to avoid the risk of losing sight of each other, and they can be disorientating. Block or spiral searches cover the nearby ground completely and methodically, and are best for small-scale searches where the margin of initial error is unlikely to be more than 100m. All searches should return to the original point of arrival, which should be clearly marked. In the event of failing to find the landmark, the team must swallow hard and continue navigating on the presumption that they had actually reached the correct point.

Failing to find a summit cairn can be frustrating and disappointing, but the hill will always be there for another day. The loss of one's shelter, and all one's equipment within it, is an altogether more serious matter ...

An Elusive Snow-hole

At the beginning of February four of us were dwelling in the snow-hole 'city' that is constructed by Glenmore Lodge parties in Coire Domhain (Fig 6.10) on Cairn Lochan each season and offered ready-made 'bed and board' less than a kilometre from the top of the climbing routes on Hell's Lum Crag. However, convenience tempted laziness. We slept long in the hole, and left late the next day for Garbh Uisge cliff, not arriving below its central gully

until well after midday. The gully's four pitches so wholly absorbed our energies that the glowering sky and whirling spindrift on the plateau top received no more than a cursory glance through the afternoon.

So the sudden blast of a south-west gale when we reached the cornice rim arrived as a rude surprise. Hell's Lum Crag was a rapidly dimming blur in the dusk, and our sanctuary no longer seemed so close to hand. We strode briskly down over ice-clad boulderfields to escape the wind under the Feith Buidhe headwall. If we could pick up the base of the Lum cliff before total blackout it would be feasible to retrace this morning's approach. To our fortune, as soon as the open slabs of the lower cliff were located in the murk, we picked up lines of tracks – possibly our own. The problem was solved, or so we thought, until we emerged over the lip of Coire Domhain and found that all footprints had vanished under a sheet of new drift. Strangely there was little wind, but a dank and silent mist choked this upland coombe. Our shelter, food and sleeping-bags lay a kilometre away – but with a deft turn of the compass dial we'd be there.

Ploughing up the valley bottom, its incline

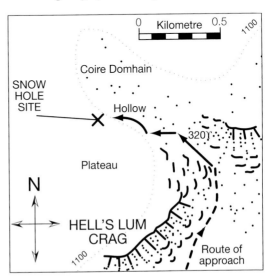

An elusive snow-hole: Coire Domhain

barely perceptible, 320 degrees for 210 double strides, torches throwing searching shafts that rebounded on the wall of fog at forty metres, now turning left to meet the corrie side-wall; then contouring the bank until it curved west into the little fold that harboured the holes – all checked and double-checked; as the terrain complied with each command and our goal drew near, our confidence mounted into absolute certainty.

But to our utter dismay, not the faintest smudge of snow-hole debris appeared. As the contours bent out of the fold and back to a northward pitch, the first nervous tingles went coursing down our spines. Was there another fold, were we too high on the bank, or were we too low, had we paced the right distance, or was the map disguising the truth? Yet our many musings misted the crucial clue even though we wallowed knee-deep in it: an afternoon of spindrift had not just covered tracks, but in the sheltered fold had buried four large holes with new-blown snow – recessed tunnels, metre-high walls and debris fans – the lot! Not a trace was left to behold! So complete was the process, it wholly escaped our credence that we might have been standing right on top of them.

Meanwhile we had formed a sweep search to scour the area. Four bobbing lights of flickering hope strung out across the slope thirty metres apart, first north two hundred strides, then doubling back south and over the fold again until we met the rush of wind and the stones of the plateau top, so back again into the fold, east a hundred steps, then west again. Panic rose. How could we possibly be lost? But then a shout came from Dave: 'It's the shovel!'

The orange plastic tip and 15cm of its wooden shaft, no more no less, stood proud of the drift. A stronger wind or an hour longer and it might have disappeared; we suppressed the thought and just thanked the heavens that

we'd left a marker. It remained to probe and dig for an hour and a half until the entrance door was found and cleared, and at half-past eight the soothing purr of stove and pan announced us safely lodged.

NIGHT MOVES

If a night finish is predicted, then one must have the wherewithal to handle the difficulties of navigating in the dark, and these problems cannot be imagined until they are experienced. Any night sections on the tops should be timed at half one's normal daytime pace, and those who wish to avoid nocturnal groping should set routes with a safe margin of daylight, or which will get down onto easy ground by nightfall; a late finish can be more acceptably entertained if the well tracked length of a Glen Tilt or Derry comprises the homeward trek. An early start is the best means of averting navigational problems at the end of the day; however, the morning sloth of the Scottish winter climber has evolved from a tradition into something of an institution.

If one is caught out on rough ground after dark, the value of torches is well appreciated. In the carefree days of the 1930s, many parties never took torches on winter expeditions. Alastair Borthwick recalled the amusing consequences of such an oversight when he was trying to locate Forest Lodge by Loch Tulla after battling over Stob Ghabhar in a blizzard with Hamish Hamilton and Mary Stewart. While lacking torches, they did have matches, although these had been brought for lighting cigarettes rather than for illumination. Now the three huddled together, each holding different sections of the map and one the compass. There were ten matches left. As each was struck, a gust of wind would extinguish the spark. After seven matches had been wasted, tensions and tempers were rising, but the eighth burst into flame, giving five or ten seconds of flickering light in which to read the map, fix the location and set the compass. However, even with a rough estimate of the direction of the Lodge, the compasses of the 1930s were of little use in the dark, lacking the luminous markings of the more modern Silva models. Borthwick's party did eventually find Forest Lodge, but only thanks to the car headlamps of their waiting friend, which provided a guiding beacon.

CUTTING THROUGH THE GADGETRY

Winter navigation used to be a simple mixture of map, a cheap compass, common sense and a little skill. Now there are two more aids to progress, namely the altimeter and the global positioning satellite (GPS) navigational system – each adding significantly to the cost and complexity of navigational methods.

Altimeters

These are available either as mechanical analogue barometers, as traditionally made by Thommen of Switzerland; or as digital electronic alti-watches, of which there are now numerous models. Although the mechanical barometers give better precision, most mountaineers use the cheaper and smaller watch-altimeters. These claim accuracy to within +/–5 or 10m. They have several particular uses in Scotland's winter environment:

- In the necessary event of a long traverse, an altimeter can provide a constant check that height is being maintained, and prevent down-slope slippage.
- Ski-tourers find altimeters essential for two reasons: first, on skis and particularly on downhills, one has no gauge of one's speed

of travel nor any means of pacing, so that a knowledge of altitude becomes an essential aid to positioning. Second, the skier will often – and on alpine equipment will nearly always – seek to traverse around intermediate relief on a ridge in order to save both effort and the constant delay of taking skins on and off.
- On the Cuillin Ridge of Skye the compass can be magnetically distorted by up to 40 degrees on the crest, and the OS maps are an indecipherable mass of cliff, gully and screes. An altimeter could be invaluable to check summit and bealach heights against the guidebook lists.
- The altimeter can be used on overnight expeditions to monitor changes in air pressure and thus predict weather changes (see Chapter 2, page 59).

There are two main arguments against their use:
- The altimeter is not an infallible device, and the actual accuracy of digital altimeters is variable. In any event, readings rise and fall with the prevailing air pressure to produce small but sometimes crucial errors over the course of a day. Unless one remembers to reset the height on known landmarks, a pressure drop of six millibars, which is quite normal over three hours in frontal weather as a depression approaches, can produce an apparent height gain on the meter of 50m. Secondly, an altimeter can introduce an unnecessary extra complexity into the navigational arsenal – as if timing, pacing, map-reading and compass-watching are not sufficient additions to the problem of looking where you are putting your feet.

GPS Receivers

The global positioning system consists of twenty-four navigation satellites in orbit which are owned by the US Department of Defence.

There are now many models of receiver on the commercial market and their price has fallen within the range of many of today's mountaineers. A GPS receiver has two particular uses in mountain navigation:

- as a means of route planning, whereby a series of grid references can be input and the resultant route with bearings and distances is displayed;
- as a means of accurately checking one's actual location, or one's current location in relation to a selected destination.

The route-planning function is limited in that the GPS receiver navigates by straight lines and makes no allowances for deviations and detours in the route. Only if the specific grid references for each individual leg of compass-bearing were input would the result be meaningful.

As a locator in the field, especially in relation to predefined way points, the GPS receiver might be of enormous help, less so in well defined relief of the Western Highlands, but definitely on the featureless plateaux of the Cairngorms and Grampians. After stages of improvised navigation without any guiding features, the GPS can be used to pinpoint position, and will give distance and bearing to a pre-set waymark on the map; I could imagine finding an occasional GPS reading very reassuring on that long, featureless trek from Braeriach to Cairn Toul. Such application requires the device to be both reliable and simple to operate under difficult conditions. Here there are some limitations:

a The positioning accuracy of civilian GPS receivers has been deliberately reduced by the US military by introduction of a random error component known as 'selective availability' (SA). Although the positional fix on the GPS will be within a 100m margin of error 95 per cent of the time, the maximum possible error that might be encountered with a 1 per cent

frequency is about 300m, which is significant in Scottish mountain terrain.

b The receivers are battery dependent, and if used continuously in cold conditions may exhaust a full set of batteries within a single day. Spares must be carried.

c GPS receivers take between one and two minutes to get a positional fix from three or four satellites. If the device is used repeatedly through a mountain day, this accumulates into a considerable overall delay.

d Operation of the receivers requires good manipulative ability with small and sensitive buttons. This may be difficult with gloved hands on a stormy day.

e Just like cameras, GPS receivers can easily be dropped, and can be damaged by moisture penetration.

The only wise conclusion is that the GPS should never be used as the sole means of navigation. Map and compass work is quicker, simpler and more adaptable when on the move. However, as a back-up check on position when the going gets tough, or if you are genuinely lost, the GPS is a welcome addition to the navigator's armoury. Whether that justifies their expense is another matter.

From all my own experience of Scotland's winter mountains, I would conclude that route-finding is the most crucial and demanding skill of all, more than any of the individual techniques of steep climbing. In contrast to the cavalier attitude of some climbers, mountain walkers tend to realise its importance and place navigation at the forefront of their learning and practice on the hills. It may lack glamour and excitement, but there is an equal mastery to win over map and compass as over any of the other tools of the mountaineer's trade, and a quiet pleasure to be gained both in its acquisition and effective application.

7: THE SURVIVAL INSTINCT

FACING THE COLD AND PASSING THE WINTER NIGHT

To the critical but uninitiated reader, a snow bath may appear to be an extreme of asceticism or bravado. In fact it is neither. It is far less of a shock to roll about in deep powdery snow on a calm sunny afternoon than to dive into ice-cold water, and enormously less than the revolting chill of the domestic cold bath. In any case, whoever indulges in a snow bath on a mountain crest will continue his progress along the ridges with renewed zest and vigour.[1] (Dr J.H.B. Bell)

Doctor Bell's prescription for bodily refreshment is one that few winter mountaineers would willingly emulate. More usually the 'cold' of winter is stoically endured rather than gleefully indulged in – yet it is essential to the challenge of the sport. The seasoned hillgoer comes to memorise and minutely differentiate every degree and variety of chill, and in the Scottish climate these are many: there is the creeping cold of the deep night-frost that enters at the soles and stealthily ascends the lower limbs as you linger on the tops at sundown. Then comes the searing dry cold of the easterly gale that cuts straight through every garment and sucks away your heat without mercy. More gradual, but no less penetrating, is the insidious wet cold of the westerly storm of sleet and moist snow. As the clothes slowly saturate, an eruption of goose-pimples gives way to a tingling chill, then a chattering of teeth and finally a convulsive shivering.

Most painful, though, is surely the cold that attacks only the extremities. Fingers and toes turn to venous blue, then deathly white. An unpleasant and distressing numbness is sensed, and when the circulation returns the nerve-ends are reactivated and inflict a throbbing torture. The 'hot aches' or 'freezing hots' as they are variously known, are so exquisite as to bring tears to the eyes of the toughest countenance. The agony subsides only once the blood vessels are fully flushed. Then one can savour the pleasure of glowing warmth and relief from the risk of frostbite.

Undoubtedly the most dangerous form of cold is that which gives no pain. If the body is sufficiently cooled, the nervous system is suppressed and will fail to sense the chill. Frostbite or hypothermia can then make a stealthy attack without alerting the potential victim.

COMBATING THE COLD

Besides basic survival, a winter mountaineer has two overriding priorities: the successful completion of the expedition, and the maintenance of an acceptable degree of personal comfort. In scientific terms, personal comfort means keeping the inner body temperature close to its norm of 37.5 degrees C; in reality, the first goal is hardly feasible without a proper regard to the second.

Man is a warm-blooded animal, and our survival and physiology are geared to our sustaining a constant core temperature. Faced by the cold, the body protects its vital organs by way of three mechanisms which become automatically activated below a certain temperature:

- the accelerated breakdown of fats to provide extra heat;
- the cutting off of the blood supply to the extremities, which is termed *vasoconstriction*;
- involuntary shivering.

If these are not sufficient, then the body progressively cools, and incipient exposure will commence as the core temperature dips below 34.5 degrees C. At around 32 degrees C, shivering stops and the brain becomes helpless to resist the onset of severe hypothermia, which will prove fatal without treatment.

As well as the involuntary reactions of the body, the climber has a threefold armoury with which to combat the cold:

- **clothing** to provide insulation and minimise the rate of bodily heat loss;
- **nutrition** to provide reserves of heat energy in the body;
- **fitness** to minimise the rate of expenditure of the body's heat reserves.

To these must be added a fourth vital weapon: a determined mentality. You need a focused attitude, a high level of enthusiasm, and a strong commitment to cope with all that the elements can throw at you and to complete a winter expedition successfully.

THE CLOTHING SYSTEM

The prime function of clothing is the prevention of heat loss from the body, but many people who climb in Scotland for the first time make the error of believing that personal warmth depends on insulation of maximum thickness and bulk. However, this supposition is incorrect, and in fact the body loses heat by three main mechanisms:

1. direct conduction to the air;
2. conduction by water;
3. convection by wind.

In the Scottish climate it is 2 and 3 that greatly accelerate heat loss and create the risk of hypothermia; insulation will only satisfy the first requirement, but cannot combat the rain and wind. Thus a clothing system must protect against all three heat losses and must also be easily adaptable or removable so as to prevent overheating. Basically, when dressing for the winter hills one must consider all extremes of temperature, and there are five fundamental operational requirements of a clothing system for the Scottish winter: insulation, waterproofing, windproofing, moisture transmission and layering.

Insulation

The insulation value of one's clothing is derived not from the material fibres themselves, but from the volume of air which those fibres trap, both within each garment and between the garment layers. This is because the thermal conductivity of air is many times less than that of a solid material. In other words, still air is far more resistant to heat transfer. A good insulating material is therefore typically composed of 10–20 per cent by volume of fibre, and 80–90 per cent of air, and a good clothing system is one which comprises several layers. The standard measure of insulation or thermal resistance used by clothing manufacturers is the TOG.

Waterproofing

Wetting eliminates the air spaces that are trapped by the material fibres: in other words, they lose their loft. Moreover the greater weight of wet garments causes them to become compressed, which eliminates the air layers between each garment. Water has a conductivity some 240 times greater than air, so the insulation value of any clothing system is rather more than halved, even when it is only partially saturated. It is therefore essential to keep one's clothing dry in the wet cold typical of Scotland's winter climate, and a waterproof shell is worth four times its weight of absorbent insulation material. Keeping dry is therefore the key to keeping warm.

Windproofing

Effective insulation requires that there should be minimum movement of the trapped air within one's clothing. A wind causes continual displacement of trapped air by colder air from outside, so that the body is unable to create and maintain a cocoon of warmth. This 'convective loss' of heat is hugely accelerated by the wind – the rate of cooling of bare skin is trebled in a wind of 64kmph compared to still air. All other forms of heat loss – radiation, evaporation and still-air conduction – are relatively insignificant when the wind blows.

All clothing offers some degree of protection from this effect, but an outer shell of closely woven material provides the main barrier. Happily, wind- and waterproofing are achieved by the same type of garment. While an impermeable shell is of paramount importance, it also helps to have closely woven undergarments which offer some additional wind protection.

Moisture Transmission

As well as providing external insulation in a cool, moist environment, winter clothing should effectively dissipate the internal moisture that is produced by bodily perspiration. The high work rates involved in winter mountaineering are often underestimated, and despite sub-zero temperatures, a clothed body walking or skiing uphill with a pack can produce a sweat volume of more than 600ml (1pt) per hour. If this moisture is unable to escape through the clothing, the skin surface becomes saturated so that the body is unable to disperse its heat by further sweating. Paradoxically, overheating then results, which impairs the regulation of the body's temperature and quickly reduces the efficiency of the muscles, leading to early exhaustion. At the same time the clothing becomes damp, and a 15 per cent saturation level in absorbent undergarments reduces their insulation value by approximately one half. Therefore, overheating on an initial climb may lead to serious chilling on the summits when the perspiration rate falls but the cold is more severe.

Modern thermal underwear is effective in 'wicking' moisture and transmitting vapour away from the skin and, for winter use, it is strongly recommended to invest in a breathable shell garment, which can transmit a high proportion of the internal vapour created by perspiration while remaining absolutely resistant to external liquid moisture.

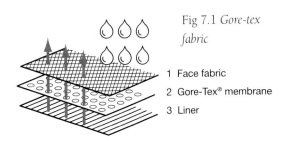

Fig 7.1 *Gore-tex fabric*

1 Face fabric
2 Gore-Tex® membrane
3 Liner

Gore-tex (Fig 7.1) remains the field leader in such fabric. Non-breathable waterproofs such as simple polyurethane or neoprene-coated nylon produce a 'Turkish bath' effect during prolonged exertion which cannot be tolerated in winter, and the extra cost of Gore-tex or comparable breathable materials should not be spurned. Of all clothing items, the outer shell is by far the most important.

Layering

As regards pure insulation, the demands of the Scottish winter are not often that great, and it is a big mistake to wear thick, integrated garments such as down duvets, synthetic fibre-filled jackets or fur-lined parkas. These are designed primarily for the extremes of a polar or Himalayan climate; they provide beautiful warmth when one is stationary at a camp or bivouac, but cause desperate overheating when one is on the move in all but the worst Scottish weather. Yet if a single garment forms 90 per cent of one's insulation it cannot be removed without causing severe chilling. A layering of clothing is essential to provide a flexible response to the wide range of temperature, and to changes in one's work rate.

The layered system should be easily interchangeable to enable quick adjustment as the wind rises or the sun begins to burn; however, this is not feasible with regard to one's choice of underwear – thus thermal long-johns tend to go on at the start of the day and stay on, or are not worn at all. I prefer not to wear these, and instead pull on Gore-tex overtrousers as soon as the wind chill bites. The delay and temporary discomfort of changing layers when one is on the hill is fully repaid in terms of comfort and warmth. It does help to anticipate changes in clothing demands: extra layers can be donned with ease and comfort in the lee of a summit so that one then emerges into the gale on the crest well wrapped and fully prepared for the blast. This is preferable to grappling with flapping sleeves and cords on the summit itself, when valuable bodyheat is lost and discarded clothes and gloves can be blown away during the changing operation.

The clothing needs of the Scottish winter are therefore simple but specific: a top-quality, breathable weatherproof shell, backed by a series of under-layers to enable balanced insulation over a 40-degree range of sensed temperature. There are four supplementary needs on top of the main functional requirements:

- **durability:** Scotland's winter climate takes far more out of clothing than an alpine environment;
- **suppleness** for ease of movement: many modern materials, especially trousers and salopettes, are made from stretch material;
- **speed of drying;**
- **minimal garment weight**.

Designer styling and fashionable colours may also be a desirable option for photogenic posing or mooching round Fort William.

A Historical Perspective

Those who complain of discomfort, or pick fault with their modern clothing, should look at the clothing systems of past generations:

Pre-1914 Traditional wool and tweed: wool vest, long-johns, shirt and jerseys; and tweed breeches and jacket (possibly proofed with alum solution) (Plate 7.1).

The early pioneers could enjoy the excellent insulation of wool and tweed when the weather was dry, but undoubtedly they suffered untold discomforts in rain, wind or blizzard: although wool retains around 50 per cent of its insulation when saturated, it almost trebles its weight, giving an extra 5kg deadweight of clothing on the body. Moreover, the tweed jackets were no more than showerproof, nor were they fully windproof, with plenty of gaps for spindrift to penetrate. Worse still, the whole outfit could shrink and then freeze solid if it got wet on the approach to a climb. And the possible, indeed likely, chafing around the nether regions hardly bears thinking about!

Although they could not operate in the extremes of weather that modern mountaineers tolerate, the early stalwarts still managed to drag their stiff, heavy garments up

Plate 7.1 *Traditional winter clothing: tweed jackets, plus fours, puttee gaiters, wool balaclavas plus a liberal coating of snow! (SMC Collection)*

many remarkable climbs, and for this achievement deserve our undying admiration.

The 1960s Cotton, wool and nylon (Plate 7.2, page 156): cotton or wool underclothing, and wool jerseys; mole-cord breeches; Ventile cotton anorak and/or polyurethane-coated waterproof cagoule; and perhaps an optional down-filled duvet jacket for extra warmth.

Specialist outdoor clothing was becoming available in the 1960s, but much of it was singularly unsuited to the rigours of Scotland's winter climate. For instance, the coated nylon cagoules in regulation fluorescent orange were veritable sweatboxes; cord breeches sagged and chafed terribly when damp; and cotton undergarments were quickly saturated and then lost three-quarters of their insulating strength. Many climbers used down jackets which were designed for the dry cold of the Alps or the Himalayas; these usually got wet and compressed in Scottish conditions, whereupon they lost 80 per cent of their insulation. The Ventile anoraks of this period as made by Blacks were perhaps the best adapted to Scottish needs: Ventile is relatively light and breathable when dry, and although when the material 'wets out' and the fibres expand it becomes heavier and is no longer breathable, it does remain impermeable to both wind and snow. Manufacturers still use similar cotton weaves for pure windproofs.

PROTECTING THE EXTREMITIES

The feet and hands require particular thermal care in winter. They are the most remote as well as the most exposed parts of the blood circulation, hence their vulnerability to frostbite, while the retention of a basic manipulative capacity in the hands is essential to one's operational efficiency on the hill. Apart from the pain and discomfort of cold digits, the muscular efficiency of the arms and legs is also dependent on their maintaining an adequate warmth. The skin temperature of limbs may be halved from their norm of 20–25 degrees C during exercise in wet, cool and windy conditions without adequate weatherproofing, and at such reduced levels, severe muscular impairment may be suffered. Some people experience a sudden and complete cut-off in circulation to the fingers when cold, which leaves the victim vulnerable to frostbite, and it takes up to an hour of slow re-warming to rectify. Even taking the greatest of care, I frequently find myself hard-pressed to turn the key in the car door at the end of a mountain day. One simply has to acknowledge that on occasions the hands and feet will refuse to maintain an acceptable level of warmth despite constant attention.

There are two main factors in the protection of the hands and feet: insulation and weatherproofing, and keeping the body-core warm.

Insulation and weatherproofing

This reduces the rate of heat loss from the extremities. Most of the qualities of a good clothing system apply in the same way to the choice of gloves or mittens: thin inner gloves for manual dexterity, thick wool or fleece mittens for warmth, and Gore-tex overmittens for total weatherproofing in the worst conditions; these form an interchangeable layered system. The 'Dachstein' wool mittens have been the cheapest and most adaptable hand protection for the last thirty years, and are as warm as the more sophisticated mitts. Integrated fleece-lined Gore-tex gloves and mitts offer better grip and technical performance, but when paying five times the price, the great fear is of losing one. Mittens are to be preferred to gloves for basic warmth because they allow the fingers to remain in contact with each other. On the feet it is best to wear a thin pair of nylon or polyester inner socks which 'wick' away moisture from the skin and maintain a feeling of dry comfort. Thick wool-mix socks are then worn over these. Gloves, socks and indeed boots must not be tight-fitting, in order to maintain circulation and to keep plenty of air trapped in the garment fibres.

Keeping the body-core warm

Unless the body is generally warm, vasoconstriction in the extremities will occur, and in this situation it does not matter how good socks and gloves are, the hands and feet will stay cold because the body will always give priority to the warmth of its essential organs by restricting the circulation elsewhere. In severe cold, the rate of blood-flow to fingers and toes may drop to just 1 per cent of its normal level during enforced inactivity. By wrapping up well, a good flow of blood to the extremities is readily available and it is then possible to re-warm hands quickly by rubbing, shaking, slapping, blowing or, most effectively, by shoving them into the bare armpits. If, however, one is bodily cold, such tactics will ultimately fail.

The warmth of the hands is also effectively conserved by learning to execute intricate tasks while one's hands are gloved. It is rumoured that the most prized skill of Glenmore Lodge instructors is the ability to unwrap the silver paper from a Kit-Kat bar with iced-up Dachsteins in a force 10 gale.

Finally, preventive care of the hands and

feet should not be overlooked. Mistreatments at home such as overheating, wearing ill-fitting footwear, and failing to wash and properly air the feet, predispose the extremities to cold injury when on the hill. While severe frostbite is rarely suffered in Scotland, superficial frost-nip and chilblains can still cause considerable pain and tissue damage.

Headwear

Protection of the head deserves special attention in winter. As opposed to the hands and feet, there is a strong and copious blood-flow to the scalp, and vasoconstriction does not operate. Thus between 30 and 50 per cent of bodyheat may be lost through an exposed scalp, and this rises greatly at low temperatures. Furthermore, if the brain is allowed to cool by direct exposure, the onset of the light-headed state of weakened concentration is inevitably more rapid. Good headgear is therefore essential to sustain general bodily warmth and mental control. Balaclavas or fleece ski-hats which cover the ears are ideal. Climbing helmets are also remarkable insulators.

A FURTHER LOOK AT WIND CHILL

Wind chill is the predominant cooling agent on the hills in winter, and yet is frequently misunderstood.

Most quoted wind-chill factors take no account of clothing insulation or windproof-ing, and the results could only be applied to exposed flesh. They give an idea of frostbite danger to the extremities, but vastly overstate the overall rate of bodily cooling. More recent work by Steadman incorporated the insulation value (TOG rating) of one's apparel in estimating the total heat loss from the body; though ignoring the degree of windproofing of the clothing.

Fig 7.2 gives Steadman's predictions of total rate of heat loss from an average human body at an air temperature of 0 degrees C and given three different clothing combinations and windspeeds from 0 to 64kmph. The figures are given in calories and therefore equate directly with our energy intake in the form of food. Exposure to a 64kmph wind without a windproof clothing shell will double the rate of heat loss from the body compared to a calm day (column 1 of the table). Heat loss and energy expenditure are one and the same thing: therefore, four hours hard walking when exposed to such a wind would consume approximately 4,000 Kcal, in other words the body's entire daily supply of food energy. Once depleted, the body is able to produce little further energy for progress, nor the additional heat to keep warm.

A second important message from Fig 7.2 is that if the clothing is wetted so that its insu-

Fig 7.2 *Rates of body-heat loss at 0°C at different wind speeds in calories (KCals) per hour*

(Derived from Steadman's 1971 wind-chill equation. Assumes the person is walking at 4.8kmph; the heat losses in nil wind would be considerably lower if the person was stationary)

Wind speed	Wearing dry undergarments	Wearing wet undergarments	Nude
	Vest, shirt and fibre-pile jacket	Vest, shirt and fibre-pile jacket	Nil insulation
	TOG value c4.0	TOG value c1.3	TOG value zero
Nil	450–530	550–630	650–750
32kmph	750–850	1,030–1,130	1,300–1,400
64kmph	1,000–1,100	1,400–1,500	2,000–2,100

Plate 7.3 *Modern gear under test: storm and spindrift during a new route attempt on Beinn Alligin's Cleft*

lation drops to one third of its dry value (column 2), the chill effect is increasingly more severe as the wind speed rises. In nil wind, the rate of heat loss is 15–20 per cent greater because of the wetting, but at 64kmph the increase is around 40 per cent. Thus it is easy to perceive from these figures just how rapid the onset of hypothermia can be in wet, cool and windy weather.

Fig 7.3 (page 158) translates Steadman's formula into the wind-chill equivalent temper-atures. These are the lower temperatures which would produce the same rate of heat loss if the person was walking in calm conditions. For example, at 0 degrees C and at 64kmph, the equivalent temperature is −14 degrees C. The graphs demonstrate that the rate of wind chilling rises slightly in colder air; this is because the initial temperature difference between skin and air is greater.

The regular use of wind-chill graphs has caused the widespread misconception that the

Plate 7.2 *Winter clothing c1960: Tom MacKinnon on Beinn a'Bheithir when voluminous breeches were* de rigueur *(SMC Collection)*

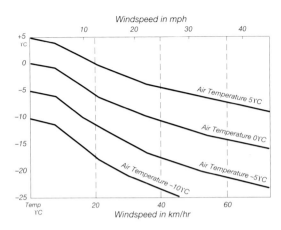

Fig 7.3 *Wind-chill equivalent temperatures. The
equivalent still air temperatures which would produce
the same rate of cooling*
(*From Steadman's 1984 wind-chill equation*)

pleasant	100–200 *Kcal/m2/hr*
mild	200–300
cool	300–400
very cool	400–600
cold	600–800
very cold	800–1000
bitterly cold	1,000–1,200
exposed flesh freezes	1,200+

As a guideline, at 0 degrees C the rate in still
air is 350 (cool); at 30kmph it is 950 (very
cold); and at 60kmph it is 1,150 (bitterly
cold). At an air temperature of –10 degrees C
wind chill enters the 'exposed flesh freezes'
category at speeds of greater than 25kmph.

The wind is a double-edged sword. It does
not just chill but also demands a huge extra
output of energy to maintain progress. In severe
combination, these two effects place mountaineers under an intense physiological stress.

THE TREATMENT OF HYPOTHERMIA

Mild Hypothermia
The onset of hypothermia is often hard to
detect either in oneself or in companions on
the hill, yet it is vital to recognise and treat the
condition in its early stages. Symptoms of mild
hypothermia, where the core temperature has
fallen to between 33 and 35 degrees C,
include:
• involuntary shivering;
• pale cold skin;
• muscular impairment;
• mental confusion, apathy and irrational
  behaviour.
Most climbers experience these symptoms
when marooned on belays during winter
climbs. The loss of mental focus is the most
worrying, where complex tasks such as tying
knots seem to take longer, and precision in
placement of axes and crampons is temporar-

equivalent temperature is a real air temperature. It must therefore be stressed that at an air
temperature of +5 degrees C, there is no risk
whatsoever of frostbite, however hard the
wind blows.

Even when wearing a windproof garment,
wind chill is by no means entirely eliminated
for several reasons: firstly, the extremities
remain exposed, also the wind compresses the
clothing, eliminating trapped air layers and
accelerating the rate of conduction heat loss,
thirdly, some wind will almost certainly still
get through to inner garments via the neck,
sleeve cuffs and skirt, and the moving body
creates a 'bellows' effect within the clothing,
causing an extra convection heat loss.

It should also be appreciated that a moving
body itself creates a chill effect because of air
resistance, even when there is no wind at all.
This is especially significant when one is skiing.

Specialist mountain weather forecasts now
give wind-chill indices which are based on the
rate of heat loss from exposed flesh as measured in Kilocalories per square metre per
hour (Kcal/m2/hr). The range of quoted wind-
chill ratings is as follows:

ily lost. Alastair Borthwick's intimate analysis of this condition could not be bettered. After standing motionless for two hours in Stob Ghabhar's Upper Couloir belaying his leader during a storm-whipped ascent of the 1930s, he was well qualified to comment as follows:

'Intense cold has a strange numbing effect on the brain as well as the body, and both reach their limits of endurance before very long. Thereafter those parts of the brain which register pain and fear hibernate. A body is cold and miserable, but it is not, somehow, quite one's own body. The brain has retired into a protective casing, from which the circumstances glance off, leaving no mark. He who is cold lives in a passionless and almost painless world. That is why death by exposure must be, contrary to popular opinion, one of the more pleasant routes to Paradise.' [2]

Shivering, both voluntary and involuntary, usually helps allay the condition, while the eventual call to climb ends the torment.

Similar symptoms experienced in the full blast of the storm on the summits could rapidly lead to more serious hypothermia, and an immediate retreat to shelter is then essential. This must take priority over any other treatment so long as the victim is in the early stages. Once a degree of shelter is found, the ideal means of stabilising the sufferer and rekindling the party's spirit is a nylon 'group shelter' (also known as a 'Kazoo'); these can be purchased in rip-stop nylon at a reasonable price and allow a group of four or five to share their communal warmth. Those in the group use their backs to provide a frame to the shelter, and can sit on their rucksacks. The shelter is preferable to the one-person bivouac bag, which might otherwise be carried.
Contrary to traditional thinking, active external rewarming of a mildly hypothermic casualty is no longer recommended. Applying direct heat to the body can stop the shivering reflex, thus preventing spontaneous heat gen-

eration. The warm atmosphere and windproofing of a group shelter will usually be sufficient to allow the body temperature to recover. A change into dry clothing and a warm drink may also assist.

Severe Hypothermia

Once severe hypothermia (core temperature below 33 degrees C) has set in, the victim ceases to shiver and may quickly become unconscious. The party must stop immediately, then shelter and insulate the victim as best they can while a rescue is sought. Above all, any unnecessary disturbance must be avoided: attempts to change clothing or directly apply heat could be disastrous because a sudden rush of circulation can cause an 'afterdrop' in core temperature, and the return of toxic blood from the peripheries to the heart may trigger fatal ventricular fibrillation. To quote current mountain rescue guidelines:

'Re-warming on the hill in severe hypothermia is unrealistic, potentially detrimental to the casualty and outdated, and cannot be recommended. Our aim should be to prevent further heat loss and transfer the casualty as quickly and smoothly as possible to a hospital.' [3]

THE WINTER MOUNTAIN DIET

How does he climb
Solo and briskly
On twenty fags a day
And Scotland's good malt whisky?

This parody of the late Tom Patey should serve to scotch the myth that an Olympic regime of diet and training is essential to the enjoyment of winter mountaineering. Indeed, a liberal consumption of tobacco and alcohol might even be recommended as anaesthetising the brain to both cold and fatigue. The mountaineer who grimly endures hard winter days on the hills understandably develops a craving for pleasurable indulgences in the bar-room and chip shop on returning to civilisation. This psychological rebound is often necessary to muster the courage to go out and face another storm on the morrow. However, such apparently unhealthy practices among some leading mountaineers should not obscure their underlying reserves of stamina and experience. Patey's own career demonstrates better than most how an unwilling body could be dragged to remarkable achievements when possessed of limitless enthusiasm and determination.

The relaxed and vaguely alcoholic social image of Scottish winter mountaineering is, of course, renowned. Nevertheless, performance, pleasure and safety on the hills are all improved if one starts the day with a clear head, clean lungs and well rested muscles. The winter mountaineer is also wise to pay the same attention to the quality of nutrition, as one would in any other endurance sport. So how does your mountain diet measure up?

Total Intake

Humans have a basal metabolism of 1,200–1,800 calories per day. To this minimum survival requirement must be added the energy demands of physical activity, which are of the order of 300 calories per hour of active mountaineering, plus a supplement of some 15–20 per cent to counter the extra cold of winter. Therefore, as much as 4,000 calories might be expended on an average seven-hour day on the hills. While it is not absolutely essential to consume this amount of energy in direct sequence with its expenditure, over a period of several days the total should be fully replenished; otherwise the body is forced to live partly on its reserves of fat and muscle protein in order to make up the shortfall, which is a most inefficient source of energy conversion and cannot alone sustain the speeds and strengths required for mountaineering.

Composition

If 3,500–4,000 calories is a reasonable daily target, a reasonable balance between carbohydrate, protein and fat is desirable.

As Fig 7.4 demonstrates, each plays a necessary role in bodily maintenance and energy output during intensive sporting activity. For instance in endurance running, carbohydrates (CHO) are the crucial source because they provide an immediately accessible store of energy in the form of glycogen in the liver and muscles. The marathoner's best balance is around 62 per cent CHO, 25 per cent fat and 13 per cent protein.

The mountaineer's exertions, however, are three times as prolonged but at a much lower intensity, and will therefore benefit from a 5–10 per cent higher proportion of fat, which in weight is over two times more concentrated as a source of energy but is released at a much slower rate. Fat therefore extends the CHO reserves which would otherwise be exhausted within three or four hours of hard walking; it gives a stable sustenance over a long day, is excellent protection against continual cold, and reduces the risk of sudden and dangerous exhaustion.

CHO should still constitute at least 50 per cent of the total intake, however, although the exact form in which it is taken is important, since the simple sugars and complex grains and cereals have rather different energy effects. For example, a high reliance on pure glucose, as found in sweets and chocolate, may have a detrimental effect on the body's sugar balance whenever such a concentrated sugar intake is followed by heavy exercise. This is because the body over-reacts in its production of insulin in order to rid the system of the excess sugar, and so a sudden burst of energy may be followed by a mental and physical low, commonly known as the 'Mars Bar syndrome'. Complex CHOs in the form of bread, cake, biscuits and

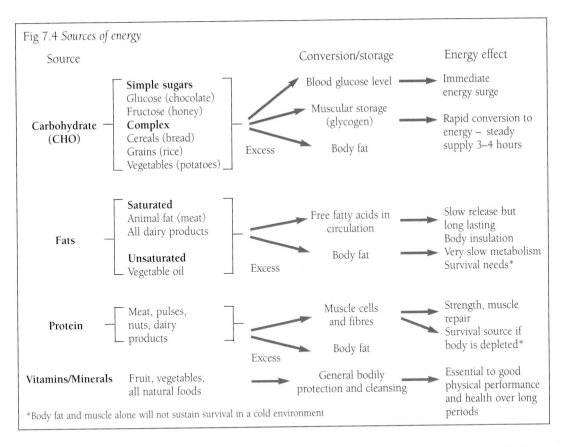

Fig 7.4 *Sources of energy*

Source		Conversion/storage	Energy effect
Carbohydrate (CHO)	**Simple sugars** Glucose (chocolate) Fructose (honey) **Complex** Cereals (bread) Grains (rice) Vegetables (potatoes)	Blood glucose level Muscular storage (glycogen) Body fat	Immediate energy surge Rapid conversion to energy – steady supply 3–4 hours
Fats	**Saturated** Animal fat (meat) All dairy products **Unsaturated** Vegetable oil	Free fatty acids in circulation Body fat	Slow release but long lasting Body insulation Very slow metabolism Survival needs*
Protein	Meat, pulses, nuts, dairy products	Muscle cells and fibres Body fat	Strength, muscle repair Survival source if body is depleted*
Vitamins/Minerals	Fruit, vegetables, all natural foods	General bodily protection and cleansing	Essential to good physical performance and health over long periods

*Body fat and muscle alone will not sustain survival in a cold environment

cereal bars are often hard to eat and digest when the body is stressed, but they form a better basis of nutrition on the hill. Sugary foods should ideally be kept in reserve for a quick top-up, and are particularly beneficial if one is exhausted near the end of the day.

Timing

Regular snacking rather than prolonged lunching is recommended on the mountains in order to give a steady supply of energy. A large lunch can also easily overload the stomach and valuable energy is expended simply in digesting the excess over the subsequent hour. It is wise to eat early in the day rather than keeping food for that sheltered summit cairn that never seems to arrive; food is better stored in the body than in the rucksack. Snacks should also be taken *before* one feels desperately hungry or tired, because once the threshold of depletion is passed, it is extremely difficult to refuel and regain one's strength.

Liquid

Water constitutes around 60 per cent of our total bodyweight. It is essential to efficient digestion so that nutrients are carried through the bloodstream and the body's temperature balance is maintained. Without a sufficiency of liquid, the best planned diet is of no avail.

As has already been explained, dehydration and overheating are more frequently suffered in winter than is supposed, and serious physical and mental impairment is experienced with just a 5 per cent loss of body water. This equates to around 2.25 litres and might be expended in four or five hours of sustained strenuous mountaineering if the mountaineer is wearing protective clothing. In winter, it is often impracticable to replace this volume of liquid on the hill – one might at most carry a litre of liquid in the rucksack while streams are frozen or absent. Some degree of fluid deficit is therefore inevitable, but all measures should be taken to restrict the loss. Copious mugs of tea at breakfast-time will top up the initial fluid reserves, and a generous CHO intake fixes and stores liquid in the muscles in the ratio 2.5:1 by weight of water to glycogen, which can give a reserve of over a litre for release during prolonged exertion. Finally, clothing and walking speed should be continually adjusted to minimise sweating whilst maintaining adequate warmth.

It is as well to note that the sensation of thirst is triggered by rising salt concentrations in the cells. If both fluid and salt are equally depleted by sweating, the salt concentration will be unchanged and dehydration may develop unnoticed. Therefore like eating, it is wise also to drink regularly on the hill even though one might not feel particularly thirsty.

If the colour of your urine turns dark yellow, it is a fairly sure sign of dehydration.

Although hot drinks may be thought highly beneficial in winter, their bodily warming effect is in fact negligible, a flask of hot soup giving only six calories of extra heat as compared to it being served cold. However, a hot drink has a marvellous 'placebo effect' in that its heat is immediately perceived, and the cup is ideal for warming the hands.

WINTER FITNESS

There is no simple medical definition of fitness: it is a phenomenon that is highly specific to the activity being undertaken, and the only wholly effective physical preparation for mountain walking, climbing or skiing is actually to walk, climb and ski. General endurance training, in the form of running, cycling or circuit training will undoubtedly help, but any exercise should be designed to replicate the

Fig 7.5 *Getting fit for the winter mountains*

Activity	Physical requirements	Training ideas
Mountain walking	Low intensity but prolonged energy output; general robustness and endurance in leg muscles.	Long hill-walks in autumn (a fine season for tramping). Jogging on hilly or rough country, orienteering.
Ski-touring	Sustained medium intensity aerobic demands on climbs. Specific strength, resilience and flexibility in leg muscles and joints for descents.	Aerobic training: running, cycling, circuits. Roller ski-ing. Stretching and flexibility exercises (yoga).
Snow- and ice-climbing	Specific stamina and strength in calves, wrists and forearms. Aerobic endurance, especially on easier routes.	Specific weight-training: leg presses, toe raises, pull-ups, wrist curls; high repetitions to develop stamina. Hill running for calf muscles.
Mixed climbing	Variety of bodily contortions as for rock-climbing; suppleness and strength in specific muscles. Aerobic stamina less important.	Autumn rock-climbing. Strength and power in wrists, calves and arms by lower repetition weight-training plus stretching exercises. Cultivation of tolerance of cold and patience; psychological training.

General tips: Lay off training at least three days before a major trip; rest and plenty of sleep is the best immediate preparation. Don't blunt enthusiasm for the 'real' event on the mountains by overtraining.

intended activity as closely as possible.

Fig 7.5 suggests suitable training routines for each winter activity. The rapid spread of indoor climbing walls in the last decade has enabled winter climbers to keep fit throughout the autumn – in one or two centres there are now even indoor ice-climbing practice walls made from plastic. For hillwalkers and all-round mountaineers, the facilities of urban leisure centres provide sophisticated weight or circuit training that can be closely geared to the real task of pumping the legs uphill. When training outdoors, note that the correct muscle groups will be developed for mountain climbing by jogging on the hills rather than on the flat. If you cannot partake in any suitable physical preparation, then it is only sensible to plan initial excursions in the hills with a high degree of prudence, until individual power and potential have been proved. Three or four days' climbing is usually sufficient to gain a semblance of fitness. Vaulting ambition and an untrained body are a dangerous couple to take on the winter mountains.

There are several components of mountain climbing fitness:

- **Aerobic efficiency:** An increased capacity for oxygen uptake reduces the heart rate and the rate of respiration; work rate and energy expenditure are lowered; energy is conserved and sweating reduced.
- **Muscular efficiency:** In trained muscles the size, number and alignment of the muscle fibres are increased; the blood supply is improved, and the rate of energy output is reduced: with energy conserved and oxygen requirements thus reduced, the ability to sustain aerobic exercise is developed.
- **Energy reserves:** The storage capacity of the muscles is expanded, and the body becomes more efficient in converting fats to

energy. Endurance is increased provided the body is fully fuelled with food.
- **Recovery period:** The body is able to restock its muscles with energy more quickly, so that the mountaineer can climb on successive days without depletion.
- **Technique:** Style implies a neatness and efficiency of movement and is the most specific aspect of fitness. Energy is conserved, and a style born from experience can compensate for a lack of physical fitness.

There is an enormous psychological benefit from gaining fitness: a confidence in one's ability to keep going, a knowledge that the body is capable of fighting the cold, that it has the survival reserves for an emergency, as well as a feeling of well-being and attunement to the hills.

THE LONG DARK HOURS

Winter's nights cannot be ignored since they occupy the greater part of the twenty-four hours, and whether by mischance or design, they will inevitably be encountered, in part or whole, by all who frequent the Scottish hills. However, they are to be enjoyed as often as they are survived. As much as the gathering night looms as a major hazard and challenge to the winter mountaineer, never to be treated lightly, then equally its quality is to be appreciated, whether one is crouched beside a bothy fire, roaming the moonlit tops, or pushing for the top of a hard mixed climb.

The first Scottish winter mountaineers disdained to challenge the night. The idea of deliberately forsaking the comforts and victuals of the Highland hotel in order to camp or bivouac in the hills was so immoderate as to be wholly unknown before the 1920s. While pre-dawn starts and late evening returns were

Pages 164–5 The Cuillin Ridge in full winter raiment from Auchtertyre (photo: Clarrie Pashley)

normal practice, and even a sign of good form among the more ardent enthusiasts, a very clear line was drawn against benightment on the tops, and it became an essential and enduring code of winter conduct to take all precautions to ensure a safe return to lodgings. Sir Hugh Munro was particularly severe in his condemnation of benightment. In 1892 he wrote, 'solitary winter climbing with proper precautions is perfectly safe. The one inexcusable fault is to allow oneself to get benighted.'[4]

This aversion to spending a night in the mountains necessitated some phenomenal treks. In March 1891, Munro based an exploration of Ben Alder Forest at Dalwhinnie. On the 22nd, he traversed the Aonach Beag ridge to its furthest point at Beinn Eibhinn, then returned to his hotel, a fourteen-hour round trip of some 48km. The next day he fully retraced the 13km approach by Loch Ericht in order to traverse the neighbouring Beinn Bheoil and continue to Rannoch. Such behaviour would be regarded as totally eccentric today, when either a camp or a bothy would be used as a more accessible base. However, in March 1901 Munro was finally obliged to endure the bivouac he had so strenuously sought to avoid: descending late from Sgurr nan Each to Loch a' Bhraoin after a traverse of the Fannichs range, the way was barred by swollen torrents, forcing his companion Lawson to the admission: 'the truth is that two SMC members disgraced themselves by failing to get home on the evening they intended.'[5]

Their night was passed alternately sitting damp and despondent through the showers, then searching for a passage in the moonlit interludes. Unfortunately, the escapade also imposed an unsolicited bivouac on the carriage driver who had come from Aultguish Inn to collect the pair, but at least their faithful attendant found shelter in the now-ruined boat-house at the Loch a' Bhraoin outlet. After

some tricky river-crossings, Munro and Lawson attained their rendezvous and faced their embarrassment in the morning light.

Viewed with the perspective of the times, there was neither the equipment nor the facilities upon which nights out could be planned in winter. Camping equipment was impossibly bulky and heavy, while the open bothy system of today did not exist, many cottages which are now bothies being still inhabited by shepherds or stalkers. Most importantly, the early climbers, being largely of the professional middle-classes, had no pecuniary need to endure nights under canvas or in draughty barns. The luxury of a steaming bath, roast venison, wine and clean white sheets would surely exert the strongest attraction to us today, even at the effort of a few hours' extra walking, were it affordable.

HOWFFS, BOTHIES AND HUTS

The style and tradition of rough living in the hills was born out of necessity during the interwar years when growing numbers of the working-class sought escape from the Depression and so turned to the wild places. Without the means to afford even a tent, the 'howff' formed their cheapest and most convenient accommodation.

The 'howff' may be properly defined as a natural haunt in the hills, a cave or boulder cleft which, by fortification and cladding, can be rendered ostensibly watertight and windproof. There is no shortage of such shelters in the high-cliffed corries of the Highlands. Boulders beneath the Cobbler, Ben Narnain and the Brack came to be the main bases for exploration of the Arrochar cliffs, and their habituees formed the nuclei of such famous clubs as the Creag Dhu and the Junior Mountaineering Club of Scotland (JMCS).

Plate 7.4 *Culra bothy in the Ben Alder Forest with the Lancet Edge to its right (Roger Stonebridge)*

Hard climbing, camaraderie and close communion with the mountains were symbolised by the howffs, and they were used in all seasons, but particularly at New Year.

Jock Nimlin, the pre-war pioneer of many rock climbs on the Cobbler and Buachaille Etive Mor, remembered 'seeing in' 1936 under the Shelter Stone of Loch Avon, without a sleeping-bag and squashed between two companions for warmth. The blowing snow had sealed all external draughts and he enjoyed an eight-hour sleep – but: 'True again I have to confess that our nightcap was a peculiar mountain brew, potent as heather ale.'[6] When its effects subsided, he recalled being awaken by the chattering of his teeth. Hard times indeed!

Another sour-dough of the hills was Ben Humble, who argued: 'Mountain camping is all very well, but the inside of a tent is always the same, and once inside, there is nothing to do.

Each howff is different, each has its own building problems, each its own charm, each its own memories. And there is always so much to do, for howffing refinements are endless.'[7]

While the established howffs in the accessible corries became much frequented, the idea of climbing up into an unknown corrie on an arctic night, without the surety that a suitable natural shelter could be found, offered an extra dimension of adventure that could scarce be ignored.

The challenge and fun of winter howffing remain undiminished, and it should never be forgotten that nooks and crannies in the boulderfields can provide vital shelter in an emergency. Nevertheless, apart from popular sites such as the Shelter Stone, the howff has largely been supplanted as a winter mountain base by purpose-built huts and bothies. Between 1950 and 1970 several rudimentary aluminium shelters were installed at high altitudes in the Cairngorms and on Ben Nevis specifically for emergency use by mountaineers, especially in winter. Their siting was prompted by increasing public concern for mountain safety following tragedies in the Cairngorms in 1928 and 1933, and the blizzard at Corrour in December 1951 in which four perished.

Such good intentions sadly backfired, however, because their very existence made them legitimate targets for planned stays by parties who often lacked the experience or self-reliance to survive on the tops without them. In this way the circumstances were created for the worst tragedy so far to occur in Scottish mountaineering history: in a November blizzard in 1971, a school party failed to locate the Curran refuge, sited at 1,125m by Lochan Buidhe on the Cairn Lochan-Macdui plateau, and five children and a student teacher died in the resultant open bivouac.

The Cairngorm disaster prompted the removal of both the Curran and the St Valery shelters from the plateaux, although those on Ben Nevis remain.

At lower levels in the glens, more commodious 'bothies' have proliferated since the war. A few in the Cairngorms such as the Hutchison or Garbh Choire huts are purpose-made, but the majority are adapted and renovated crofts, barns and shielings which were once permanent habitations. Thanks to the dedicated conversion and maintenance work of the Mountain Bothies Association, they are available, unlocked, for use by all mountaineers. Sadly, there is a minority who fail to respect open bothies and cases of vandalism are threatening to destroy the bonds of trust and respect upon which the system depends.

As winter accommodation, bothies are a blessing, and they have their particular uses,

too: continuing the tradition established by the howffs, Hogmanay always sees an exodus of enthusiasts to every bothy in the Highlands, armed with wood, coal, food hampers and maybe a dram or two, their numbers such that overcrowding can become a problem. While the hills are first-footed by day, their pleasures are largely secondary to the warmth and friendship of fire-lit bothy nights.

I have many special memories of winter bothy nights. Some are sublime, like the night we watched the Northern Lights from the door at Berneas, having first mistaken them for some neon pyrotechnics from Lochcarron village some ten kilometres away! Others are bizarre, none more so than the January night in 1991 when we encountered a paranoid youth at Camasunary, who was 'hiding' there during the Gulf War. Convinced that Saddam Hussein was about to launch a nuclear attack on Britain, he had fled the city and spent a fortnight holed up in the bothy. He proudly showed us a food cache which he had buried on the moors so that it wouldn't become irradiated. I was thankful I had other companions on that night!

One or two nights might best be described as character-building:

FORCED MARCH

One evening in mid-December 1996 I trekked from Cluanie to Alltbeithe Youth Hostel with a group, on 'reliable' advice that an annexe of the hostel had been left open for winter use. Heavy rain, chilled by a strong east wind, drove across our tracks and the path was a ribbon of flowing water; when we arrived at 5.30pm, we were already half-soaked and in need of succour. The discovery that every part of the hostel was securely locked was something of a shock. **Readers should note that both**

Alltbeithe and Corrour (Loch Ossian) hostels are now fully locked in winter and can only be used by special arrangement with the Scottish YHA. We huddled in the lee of the main building pondering our options. The tops were blotted out by low cloud, leaving a leaden gloom in the glen. Casting our torch beams skywards we could see nought but a wall of gleaming, strafing raindrops. Camban bothy was some 4km away to our west, but the realisation that the wind would be at our backs decided our course. A silent, potentially mutinous group splashed after me across swelling streams and out along the jeep track to the Affric–Lichd watershed where Camban sits squat and lonely. The hillsides above us were now whitening as the rain turned to snow at higher levels. This was exactly the sort of storm every winter needs but so rarely gets nowadays, creating the worst imaginable conditions for survival.

Soaked and shivering we assembled in the byre which forms Camban's ground floor. Leaks in the roof had partially wetted the sleeping loft above, but we reckoned we could all just squeeze in. Only the novelty of the situation compensated for the discomfort. The guides performed a Herculean task in cooking a palatable pasta and vegetable stew, and the predicament was fully redeemed when a bottle of 'Whyte & Mackay' was produced. Then came the test of the night: how well would chilled bodies recover in damp sleeping bags? Outside the temperature plunged, and on venturing outside to answer Nature's call at 3am, I met a swirling blizzard.

Everybody survived, and some even slept. After breakfast of porridge, jam and bread, we pulled on ice-cold boots and ventured outside into a clear and bitterly cold morning. The direct way back to Cluanie lay over the summit of Ciste Dhubh (982m): could we all make it, and so pull some small achievement out of

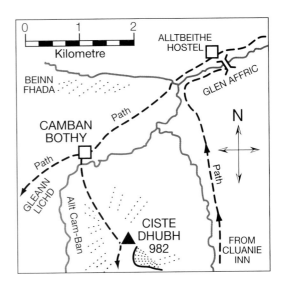

adversity? First, the Allt Camban had to be crossed. The river was dropping, but every stepping stone was covered in ice with a topping of powder snow. Having warmed clothes, socks and gloves next to the body through the long night, two of the group managed to fall full length into the water and everyone else filled their boots. Our toiling caravan then struggled up Ciste Dhubh into a keen wind which blew the fresh snow into tendrils of spindrift. But soon the sky brightened and sunlight began to cast a pale glow over the giant whaleback of Sgurr nan Ceathreamhnan, and the increasing reward of the day put the previous night into perspective. We had a businessman from South Africa in the party who was making his first trip to the Scottish mountains, and I had feared his reactions to the adversity he had experienced; but at the summit he slowly scanned the hills, then turned to me and said: 'You know, this is *really* wild country!'

He was genuinely impressed and possibly even satisfied by the bothy experience, despite the miseries of the previous night. Hardship is an inseparable part of winter expeditioning, and helps enrich us in a way that brief one-day trips from car to car do not.

All that is needed is sufficient excuse, coercion or commitment to set forth.

The CIC Hut

The Charles Inglis Clark memorial hut, sited at 670m beneath the north-east face of Ben Nevis and owned by the SMC, is the only high-mountain club-hut in Scotland. With its unrivalled location and the facilities of fuel, cookers, stove, mattresses and blankets, the CIC has always been most popular in the winter season, and the exploits of its denizens, whether members, guests or gatecrashers, both on the cliffs and in the hut, have attained a legendary fame. With the necessary materials hauled up by pony, the hut was constructed in the space of ten months, and its purpose was very promptly justified. At the opening ceremony and dinner on 1 April 1929, the Rev A. E. Robertson (the first Munroist) said the grace and prayed that the hut should be a refuge in true danger. A moment later '... the inner door of the hut was violently thrust open and two stalwart climbers lurched in, covered with snow and evidently in a state of exhaustion.'[8] They had just been avalanched 200m down Observatory Gully!

With just eighteen bed-places the hut has, since the early 1970s, been overwhelmed by demand in winter. Overnight occupancy between December and April is of the order of 90–95 per cent, an approximate total of 1,700 bed-nights, all for the purpose of snow- and ice-climbing. In winter it is also besieged by hundreds of would-be daytime visitors seeking shelter for sandwiches and a brew. Consequently the hut now has to be locked, or guarded like a miniature Fort Knox, with access restricted to members or those authorised by password systems. Moreover the absence of toilet facilities at the hut has created a potential pollution problem in the Allt a'Mhulinn glen.

All this is sad but inevitable, given the booming numbers of winter climbers.

THE HIGH CAMP

To camp in the hills in winter is rarely an act borne of necessity. On my ascent of all the Munros in the 1984–5 season, guided by the principle of least effort, I needed to camp just once, whereas twelve nights were spent in bothies.

Winter camping only became a 'pastime' in the interwar years. G. B. Speirs wrote in the *SMC Journal* that December camping was good for 'toughening up' purposes – yet his recollections smack of sybaritic rather than Spartan pleasures. Of one pitch in Glen Keltie by Rannoch he recalled: '...seldom if ever can such a dinner have been cooked in the wilds. It began with oxtail soup, then came roasted blackcock with potatoes, peas and bread sauce. The sweet was trifle, and the meal finished with port and cigars.'[9]

High camping on the summits in winter required considerably greater toil, sacrifice and risk. Bill Murray and his friends were among the first with the commitment and enthusiasm to take up this particular gauntlet. So 'in a fit of ascetic resolve', Murray with Donaldson and McCarter decided to 'sever all ties with the triumphs of 1939 civilisation in order to mortify our flesh on the icy summit of Ben Nevis.'[10]

For the three-hour effort of hauling 15kg loads up to the top, and the privations of their accommodation, recompense was granted in the majesty sunset, midnight and dawn views whose sight was denied to every other living mortal in the land, but which Murray bequeathed to future generations of mountain lovers in his descriptive prose: 'Minor hardships are far outweighed by the joys of dwelling for a space on snowfields close to the sky where the dawn and sunset come like armadas in slow and solemn grace.'[11]

Conditions were not always so idyllic, however, and one week previously a preparatory camp on the top of Clachlet in the Blackmount had proved altogether less sublime. Mountain tents of the time were made largely for use on Himalayan expeditions and were snowproof rather than rainproof, and Murray and Donaldson discovered this awful truth when the moon disappeared behind a sheet of encroaching cloud and a deluge commenced: '...the remainder of the night was indescribable, but anyone may sample the same experience in his own house. Let him step fully clothed into a cold bath at 2am in midwinter and recline there with a cold shower playing overhead until 8am. He will then know, like Donaldson and me, what it means to be grateful for the dawn.'[12]

Even on a dry cold night, the equipment available in the 1930s could not meet the rigorous demands of the Scottish mountain summit. Indeed even today, with our double-skinned nylon tents and all the other products of the lightweight camping revolution, it is hard to strike a successful bargain between the needs for warmth, ventilation and lightweight gear.

Accepting as inevitable the evil of internal dampness, the high campers of the 1930s would use two down sleeping-bags in order to provide the compensating warmth. Unfortunately the mere addition of feather-down filling is not an efficient answer to the insulation problem in the wet, because while the thermal performance of down is unchallenged when it is dry, its insulation factor drops dramatically with increasing moisture content – thus two sopping-wet down bags are not much more effective than one. Nowadays we can use a Gore-tex bivouac bag as a waterproof sleeping bag cover or else use fibre-pile bags which have a higher insulation retention when wet.

Effective insulation from the ground is especially crucial to bodily comfort in winter. Bill Murray tried absorbent rubber sponge in his high-camping experiments, but on discovering its exceptional hydrophilic (water-loving) quality, turned to sandwiched layers of tar and paper with more success. Others preferred to take an inflatable air-bed at the cost of another 2kg in the load. Today we can choose between open-cell foam-mats or slim inflatable 'Thermarests', which are minimal in weight and water-resistant. Rucksack, waterproofs and rope can also be stuffed under the body for extra insulation.

However strong the tent and sophisticated one's gear, successful winter camping remains ultimately dependent upon personal sense and organisation, particularly in siting and pitching relative to the expected winds but also in every miniscule task and refinement once inside. The winter camper is ever-prey to the approaching storm, and is never released from the sound of nature's fury. Yet as products of a centrally heated civilisation, we occasionally need to relearn the fundamentals of taking care of ourselves, and therein lies the fun in winter camping, whether one is on the summit or in the glen. And as training for expeditions to the greater ranges, a dose of winter tent-life in Scotland could not be bettered.

SNOW-HOLES: COFFINS AND PALACES

Given a widespread snow-cover on the hills, snow-holes form a more secure shelter than tents. However, they can only be dug in those few locations where well packed drifts form to a substantial depth, such as stream beds, overflow channels or lee hollows; and such sites are rarely found in the steeper relief of the Western Highlands. Since its inception in 1948, Glenmore Lodge has used snow-holes on the Cairngorm plateau for survival training courses, using specific sites selected for the consistency of their drift even in the leanest of seasons. Many students might have easily been

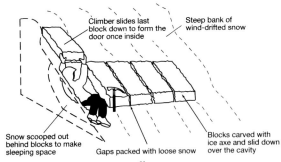

Fig 7.6a *Emergency coffin*

Climber slides last block down to form the door once inside

Steep bank of wind-drifted snow

Snow scooped out behind blocks to make sleeping space

Gaps packed with loose snow

Blocks carved with ice axe and slid down over the cavity

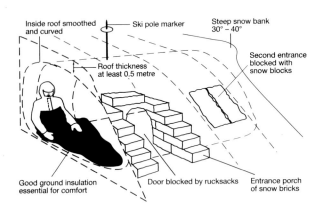

Fig 7.6b *Snow cave*

Inside roof smoothed and curved

Ski pole marker

Steep snow bank 30° – 40°

Second entrance blocked with snow blocks

Roof thickness at least 0.5 metre

Good ground insulation essential for comfort

Door blocked by rucksacks

Entrance porch of snow bricks

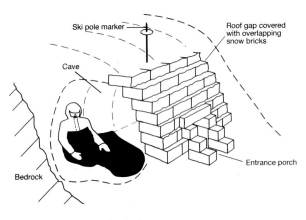

Fig 7.6c *Hybrid igloo*

Ski pole marker

Roof gap covered with overlapping snow bricks

Cave

Entrance porch

Bedrock

deceived by the experience into thinking that snow-holes can be made at whim anywhere on the high tops. In reality, considerable skill and intuition are needed in guessing where suitable sites exist, whether as a luxury snow-hole base for multi-day expeditioning, or as an emergency shelter when benighted in the storm.

Emergency Coffins

An emergency one-person hole, known as a 'snow coffin', can be dug with an ice-axe in less than half an hour provided the snow texture is suitable (despite its unfortunate appellation, the 'snow coffin' is designed for self-preservation rather than consecration). The coffin is formed simply by carving a series of rectangular blocks across the surface of a drifted slope, removing the blocks and then scooping out a cavity behind. The blocks are then slid back into place over the cavity, all except the last which is not replaced until the climber has crawled inside. A great advantage of the coffin is that it can be successfully fashioned in snow little more than 1m in depth. However, it is only wholly successful on wind-slabbed drifts where 'gravestone' blocks can be carved with ease. In a harder, homogenous snowpack, a simple burrow might be the more rewarding design, although it could take three times as long to dig.

Snow Caves

A 'fully furnished' snow cave makes an excellent group base, but such a major excavation requires the use of lightweight aluminium snow shovels. Before commencing it is essential to check that the snowdrift is sufficiently deep, at least 3m being needed, for which purpose an avalanche probe might usefully be carried. Excavation is much facilitated if digging sideways into a slope of 30–40 degrees in angle rather than downwards into a shallow

Plate 7.5 *Snow-hole palace : luxury interior of a snow cave with furniture carved to requirements*

slope. Two entrances should be started, allowing two people at a time to get to work tunnelling inwards. Once the required depth is attained, the two tunnels can be joined. The cave is then enlarged and sculpted to requirements. Finally, one entrance is blocked off and a protecting porch of snow bricks constructed around the other. Even with accommodating windpacked snow it can take anything up to three hours of hard work to create such a home for four or five people; but once complete, such habitation is both spacious and luxurious (Plate 7.5). However, the problems and dangers of snow-holes are several:

- The snow texture must be cohesive yet yielding. Snow-holes cannot be dug in unconsolidated powder snow, nor in hard, crystalline névé.
- An insufficient depth of snow, or an impen-

etrable icy underlayer can leave you with an open scoop instead of a full cave; if this happens, a hybrid of cave and igloo must be fashioned (Fig 7.6c). A snow saw will help in the cutting of the bricks, which should be built up in overlapping layers to form a roof. Sometimes the snow is simply too soft to form cohesive roof bricks, in which event a bivouac bag or tent flysheet could be used to bridge the skylight.

- Adequate ventilation must be ensured inside the hole: further snow drifting may block the entrance, and the use of candles and gas stoves inside the cave can quickly deplete the available oxygen. As well as keeping an air gap in the entrance, an avalanche probe could be used to keep a separate ventilation shaft open.
- Snow-hole sites must be marked with ski-

sticks or similar markers in order to warn others not to step on the roof, and to help in relocating the hole (see Chapter 6).

- Suitable lee-slope sites for snow-holes may also be prime locations for windslab avalanches, and Glenmore Lodge has had more than one scary experience in this regard. To be avalanched while excavating or, even worse, while sleeping in a hole, is the scenario of nightmares.

Neverthless, a successful snow-holing trip gives one great confidence in one's survival capacity, and enables novel mountain excursions to be completed.

A Snow Cave on The Saddle

One February I took a group of four to The Saddle with shovels strapped to their sacks. From Shiel Bridge we walked up Gleann Undalain and into the mountain's northern corrie, Coire Uaine. I guessed that a hollow right on the summit would probably provide the needed snow-depth, yet heavy squalls and gusting winds deterred us from going higher. We spent an hour checking out possible sites in the corrie, but by 3.30pm had found nothing that would ensure a comfortable night. The commitment had to be made. Up we went, moving roped up the grade I Little Gully, our nerves tensed by unstable snowdrifts, the prevailing storm and the oncoming night. Would I even be able to find the crucial hollow in the dark? Then, just as we ploughed up the exit runnel of the gully, the blizzard eased and the wind dropped. Ten metres back from the edge of the cliff, our torch beams found the hollow with a huge bank of snow on its far side. Working in shifts we took three hours to make our cave, and at 8.30pm moved in. Freed from the wind and stretched out in our sleeping-bags we could enjoy some good food and a

feeling of camaraderie, plus the tingling excitement that we were perched right on the top of a Munro.

We rose to see a splendid dawn develop over the South Cluanie Ridge. Packing up was agony, trying to thread frozen harness tapes, and tie into a rope as stiff as piano wire in a bitter breeze with hands that burnt with the cold. But once we were moving, we realised that we could enjoy a descending traverse of the Forcan Ridge in perfect conditions without the usual two-hour approach march. By 11.00am we were off the ridge and striding happily across the bumpy tops of Biod an Fhithich. Supping a lunchtime pint in the Kintail Lodge Hotel we were forgetting the rigours of the previous evening, and deciding that snow-holing wasn't a bad ploy for getting back early.

The Longest Bivouac

No one venturing into the hills in winter should discount the risk of an eventual bivouac – the torch may fail and the weather turn, or an ankle may snap without shelter close at hand; but the epic endured by Christopher Nicholls in February 1993 defies comparison in Scottish winter history. Having walked up Slioch by Loch Maree, he was caught by mist on the top. According to his account, he was jogging about at the summit in order to keep warm while waiting for the visibility to improve, when he tripped and sprained his ankle. Crawling to a low-walled shelter nearby and with the security of having a sleeping-bag and bivouac sack, he decided to stop and await the arrival of either a rescue party or of other walkers who might assist. Unfortunately, no one had any details of his route: his family in England knew only that he was away on a week's walking holiday, and he had failed to realise that casual visitors to the top of Slioch in a driech February are few and far between.

So he stayed, eating spare food and listening to a transistor radio which he had brought with him. The mist stayed firmly clamped on the summit, so he did not dare to budge; he was only lucky that the weather was remarkably mild and windless for the time of year. After three days his sandwiches ran out. For another two days he sucked ice to ward off dehydration. On the sixth day he was sufficiently alarmed by a stormy weather forecast on his radio that he decided he had to get down. Despite advancing hypothermia, a swollen ankle and frostbite in his toes, he managed to crawl all the way down, and a farmer found him stumbling around a field near Kinlochewe on his eighth day out.

This is one of the rare occasions when Inverness's Raigmore Hospital has been presented with a case of serious frostbite. Nicholls had, through inexperience, broken the golden rule of self-reliance in solo mountain travel. He should have got himself down the hill, whether by crawling or limping, as soon as the sprain occurred, especially since nobody had an inkling of where he was. By staying on the summit in a mood of growing apathy, he assigned his life to luck and good fortune. That he was able, six days later, to get down when death was staring him in the face, shows the strength of Man's base survival instinct. Nicholls was courageous in acknowledging his mistakes, and admitted that, lacking any previous experience of Scotland in winter, he had been overawed by the scale and desolation of the mountains.

NIGHTSHIFTS ON THE CLIFFS

The winter night stalks the climber with particular menace. Benighted near the top of a big winter cliff there is no defence or haven from the storm, and no chance to retreat or escape: either the route must be fought to an issue, or an open bivouac endured, where only will and resolve can see the long night through.

The big Scottish cliffs are just of that height between 200 and 400m where even the hardest routes can feasibly, but with no certainty, be completed in a day. So stark is the prospect of benightment that some might consider it wise to carry stove, spare food and a sleeping-bag on big remote routes. However, the motto 'If you take them, you'll need to use them' holds good. Speed is the best guarantor of security, so the climber takes to the mountains with the most slender resources and knows the thrill of fighting the night with no more than a head-torch for comfort.

The early 'ultramontanes' of the SMC achieved a remarkable record in avoiding the bivouac, despite tackling the long buttress routes of Nevis which today are notorious night-traps. However, most early climbing was done at Easter and past the equinox, when daylight has flowered to twelve hours, and few major climbs were undertaken in the shadowed depths of the winter solstice.

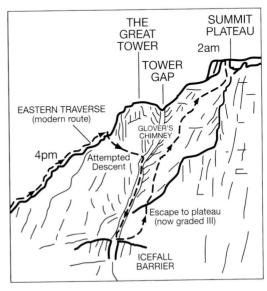

Fig 7.7 *Thirty hours on Ben Nevis*

However, on 28–29 December 1907, the first (and by no means the last) nocturnal epic was enacted on the Tower Ridge (Fig 7.7). Charles Inglis Clark (in whose memory the Nevis hut was bequeathed), Goodeve and MacIntyre arrived at the foot of the great ridge as late as midday, in CIC's opinion '... extremely fit after a good season's dances and other energetic amusements'.[13]

At 4pm the three were assembled below a heavily iced Great Tower. How many climbers since have felt the deepening pit of despair in their stomachs as dusk has left them marooned at this notorious impasse? Yet few have shown the courage and tenacity of Inglis Clark and friends in forcing a passage. Unaware of the easier Eastern Traverse, they made a long and harrowing rightward movement to completely outflank the Tower and land in the gully section of Glover's Chimney. Not realising that the gully mouth was barred by a vertical ice-fall, their attempted descent was blocked just 30m above easy slopes. All of Clark's prized fitness was now required as the party climbed back up, heading directly towards the plateau to the right of the gully, secured by naught but ice-axe hitches, 300m of mixed ascent that today is considered grade III in standard.

At about 2am they hauled themselves over the cornice into a calm but cloudy night, freed from the depths, but not out of trouble. Lacking a light by which to set the compass, they wandered south of the Nevis summit onto the craggy slopes of Carn Dearg and only at dawn were met in upper Glen Nevis by a scratch rescue team from the SMC. Thirty hours after departure, they re-entered Fort William's Alexandra Hotel, having completed the most devious ascent of the Tower Ridge on record.

The choice between bivouacking and pressing on in the dark is crucial to survival. Facing a sixteen-hour night without spare equipment, and sixty years before the advent of helicopter rescue, Clark's party chose well, and preserved their pride at the same time. To extricate oneself successfully from a winter benightment is perhaps the mountaineer's greatest test of skill and courage. In December 1936, Mackenzie, MacAlpine, Dunn and Murray effected an equally audacious all-night retreat from the crux of Garrick's Shelf (IV) high on the Crowberry Ridge of Buachaille Etive Mor, without any of the modern abseiling aids of pitons, nuts and slings, regaining the road at Coupal Bridge twenty-one hours after setting out. In the following March, Mackenzie and Murray went back to complete the first ascent.

Occasionally, however, safe judgement decrees that there is no way out or back, and the night must be endured in icy petrifaction. The bivouac of Hamish MacInnes 3m from achieving the first ascent of the Buachaille's Raven's Gully (V) in January 1953 was as desperate and precarious as any before or since. Leading the final hard grooves in total darkness, his rope jammed irreversibly. Leaving his companions Vigano and Cullen of the Creagh Dhu to the relative comfort of a bivouac in their motor-cycle suits, MacInnes, feeling that he could not survive the night in such a position, untied and soloed towards the top until a verglassed chimney barred the exit. Jammed across the cleft, he somehow did survive for eight hours clad solely in jeans, shirt and anorak until a rescue party arrived and dropped down a top rope.

A few of the longest and hardest mixed climbs have demanded two days for completion. They are too hard to be climbed by night and siege tactics using fixed ropes from the cliff-base are ethically out of order in Scotland. Where bivouacs have been premeditated, food and gear has been hauled up the route – but no amount of equipment can eliminate the discomfort of a night spent in semi-suspension on a buttock-wide ledge. To embark on a climb knowing that a fourteen-hour bivouac is to be included requires an almost biblical zeal and faith that the route's quality will match the hardship involved.

Most climbers, however, have preferred to try a bold one-day push on big routes without spare gear, knowing the score and taking the risk that a bivouac might be enforced – and on occasion the consequences have been dramatic. In a bold first-ascent attempt at New Year in 1971, John Cunningham and Bill March were benighted below the crux and final pitch of Citadel (now grade VII) on Shelter Stone cliff. Having gained their high point by a series of traverses above overhanging walls, retreat was impossible. They had naught save the clothes they stood in and an uneaten lunch-pack – and then the weather turned, the wind rising to send spindrift whirling across the cliff. March recounted:

'Hell,' I thought, 'what am I doing here?' I was barely sitting on a sloping ledge the size of a small tea-tray with my head between my knees 800 feet up Citadel. My teeth were chattering uncontrollably with the cold. The time was 9pm – only eleven hours to go until daylight and we had already been on the ledge three hours ...

At about 2am I gazed wearily across at JC. The temperature had risen and wet snow-slides were hitting us at intervals. JC was on his knees. For one split second I thought he was praying and fear gripped me. All was lost.'[14]

In fact Cunningham was desperately searching for relief from cramp. They weathered out the night and retreated by some hair-raising pendules and abseils in the dank chill of dawn.

Only once on the first ascent of a hard mixed climb has an all-night push been successfully achieved, when in January 1986 Sandy Allan and Andy Nisbet spent nineteen hours climbing The Rat-trap (VIII,8) on Creag an Dubh Loch. The pair had taken an extra haul-sack with bivouac gear, but this became inextricably jammed at an overlap and had to be jettisoned. Having made several long traverses above roofs and with night already upon them, Nisbet commented somewhat enigmatically: 'Retreat was not an option, but upward progress also seemed unlikely.' However, helped by the light of the moon and a few aid-pegs they fought their way to the top at 3am.

Given a full moon and good conditions, pure ice routes are more amenable to a night ascent as their technical content is considerably more straightforward. To 'whoop' and 'shriek' up the gleaming ice of Nevis in the dead of night is for warmth and elemental thrill to be favourably compared with the dour communion of the bivouac. The great ice-climbers of the late fifties and early sixties were masters of the art of leaving late and somehow forcing a conclusion to their routes around the midnight hour. Smith, Haston and Wightman's 'nightshift in Zero' in March 1960 was probably the most outrageous of these ascents, starting at 2pm with a borrowed rope and the CIC hut poker for belays on a grade V gully that had been climbed only once before. Inevitably, the climb finished in the 'wee small hours', the protagonists jubilant although slightly chastened.

Whatever the chosen style, to live through the full span of the winter mountain night completes an education in the ways of the wild. Successful survival is not an aim that stands alone, but is the means to know the hills at every hour and in their every mood, as well as to know oneself a little more closely.

8: AN AVALANCHE AWARENESS

ASSESSING AND AVOIDING THE HAZARD

'Dangerous avalanches are not likely to be encountered in Scotland.' (W. Naismith, 1893)

'We have practically no avalanches and no fear of ice cornices.' (Prof G. Ramsay, first President of the SMC, 1896)

'Fresh powder snow lying on old hard snow, which is so frequently the precursor of avalanches in the Alps, is not often encountered in Scotland.' (Graham Macphee, author Ben Nevis guidebook, 1936)

To our generation, accustomed as we are to regular news reports of avalanche accidents and educated by a growing technical literature on the subject, the comments of these early notables of winter mountaineering seem astounding in their complacency. The neglect of the avalanche hazard was due to several reasons. First, Scotland does not produce the large-scale destructive avalanches which in the Alps can overwhelm valley habitations. By comparison, our avalanches are mostly minor localised events, easily ignored although no less deadly to climbers caught up in them. Secondly, there were only tiny numbers of mountaineers on the hills in winter prior to 1945 compared with today. Those incidents that did occur were regarded as isolated mischances and did not arouse suspicion of a general hazard.

Thirdly, most early snow-climbing was done late in the season around Easter, when the dry windslab hazard is less likely to be present and the main danger is the more obvious wet-snow avalanche or cornice collapse during thaw.

Indeed, the first recorded avalanche involving climbers in Scotland was a cornice collapse and wet-snow slide which snubbed a presumptuous attempt on Creag Meagaidh's Centre Post in April 1896. Just two windslab avalanches were reported prior to 1914, neither fatal but both on Ben More, Crianlarich, which is still a notorious site. Only with a series of gully avalanches in the 1950s, several of which were fatal, was a proper awareness stimulated, although the misconception that open slopes of medium angle (25–45 degrees) were relatively safe still prevailed until the 1970s.

The regularity of recent avalanche events makes sombre reading. A total of 458 people have been involved in reported avalanches in Scotland between 1985/85 and 96/97, and I would guess that as many again have walked away unhurt from avalanches but have not reported their experience. Of those 458, thirty-five have died and 109 have been injured. The year-by-year volatility of avalanche accidents is shown by the graph of Fig 8.1. The incidence of avalanches correlates closely with years of heavy snowfall and unstable weather, 1994 and 1995 being the most recent examples.

Figs 8.1 and 8.2 *Reported avalanche events in Scotland 1985/6–1996/7*
(figures supplied by the Scottish Avalanche Information Service)

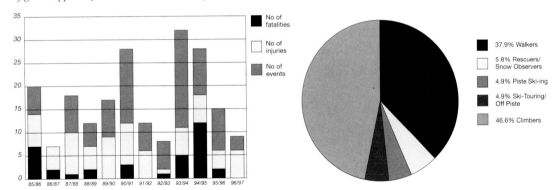

The upward trend in the occurrence of avalanches does not arise from natural factors; the great majority of Scottish avalanches are triggered by the victims. Given the rising number of hillgoers in winter, an increase in incidence is not surprising.

ARE YOU AT RISK?

Hillwalkers: The erroneous impression still persists that avalanches only occur to climbers operating on steep slopes. As Fig 8.2 shows, 38 per cent of recorded avalanche 'events' in Scotland in the last twelve years involved walking or hillcraft parties, that is a total of seventy-eight serious incidents. There are few mountain traverses in the Western Highlands that do not encounter slopes of 30 degrees or more with the potential for avalanches. The standard route to the Buachaille up the headwall of Coire na Tulaich is a notorious slope where the mountain offers no easier alternatives. The Red Burn on Ben Nevis seems a secure location, being close to the tourist path and offering a quick route down the mountain. Yet avalanches occur here regularly; indeed one of them claimed two lives in 1985. On days of severe summit winds, walking parties are often compelled to seek an escape route on the lee slopes of their mountain where

avalanche risk is likely. And because it is the usual tendency of walking parties to avoid steep open slopes, they are all the more vulnerable when they do have to make a descent over such ground.

Climbers: The great climbing corries harbour the greatest potential for avalanches. Most climbing routes involve either an approach across steep open ground at a 35–45 degree angle, or else exit on a 45–50 degree headwall with associated cornice problems. The big, easier gullies are the most prone to risk; Easy Gully and Raeburn's Gully on Creag Meagaidh are typical avalanche locations. The great majority of winter mountaineers operate within the range of grades I to III, and thus spend most of their time on just that type and angle of terrain where avalanches are most likely. Buttress routes, especially in the higher grades, are the safest option. There can be very few regular winter climbing activists who have not had at least one avalanche 'experience' in their careers.

Ski Tourers: Skiers are vulnerable by reason of the speed with which they can find themselves on dangerous ground. On descents the skier has little time to assess the changing snow conditions; gliding over the surface it is hard to sense subtle but crucial changes in the snowpack. Contrast the toiling walker who has

Plate 8.1 *Massive avalanche debris at the foot of Observatory Gully, Ben Nevis; cornice collapse after prolonged snowfall probably triggered accumulations in gullies and on faces. The debris fan, extending 200m across the valley floor and containing ridges over 3m high, is ample evidence of the potential scale of Scottish avalanches. Judging from the volumes of snow still sticking to the cliffs above, this is decidedly not the day for climbing!*

ample opportunity to consider the change from deep but harmless loose snow to potentially dangerous cohesive windslab.

Avalanche Forecasting

The Scottish Avalanche Information Service (SAIS) commenced its work in the winter of 1988–89. Known initially as the Scottish Avalanche Project, data was gathered from Glencoe and the Northern Cairngorms, with Lochaber being added the following year. The service is funded by the Scottish Office, and it added Creag Meagaidh and Lochnagar to its reporting areas in 1996–97. Daily observations are made by hardy, and on some days courageous teams who dig snow pits at relevant sites in the massifs. From the profiles they measure snow depths, hardness and temperatures, and make assessments of layering, faceting and snow types. Faceting refers to the deposition or formation of weak bands of crystals within the snowpack. Back at base by early afternoon, the observers feed this data into a computer model, together with the meteorological data forecast for the following twenty-four hours.

Up to sixteen separate data variables can be input, and each is a relevant indicative factor towards avalanche risk. The NXD model then finds the ten past days from its database which fit the current day's data the most closely; the degree of fit is quantified by a

Plate 8.2 *Slab avalanche under the summit of The Saddle, 2 January 1995. The crown wall can be traced across the top of the slope. This avalanche was triggered by an erring walker who ventured towards the top of the slope*

weighted numerical scale. Reported avalanche activity for these ten 'nearest neighbour' days is then analysed by the observers together with the service co-ordinator, Blyth Wright. If there have been avalanches reported on more than three of the ten most similar past days, then the team will issue a report that avalanches are 'likely' in the next twenty-four hours, which means a 'high Considerable' (3+) or else a level 4 category of risk (see Fig 8.3, page 182). However, inevitably there are imperfections in the working of the model:

1 Many of the input figures are not exact readings but are subjective indices as estimated by observers at the snow-pit sites.

2 There are a great many days when no avalanche activity can be observed due to bad visibility, or when few people are out on the hill to witness avalanches.

3 The data bank stored on file is still relatively limited in volume; data fits will become more accurate the longer the scheme operates.

4 The weather data used in the model is based on the forecast values; if the weather changes unexpectedly then the avalanche predictions could go awry.

5 Practical limitations mean that the avalanche predictions have to be based on snow-pit observations made twenty-four hours before the forecast day.

However, despite these drawbacks the forecasting system is achieving an impressive rate of success. By 1997 the service was recording only a 5 per cent error rate in failing to predict days on which avalanches were reported, and a 15 per cent miss rate in forecasting avalanche activity for days when no avalanches were reported.

It is also interesting that the model is proving better at forecasting than the observers themselves: thus on days when the model's predictions are at variance to the observers' intuitive assessments, the model is more often than not correct.

As the avalanche data bank grows, and as the input variables are further refined and tuned, avalanche forecasting in Scotland will become ever more sophisticated and accurate. Despite the black winter of 1994–95 when twelve died in Scottish avalanches, it is certain that the SAIS reports and forecasts have already prevented many accidents and fatalities. The SAIS is, however, highly dependent upon the information on avalanches it receives from hill-goers. Any avalanche observed on the hills should be reported to the team (see Appendix V), whether or not anyone is caught in it.

INTERPRETING AVALANCHE REPORTS

The '1 to 5' Common European Hazard Scale of avalanche risk (Fig 8.3) provides a basic framework for the reports, although the numerical grades are not always quoted in the bulletins. Risk level 1 is applied when there are only limited snowfields or else no snow at all on the hills, and level 5 only applies to 'generalised' avalanche risk at all altitudes and on all aspects of slopes, a situation which very rarely pertains on the Scottish hills. Therefore, the usual oper-

---

Fig 8.3 *The avalanche hazard scale*
(based on the European Common Hazard Scale)

Degree of hazard	Snowpack stability	Avalanche probability
1 Low	The snowpack is generally well bonded and stable	Triggering is possible only with high additional loads on a very few steep extreme slopes (**2**). Only a few small natural avalanches (**3**) possible
2 Moderate	The snowpack is moderately well bonded on some steep slopes, otherwise generally well bonded	Triggering is possible with high additional loads (**4**), particularly on the steep slopes indicated in the bulletin. Large natural avalanches not likely
3 Considerable	The snowpack is moderately to weakly bonded on many steep slopes (**1**)	Triggering is possible sometimes even with low additional loads. The bulletin may indicate many slopes which are particularly affected. In certain conditions medium and occasionally large sized natural avalanches may occur
4 High	The snowpack is weakly bonded in most places	Triggering is possible even with low additional loads on many steep slopes. In some conditions frequent medium or large sized natural avalanches are likely
5 Very high	The snowpack is generally weakly bonded and largely unstable	Numerous large natural avalanches are likely, even on moderately steep terrain

(1) **Steep slopes**: slopes with an incline of more than 30 degrees
(2) **Steep extreme slopes**: those which are particularly unfavourable in terms of the incline, terrain profile, proximity to ridge, smoothness of underlying ground surface
(3) **Natural avalanches**: those triggered without human assistance
(4) **Additional load**: high – eg group of skiers/walkers, piste machine; low – lone skier/walker/climber

ative range of risk scores is from 2 'Moderate', through 3 'Considerable' to 4 'High'.

During a spell of snowy or unsettled weather it is not unusual for the forecast risk levels to remain at Considerable or High; in January 1994 the forecasts never dropped below level 3 for the whole month. Yet it is during cool snowy spells that the most exciting and challenging conditions for winter mountaineering can be found. Such a situation could produce two very different responses: first, cautious climbers might take such forecasts as sufficient reason to stay off steep ground altogether for long periods, and would thereby miss out on some great conditions.

By contrast, those with a cavalier attitude to objective danger might pay little heed to forecasts if the risk levels never seem to change. They will go out repeatedly, and the more they enjoy successful climbs, the less attention they might pay to the forecasts. And then the black day cometh.

In fact neither response is healthy. The forecasts are written with great care and must be studied in their verbal detail if they are to be interpreted correctly. They do not adopt the stance of 'stay off the hills' when avalanches are likely, but indicate the areas and aspects of greatest risk (Fig 8.4). Sufficient information is given that users can make an informed and reasoned decision as to where they might climb with an acceptable margin of safety. Several points in the details are important: first, categories 3 and 4 indicate 'localised' hazard which is largely confined to particular slope aspects, or lies within a limited range of altitudes; by avoiding these aspects, exposure to danger can be reduced to a much lower level. However, the indication that south-facing slopes might be dangerous does not mean that all north slopes are entirely safe. Wherever open slopes with fresh, dry accumulations of snow are encountered, full precautions should be taken, irrespective of the aspects indicated by the avalanche forecast.

The indications that 'avalanches are likely' or 'avalanches will occur' in the forecast is significant, because such predictions are made on the basis of past avalanche experience from the running of the nearest neighbour model. A level 3 Medium-risk forecast is enhanced to a 3+ level by the wording 'avalanches are likely', and users should be especially wary on the indicated slopes.

Snow and Avalanche Report

LOCHABER

Avalanche hazard at 15.00 hrs on Thu 23/2/95
Extensive areas of deep unstable windslab are present on all easterly aspects above 800m. Large unstable cornices are also present above easterly aspects. The avalanche hazard is Considerable where this windslab exists.

Avalanche hazard outlook for Fri 24/2/95
Large areas of deep unstable windslab will be present on all easterly aspects above 800m. Fresh snow overnight will form areas of unstable surface slab, mainly on E and SE aspects. Avalanches are likely on easterly aspects. The avalanche hazard will be Considerable. Cornices will remain unstable and prone to collapse.

— Ben Nevis, Aonach Mor/Beag, Grey Corries and Mamores ranges

— Existing hazard assessment

— Clear indication of hazard areas

— 'Considerable' hazard is level 3

— Forecast hazard for next 24 hours

— Dangerous aspects and altitudes specified

— Avalanches are expected on indicated slopes

— 'Considerable' risk plus likelihood of avalanches means a '3+' forecast

Fig 8.4 *A typical avalanche forecast · 24th February 1995*

The forecasts should provide an extra basis of awareness, but should never be regarded as a substitute for personal judgement on the hill. Nevertheless, ignorance of the prevailing snow conditions is no longer an excuse for getting avalanched in Scotland, as it might have been twenty years ago. The avalanche reports and forecasts are available on freephone and fax, and on the internet throughout the winter season (see Appendix V).

PERSONAL PRECAUTIONS

An avalanche awareness can be gained in four ways:

1 Studying the broad principles of snow conditions and avalanche genesis through the available literature gives a vital theoretical grounding (Chapter 3 has attempted to do this!).

2 Regularly performing snow-pit examination and analysis on the mountains, whether or not any significant danger is initially perceived. To witness a layer of snow shear and slide on its base in a test pit gives graphic indication of the potential of a seemingly benign snowpack to avalanche.

3 Seeing avalanches on the hills, or observing avalanche debris. A cornice collapse on the South-East Coire of Fuar Tholl at Easter 1986 gave me my most vivid memory of the potential scale of Scottish avalanches. We were walking up towards the rim of the upper corrie when we heard the crack as the edge gave way 300m above us. The resultant mass of powder mushroomed on impact with the corrie floor. As the cloud threatened to spill over the lip our attitude turned from open-jawed admiration to one of panic-stricken flight. Thankfully, the dust settled within a few seconds. Had the avalanche occurred twenty minutes later we would have been sitting close to its point of impact preparing to start a snowcraft session! If the avalanche is not actually witnessed, then it can be almost as sobering to see the scale of the resultant snow debris (Plate 8.1).

4) Getting caught in a couple of real avalanches does wonders for one's awareness. This cannot be proposed as a conventional means of enlightment, but it is true to say that most of today's avalanche experts have gained their respect and interest in the phenomenon from their own experiences...

11 JANUARY 1980: A BLACK WEEKEND

The freeze came early, and I was itching to be back on Scottish ice. Having expended last year's energies on the Ben I fancied a visit to Lochnagar; Eagle Ridge and Parallel 'B' would do nicely for this first foray.

I left Sheffield after work on Friday, and collected Kevin McLane from Newcastle. Bitter east winds, intermittent blizzards and straying deer enlivened the drive over the Cairnwell. But driving up Glen Muick past swaying pine stands and out onto the icy moors I was assailed by fear. We were stiff and exhausted from the journey, and there was nothing out there to comfort, only elemental hostility. Why have we come, I thought?

As we had planned to bivouac beside the car, the discovery that the roadhead toilets were open and habitable was welcome. Yet kipping in their shelter seemed a concession to nature, a forfeit of pride that rankled. Morning's only comfort was the sight of other parties hiking up the Land Rover track towards the Lochnagar corrie. The wind was cutting at the corrie rim, the spindrift whipping wildly. We paused five minutes to eat and reorganise.

Our silence betrayed our trepidation, but even here neither of us thought to question our objectives. Maybe we didn't know each other well enough to dare show a doubt, or maybe we believed too blindly in the virtues of endurance.

We dropped into the corrie and began a long traverse on steepening snowfields towards Parallel B Gully. The wind dropped in the shelter of the bowl, the blood returned to my limbs and this, coupled with the sight of the cliffs, revived my spirit. After all the self-doubt, there was the gully just 200m away. At first we plugged deep steps, but then the snow became more supportive, giving another fillip to our rising mood.

Then a crack, and everything was moving – me, the slope and the mountain. I tried to run, but was thrown head-down on my chest. The snow below broke into blocks, and then I felt an overwhelming surge from above, tipping me completely upside down. This was the end. One despairing pang of regret, a final thrust at the snow with my arms, and then silence.

My chest heaved against the casing of snow. I had a small cavity at my mouth and gasped in short shallow breaths. My left hand was pinned painfully behind my back, but the fingers of my right hand felt the chill of air: they were sticking three inches out of the surface, allowing me a tiny flow of oxygen. Panic subsided, and I worked my free hand feverishly in circles to open a hole. After a minute my forearm could move, another two and I could just rotate my shoulder; I began to believe that in time I would be able to dig myself out and look for Kevin.

Then I heard voices, and Kevin's Geordie accent called my name. Within seconds several axes were scraping at my body, and I was freed. Kevin had been only half buried and had dug himself out, and two Scots lads had rushed over to help – they had seen the windslab go.

Surrounded by debris, I sat down for five minutes to recover, then we checked our belongings and turned tail. Before we reached the glen, we saw a helicopter going in to the mountain: somebody had fallen off Black Spout Buttress. The next day two more were avalanched in the corrie; one of the victims was buried unconscious for 8½ hours, yet remarkably he survived. For us, the weekend might have been so much blacker.

We drove the long road home in silent shock, plagued by a growing sense of guilt. After all, we had committed just about every elementary mistake in the avalanche book, from ignoring the warnings of weather and blowing snow to walking straight across the most vulnerable part of the slope. Would we learn the lessons?

THE WARNING SIGNS

It is possible to climb throughout a whole winter season without encountering a single day of high avalanche risk. Then, quite suddenly, the weather factors combine to produce conditions that are ripe for a spate of accidents. Those travelling north to the Highlands without recent experience of the conditions, like ourselves in 1980, must consider every possible sign of avalanche risk before they become committed on the hills.

Weather History: A combination of sub-zero temperatures and recent snowfall and/or high winds over recent days urges caution. By keeping tuned to weather and avalanche forecasts in the days before a visit a clear picture can be built up of the evolving snow conditions. Knowledge of recent wind directions can help to specify high-risk zones.

Visual Signs of Wind Action: There are several signs of high winds and snow drifting on the tops which can be perceived from the valley:

1 Plumes or streamers of spindrift billowing off the summits.

2 Cloudbanks shearing off on the lee sides of the massifs; this is a particularly good indicator of high winds over the Northern Cairngorms.

3 Scouring of the windward side of the mountains, leaving them bare of snow while lee slopes are loaded.

Snow Conditions Underfoot: On days of high-risk conditions, unstable snow can be sensed on the walk into the mountains: surface snow may break off in cracks under the weight of the boot; stamping on fresh drifts releases miniature slabs; when walking on hard slab, the snow feels strangely supportive; rotation of the ice axe in the snowpack may produce a squeaking noise. Conversely, there may be duning of the snow or sastrugi on exposed ridges indicating wind erosion of lying snow. All these features are saying 'Watch out'!

DIGGING FOR INFORMATION

The excavation of a snow pit is the only formal means by which an assessment of the prevailing avalanche risk can be made, and it should be a standard skill for every party leader. The main considerations when choosing to dig a pit are:

Location of site: The pit should be dug in a relevant place, in other words as close as is feasible to the height and aspect of the slopes which might present the danger. There is little benefit from digging a pit 300m below the likely hazard area; indeed, such practice might lead to the erroneous pronouncement that the mountain is safe when localised windslabs are in fact lurking up higher. Similarly, snow profiles taken at the entrance of a gully are often worthless as a guide to the conditions at the gully exit.

Yet there is no sense in wandering out onto the most vulnerable open slopes and proceeding to 'dig your own grave'! The first snow pit should be dug to the side of, or a little below risk-prone slopes, never in the middle of them.

How deep to dig: The profile should be excavated down to ground level or, failing this, to a stable layer, either frozen névé or old 'spring' snow which has been through several meltfreeze cycles. If seven or eight minutes of digging with the axe adze fails to find such a 'stable' layer, the slope might be presumed dangerous purely because of the volume of fresh snow, without the need for further analysis.

Subsequent pits: The initial pit may show little risk of avalanche, but further investigation of the snowpack should be made during the course of a climb or ski tour, whenever a slope aspect alters, or a change in the resistance of the snowpack is encountered, or if heavy drifting of snow occurs during the course of the day. This need not take the form of the elaborate trench: half a minute spent scraping down the top layer and performing a quick 'shear test', repeated several times during a climb, is quite sufficient. Chopping out belay stances automatically reveals the upper snow profile, so no extra effort or time may be needed to do this.

What to look for: Having fashioned a vertical back wall to the pit and brushed it clear of extraneous snow, the profile can be formally examined. Four tests should be made:

The visual check: Is there layering visible in the snow? Old 'spring' snow or névé bands are visible as discoloured crystalline layers: they appear bluish in sunlight or slightly grey in flat light, and the grain of their sugar-sized crystals is usually obvious. Windslab is generally chalky white and less reflective than unaltered

Plate 8.3 *Powder-snow avalanche in Coire an t-Sneachda, Cairn Gorm (climber: Iain Peter) (Dave Willis)*

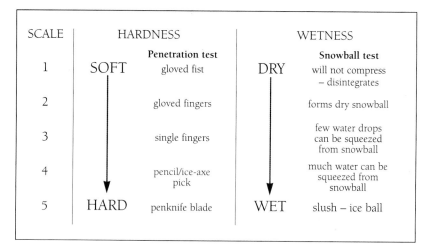

Fig 8.5 *Examining the snow profile: the rule-of-thumb scales. Note: Sharp differences in hardness or moisture between adjacent layers indicate instability and avalanche risk*

SCALE	HARDNESS		WETNESS	
		Penetration test		**Snowball test**
1	SOFT	gloved fist	DRY	will not compress – disintegrates
2		gloved fingers		forms dry snowball
3		single fingers		few water drops can be squeezed from snowball
4		pencil/ice-axe pick		much water can be squeezed from snowball
5	HARD	penknife blade	WET	slush – ice ball

snow crystals. In good light the eye can detect marginal changes in the tint of white between different layers of freshly deposited snow. Close visual inspection may detect air gaps between different layers of, or thin weak bands of graupel pellets, buried hoar or depth hoar, and these greatly increase the avalanche hazard.

The hardness test: A 'rule-of-thumb' scale from 1 to 5 is usually applied to give an index of the relative hardness of snow layers (see Fig 8.5). Sharp discontinuities in hardness are indicative of a slab avalanche risk, especially when a weak layer is revealed buried in the pack.

The wetness test: The relative 'squeezability' of adjacent layers of snow suggests the degree of wet-slab avalanche risk, as for example during a sudden thaw when slush is lying on top of hard névé.

The shear test: This is the most direct way of determining slab avalanche risk (see Fig 8.6). If the briquette of snow slides while being cut, a High-risk level is obvious, and the slope should be evacuated! If shearing occurs with little or no leverage once the brick is cut, a Considerable risk is suggested. If considerable leverage behind the block is needed before it slides, or if the block disintegrates without sliding, a Low to Moderate-risk range applies.

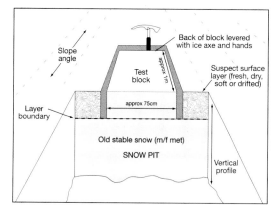

Fig 8.6 *The shear test: tests slab avalanche risk. The block is cut at the back of the snow pit with the axe adze to the full depth of the surface layer, then levered. Further tests are performed if lower layers are suspect*

The shear test should be applied to successive layers if there is multiple stratification in the snowpack.

AVOIDING ACTION

Having assessed that there is some degree of risk in proceeding on the planned route, the options are threefold:

1 **Turn back:** The only sensible option if there is no safe way to get to a route or summit in conditions of high risk, particularly if visibility is poor due to spindrift.

2 Alter the route: Go for ridge or buttress routes instead of gullies or faces, provided they can be accessed safely, or take the option of a ridge walk instead of a steep climb.

3 Proceed with safeguards: If the risk is not acute it may be considered reasonable to continue with the help of extra precautions, for example:

Avoid unbroken areas of snow by linking islands of bare ground to reach the objective.

Avoid open slopes by approaching a climbing route around the uppermost limit of snow where it meets the rocks of the cliff (ie actually touching the rocks with axes).

Rope up and belay on the approach to a climb if there are rock anchors available.

Cross any open areas of snow one at a time. Loosen sack straps and remove axe or ski-stick wrist loops (any impedimentia attached to the body increase the chance of injury during an avalanche).

On days when there is no obvious avalanche risk it is wise to select the safest route options wherever possible, for instance keeping near the edge of gullies or open slopes instead of their centre. However, even with the best intentions, the day may arrive when you get stranded with no place to hide …

LIATHACH, 8 MARCH 1995:

A cool bright morning with the promise of frost on the cliffs, our chance to get on some ice had arrived. The 750m haul up to Pyramid Buttress on the south face of Liathach provided a rude start. By the time we gained the snow-line at 500m a gentle snowfall had begun. A weak trough was forecast to pass through during the day but heavy precipitation was not anticipated, so I was not unduly concerned.

To reach the routes one must traverse exposed terraces across the banded face. Today they were thickly and steeply banked with soft snow. We roped up and I led the way 15m ahead of my three clients, working up between rock outcrops and putting in running belays from time to time. Despite a worrying volume of snow there were no indications of avalanche risk; the snowpack was one damp amorphous mass. Yet I couldn't relax in view of the crags below us. Near-vertical wading got us to the bottom of the Right Hand icefall, which rewarded our effort by sporting some ice. By now the snowfall was steady and visibility had dropped to 20m, but we supposed it would soon ease. In any event we were already considerably committed to the climb.

With three on my ropes, the two main ice pitches took us four hours. The ice was soft in places, but I found decent protection and belays. By half-past three we were ready to start the exit gully. The snowfall hadn't ceased for a minute. While belaying the team up the second pitch I watched how the gentle drift of the wind was brushing waves of snow up the slopes, and noted that there was already half a foot of fresh stuff banked uniformly on top of the existing pack. I got the distinct and creepy hunch that all this soft snow was being laid as soft slab, despite the lack of strong winds and despite the fact that we were not on the lee slope.

The proof came as soon as I set off up the gully, because at every step the snow broke away in little plates. To be sure, I put in a good runner, stood up on the side rocks and gave the snow surface a smack with the side of my axe. Instantaneously, a six-inch surface slab sheared off right across the gully.

We completed the climb by linking outcrops of rock, and emerged on the summit ridge of the mountain in dense fog at something like five o'clock.

If there is ever a place you don't want to find yourself in extreme avalanche conditions it is the main summit of Liathach. I considered every possible route off, but with every slope aspect likely to be loaded with surface slab, I forsaw us being avalanched on seriously exposed terrain on every option save one. Therefore we would descend the gully south from the first col east of the main summit, cross the little plateau of the upper Coire Liath and drop directly down the continuation fault line close by the side of the Pyramid. We might well get avalanched on this line, but at least there were no .major crags en route which could prove fatal in a slide.

In thick mist and ungodly silence we swayed down through the blanket of new snow. At the col we made our plan. I would go first and would call the others to follow one at a time after 50 or 60m. I dropped into the gully, quickly scraped a pit and did a quick shear test. Nothing happened. Perhaps the snowfall had channelled down this gully, and had therefore deposited itself in a more stable manner. For a few steps I waded down, then

decided that I might cause less disturbance to the snowpack if I did a surface 'bum-slide'.

Soon we were all doing likewise about 50m apart, and we arrived on the plateau in much better spirits. I now became hopeful that the continuation fault would also be safe, but we adopted the same precautions, only now we couldn't glissade because of outcrops and the absence of a runout. With much wallowing we were soon down below the Pyramid. We passed the point where we had begun traversing towards the climb seven hours previously, but the morning's steps were now completely covered over.

Still well ahead and now sure of success, I commenced another sitting glissade. But as my momentum rose, a glance to the side made me strangely aware that the slope was moving as well as myself. A second later a mass of snow hit me from behind, throwing me forwards, and together we slid another 10 or 15m downslope. I picked myself up and spotted a thin windslab fracture above my slide. Even here, at 600m in altitude and well below the freezing level, the slopes were no longer safe. If nothing else my little slide justified every ounce of fear and caution we had applied since the top of the route.

The touch of Liathach's tangled heather braes brought us back into the land of the living. Down in Glen Torridon it was just another damp March evening.

CAUGHT IN THE LANDSLIDE

Only a few unlucky people will be struck by an avalanche from above. The loss of a father, his son and a friend, taken by a massive natural avalanche while walking in the bottom of Coire na Tulaich on the Buachaille Etive Mor in February 1995, is the most tragic such example, but such eventualities are relatively

Liathach
Winter Descent
● ● ● Route followed 8 March 1995

Top 983
Col
Gully 1
Gully
Spidean A'Choire Leith 1055
Main Ridge
Pyramid Buttress
N
0 250
Metres
Plateau
Fault
Avalanche
Coire Liath More
Summer approach path
To Glen Torridon

uncommon. In 95 per cent of cases, the victims will themselves trigger a slab or cornice collapse and will therefore be somewhere near the top of the avalanche debris when it settles. Of the 458 folk involved in reported avalanches from 1985–86 to 1996–97, only forty-eight were actually buried, and in fact most injuries and fatalities are sustained during the falls resultant from an avalanche. Provided the fall-line is free from crags or sheet ice, there isevery opportunity for a happy outcome provided victims can quell panic and make intuitive reactions during the slide.

When avalanched for the first time the predominant emotion is one of total helplessness, yet it is the worst possible reaction to abandon one's fate to chance. Several practical things can be done, which in themselves foster some slight sense of control, besides much improving survival chances:

1 Spread the legs and arms to enable the body to rotate into an uphill position on the slab. This reduces the chance of the chest and face being buried, and of suffocation in the event of ending up in a totally inverted position.

2 Raise the heels and hands to prevent the limbs from getting caught under the snow.

3 If falling free over outcrops tuck the head, knees and arms into the chest to minimise the chance of head injuries

4 At the moment of being overwhelmed by the mass of snow, push the elbows out in front of the chest and cup the hands over the face. This will simultaneously prevent crushing of the chest by the snow, allow a small cavity of air to remain around the face, and prevent the swallowing of dry snow which could cause suffocation. For this last reason a final despairing yell is not advisable: keep the mouth shut tight!

To the Rescue: For anyone seeing a companion swept down by an avalanche, it is vital to realise that unless the victims are located and dug out within a few minutes their survival chances are very low.

1 Before rushing headlong towards the debris, rescuers should consider their own safety. Although a windslab avalanche usually clears a slope of all its unstable snow, the possibility of further avalanches should be considered. Rescuers should if possible keep off remaining areas of unbroken snow and watch out for further avalanches from above.

2 The initial search area should be defined by marking the point where the victim was avalanched and working in the debris area directly below this spot.

3 Even if there are several witnesses to the avalanche, everyone should spend some 10 to 15 minutes in the first search of the debris before a team is sent off to get a rescue.

4 Rescuers should not be deterred from vigorous probing of the debris with axes or ski-sticks for the fear of injuring a buried victim.

5 If any of the rescuers has a mobile phone, a call to the emergency services should be made if the first search has failed to find all the victims. However, avoid calling for the rescue team too early, because it is not unusual for everyone to be dug out without serious injuries.

6 A lone rescuer must spend at least half an hour searching before going for help. Once the decision is made to get help, the subsequent time delay means that the victim is unlikely to be alive when eventually found.

7 On finding anyone unconscious in avalanche debris, the rescuer's first actions should always be to open the victim's airway by tilting the head back and clearing any snow or loose matter out of the mouth and throat; then check if he or she is breathing. Subsequently the normal sequence of emergency resuscitation should be followed: rescue breathing (mouth-to-mouth) and

checking for pulse. As soon as a victim is breathing unaided, he or she should be rolled into the recovery position and monitored for pulse and breathing every couple of minutes.

8 Anyone dragged out of avalanche debris after being trapped for more than a few minutes is likely to be hypothermic and should be treated as such.

23 FEBRUARY 1995:
NEVER DROP YOUR GUARD

The week had been wild in every respect, with big winds and massive volumes of snow. We had to seek a challenging route which stayed well clear of any steep slopes or gullies, and the Forcan Ridge of The Saddle fitted our requirements. One can stick to the ridge crest all the way to the summit. With a fit party we had made the top in four hours from the road, this despite heavy work in trailbreaking on the lower slopes. The instructional part of our day was wholly focused on the snow conditions. We dug little snow pits, performed telling shear tests, and I verbally justified our choice of route at every opportunity. At the summit we sat and enjoyed our lunch in dull, calm conditions with the temperature just below freezing.

I recounted to my three students how I had been here two months ago at New Year when the snow slopes were similarly unstable. Another party had arrived and casually decided to descend the south-east slope direct off the summit instead of following the low-relief ridge which curves away to the south. Their leader had taken six steps down the slope when he stopped suddenly; ten seconds later he was back at the summit trig point, having triggered a huge slide of soft windslab – on examination a fracture line was found to have run diagonally downslope from his last boot-

mark, and had released the avalanche just where the ground steepened (see Plate 8.2).

'That just shows how easy it is to walk into trouble,' I burbled between mouthfuls of fruit-cake. 'So today, of course, we are going to follow the curving ridge.' And down the ridge we went.

'We can't be sure about the snow even here, so I'll go first. You follow one at a time when I shout,' I commanded. I worked my way down in short zig-zags. Once off the convex breast of the ridge my confidence returned, and I called the others. The ridge soon levelled into the sloping floor of Coire Mhalagain. With the steep stuff over, and feeling pleased as Punch that all my judgements had paid off, I gathered my group for a final debrief.

'We've beaten the conditions today; it's been a model of how to deal with avalanche risk,' I proudly concluded, and adjusted my instructor's hat. Off we marched. A little bowl of snow no more than five metres deep developed to our left, and the recent release of tension made me want to jump into it.

'I'll just have a bit of fun here,' I announced, and took two steps towards the hollow. Ready to leap and a metre from the edge, I suddenly felt the whole snowpack give from under me. A second later and I was deposited at the bottom of the bowl, jammed between two cabinet-sized blocks of snow, either of which could have crushed me. My students helped me out, their bemusement turning to amusement as they realised that I was unhurt. I was dumbfounded that a 10m length of snowbank could have collapsed in such an innocuous place. We examined the remains of the edge and discovered a concealed cavity running under the whole length of the snowdrift, probably the remnants of a former cornice.

Red-faced and apologetic I faced my smirking students. The talking was over, and the mountain had won again. It always does.

Plate 8.4 *The layered profile; windslab lying over old névé on The Saddle (Martin Welch)*

9: FROM TOWER RIDGE TO CITADEL

SCOTTISH WINTER CLIMBING:
ITS EVOLUTION AND TECHNIQUES

THE EARLY SPIRIT

Easter 1903 on the Cuillin of Skye

'...the writer has a vivid recollection of being spread-eagled and clinging with every available portion of his anatomy to the ice-covered 'easy' ridge of the Inaccessible Pinnacle, while the level hail drove fiercely past, expecting every moment to see his legs raised in the air, his hobnailers crack together once or twice like the tails of a pennon, and then, converted along with his three companions, like the crew of the Hesperus, into icicles, hurled away into Coruisk on the wings of the arctic blast. Needless to say, we did not get up.'[1]

(Harold Raeburn)

The climbing potential of Scotland's mountains in winter was not recognised until the last decade of the Victorian era. English climbers had played a dominant role in the golden era of alpine exploration through the middle of the nineteenth century, yet they cast not so much as a single northward glance upon the availability of snow- and ice-mountaineering within Britain's own shores.

The neglect was not deliberate, however: in the nineteenth century, the Highlands were as remote to London-based members of the English Alpine Club as the Alps themselves, particularly in winter, and it is therefore unlikely that the existence of vast quantities of snow and ice on British hills was even realised

by climbers living south of the Border. Furthermore, this was the era in which mountains were being climbed for the first time in any season, so a winter ascent carried no additional relevance or kudos, while our own hills could not compare in scale with the giants of the Alps. Nor was there yet a tradition of seeking difficult routes for their own sake. Rock-climbing was in its infancy, while mountaineers saw the summit as the all-important goal and felt no obligation to seek out steep cliffs unless they formed unavoidable obstacles en route to the top, a circumstance unknown in Scotland except on the Cuillin.

The development of snow- and ice-climbing on home hills was therefore left for a generation which in the first place perceived an added challenge in the winter ascent, and then sought difficulty for its own intrinsic merit. Most importantly, it awaited a band of committed Scottish climbers, a caucus of local activists wherein great deeds might be stimulated, and a tradition established. The formation of the Scottish Mountaineering Club (SMC) in 1889 brought together such a nucleus, within which new ideas were quickly accepted and fermented – and once the spirit was kindled, it burned brightly and undiminished for the next twenty years. With remarkable speed a level of technical achievement in winter climbing was attained that was not surpassed until the late 1930s; it was as if the latent talent of Scots mountaineers suddenly erupted in an attempt to make up for lost time. Certain individuals played a key role in the new movement: William Naismith at the outset, then Norman Collie and later Harold Raeburn, undoubtedly the outstanding pre-1914 pioneer.

A schism within the SMC membership quickly became apparent between the 'ultramontanes' and the 'salvationists' – in other words, the true climbers who revelled most in the physical difficulties, and the scenic mountaineers who gloried primarily in the views. In fact these two groups have co-existed amicably in the club up to the present day.

The winter faces of Ben Lui, Ben Cruachan and Stob Ghabhar on Blackmount became initial testing grounds for the new mode of expression, and interest quickly spread to Glencoe, Lochnagar and the icy crown of Ben Nevis itself. The good news travelled fast, and by 1897 the English Alpine Club itself was holding an Easter meet in the Highlands, its interest aided to a degree by the completion of the West Highland railway to Fort William in 1894. Even among the tiny fraternity of mountaineers, the first Scottish activists were a bold avant-garde: not only did they go out of their way to seek the deepest chasms and steepest crags, but they had to do it without guides, and this was a complete departure from normal alpine practice. In the words of a modern commentator: 'There is no doubt that the pre-war ice climbers were regarded by the bulk of their contemporaries as the most Desperate and Dangerous Radicals – and that they achieved as much as they did under the circumstances was remarkable.'[2]

What, then, were their specific achievements? The web of elegant face-climbs on the north-east face of Ben Lui typified the first wave of exploration between 1890 and 1892, snow routes without complication, but exposed at angles of up to 55 degrees, and descended as well as climbed by many early parties.

Then came forays into short but steeper rocky clefts where ice-draped chock-stones might be encountered. The ice-fall in the Upper North-East Couloir of Stob Ghabhar was investigated as early as 1892 and climbed direct in 1897, while the Black Shoot on Beinn Eunaich (by Cruachan) became an infamous challenge, its winter ascent repulsing a host of suitors until December 1900. Retreats from this type of climb were often problematic, as Gibson and Robertson discovered in 1891 when they were rebuffed by a chimney cleft on Beinn a' Bhuiridh in the Cruachan range, having already surmounted a 10m frozen waterfall: 'One man had to be let down by the rope, and the last man had to jump the thirty feet! This he did, sinking into soft snow up to his waist.'[3]

With this grounding of experience, the great ridges of Ben Nevis were tackled with astonishing élan. Between 1894 and 1896, the Tower and Castle Ridges and the Castle and North-East buttresses received their first winter ascents, together with the North-East Ridge of the nearby Aonach Beag. Tower Ridge was repeated no fewer than five times at Easter 1896, its status quickly demoted to that of a 'trade route'. These were routes of great length, commitment and variability of condition, grade III or occasionally grade IV by modern reckoning and still retaining their aura of difficulty in the present day. The pioneers had no hesitations in tackling steep, snow-covered rock. Thus, J. H. Gibson raced up the sensationally

Overleaf Plate 9.1 *The North-East Face of Ben Nevis: crucible of Scottish snow and ice climbing, with the CIC Hut at bottom left*

Plate 9.2 *Early pioneering style on steep snow: party moving together 5m apart on manila hemp rope and belayed direct to the leader's ice axe (A.E. Robertson/SMC Collection)*

Plate 9.3 *Early pioneering gear c1909: ice axe (wood-shafted and over 1m in length), nailed boots, manila hemp rope, wide-brimmed hat and sundry other accoutrements (SMC Collection)*

exposed East Ridge of the Inaccessible Pinnacle at Easter 1893, clearing fresh snow off the holds as he climbed. Nor did bad weather dampen the fire, as when Raeburn attempted the pinnacle in a veritable whirlwind ten years later.

Equally the yawning gully lines on the big cliffs were not ignored for long. Many were straightforward save for the cornice, but in March 1893 Douglas and Gibson skirmished with a climb of an altogether different calibre in the north-east corrie of Lochnagar, their presumptuous attempt being halted by a near-vertical 60m headwall. The Douglas-Gibson Gully, as it became known, waited until 1950 for its first ascent by Tom Patey and 'Goggs' Leslie, and was initially regarded as Scotland's first grade V winter climb. Harold Raeburn's two great gully routes were Crowberry Gully on the Buachaille Etive Mor,

climbed under true winter garb in April 1909, and Green Gully on the Ben climbed in April 1906. Both are still considered grade IV, even with modern equipment. These epoch-making ascents remained clouded in obscurity and their records were only 'discovered' around 1970, the routes having been wrongly credited to parties in 1936 and 1937 respectively in SMC guidebooks to Glencoe and Ben Nevis.

The early pioneers were therefore formidably competent in every aspect of the winter climbing art. Furthermore, their achievements were founded wholly on personal skill and fitness, because the available equipment and rope techniques of the era were primitive in the extreme. Parties carried the same full-length ice-axes as were used for winter walking, and manila hemp rope in the length of 6 or 12m per man, plus 18m for the leader.

They wore 'hob-nailers', which were labourers' boots with clumsy, wide sole welts, but adapted for climbing use by tacking 'clinker' nails to the sole edges.

Belays were effected solely by driving the axe shaft full-length into the snow and hitching the rope around the head (Plate 9.2), or by the climber bracing the body on a good rock ledge. Waist and shoulder belays were unknown prior to the 1920s. The security of these methods was tenuous in the extreme, and neither the wooden ice-axe shaft nor the rope itself could withstand the strain of a long fall.

With so little rope, the early climbers either moved together or proceeded by short staccato pitches. The system afforded the seconds a degree of security, but left the leader under no illusion as to the consequence of a slip. Yet during the first twenty-five years of Scottish winter mountaineering, there was not a single serious accident.

The speed of early ascents was further testimony to the skill of the pioneers. Collie led the Tower Ridge in a brisk five hours, and Raeburn acquitted himself on Crowberry Gully in 1909 in a mere four hours twenty minutes, despite a rope of three and an alarming avalanche incident. These would be respectable times even for today's climber, aided by crampons, two curved-picked axes and the tracks of previous parties to show the way – on stepcutting first ascents a century ago, they were quite incredible. Of course, the overall speed stemmed partially from the absence of delay in belaying operations, whereas over half the duration of modern ascents of these routes might be spent in searching and digging out solid anchors. The early practitioners had minimal security, but this was more than compensated for by skill and speed. Their example is too often ignored in the present era: we tend to be preoccupied with security of attachment, and thus sacrifice

the rhythm and style which are equally important to ultimate safety and success on the classic winter climbs.

The style of ice-climbing which developed prior to 1914 remained little altered in Scotland for the next fifty years. Dependent solely upon the nailed-boot edge and straight-picked axe, the original art was gloriously simple, but demanded excellent balance and superb precision in the wielding of the axe to cut steps. Long ice pitches also called for great arm and wrist stamina, although success lay in the conservation of energy through skill rather than in brute strength. Raeburn expressed it thus: '... the cultivation of coconut-like biceps by any of the modern methods of muscle-growing may possibly be of some use to climbers. But man, after all, is not a monkey, and the mountaineer, even though the angles approach 80 degrees, travels mainly by his feet.'[4]

Indeed, the straight-picked axe was simply not reliable for a pull on the arm when it was driven into steep ice. Thus, footsteps had to be cut in order to support the full bodyweight, with the axe shaft being used merely as a prop or strut for balance across the body. Where the angle steepened beyond the limit of foot balance, handholds as well as steps had to be hewn for support. This was necessary on Green Gully's first ascent where pitches of 70–80 degrees were encountered, an angle which seems quite perpendicular when spread-eagled on an ice-sheet. The immense labour of chopping out four holds for every move at this steepness with a metre-long axe can only be realised by a personal trial. Nor did the deepening of steps serve to improve security or ease the strain, because at 70 degrees the knees and elbows tend to interfere with balance.

The good stepcutter always thought ahead and fashioned two or three holds above before making each move. While the arm swung and flailed the axe, the feet had to remain absolutely still and steady in their holds, the heels held horizontally to maintain the grip of the nail edges, and the weight pivoting on the calf muscles which likewise were flexed in support. Sustaining of this position over long shifts was tantamount to static torture in all save the fittest.

By 1914, the hardest Scottish ice-climbs surpassed anything that had been achieved in the Alps in terms of pure technical difficulty, while the standard of winter buttress climbing was hardly a whit less advanced. The culmination of this great era was the first winter ascent of the Observatory Ridge (IV) on Ben Nevis on a snowy day in April 1920 by Raeburn, Mounsey and Goggs in a startling five hours. Goggs was sufficiently enraptured by the climbing and the situation to write later:

We inhabited:

'The palaces of Nature, whose vast walls
Have pinnacled in clouds their snowy
    scalps,
And enthroned Eternity in icy halls
Of cold sublimity'[5]

Such was the early inspiration of the Scottish winter climbers.

RETRENCHMENT AND RENAISSANCE

At 7.30pm on 17 March 1935, in Glover's Chimney, Ben Nevis, Graham Macphee was leading the crux by diffused moonlight, with George Williams belaying:

'I could now but dimly see him as he moved slowly and steadily upwards. Now and then, when in clearing holds of ice, his ice-axe struck the bare rock, I could see sparks fly out. Above the chockstone the conditions became harder. The entire chimney was sheeted with ice, and there was no place where the leader could take a proper rest, much less to where he could bring me up. He had

now run out over 30m of line, and the situation was very sensational. It was a thrilling experience watching the leader's figure dimly silhouetted against the sky as he got nearer the Tower Gap. By superb climbing he reached the Gap and announced his arrival there in no uncertain manner.'[6]

This ascent, together with that of SC Gully on Stob Coire nan Lochan in 1934, re-established the vogue for winter climbing which had lain dormant for the previous fifteen years. The lull in activity was largely due to the heavy toll of climbing talent and energy taken by World War I; moreover it is understandable that after the war experience, those remaining of the older generation no longer saw any worth in hazardous pioneering. There was also a series of mild winters in the 1920s and early 1930s, and a lack of inspiring personalities capable of initiating a new movement, Raeburn having died in 1926.

When the revival did gather impetus, the basic style and techniques of the pre-war period were reinstated intact. A distinctive 'Scottish' tradition was thus perpetuated, and such modifications of ropework and equipment as were effected did not threaten its essential quality. The changes were individually important, however, and owed much to the innovative attitude of the group of activists who emerged within the Glasgow section of the Junior Mountaineering Club of Scotland (JMCS), led by Bill Mackenzie and Bill Murray. First, ice-axe shafts were shortened in length from 100 to 85cm, and slater's picks just 35cm in length were procured. Both were carried by the leader, the short pick for cutting on pure ice and the longer axe-adze for easier angled névé. In particular, the short pick greatly increased the potential scope of winter ice-work, as nicks just sufficient to take the fingertips and a nailed-boot edge could be cut on steep ice.

Then, rope lengths were greatly increased

to 25m per man and 45m for the leader in order to handle long-sustained runouts. After their all-night retreat from Garrick's Shelf on the Buachaille (see Chapter 7), Mackenzie and Murray's parties always carried a couple of rock pitons, karabiners and slings, but only for the occasional belay or in case of retreat. By this time boots with narrow welts were especially manufactured for mountaineers.

With these few changes, the existing routes were repeated with aplomb, and the group went on to pioneer several new lines in Glencoe. In particular, Garrick's Shelf on the Crowberry Ridge represented a step forward in commitment and vision, meriting a technical rating of 6 under the modern grading system. They were also climbing regularly at all times during the season rather than only during the more kindly climes of late March and April when most early pioneering was achieved. However, the activities of Murray, Mackenzie and company were viewed with alarm by the rather moribund climbing establishment of the day; twenty-five years later, Murray remembered that, while attempting new ice routes in the thirties, he was: '... *damned in official letters from the JMCS for bringing Scottish climbing into disrepute – that is, by trying climbs that were not thought justifiable. Indeed, when I first produced my slater's hammer it was denounced as exhibitionism. Nowadays no such mistakes are made.*'[7]

Yet while these modest advances were being wrought in the face of entrenched conservatism in Scotland, the Alps were experiencing a revolution in techniques, attitudes and achievement. The great ice walls of the Bernese Oberland, the Pennine Alps and the Mont Blanc range fell during the late 1920s and early 1930s to such illustrious exponents as Wilo Welzenbach and Armand Charlet. Then the awesome, mixed north faces of the Jorasses, the Matterhorn and, of course, the Eiger were tackled and conquered. For length

and sustained technicality, these routes outstripped the Scottish standards. A new spirit of extremism, coupled with competitive rivalry between the national groupings in the Alps, stimulated this wave of development, but it was highly dependent on the wholesale acceptance of new equipment and techniques – rock and ice pitons for belays, protection and direct aid, short axes and northwall ice-hammers and, most importantly, the use of crampons.

Ten-point crampons were already in widespread use in the Alps in 1930, even by the visiting British as well as by the continentals. For speed over glacier ice and on long medium-angle snow faces, they were regarded as indispensable. Twelve-point models with two front claws were made by Grivel in 1932, and then by Stubai; they were used with crucial effect on the first ascent of the Eiger North Face by Heckmair and Vorg in 1938. On ice-fields of between 50 and 60 degrees in angle, the front points allowed them literally to 'run up' the slope, relying on their axe picks for balance, thus pre-dating the so-called 'front point revolution' in Scotland by thirty years.

However, crampons were disdained in Scotland for a variety of reasons. Availability and expense constituted a restriction for some – it is easily forgotten that many climbers of the 1930s were sorely pressed to afford more than a rope and an ice-axe – but more importantly, there was an affinity for the stepcutting art, and a belief amongst both old and young that it was the natural foundation of winter-climbing skill. Raeburn had commented: '... an alpine climber who starts by using crampons and employs these on every occasion will never learn to be a safe and competent mountaineer...'[8] – an assertion which retains a certain relevance today.

Stepcutting was regarded as a subtle craft to be applied with loving care, as Bill Murray explained: 'The craft used varied accordingly

Plates 9.4a and b *Stepcutting on a 1950s ascent on Lochnagar (Bill Brooker)*
a) With the adze (note the handhold for balance)

b) With the pick in hard watery ice (no wristloops were used for support while cutting)

to the quality of the ice: black, white, green, blue, brittle and watery, they all had their quirks, which had to be learnt until one could tell them apart at a glance and cut accordingly.'[9] And crampons could spoil the purity of that art, interfering with the communion between the climber and his medium. Besides, there was also the practical aspect, whereby the Scots maintained that on steep ice above 60 degrees – an angle rarely tackled in the Alps, and where steps had to be cut whether the mountaineer was wearing crampons or not – crampons tended to sit awkwardly in the holds, while on thinly iced rock they could not nearly match the precision of the nailed boot.

Only J. H. B. Bell of the great pre-war Scots climbers flirted seriously with the new alpine methods. He often wore crampons, and in March 1939 he made a rendezvous with Murray for an attempt on Centre Post Direct (now a good grade V) on Creag Meagaidh,

'armed with a big bagful of sawn-off curtain rods', their tops ringed and bottoms filed, with the intention of 'nailing' the steeper ice in the best Teutonic style. Murray, the purist, was amused at the daftness of the idea, and must have harboured a genuine fear that Bell's home-made ice pitons would simply buckle under load. In the safety of posterity, we might be disappointed that bad weather prevented their test. Of all the ethical considerations, the notion of using pitons for aid on rock and ice was the most stoutly resisted among both the vanguard and the old guard before 1939.

So, these experiments apart, the Scottish tradition was little altered and thus became isolated from events abroad, its style unique and distinctive – indeed, a separate sport from alpine climbing, no less skilled, certainly more admirable in its ethics, but undoubtedly a major step behind in the scale of its achievement. After 1945, when a new generation turned its eyes to the near-vertical buttresses and gullies that were as yet unclimbed in Scotland, the pre-war style was found wanting in both technique and security. Further compromises of tradition had to be conceded for the next advance to proceed.

Perhaps the most significant legacy of the burst of activity in the late 1930s was the publication of Bill Murray's *Mountaineering in Scotland* in 1947, encapsulating within its pages all the thrill and beauty of winter climbing. The 1930s climbers had little inspiration from the great deeds of pre-1914, which were either wholly unknown at that time or were hidden in obscure journal sources; but now a fine literary tradition had been created, and was available for the eager consumption of the post-war generation.

1950–70: A FRUITION; THEN IMPASSE

The following is from the 'new climbs' section of the 1954 SMC Journal:

'Raven's Gully – found Very Severe and climbed by H. MacInnes (CDMC) and C. Bonington (JMCS London) on 14th February 1953.

Crampons used on pitch 4, which, using two pitons, required 1½ hours. Socks used above this although crampons used on the final slopes. The chock-stone in pitch 5 was lassoed, allowing pendulum action, and saving hours of struggle as the pitch was very much iced. Two pitons used on pitch 6. The ascent took 6½ hours. 10 hours or more might easily be needed.'[10]

These few clipped phrases capture all the skill, cunning and epic atmosphere of the new wave of post-war pioneering; and the wearing of crampons, the acceptance of rock pitons, and the use of socks, lassoes and pendules, all point to the feeling of being prepared to break

loose from the mould of conventional winter tactics. With its series of chock-stone pitches, Raven's Gully is a notoriously unaccommodating route, and its perpetrator Hamish MacInnes was above all others the one personality who was ever willing to stretch the bounds of convention and plough his own innovative furrow. His ethics and methods were controversial at times, but he had a significant influence in accelerating the changes in techniques that were needed to tackle the great outstanding lines on even terms.

Raven's was the first major grade V gully to be climbed in the west, and was undoubtedly the harbinger of a stride forward in standards; but it was accompanied by a series of equally significant buttress climbs, evidence that climbers were prepared not just to extend the technical repertoire of winter climbing but to venture boldly onto new terrain in search of the metaphorical Grail. As Tom Patey wrote in 1960: '... All conditions were (now) regarded as climbing conditions. It merely became a question of adapting the techniques to meet the prevailing conditions – névé, powder snow, verglassed rocks, frozen vegetation etc.'[11]

Scabbard Chimney and Crowberry Ridge Direct in Glencoe, and Scorpion, Mitre Ridge and Eagle Ridge in the Cairngorms were representative of the new attitude. All are still grade V, and Eagle Ridge is a benchmark of grade VI under the modern grading system. Under the inspiration of Patey, Cairngorm mixed climbing was launched as a distinct brand of winter climbing that has warranted a separate niche even to the present day (see Chapter 12); but over in Glencoe and on Ben Nevis it was the ice gullies which posed the obvious challenges.

Ice-climbing style saw two main developments in the 1950s: most important was the gradual acceptance of crampons, and in particular front-point models – though to a degree this was enforced by the introduction of vibram-soled boots in the 1950s and the declining availability of nailed models. However, the Aberdonian school stuck loyally to nails throughout the decade, finding them more adept for their buttress excursions yet perfectly adequate in the gullies. Others were gradually converted to the real benefits of crampons on pure snow and ice, in particular on medium-angled ground where crampons enabled swift, continuous movement without the labour of step-cutting. Two styles of cramponnage can be identified, although in reality they have always been interchanged according to the demands of the terrain.

The French technique, using the sole flat on the slope, maximises the use of the sole of the crampon, involving awkward ankle flexion but giving better grip and saving strain on the calves; when expertly applied it is elegant and stylish, but it requires a hard, reliable snow surface.

The alternative German method is effectively the front-pointing technique that we know today, and it therefore needed the twelve-point (or 'lobster claw') crampons. The front-pointing technique is stressful on the calves, but more adaptable to the wet or loose snow which is so regularly encountered in Scotland. By kicking steps with the toes and thrusting the ice-axe shaft down into the soft snow as a prop, an admirable stability can be achieved, which is further improved with a second axe. By 1965 even Patey was converted to crampon technique for middle-grade ground, a winter traverse of the Cuillin Ridge being otherwise inconceivable and of which he wrote: '...Without twelve-point crampons we would have needed to have cut thousands of steps and might easily have spent the better part of a week on the climb.'[12]

On steeper ice, however, steps remained obligatory because of the unreliability of the straight-picked axe for traction – though the idea of spiking the pick above the head for a quick pull was undoubtedly tempting. Hamish Hamilton had tried it, and peeled off at the top of one of the pitches in Crowberry Gully in 1936. It is therefore surprising that the dropped or curved-pick principle was not considered as a solution to this obvious inadequacy, especially since axes were modified in other ways. For instance, as early as 1947 MacInnes made an all-metal hammer-axe which became known as 'the message': fabricated from tool steel, it was a weighty but effective ice-breaker, yet the pick was straight. Other leading climbers replaced the long axe and slater's pick combination of the thirties in favour of a short 50cm axe, used for all cutting, plus a heavy hammer for pitonning, with a short, pointed hook that could be used if the axe was lost.

A more significant departure was the use of ice pitons for climbing steep ground. These were simply long metal blades 15–30cm in length, hammered directly into the ice and used for immediate protection or rope tension while the next steps were cut. They greatly facilitated the climbing of steeper ice, enabling two-handed cutting under tension; but they were almost useless in holding a fall. The commitment of the leader on pure ice pitches therefore remained undiminished, as Joe Brown found out when an ice bulge fell away under his weight two pitches up Point Five Gully during an early attempt in January 1956. So too did everything else – ice-piton protection, belays and his belayer, Nat Allen – and *en masse* they tumbled some 45m to a fortuitously soft landing at the bottom, where they were brought to a halt by their third man who was anchored at the foot of the gully. The near demise of 'the human fly' on Nevis ice remains a fond legend among Scots climbers.

Two methods of climbing steep ice during

the 1950s and 1960s can be identified. Both were employed on the first ascent of Zero Gully in February 1957 by MacInnes, Patey and Nicol, this being the first of the major gullies to fall. Patey led the first four pitches in nails, and thus was forced to take the fullest assistance from ice pitons on the vertical bits: '... The technique is to take tension through an ice piton placed as high as possible above the climber until the next few handholds have been cut. Then, hanging on with one hand, a higher piton is inserted and the lower one removed for further use. This is all very delicate work, as any outward pull on the piton will have the maximum result.'

Contrast MacInnes out in the lead on pitch five using front-pointers and the 'message'. Patey observed: '...In went the first ice piton, and with a violent heave Hamish got a crampon level where his nose had been. The only indication of his passing was a large bucket-hold every six feet.' Then, after a pause: 'All that was now visible of Hamish was the soles of his boots outlined against the sky – an apparent contradiction of the laws of gravity until you realised that his weight was supported by the angled points on the front of his crampons.'[13]

The crampon method thus enabled holds to be cut at wider spacing, and linked by a few quick 'kick-ins' of the front points, with less dependence on the pitons.

The security of belaying on these new routes was improved from minimal to marginal by reinforcing the vertical axe with ice pitons, and wherever possible by the excavation of rock-piton anchors. But the direct axe belay was proved inadequate on near-vertical ground by a series of accidents, most tragically the death of three English climbers who fell out of Zero in 1958 when their wooden axe shafts broke under load. This incident stimulated MacInnes to manufacture a much

stronger, metal-shafted axe in 1964.

Stronger and more supple nylon ropes replaced hemp lines after the war, and on hard routes there was also a shift away from direct belays to the indirect waist belay where the belayer is tied separately to the anchors. Prior to 1970, climbers were largely taught by experience and their achievements cannot be properly appreciated without an awareness of the singularly rudimentary protection techniques that were available to them. Indeed, the lack of protection was consciously accepted as part of the game.

Innovative technique was stimulated during the 1950s by the regular visits of Scots climbers to the Alps where mechanised climbing methods were fast evolving and by increasing rivalry between the various groups of activists for the 'plum' lines. Thus the strict practices of tradition were slowly levered open. However, the door was not allowed to swing beyond a certain point, and the hinges stuck at the first ascent of the biggest plum of all: after countless attempts, Point Five Gully was eventually sieged into submission by Ian Clough and party over a five-day period in January 1959, fixed ropes, expansion-bolt belays and etriers all being liberally employed. The shabby style of the ascent caused a furore, as it was considered that the grand tradition of winter climbing in Scotland was being threatened in a competitive free-for-all. However, Scottish climbing was spared a protracted ethical debate. A swifter and far more effective response came on the cliffs themselves in a brilliant series of ascents by Jimmy Marshall and Robin Smith of Edinburgh, Marshall reaping the fruits of a ten-year winter apprenticeship in the JMCS, and Smith unleashing a tidal wave of youthful talent and enthusiasm onto the climbing scene.

In 1959, Marshall accounted for Minus Two Gully on Nevis and Smith's Gully on

Creag Meagaidh, both a notch steeper than Point Five, while Smith made ascents of the Orion Face via Epsilon Chimney and the Tower Face of the Comb, the latter only recently rediscovered as a fine grade VI mixed climb. Then, in superb conditions in February 1960, they combined their abilities for a devastating eight-day campaign on Nevis, during which six new routes were made, including the futuristic face climbs of Orion Face Direct and Gardyloo Buttress, plus a highly significant second ascent of Point Five in a mere seven hours. Within two years, a new high-water mark was reached in Scottish winter climbing, and the sour taste of the Point Five saga was washed away.

The Marshall-Smith style struck a fair balance between modern technicality and traditional purism, their use of crampons and pitons being not such as to devalue the essential skill of ice-axe work. Thus the link with Murray and Raeburn was preserved, yet at a level of performance two grades higher than anything achieved before the war: theirs was a 'real' as opposed to a 'technical' advance in achievement. Looking back, Jimmy Marshall recalls:

'We were very aware that we were breaking new ground. Smith and I were leading a crusade, and from our Scottish experience we felt we could climb anything on ice. Our writings were specifically aimed to incite the young mountaineers of our day to get off their butts, climb the ice-bound walls, and discover this magnificent, wild and rewarding backwater of mountaineering.'[14]

So at the dawning of the 1960s, Scottish winter climbing was indeed a lion rampant. Once again, technical standards in both pure-ice and mixed-buttress climbing had moved ahead of those practised in the Alps, yet the distinctive character and adventure of the sport had been maintained. The introduction of a specific grading system for winter routes

in 1961 was a clear confirmation of the independence of the Scottish sport from other types of climbing. The original I–V scale (Fig 9.1) was never intended as more than a general guide, for a route's standard could vary widely according to the conditions, and the same system had to cover gully and buttress routes of wholly different character. Yet it captured imaginations and fairly assessed the overall 'grip factor' of a winter climb. Although more recently the ratings have been elaborated and extended, the basic I to V scale still covers the full range of classic snow and ice mountaineering, and remains the yardstick for any aspiring winter climber.

When the spindrift finally settled from the flurry of activity in the late fifties, a quiet period of consolidation was inevitable, especially with the tragic death of Smith in 1962. There was no shortage of new climbing ability, nor was there any lack of good winter conditions – though indeed, mild seasons have rarely deterred the determined winter pioneers. Rather, the potential for new routes other than those of extreme difficulty on the mainstream cliffs had been in large part exhausted, and the best energies were expended in repetitions of routes like Zero or Point Five, and the exploration of new cliffs, in particular Creag Meagaidh. The Marshall-Smith routes remained inviolate.

There were a few developments in equipment, most notably the manufacture of ice screws, which greatly improved security on steep ice; the widespread adoption of Salewa twelve-point crampons; and experiments with ice-daggers. However, these were not sufficient to enable a sustained advance onto the remaining unclimbed winter ground, and the 'high-water mark' was also an impasse. Thus the technical limits of the stepcutting art had been reached. The Curtain on Ben Nevis, climbed in 1965 by Jock Knight and Dave

Bathgate, although short, was one notable new climb, tackling a continuously steep ice-fall out on a face – but oh, the labour involved. After two hours' cutting up the last near-vertical pitch, Bathgate complained that his left arm was 'as strong as a wet newspaper'.[15] In similar vein, the pace of development was also wilting by the late 1960s. The time was ripe for a new style of attack which could liberate the last defences of the winter cliffs to successful attack. When it came, the change signalled a definite and irreversible break with tradition.

New Tools, New Angles

1970: The following is a passage from the *Guide to Winter Climbs, Ben Nevis and Glencoe,* by Ian Clough:

'The big bay above and to the right of Minus Three Gully and to the left of Observatory Ridge harbours some of the most ferocious ice climbs in Scotland. These routes brought standards of difficulty much in advance of anything previously achieved. After the passage of ten years, experts still regard them with considerable awe, and they give a challenge and inspiration for the future. Suitable only for the most expert of ice climbers.'

In 1970, an aura of impregnability still hung over the great Nevis ice routes. They inspired a reverent fear among leading climbers, and the guidebook's chilling assessment was stern warning that anyone else should stay well clear. Despite their shorter length, they were ranked as seriously as alpine north walls in commitment and danger.

That within the next five years this aura should be completely shattered was the remarkable result of one relatively minor technical adjustment: the idea of dropping the angle of the ice-axe pick by 3–4cm to give a better grip for a direct arm pull. In the late 1960s, Hamish MacInnes in Glencoe and John Cunningham at Glenmore Lodge training centre were independently scheming on ways to make stepcutting redundant. MacInnes's metal axes were already slightly drop-picked, but the incline was insufficient for reliable traction. Cunningham was experimenting with twin hand-daggers that could be jabbed overhead. In 1970, he and Bill March used the dagger system to make the first ascent of the Chancer, a vertical icicle on Hell's Lum crag, but a considerable amount of artificial aid from ice screws was still required.

The real catalyst for these formative ideas came with the visit of leading climber and equipment manufacturer Yvon Chouinard from the USA in February 1970. He brought with him prototype axes and hammers with curved picks and shafts 40–50cm in length, which he had developed in the USA, and demonstrated their effectiveness in meetings with both Cunningham and MacInnes. With front-point crampons and two curved pick-axes with loops fitted for wrist support, it was patently clear that vertical ice could be climbed without recourse to steps or artificial aid. Immediately, Cunningham was converted to the curved-pick school, while MacInnes promptly steepened the angle on his pick to 55 degrees to produce the alternative droop-picked 'terrordactyl' axe, which gave a similar grip but with a jabbing action rather than the smooth swing of the curved pick. Both had their minor practical problems, namely 'terrors' tended to bruise the knuckles on insertion, whereas curved picks were often difficult to extract. Within a year, however, 'terrors' were in commercial manufacture and Chouinard curved tools were being imported to Britain.

The subsequent upheaval in ice-climbing styles and standards has become known as the 'front-point revolution', but this is strictly a misnomer, for it was the change in axe design and the adoption of two axes that was critical; 'front-pointing' with one straight axe had long been practised on medium angles in both the Alps and Scotland. Nor is it fair to say that the revolution originated in Scotland, given Chouinard's vital role. In reality there was vertical ice waiting to be climbed in both Scotland and North America; several similar ideas had been germinating as to how to do it, and the common solution was forged by the meetings of 1970. However, Scotland undoubtedly became one of the major testing and forcing grounds for the new methods, for once leading the alpine countries in technical development.

Yet before they could be exploited to the full, there was an enormous psychological barrier to overcome, and this is easily overlooked by the young generation who have been weaned on front-points. To abandon all recourse to steps and to trust one's survival to the centimetre tips of axes and crampons, required a bold nerve, especially as early front-point ascents were done without wristloops to support the grip on the axes. As Cunningham and March wrote in 1972: '... a strong mental attitude is necessary, as the apparently precarious nature of the climbing induces "psyching out".'[16]

Whereas a ladder of steps could usually be reversed, it proved extremely difficult to climb down vertical ice on front-points. Also, an even greater localised strain is imposed on the calf, wrist and forearm muscles. With the new method, the climber has to weigh anchor and 'go for the top', which is contrary to the more cautious traditional climbing styles. An initial period of trial and mental adjustment was therefore understandable. The broader mass of climbers remained intrigued but sceptical, until a stunning series of fast repeats of the existing desperates by the avant-garde proved beyond doubt the potential and safety of the new style – Point Five Gully in 2¾ hours by Cunningham and March in 1971, second ascents of Orion Direct, Minus Two and Gardyloo Buttress by Mike Geddes, and then in 1973 the mind-boggling solos of both Point Five and Zero in a combined time of three hours by Ian Nicolson. Nicolson was attributed with the superbly laconic comment on this feat: 'You know, when you're doing these big icy climbs solo you sometimes wonder what might happen if you fell off!'[17]

By 1975 there were no waverers or lingering recalcitrants, and everybody was front-pointing with two axes. The simplicity and speed of the style, coupled with much improved protection methods, devalued Scotland's fearsome grade V's to classic status – indeed, the grading system was thrown into disarray. Pure ice routes became a full grade easier than their buttress equivalents, which benefited less from the new techniques. Either climbs like Point Five had to be downgraded, or the system needed to be extended above grade V. The debate continued until 1991 when the option of extension was taken, preserving the grade V status of the 1950s to 1960s classics. Even so, were routes like Orion Face and Gardyloo Buttress repeated nowadays with the styles and equipment used in 1960, they would doubtless be ranked in the region of grade VII under the new scale. The Dundonian team of Neil Quinn and Doug Lang was the last to resist the change, less from caution than from the conviction that front-pointing was somehow cheating; but when they took 17½ hours to cut steps up Hadrian's Wall Direct in 1973, they too were persuaded that the defence of traditional ethics was no longer relevant.

With the barriers of tradition removed, the numbers of winter climbers active on ice of grade III and above vastly increased, creating the new threat of overcrowding and queuing on routes. At the same time, the new style generated a fresh wave of winter pioneering on steeper and thinner ice. The climbing of Labyrinth Direct on Creag an Dubh Loch (without wristloops) by Bolton and Arnold (now graded as high as VII under the extended system) in 1972 and Minus One Gully (VI) on Ben Nevis by Crocket and Stead in 1974, signalled the final maturity of an eighty-year era of gully exploration. Both had been inspected by Marshall, but the right team had never arrived in the right conditions to enable an earlier step-cutting attack.

Front-pointing effectively brought the gully climbing era to a conclusion, and encouraged the popularisation of Scottish ice climbing as a sport; the new equipment also allowed a fresh evaluation of mixed climbing. Whilst public focus rested on the ice-climbing feats of the 1970s, a few leading activists were also using 'terrordactyls' to push buttress-climbing standards forwards. By using the drop-picked axes to hook on rock and turf and to torque in cracks, steeper and more sustained mixed routes could be attempted. Kenny Spence was the first to explore this potential, and his ascents of Central Buttress, Beinn Eighe (VI) and Sleuth, Mainreachan Buttress (VI) in the North-West in 1971 were definite advances, whose significance was not realised for several years.

On the Ben, attention turned from the gullies to the intervening faces and the front-point style proved greatly effective on the thin ice smears of the Nevis open slabs, 'terrordactyls' hooking particularly well on ice just an inch or so in thickness. Astronomy (VI) on the Orion Face climbed in 1971 with 'terrors' by MacInnes, Allen Fyffe and Spence was the first such excursion, combining thin ice and mixed climbing. This was the precursor of a series of similarly bold new climbs in the mid-1970s. Minus Two Buttress by Docherty and Muir, 1972 and Slav Route by Lang and Quinn, 1974 established the trend, and then, in the excellent conditions of 1978, new climbs were made on every major face of the mountain. Journey into Space by Con Higgins and Alan Kimber, Galactic Hitch-hiker by Mike Geddes and Con Higgins, Pointless by Nick Banks and Gordon Smith, Albatross by Geddes and Higgins, Pyschedelic Wall by Arthur Paul and Norrie Muir and Route II, Carn Dearg Buttress by Geddes and Alan Rouse set new standards in thin ice climbing. Long, bold runouts and poor belays were the hallmarks of these routes which are all now graded VI or VII. Then in 1979 Mick Fowler and Victor Saunders climbed the stupendous line of The Shield Direct on the right side of Carn Dearg Buttress, which was especially significant as the first route to be acknowledged as grade VI in the SMC Journal (it now rates grade VII, 7 under the extended grading system). Thin icing, intense competition and bold attitudes fuelled this wave of development, which consolidated the status of Ben Nevis as a crucible of ice climbing to rank with any in the world at that time.

Until the 1970s Scotland had enjoyed relative isolation in both the techniques and spirit of its winter climbing. However, the front-point technique was uniformly adopted worldwide, precipitating a decade of 'goulotte' climbing in the vertical couloirs of the Western Alps and giving the means to climb amazingly steep and long waterfall ice in Colorado, the Canadian Rockies and Norway, their scale dwarfing anything the Scottish mountains could offer. In the seventies, ice-climbing became a truly international sport in that national barriers could no longer withstand the tide of popularity and competition. So, just as its standards were reaching new heights, Scottish ice climbing was losing its aura of mystery and impregnability, and the limitations of scale and climate were soon to become apparent.

THE 1980s:
BACK TO THE BUTTRESSES

The winter climbs of tomorrow will be rock climbs under hellish conditions.
Jimmy Marshall, writing in 1961

In the mid-1970s a new dawn in mixed climbing was rising in the east, and the renaissance of the Aberdonian school was influential in swinging attention back to mixed buttress climbing. The relative lack of ice and abundant rime icing of the cliff faces in the drier Eastern Highlands, and the traditions established by Patey *et al* in the 1950s, made buttress-climbing the natural option on Lochnagar and the Cairngorm cliffs. The Aberdonians were also prepared to adapt their equipment to the

needs of climbing rimed granite faces where tiny rock edges are essential to progress. One of the mentors of the revival, Norman Keir, designed and used strap-on tricouni plates, known as 'trampons', on first ascents in the mid-seventies. The routes of Patey's generation were repeated, and young climbers such as Andy Nisbet and Dougie Dinwoodie then turned to the unclimbed bastions. A psychological breakthrough came in December 1977 when Andy Nisbet and Alf Robertson succeeded on Vertigo Wall on Creag an Dubh Loch, a route rated Very Severe in summer. Although the ascent was partially aided and protracted over two days, it brought down the barrier to a new wave of exploration. After Vertigo Wall, the Link Face on Lochnagar became the big prize, and was claimed by Nisbet and John Anderson in January 1979. From then until 1986 the Cairngorm cliffs presented a succession of 'last great problems', which were plucked one by one. Nisbet went on to establish himself as the keenest and most prolific mixed climber of his generation. Combining total personal determination with a choice of very able partners like Dinwoodie, Colin MacLean, Andy Cunningham and Brian Davison, Nisbet presided over Cairngorm developments for a decade. His Scottish new route output, which by 1998 was approaching 400, far outstrips that of Tom Patey.

However, the Aberdonian climbers by no means had things all their own way. A new breed of climbers from Edinburgh was pushing up Scottish rock-climbing standards in the late 1970s, and made a conscious decision to apply their technical ability in raising the stakes of mixed routes. Joining forces with the experienced hands of Kenny Spence, young climbers such as Murray Hamilton, Alan Taylor and Rab Anderson formed an able and competitive team. In the remarkable winter of 1980 they solved several big lines, culminating in the coveted first ascent of Citadel on Shelter Stone Crag by Hamilton and Spence using a single point of aid. Citadel became a touchstone of modern mixed climbing, long and sustained with a very hard crux. It is graded VII,8 under the modern system, and it was only in 1996 that it was climbed completely free in a single push.

Significant advances in equipment underpinned these developments. Rock protection methods vastly improved in the 1970s with the manufacture of wired nuts, 'hexentric' chocks and 'Friends' camming devices, and hard, mixed pitches could now be well protected provided the climber had the strength and energy to scrape out cracks and place the gear. As a result, the technical standards of the new mixed climbs far outstripped those on ice. With improvements in the design of axes – notably the 'reverse-curve' or 'banana-shaped' picks which first appeared in 1978 – some bizarre techniques could now be attempted. Experimentation in the torquing of axes in cracks gave birth to a new style of buttress climbing. No longer were holds cleared and then climbed with hands, as in the 1950s: instead, every part of the ice-axe – pick, adze and even the shaft – was used to effect weird and wonderful moves, and thus a whole new world of gymnastic pleasure was opened, far removed from the grim, tortuous struggles of traditional routes.

In similar vein, the long 'walk-in' was no more a requisite part of the winter's day. While the big multi-pitched mixed routes required outstanding commitment and prolonged engagement, and although lonely pioneering continued on the remotest crags of Braeriach and Beinn a'Bhuird, by far the most popular cliffs for mixed climbing in the eighties became those nearest to the road or ski-lift, where a 'quick fix' of fun and excitement was on offer. First the Northern Corries of Cairn Gorm, and

then Aonach Mor were subject to intimate scrutiny, and many short but testing climbs created, such as Fall Out Corner (VI) which have become popular testpieces.

Another influence from the increasingly competitive world of rock climbing was the application of specific training for hard, mixed routes: the days when a studied indifference to training was considered a virtue among leading climbers were over, and since 1980, mixed climbers have applied high and growing levels of stamina and power to the game. Successive one-arm lock-offs on torqued or embedded axes are now integral to success on the steepest routes.

The advancing technical demands of mixed routes eventually led to the introduction of a two-tier grading system in 1991. An overall route-rating on the scale I to VIII assessed the seriousness or sustained nature of the climb, and alongside it a purely technical grade on a scale 1 to 9 is given to show the gymnastic difficulty of the hardest moves. Thus a short, hard and well protected mixed climb such as Fall Out Corner rates VI, 7, whereas a long, poorly protected but technically reasonable ice route such as Slav Route on Ben Nevis is VI, 5.

If the initial thrust of modern mixed climbing was made in the Cairgorms, the movement soon spread to other areas. Central Grooves on Stob Coire nan Lochan (VII, 7) in Glencoe climbed by Spence and John 'Spider' MacKenzie in 1983 was one of the decade's finest routes, and 'Cubby' Cuthbertson and Arthur Paul's 1984 winter ascent of Guerdon Grooves on the Buachaille at a reputed grade VIII has not yet been repeated. Even Ben Nevis, generally considered inimical to mixed climbing techniques because of its compact, crackless rock, produced one of the hardest buttress routes, the great corner line of Centurion on Carn Dearg Buttress which was winter-climbed by Spence and

Plate 9.5 *The classic shot of Jimmy Marshall leading the first ascent Parallel Gully B (V) in 1958; a stunning Edinburgh raid on Aberdonian territory which finally persuaded the locals of the advantages of crampons over nails on ice (G. Tiso/SMC Collection)*

MacKenzie in 1986. The huge potential of the north-west Highlands was steadily developed from 1986 onwards, Andy Nisbet being the main progenitor of a series of extremely steep routes on Beinn Eighe's Triple Buttresses. Excellent demanding climbs were also found on accessible cliffs in the Southern Highlands such as The Cobbler, which had hitherto been ignored.

Indeed, the 1980s saw an explosion in the number of new routes, and most of them were mixed. With the idea of tackling pure rock climbs in winter garb now fully accepted, and because of the increasing numbers of activists and also a series of good winters, the floodgates opened. Whilst the majority of climbers visiting Scotland showed a continuing preference for the aesthetic beauty and technical simplicity of ice climbing, pioneering on ice became increasingly sporadic, being dependent on prolonged winter conditions and the supply of available icefalls. Only in the north-west Highlands was there a sustained spell of ice-climbing development in the eighties, a period greatly enlivened by the raiding visits of Mick Fowler. But it was on the buttresses where the main action took place, and where, in the 1980s, the supply of new lines seemed limitless. But would that potential itself become exhausted, and would mixed climbing ever gain the popular appeal of ice?

ONE CENTURY LATER

In 1989 Scottish winter mountaineering cele-
brated its centenary and could look back on a
chequered history stretching back to those first
forays of the bearded stalwarts of the Scottish
Mountaineering Club. By 1990 Scottish winter
climbing was no longer an isolated citadel of
either style or technical expertise as it had been
in 1960, standards in ice climbing worldwide
having advanced in leaps and bounds since
1970. Official visits by top French and Polish
climbers as long back as 1979 and 1980 had
opened the eyes of their Scottish hosts to this
uncomfortable truth. Yet the basic traditions of
the Scottish sport had survived, partly by
adaptation to change, albeit reluctant, and
partly by the respect which Scotland's wild climate, its admirable ethics and colourful
history have inspired around the world.

The 1990s have not seen the same strides
in techniques and standards as earlier decades,
and the period has been one of consolidation
rather than advancement. Equipment has not
benefited from any radical development, and
the growing band of activists has been
thwarted in their plans to raid the last defences
of the cliffs by a run of poor winters. When
conditions have been good, many fine and
hard routes have been climbed, but leading
climbers have had to apply patience and
endure frustration in equal measure in order
to get them. In Scotland, climbers must always
operate in the likelihood of appalling weather
and fickle conditions, and the battle with the
elements is integral to the challenge of the
Scottish sport; inevitably, however, it obstructs
pure technical development. Therefore the fact
that many of the big routes of the previous
decade, such as Guerdon Grooves or The
Needle Variations on Shelter Stone, remained
unrepeated by 1998 says more about the rarity of suitable conditions in the 1990s than

any lack of will amongst the activists.

In ice climbing, a few of the last remaining
problems have been climbed. Those that do
remain are features which might form only
once every five or ten years – but they serve to
fire the dreams of those who watch and wait!

Since the number of winter climbers capable of operating at the highest Scottish
standards is growing, there is likely to be a
surge of winter climbing activity whenever our
climate conjures up a season to compare with
those of the late seventies and mid-eighties.
However, in order to see a step forward in
standard to match the advances made in the
Alps or North America, another tradition of
Scottish winter climbing might have to be
compromised: the noble ethic that ascents
should be made 'on sight' without prior
knowledge, and without fixed equipment or
repeated attempts 'yo-yoing' on the ropes, has
been sustained largely intact for a century –
but it is hard to see routes of grade IX being
established without some realignment of the
rules of the game.

Meanwhile there remain a host of easier
possibilities on remote cliffs for those intent on
exploring the furthest reaches of Scotland's
winter potential. However, it is fair to say that
the pioneering zeal of the last century cannot
possibly be sustained through the next.
Saturation is inevitable in the next thirty years,
but Scottish winter climbing retains an enigmatic appeal to the growing numbers of British
climbers who seek the winter experience. And
what can never be reduced to the common-
place by technical development are the
mountains themselves: the Scottish arena is
unique, and its variety of climbing styles,
weather, conditions and scenic grandeur will
always guarantee a special distinction to our
winter sport. The 'icy halls of cold sublimity'
remain as inspiring as they did in 1920. Long
may they fire the climber's dreams and deeds.

10: IN THE GULLIES

CLASSIC SNOW AND ICE:
PRACTICE AND PSYCHOLOGY

For those people who are not satisfied until they have clawed and dragged themselves through the innermost clefts of the mountains they love, gully climbing is the ultimate indulgence, and as near as you can ever get to dissecting the mountains' secrets and mysteries. And if your ardour extends to wilfully submitting yourself to the miseries of drip and deluge or spindrift and avalanche, then gullies are definitely the places to be.

The distinction of Scottish winter mountaineering owes a great deal to its tradition of gully climbing, and although the techniques described in this chapter cover both, it is to the gullies much more than to the face routes that climbing styles on pure snow and ice owe their evolution. Compared to the Alps, Scotland possesses relatively few unbroken expanses of snow and ice on the faces. Ben Nevis, of course, has the superb Orion Face and indeed its own Little Brenva, but the majority of winter ridge and face routes are mixed in their climbing character, and it is undoubtedly the gully which evokes the most vivid image of Scottish snow- and ice-climbing, and which exemplifies its uniqueness and perversity.

The Scottish predilection for the gully is not simply a matter of determined eccentricity. Our mountain geology and glacial past have created joint-line clefts at regular intervals across every cliff and corrie in the Highlands, and as the main weaknesses on the cliffs, these gullies formed the most feasible routes up faces other-wise impregnable in the early days of mountaineering, especially in winter when they are steeply banked with snow and safe from rockfall. Initial exploration quickly kindled a passion for the savage wildness of gully scenery, and the appeal of their soaring, cleaving lines has remained as powerful ever since. All the gullies' many miseries which would otherwise repel, are magically transmuted in the climber's mind into passing penances to be willingly paid *en route* to eternal redemption at the cornice crest.

ROMPING UP THE
EASIER LINES

The easier grades I and II gullies are tackled today much in the style of a century ago. The traditional method of moving together on a short rope, as elaborated in Chapter 5, remains the efficient approach, save for the odd ice pitch and the steeper corniced exits where belays may be demanded. Unfettered by any equipment above rope, a single axe, a few slings and wired nuts and perhaps a couple of ice screws, parties can enjoy the same fast-moving freedom on the easy routes as the pioneers of the 1890s. Classic climbs such as the Central Gully of Ben Lui, first ascended in 1892, still offer the first taste of real winter mountaineering for many who hitherto would have described themselves as winter walkers.

One often hears the grades I and II denounced as 'snow-plods' or 'stepladders', and it must be conceded that many of the straight, broad and open-mouthed couloirs – for instance Broad Gully on Stob Coire nan Lochan, or Numbers Three and Four Gullies on Ben Nevis – *are* perhaps lacking in distinction and intrigue. And in recent years the growing numbers climbing on the popular cliffs have hacked the easy lines to pieces at the peak of the season, leaving them largely devoid of guile or charm: a line of bucket-holds stretching skywards gives a depressing feeling of inevitability to the outcome of a climb, and even worse is a passing string of parties who are using your route as their quick descent.

Such disparagements could not be applied to as long and scenic a route as Great Gully (II) on the Buachaille Etive Mor, which counts as a real mountaineering expedition and might even be grabbed in virgin state with an early start or a midweek visit. A gully nigh on 600m in vertical height, it plays the delightful trick of eliminating the toil of the day. Hardly is there a chance to grumble at the monotony of the walk-in than one is absorbed in the little ice pitches of the lower cleft. The gully line curves upwards and disappears enticingly out of view. Raven's evil slit and the barrel-shaped bulge of the Slime Wall to its left tower above in fore-shortened dominance of the scene and beckon many a pause for closer scrutiny. In the gully bed, the textures and angles of snow and ice alter continuously as height is gained, demanding constant care and re-tuning of technique. So rapt is the attention that, before you know it, the ice barrier is behind, the final bend is turned and the summit snows are yours. With the mind thus preoccupied, the body had somehow managed the upward climb without a murmur of complaint. Perched by the Buachaille's topmost cairn, there is now time in hand to contemplate a lunchtime pint at the Kingshouse, or to consider an onward traverse of the mountain's trident of tops, because the climb itself is

Plate 10.1 *Snow and ice climbing boots and crampons: (left) leather boot (B2); crampons with toe-strap and heel-clip – all-round performance from grade I to IV; (centre) Koflach plastic boot (B2); clip-on crampons – for grades I to IV; (right) Scarpa plastic boot (B3); rigid 'footfang' style crampons – for technical ice routes from grade IV to VII*

unlikely to have taken more than three hours.

Once the 'honeypots' are left there are countless quiet refuges spread all over the Highlands for the discerning explorer, and therein an abundance of long and twisting gully clefts whose quality mocks at those who would scorn the 'snow-plod'. The massive jointing of Torridonian sandstone especially lends itself to the gouging of chasms which split the cliffs from top to toe. Try Deep South (I) and Deep North Gully (II) on Beinn Alligin as magnificent ways to reach the Horns. This pair are so sharply incised that their entrances are akin to mine-shafts and therefore hard to locate. Once inside, you climb an easy strip of snow no more than 10m wide imprisoned by rearing sidewalls which spew great torrents of ice from beneath their roofs.

Twisting Gully (II) in Coire na Caime on Liathach, and Hayfork Gully (I), The Alley (II) and Lord's Gully (II) on An Teallach are all wonderful excursions, offering close inspection of the 'innards' of their respective

Plate 10.2 *Moving together up Deep North Gully on Beinn Alligin*

verses of a mountain as fine as An Teallach, such routes give the complete mountaineering experience at a modest technical grade.

The personal skills to be applied on grades I and II gullies extend rather than replace the winter walking techniques discussed in Chapter 4. The French styles of crampon-work, in particular *'pied à trois'*, perform well on firm snow at angles of up to 50 degrees, but in soft snow such refined styles don't work and steps must be kicked rather brutishly with the toes. Full front-pointing with both feet will become necessary as the average angle rises past 55 degrees or wherever ice is found. Also, use of the axe has to be altered at angles above 45 degrees where the normal 'pick-back' walking stance becomes awkward: the pick is turned into a forward-pointing position and daggered into the snow as in Plate 10.3 – in hard snow only the pick may bite the surface, but in softer conditions a combination of pick and shaft will penetrate, providing a stable fulcrum of support. The hand should be pressing down on top of the axe in order to maximise the braking force. With either one or two axes the daggering technique is fast, simple and highly economical of energy output. The temptation to swing the axes in full *piolet traction* should be resisted until a genuine ice pitch is encountered. Good fitness is the final ingredient of personal skill for the easier gullies because long, continuous ascents on snow place a repetitive strain on specific leg-muscle groups. With good cardio-vascular fitness they become quicker and more enjoyable.

A few notes of warning must be sounded when contemplating such ascents, however. Many of the wider gullies harbour high avalanche potential, particularly those which have a broad exit fan, Great Gully on the Buachaille being a prime example, No 5 Gully on the Ben another. The gullies are best tackled when the snow is stable, and fresh

mountains, an aspect denied to the mountaineer who sticks solely to the crests. Fuselage Gully (II) in Coire Mhic Fhearchair, Beinn Eighe is a unique excursion in that the crux chockstone is formed from the propeller of a Canadian bomber which tragically crashed into the plateau on its way home at the end of World War II. Trident Gully (II) on Beinn Dearg Mor offers a line of great elegance, mounting exposure and a choice of three forks to finish right at the summit of this magnificent Corbett in the Fisherfield Forest, and is all the more to be prized because of its remoteness. A good gully is one which keeps its secrets close to its chest, offers a couple of branches to test the routefinding skill, and comes to a sudden ending at the summit ridge. If they are combined with the main ridge tra-

accumulations are either light or avoidable. Narrower clefts are much safer, but without prior knowledge of conditions at the exit one can never be sure how great the avalanche risk is – even tight clefts like Deep South and Deep North Gully on Alligin finish on open slopes with considerable avalanche potential. In any event, there is little fun in wading up a 45-degree gully thigh-deep in powder snow.

Cornices may provide a final barrier far more delicate than anything encountered on the gully itself, and parties must apply due consideration before blindly pushing up a long route without prior sight of the cornice – though narrow gullies such as No 2 on Ben Nevis hide their exit possibilities until you are almost level with the final lip. In No 2 Gully, a left-hand exit is usually, but not always feasible. Having climbed 100m of 55 degree snow/ice to reach the exit, the prospect of reversing the route may be sufficiently daunting to impel an unwise attack on an unstable cornice. Such uncertainty is, of course, part of the ultimate thrill of gully climbing, but judgements of the state of the cornice should not be taken lightly.

The sense of security engendered by the enclosing walls and the likelihood of yielding snow on the lower part of a gully climb should not seduce inexperienced winter mountaineers to ignore the very real commitment of gully climbing even at grade I level. How easy it is to kick steps up gradually steepening snow without a thought as to how much more difficult it is to climb down such an angle; and as soon as icy névé snow is encountered, a long fall will have serious consequences. Although by soloing or moving together large sections of an easy route can be covered swiftly, a party must have the common sense to decide when belays are required for its security and confidence – as, for example, when the angle gets steeper than 55 degrees, or the snow becomes icy, an

Plate 10.3 *Axe daggering and frontpointing technique on névé snow*

iced chockstone bars progress or a cornice looms – and, indeed, whenever anyone in the team shows signs of nerves or hesitation. And of course, it is incumbent upon all winter mountaineers that they are able to make safe, sure anchors and use effective belaying methods when such circumstances arrive ...

BELAYING ON SNOW

The first rule of all winter belaying is to use rock anchors wherever they are available; in terms of strength and speed of placement, a rock belay is nearly always to be preferred. Only when the rocks of the gully walls are so heavily sheathed with ice that excavation of cracks might take several minutes would I consider digging a snow belay by preference without investigating the rock possibilities. However, the rock in gully beds is typically highly compact and crackless, and such spikes or cracks as do exist are often loose and fractured due to the continued action of freeze-thaw erosion. Broader couloirs may have long sections without any accessible rock islands, especially near the exit, and most gullies tend to finish on a featureless level snowfield. In all these situations the party must have recourse to snow and ice belays, and on climbs below grade IV in standard these will invariably be on snow.

The construction of solid ice axe belays is fundamental to security on low and middle grade snow and ice climbs, and traditional reliance on a vertically driven axe has long been discredited. The vertical axe belay is suitable only for short sections of top-roping in a well frozen, stable snowpack, where it might be used as a direct belay with the live rope looped around the top of the shaft. The vertical axe anchor can be reinforced into a *boot-axe belay* by bracing the boot up against the axe shaft and feeding the rope under the instep, round the axe and up round the ankle. A more reliable modification of the vertical axe anchor is the *stomper belay* where the belayer stands on top of the axe, and by running the rope through a karabiner clipped into the hole in the axe head and around the waist, any load from below is transferred into a vertical pull down onto the anchor. However, if the belayer loses his balance, the belay may collapse completely, and the use of either boot-axe or stomper belays should be restricted to top-roping or lowering on medium-angled slopes.

It is the horizontal axe anchor which is fundamental to snow belaying. This is often termed the *buried axe belay*, which is in fact a misnomer because the axe is actually placed into a pre-dug trench. Covering it with snow does nothing to improve its strength, which

Plate 10.4 *The T-axe belay anchor*

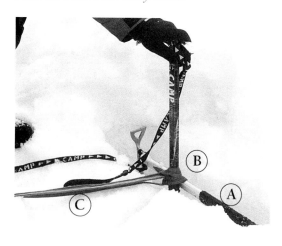

A Horizontal axe placed behind the vertical
B Clove hitch on sling tied round both axes (optional)
C Belay sling pulled down vertical trench

depends entirely on the resistance of the snow downslope of the anchor. Packing or stamping wet snow into a solid initial platform can much increase the strength of the pack, since compression of the snow allows the ice grains to make contact and bond together. The horizontal trench is then dug at the back of the ledge and the axe pulled firmly against the lower wall of the slot before attachment.

A single axe anchor may be insufficient in unconsolidated or very wet snow. Moreover, in a stratified snow profile the axe may pull through under load if injudiciously placed at a layer boundary. For belaying the leader with the attendant possibility of loading from a long fall, the addition of a second axe driven vertically in front of the horizontal axe probably triples the strength of the anchor (Plate 10.4). My personal habit is to tie the attachment sling with a clove hitch around both axes, which ensures that they are both loaded together in the event of a fall. In a party of three carrying one axe each, two axes are always available to make such a crossed- or T-axe anchor to belay the leader. Alternatively, one can use a ski-stick instead of a second axe to provide the vertical component of this kind of anchor. On névé snow with a hard frozen crust of a few centimetres the horizontal axe is best placed in a shallow trench in order to utilise the strong surface layer, so that the resultant arrangement resembles a T-shape. Otherwise both axes are buried in a deeper trench, typically 20 to 40cm in depth.

The dead-man is no longer as fashionable a snow anchor as it was in the 1970s and 1980s, but it has a decided advantage over a single axe horizontal belay on most types of snow. Measured against the T-axe or crossed-axe belay, as in Fig 10.1, page 220, the dead-man loses its edge of performance, and the disadvantages of its cumbersome weight and possible unreliability in stratified snow become more significant. Because its tendency to scoop through the snowpack if it hits a weak snow layer, the instructional advice of recent years is to dig a trench for the plate instead of hammering it straight into the snow surface, so that the underlying snow can be examined and tested before completing the belay. But this eliminates the dead-man's main traditional advantage, namely its ease and speed of placement.

I would only carry a dead-man if tackling a big gully climb in heavy snow or thawing conditions. I recall a dreich March day when a warm front fog had licked the South Post of Creag Meagaidh into a dribbling chute of slush. We had driven and walked for many hours and needed a climb. Thankfully we had brought two dead-men, and they were used on eight of the nine stances, providing the only measure of real security throughout the grade III 350m route, in conditions where axe belays could not have worked as effectively.

The use of other forms of snow anchor such as bollards, or buried equipment such as rucksacks (or frozen Mars Bars) may enliven

Plate 10.5 *The classic snow belay*

A Bucket seat stance 2m below axe anchors
B Waist belay with twist round wrist in braking arm
C Live rope on same side as belay is tied in to the harness

instructional sessions and test one's belaying ingenuity, but such ploys are rarely required on a genuine winter climb.

In terms of creating a reliable snow belay, the placement of the anchors is less than half the battle and there are three more tasks to complete before you can settle down to pull in the rope:

Digging the stance: A good stance is essential to defend the anchors. In terms of a snow belay this should always be a sitting stance between 1½ and 3m below the anchors with a bucket seat, an upraised saddle between the legs, and firm steps for the heels (Plate 10.5). By digging oneself into a miniature bunker one then ensures that little, if any of the energy of a fall is transmitted to the anchors. If the snow is frozen, the stance must be cut and dug out

Fig 10.1 *Ice-axe and dead-man belays: a comparative review*

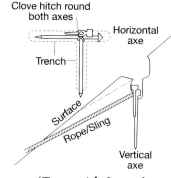

Ice-axe (T-axe with 2 axes)	vs	The Dead-man
Weight and bulk		
Multi-purpose use of climbing tools; no extra weight		Heavy – 1kg for a full-size plate and unwieldy to carry
Material strength		
Metal shafted axes essential		Reliable; strength of snowpack is always more critical
Placement time		
3 to 5 minutes to construct a T-axe belay properly		2 to 3 minutes on average
Construction problems		
T-axe requires two axes per person; otherwise a single horizontal axe must suffice which is weaker and less stable		Two dead-men must be carried if used on every successive belay
Correct loading point on horizontal axe is crucial to prevent pivoting (two-thirds of the way up shaft, ie at centre of surface area)		Angles of placement, plate to snow (40 degrees) and of anchor wire to plate (50 degrees max), are critical to the stability of the dead-man
The belay is excavated and its placement in the T-trench is visible; greater certainty of stability		Bedding of the plate is invisible once pulled under the surface; risk of unseen 'scooping' motion
Vertical section of T-trench must be same depth as horizontal to prevent an upward leverage on the axes under load		Anchor wire must be pulled straight and tight through snowpack to avoid upward leverage on the plate
Axes are sacrificed for the anchor, leaving the climber vulnerable until the belay is completed		Plate often pulls several feet through snow before bedding firmly; precarious on steep ground
Adaptability to different snow types		
A névé/hard-pack		
Highly effective		Hard to knock in unless an ice hammer is carried
B Windslab		
Secure provided horizontal axe is not placed at profile junction; the vertical axe helps avoid 'cheese-cutter' effect		Danger that plate will pull through along the base of the slab; as the profile is not excavated this danger may not be seen
C Wet snow		
Excellent in moist snow which compresses well; unreliable in slush		Dead-man is highly effective in moist snow and will lodge better than axes in slush
D Dry powder snow		
Very poor anchorage; construction of good stance and body belay essential		Unpredictable performance; may pull straight out or can dig in to lower snow layer

Fig 10.2 Winter belaying: a comparative assessment

BODY BELAY ROUND WAIST	FRICTION PLATE (eg Sticht)
Ease of construction	
Belay tied direct to front of harness; fast and simple. Belay tied to back of harness: more awkward; an in situ sling and s/g krab on back of belt helps tying in	Awkward with gloved hand
Rope handling	
No problems; rope can be paid out quickly on easy ground, therefore very suitable on easier climbs	Greater risk of jamming when leader is moving fast on easy ground. Iced/frozen ropes will not feed
Rope control	
If belay is tied direct into front of harness the 'live' rope must be paid out on the same side as the belay rope/sling; if not, the belayer can be turned in to the belay under load and the live rope snatched off his back	Once plate is clipped into harness the ropes cannot be completely lost from the belayer's grip
Control of double ropes is difficult on intricate pitches where each rope is paid out at different rate	Double ropes are separated on the plate; enables close independent control of each rope
A fall places high stress on belayer; skill required	Relatively simple to hold a fall; little strain felt
Dynamic capability	
Dynamic arrest is automatic because some slippage through gloved hands is inevitable; a good belayer can control the rate of slippage to create the optimum braking force	The plate gives only minimal slippage when applied instinctively in event of a fall; therefore, shock loading on protection points and climbers is higher
Load impact on belay	
Body belay shields the anchors and can absorb a high percentage of fall energy especially if belay is tied into back and if stance and positioning are solid	With plate and belay both clipped into front of harness as is normal any load on the plate by-passes the body and is transmitted direct to the anchors
Self-rescue situation	
It is possible but difficult to tie off and escape from a waist belay under a hanging load	Plate is easily locked off; escaping from the system is then simple; an assisted hoist can be rigged with the Sticht plate as the pulley point
Summary of applications	
Easier routes; grades I-III	Steeper intricate routes, especially mixed climbs where there is more plentiful protection
On all snow anchors (best with back tie-in) On doubtful rock/ice belay anchors Whenever maximum speed is essential In severe conditions – iced ropes	Never on snow belays except with back tie in to belt On good rock/ice anchors

before the axes are placed as anchors, a precarious operation on steep ground. There is sense in placing one axe in the belay trench and clipping your rope to it while cutting out the stance with the other.

Tying in to the anchors: Strict textbook convention advises that on snow belays the belayer should always tie in to the back of the harness, so that the body is placed directly between the anchors and the direction of load. This necessitates having a short sling threaded through the back of the harness with a screwgate krab attached. However, even with such a ready-made 'cow's tail', it is often fiddly to tie in to the back because you are unsighted and the rucksack gets in the way. Practicality dictates

Plate 10.6 *Waist belay on rock anchors: loadings to anchors equalised with rope and sling, live side of rope on same side as belay attachment*

that the anchors are more usually tied into the front of the harness. Whether tying in to front or back, it is essential that the vertical trench dug for the belay sling or rope should be as deep as the horizontal trench in which the axes are lodged so that any loading will pull the anchors down into the snowpack. Of equal importance, attachment of rope or slings must be tight so that there is no possibility of shock-loading the anchors in the event of a fall, and so the belayer cannot be pulled off the stance.
Waist belaying: On snow belays the waist belay is the method of choice. The respective merits of manufactured belay devices and the traditional waist belay are compared in Fig 10.2. Different models of belay plate do differ in their braking performance, but in the emergency of a leader fall, they are all applied in what is essentially a *static* manner – in other words, the belayer locks off the plate as soon as

the load is felt. Rope stretch distributes some of the fall energy, but otherwise the brake is sharp and sudden. Not only does this risk injury to a tumbling leader through jerking, but it also transmits an unwanted shock-load to both belayer and anchors. By contrast, an arrest off a waist belay is almost always dynamic in that there is considerable slippage round the belayer's waist before the fall is stopped. With prior practice, a belayer can deliberately allow the rope to slip several metres before the fall is arrested, and thus the fall energy is absorbed gradually, eliminating the potential for shock-loading. Since snow anchors are inherently unreliable, and fall-potentials are very high on ill-protected snow climbs, the dynamic waist belay must be used – but only in conjunction with thick gloves and clothing!

Belays should, if at all possible, be made close to the side of the gully, the leader making it clear which side of the belay he or she will be climbing, and the others keeping well out of the firing line of spindrift or falling debris. And when using the waist belay with attachment of anchors to the front of the harness, the 'live' rope should always be paid out on the same side as the belay ropes are attached. If this is done, the downward force of a leader falling directly onto the belay maintains the belayer in an out-ward-facing position where the belay can be controlled. If the loaded rope is on the opposite side to the belay attachment, the belayer will be rotated to an inward-facing position and the rope snatched away off the back. Practice trials of holding slides of 10 or 15m on training slopes are recommended to prove the point.

THE MIDDLE GRADE CLASSICS

The step from grade II to grade III and IV routes is a major advance in both technical and psychological terms because the basic snow-climbing and belaying techniques must now

Fig 10.3 *Winter climbing anchors*

Origins in Scotland	Modern applications
VERTICAL ICE-AXE Traditional; pre-1960 the universal snow belay.	Emergency brake in event of a fall when moving together Quick belay in hard snow for bringing up seconds ('boot-axe' or 'stomper' belay).
DEAD-MAN Developed in Antarctica in mid-1960s, then manufactured for UK winter use	Rarely carried on harder ice routes but useful on snow climbs in thawing or unconsolidated conditions.
BURIED AXE (Single horizontal and T-axe) Copied the dead-man principle; used since late 1960s.	Now the standard snow belay; most common usage on exit pitches especially on level ground on top of routes.
SNOW BOLLARD Traditional	Main use is for retreats and abseils (eg cornice above descent gullies); too much hard work otherwise.
ICE BOLLARD Traditional.	Sometimes used on easy angled ice (saving on ice screws) and occasionally on retreats/abseils; time and effort to construct.
ICICLE THREAD Traditional.	Regularly used on organ-pipe ice; of tangible strength round icicles of substantial girth.
ICE PITONS Home-made by J. H. B. Bell for an attempt on Centre Post Direct (Creag Meagaidh) in 1939; used widely in 1950s.	Wholly superseded by ice screws in late 1960s; pitons tended to shatter ice when driven and have minimal lateral grip.
ICE SCREWS *'Wart-hog' drive-in* Imported from Continent in 1965; used on fourth ascent of Point Five Gully in 1965.	Still available but prone to plating/shattering the ice; used in frozen turf by some mixed climbers.
'Snarg' drive-in First made in USA by Lowe in 1982; rapid spread worldwide.	Popular for protection on steep ice; extruding action prevents shattering; lightweight titanium versions available.
'Tubular' screw-in First reported in Scotland by Dougal Haston in 1965; originally made by Salewa of Germany; cheap lightweight titanium models from Eastern bloc countries flooded the market in late 1980s, now superseded by stronger quality-controlled models made by mainstream manufacturers such as Black Diamond and Grivel .	Strongest ice anchor; traditionally used on main belays; but with improved design can be placed by hand on steep ground; tapered cores aid extrusion, four bits aid penetration and now available in titanium.
NATURAL ROCK SPIKES/CHOCK-STONES Traditional.	Convenient and reliable but all too rare on pure snow and ice routes.
ROCK PITONS Soft steel pegs first used with ethical misgivings in 1930s but widely accepted after World War II; hard steel pegs developed and produced in USA by Chouinard in early 1960s.	An essential part of the gear rack on grade III and above; selection of 6 to 10 pegs usually carried (knifeblades, king-pins, angles, leepers); can be used when rocks are severely iced.

Fig 10.3 *Winter climbing anchors* CONTINUED

Origins in Scotland	Modern applications
WIRED METAL NUTS	
Used in rock-climbing since late 1960s; natural spread to winter use; curved tapered 'Rocks' manufactured since 1978, brass micronuts ('RP' and 'HB's) since 1979.	Quick to place and extract; used in preference to pitons if rock is not badly iced.
METAL CHOCK-STONES	
Simple hexagonals made c1970; offset Hexentrics (Chouinard) made since 1974.	Hexentrics have camming action in parallel-sided cracks; can be hammered into icy cracks.
CAMMING DEVICES	
'Friends' developed for use on granite rock cracks in Yosemite, USA; manufactured since 1978; well suited to alpine/ winter climbing.	Will work in all types of flared cracks from 10 to 100mm ($\frac{1}{4}$ to 4in) width, but not in verglassed rock; other trigger-operated cammers made since 1984, but Friends remain the most popular.
DRILLED EXPANSION BOLTS	
Spread in alpine big wall climbing in 1950s but only used in Scottish winter on first ascent of Point Five Gully in 1959, with much subsequent criticism.	Ethical taboo has persisted; adventure and ingenuity in making anchors remain fundamental in Scottish winter climbing.

be augmented by the full range of rock- and ice-belaying, and sustained pitches of steep ice will henceforth be encountered. A second hammer axe will be needed by each climber. Psychology plays a greater part because of the inherent unpredictability and potential objective danger of the steeper routes. Although winter walkers can happily make the step to grade I and II climbing, at grade III a background of rock climbing comes to be of direct benefit in coping with greater exposure, in arranging running belays, and in organising the ropework over a continuous series of pitches.

The key to making the transition lies in choosing the right routes in good condition. Following the steps and belay ledges of other parties up a route such as SC Gully or Twisting Gully on Stob Coire nan Lochan, Glencoe is one way of softening the impact of grade III. Waiting for conditions when Comb and Green Gully on Ben Nevis are well banked with snow

can bring these grade IVs into the realm of those whose previous experience has barely exceeded II. By contrast, an ill-timed attempt on a great classic in lean conditions can bring failure and discouragement. Crowberry Gully on the Buachaille is the touchstone of classic multi-pitch gully route, but it becomes considerably more technical when its pitches are only thinly iced and lack the banking of snow which provides an easy take-off on each pitch. In the cold but lean winter of 1996 I encountered several sequences of delicate, even scary, moves, particularly on the crux at the Cave Pitch where the guidebook's 'curtain of ice' was replaced by three or four tiny blobs of water ice. Thankfully they bore the weight of my front points or we might have faced a long retreat. For those weaned on the reliable banking of grade Is and IIs, the greater variability of condition of grade III and IV routes has to be recognised, and judicious selection applied.

Plate 10.7 *Soloing in the lower part of George Gully (III), Liathach (climber: Colin Gardiner)* (Jonathan Preston)

Plate 10.8 *Leading the first ice pitch in Emerald Gully (IV) Beinn Dearg*

and bridging contortions to minimise traction on the picks in poor ice must all be part of one's technical repertoire. In all my winter climbing I apply the maxim, 'never pull when you can push'. Such an attitude may not engender an especially glamorous style of movement, but bridging techniques have got me past rotten columns of ice on countless occasions.

An ice pitch should be approached with some of the craft and guile of the stepcutting pioneers – spying resting places and likely protection points, then splitting the pitch so as to see each easement as a sanctuary where the calf muscles can recover and ice screws can be placed for protection in relative comfort. The forethought of chopping out a big step to take the soles of both feet turns a sloping *glacis* into a genuine resting ledge which forms a haven for retreat if the ensuing section proves difficult.

The full range of possible protection anchors for winter climbing are detailed on Fig 10.3. The grade III/IV leader will be carrying a selection of four to six ice screws, six to eight pitons, a set of wired 'Rocks', two or three 'Friends' and a couple of 'Hexentrics', plus six to eight extenders with karabiners, and five or six longer slings. Longer extender slings, as opposed to the short 'quick-draws' used universally in rock climbing, are better for winter routes where protection points may be widely scattered and rope drag is often a problem. The placement of ice screws on near-vertical ground should rarely be necessary on routes below grade V, and adequate protection can usually be arranged either before or after any really steep sections; on grade IVs these rarely exceed 8 or 10m in length. Such tactics spare the energy of hanging on the tools trying to place gear, and they also develop the positive mentality needed to succeed on steep ice climbs at a higher grade. In contrast to the 'runner above the head' mentality with which many rock climbs can be tackled, on winter

The technical demands of the middle grade classics include front-pointing with both axes swung into the full traction position. This is regarded by many aspiring ice climbers as a matter of applying whirlwind energy and windmill motion. Such tactics may work when seconding on routes such as Green or Comb in good condition, but a blind faith in simple traction when leading long and poorly protected pitches on ice of variable quality is most unwise. A leader needs to develop precise judgement as to which placements will hold, recognising the resonant thud and vibration of a well bedded pick. Careful weighting of axes

routes one must arrange the best possible gear where one can and then trust it for lengthy sections of leading. This can be termed the 'bottle' factor, and is one of the features which makes snow- and ice-climbing so exciting, whatever the grade being tackled.

Very often the climbing of the ice pitches is the easiest part of a classic gully climb, and one has to reserve one's real 'bottle' for what lies above. Emerald Gully on Beinn Dearg is one of the most popular grade IVs north of the Great Glen, an appeal which is only heightened by the rarity of good conditions; but on my only visit there I can recall less of the two main ice pitches than of the 60-degree wall of rotten snow above, which led up to an unfriendly cornice. Only two rock outcrops suggested an inkling of security, but neither provided a really decent runner. Once passed, the snow became so thinly crusted that my feet broke through at every kick and threatened to topple me backwards. I started the pitch daggering the axes, but the snow soon became so soft and steep that I had to plunge axes and arms horizontally into the pack to keep in balance. Nearing the cornice bulge after 20m of unprotected mush I was close to 'psyching out' – but then my arms broke through into a sizeable cavity beneath the lip, and at its back I spied a cracked outcrop of rock tailor-made for a belay. Never have I known such a snug stance. Having brought up my team, I could tackle the cornice with gusto and we escaped by the last embers of sunset.

THE GRADE V BARRIER

An apprenticeship on Scottish snow and ice leads inexorably to that great day when a genuine grade V is tackled. Although the likes of Point Five and Zero Gully have lost some of their aura of impregnability, they remain major undertakings, with long sustained ice pitches, considerable objective danger from spindrift avalanches, and in the case of Zero, poor belays – all good reasons for a sleepless night of anticipation. My own first full grade V was Orion Face Direct, and I remember less about the route than the utter ecstasy of success as we climbed out of the final ice chimneys onto the summit snowslopes which were fired mauve by the sunset. Caring not a jot about the all-night drive back to Sheffield, nor of the prospect of turning in to work by nine the next morning, we just revelled in the glory of completing a big Smith-Marshall route on the Ben after so many years of dreaming. Without doubt it remains one of the most precious experiences of my life as a climber, and there can be few winter climbers who do not feel similar emotions on breaking through into grade V.

The use of ice anchors for regular protection and occasionally for main belays characterises the big grade V gully and face routes. Ice screws may need to be placed on steep ice at 70 to 80 degrees in angle, a tense process of hanging by the elbow from the wrist-loop of one tool while holding the screw so that it can be tapped and turned into place. Tubular ice screws with large handles have taken much of the strain out of this process, since they can be screwed in by hand in the yielding ice typical of Scottish gullies. Nevertheless, the screw has to be held initially with the supported hand and tapped with the hammer in order to get the bits embedded. A solid core of ice extruding through the tube of the screw indicates a sound placement, but very often the chosen piece of ice proves to be honeycombed or too thin, in which case one must remove the screw, shift position and go through the whole process again. If possible, ice screw runners should be placed in pairs, and the potential loading equalised by linking the two with slings.

Two screws should always be placed on

Plate 10.9 *Approaching the top of the first pitch of Zero Gully on Ben Nevis (climber: Tony Smith)*

main belays, preferably at slightly different levels and at least ¹⁄₂m apart so as not to risk weakening a single plate of ice. It is vital to equalise the pulls on the belays by adjusting clove hitches or slings, in order to maximise the strength. The belay can be additionally strengthened by bedding the axe picks into the ice as hard as possible and clipping the wrist-loops into the belay system. Icicle threads may occasionally be found to add to the protection.

Some ice climbers will place one ice screw two or three metres above the other at the stance, and the higher anchor is then used as the first running belay on the next pitch. In any event it is very important to get a runner in early on ice pitches so as to eliminate the potential of a factor 2 fall directly onto the belay. Though more dependable than snow belays, ice anchors are only as strong as the ice into which they are driven, and a dynamic waist belay might therefore be considered. ·

However, it is usual on harder snow and ice routes to use double climbing ropes (ie two ropes of 9mm diameter) and it is difficult to operate two ropes simultaneously from a waist belay. Furthermore, on steep ice the stances are too small to allow the construction of a bucket-seat belay. For these reasons most climbers revert to a plate belay at grades IV and V, and try to place a couple of runners early in every pitch as the best means of protecting the ice anchors.

On harder gully routes the use of rock pitons is essential. On many of the classics, pegs will be found in place at main belay stances, but these may be of unknown vintage and could be in an advanced stage of corrosion. If cracks are available one should place one's own pegs, and ensure that they are retrieved by the second! With the demise of aid climbing as a winter pastime on rock, few modern climbers get any chance to practise and test piton placement until they are at grips with a serious winter route. However, the place to learn the art of pegging is not on the crux pitch of Smith's Gully on Meagaidh, but on a quarry face or scruffy rock outcrop where rock scarring will not be offensive to others. Exploring the potential of piton placement means learning the difference between the singing and ascending notes of a well driven peg, and the dull rebounding tone of a blind and shallow placement; seeing the danger of knocking pegs into hollow flakes which expand as the piton is driven; exploring the torquing potential of knifeblades and leepers with offset heads; and discovering just how easily pegs can jump out of gloved hands during extraction.

In all winter climbing the placing of two or more belay anchors is regarded as standard safety practice, unless you are fortunate enough to excavate a giant rock spike or chockstone. The prevalence of iced cracks,

together with uncertainties as to the strength of *in situ* pitons (as well as one's own!) make multi-point anchorage on belays fundamental to winter security, whether they are on rock or ice. And if you have placed three or four anchors which are each of doubtful security, their strengths must be aggregated by equalising their potential loading in order to provide a belay of dependable calibre.

In tackling the grade Vs with a margin of security, there are two personal qualities which are indispensable, namely ingenuity and 'unflappability'. For example the following scenario is enacted with unfailing regularity on a long snow and ice route: 'At the top of the pitch you spy a likely belay spot and chop a resting stance. The available snow and ice anchors are investigated and reluctantly dismissed as inadequate, so you then attack the ice sheath covering the gully wall to your side in pursuit of some usable rock. A widening

Plate 10.10 *Eternal Redemption: breaking through the cornice after a first ascent on Fuar Tholl (climber: Ian Dring)*

scar of bare pink rock is exhumed, only to reveal a plethora of blind cracks, verglassed cracks, flaring cracks, expanding cracks behind loose blocks and sometimes no cracks at all! Having pounded your stock of nuts and pitons to near submission to little avail, the search is finally abandoned. Never mind, you can always move to a new stance; but try to go higher and there is never any spare rope left, and the ground is always too steep to allow you to climb back down. So in the end you conveniently convince yourself that those snow anchors weren't as bad as you initially judged, and combine them with whatever crumbs of comfort the rock has offered into at best a "scientific" and at worst a "psychological" belay. It is small wonder that nigh on an hour can have passed in the process.'

Broken axe picks, dropped gear, and 60m runouts on a 50m rope are all trials which test the ice climber's resolve and patience, and which delineate the sport from the precision geometry of summer rock-climbing. Snow and ice psychology is the knack of deliberate self-deception in the face of the undeniable disaster, and of smiling in the face of every adversity that the winter mountains can contrive. The successful winter climber somehow steers a muddled course through these mishaps and emerges unscathed.

Robin Smith was a master of this art. He dropped or lost his ice-axe no less than three times while achieving that great week of pioneering on Ben Nevis in 1960 with Jimmy Marshall. A fourth occasion came perilously close while he was leading the crux pitch on Gardyloo Buttress: *Then I dropped the axe. It stuck in the ice on top of an overhang five feet below and I crept down to pick it up in a sweating terror of kicking a bit of snow on it.* Minutes later, having just dropped an ice piton, Smith was again playing 'drum majors' with the axe: '... *it started somersaulting in the air*

with both my arms windmilling trying to grab it and my feet scarfing about in crumbly holds. Somehow all was well'[1]

Disaster really was thus narrowly averted, because Smith was using Marshall's axe – his own resting somewhere in the vicinity of Number Four Gully where it had been dropped the previous day – and the loss would have left just two short-hooked peg hammers between them: barely sufficient to complete a grade V first ascent.

In practical terms, one facet of psychological character stands out, that of keeping a cool control in the lead. On very few snow and ice routes can the leader contemplate a fall with the same equanimity as a rock-climber, even today. Protection points are too widely spaced, and when they do arrive their strength and reliability are often dubious. Not all grade V gullies are as serious as Zero where few, if any decent belays can be found on the first two pitches. Some, like Glencoe's Raven's Gully, are decorated by enormous wedged chockstones which shelter safe belay havens with 'bomb-proof' rock belays – but which also constitute the crux obstacles of the climb. Point Five Gully is regarded as a reasonably well protected route by grade V standards, but it also illustrates the challenge of leading the big Scottish gully lines:

'The first belays are usually found on the right side of the icefall of the first pitch. If thickly iced this pitch can be a straightforward romp, but invariably it features a thin section at a bulge where the gully narrows into a chimney. Here the axes may scrape through to bare rock, and should there be any parties in the gully above, you are now directly in the line of fire of their ice chippings, which whistle past at high velocity. It is at this point that you begin to ponder the security of those two lonely ice screws which you placed five metres lower. The stance above is hardly commodious, but with a foot-ledge chopped out and decent anchorage to an *in situ* peg and good "Friend" placement, you can relax and dare to enjoy the situation. Above is the iced chimney, no place to be in conditions of heavy spindrift, but otherwise a delightful exercise in ice bridging and chimneying. Just when the lead is becoming a little extended, the chimney eases and deepens, and good rock belays are discovered on the right wall. Now for the crux. The gully kinks up left to a sheer cascade of blue ice. Fix initial runners from pitons up on the right of the bay where the gully twists, then launch up left onto the cascade. At first you can bridge the feet wide, but soon you are forced into applying full traction on the axes. You know that the final bulge will not forgive a misplaced axe, and a glance down at the ropes hanging free from your waist back into the bay signals an urgent need for additional protection. The spindrift is tumbling over the bulge filling the arms and neck, and the screws refuse to lodge securely; but after anxious minutes, you have enough gear and courage to face your destiny. With the body arched at the bulge and the axes lodged in sugary snow above, there is no going back. A strong pull on the axes, a high kick of the crampon into the lip and you stand up in the upper gully. Good rock belays are close above. In another four pitches of grade II and III you'll be steaming up on top of the Ben in a dramatically altered state of consciousness.'

Crowding is becoming an increasingly serious problem on classic grade V gullies. There is no fun and considerable danger in climbing behind other parties on a narrow gully such as Point Five; moreover queuing at belays causes major delays and spoils the flow of progress. Avoiding such scenarios may require some radical behaviour. The first time I did Zero was on Easter Sunday, so I set off from the golf course at midnight, spent a couple of hours crouched in the rescue cupboard outside the CIC Hut and set off for the route as soon as the sky evinced the first flicker of twilight. The reward was a deserted climb on ice which shone green in the dawn light. In the longer days of late March and early April it is possible to embark on a route in the early afternoon after the morning rush is over, as long as daytime temperatures stay cool and the ice remains frozen. Such cavalier tactics may well lead to the added excitement of an evening tussle with the final cornice…

THE FINAL IMPASSE

A troublesome exit cornice can be the bane of any gully climb from grade I to V. To be trapped beneath an overhanging and possibly dangerous cornice, late in the day and after a taxing climb, is a predicament in which you are not likely to appreciate its magnificent architecture. However, the cornice and its surrounds possess a strange and lonely beauty which can inspire more aesthetic reflection once the problem is surmounted. W. Inglis Clark remembered the scene with particular clarity when he was ensconced under the cornice at the top of Moonlight Gully, Ben Nevis, on its first ascent in January 1898; looking out across the precipices he observed that: '... *the grandest sight was the roof of a great crag, which, projecting like some storm window into the valley was covered with unbroken snow shining like polished silver in the moonlight.*'[2]

In a wind, the cornice is a place of savage wildness. The climber grapples in a whirlwind of spindrift, face and eyes caked with ice, barely in touch with gravity. As the top is breasted, axes are plunged in the summit snows and a final heave is made onto level ground to meet a scene of peaceful beauty. A tugging rope is the only link with the cauldron of fury which has just been quitted. The feeling, then, is one of the most joyous in mountaineering – a battle won, redemption gained.

The methods employed to climb cornices have been many and varied. If some slight break can be found in the lip, then a vertical trench can be dug up the headwall, but so precarious is the climbing if the snow is unconsolidated that ladders of ice-axes have been used to give stable holds, their shafts plunged full length at a slightly downward angle into the wall. Harold Raeburn used this means to get out of Green Gully on Ben Nevis on its first ascent in 1906. Such a ladder might consume a party's entire supply of axes, however, leaving the seconds with the tricky problem of how to follow the pitch.

Where the cornice is continuously overhanging, tunnelling is the time-honoured method, which is dangerous, strenuous, highly uncomfortable and can be protracted. Raeburn recalled the record: '... *of two Alpine pioneers who, on the occasion of the first ascent of Tower Gully on Nevis, actually burrowed through the great cornice at the top, taking two days to the task – the intervening night being spent at Fort William.*'[3]

Such extreme behaviour apart, tunnelling can take many hours, and the ethics of unaided climbing are quickly abandoned if there are alternative means of assistance available, purists like Raeburn included. In 1901, he found himself extended on a cornice at the top of Gardyloo Gully: '*I had worked my hat about level with the edge when we heard the voice of an eloquent member of the SMC. A shout brought his party to the edge. I expressed a desire to shake hands with one of them, so Workman kindly extended his arm, and I was so glad to see him that I did not leave go till landed on the top.*'[4]

Seventy-five years later, on the adjacent Gardyloo Buttress, Andy Nisbet and Alf Robertson faced a major epic when they were trapped at nightfall under a 3m cornice of frozen ice that could not be tunnelled. As they pondered their options, a shout came over the plateau edge offering a top rope. The unseen rescuer belayed them throughout a 90m traverse under the roof to a point where they could abseil into the confines of Tower Gully. Once they were safely landed and untied, the rope disappeared into the darkness and their saviour has never been seen nor identified.

If climbing the cornice has its difficulties, then the experience of J. H. B. Bell should demonstrate that attempts at its descent require even greater caution. After ascending the partially snowed Slav Route on Ben Nevis in 1936, he decided to jump the lip at the head of No 3 Gully, no doubt expecting soft snow below. Unfortunately the landing was harder than he had anticipated, and he came to rest 450m lower beside the Coire na Ciste lochan, bruised but unbroken.

But enough of tales of woe: their experience is often cruel, but it trains the senses to know an unbounded joy when the gods turn to your side, when the corrie lip is mounted, when the trials of the walk in are nearly done and your gully comes to view completely formed, shining in pristine glory and just ripe for the picking. And don't be deterred to know that virtually every gully of note in Scotland has been ascended in some sort of winter conditions, from simple grade Is to the extreme grade VIs and VIIs. The winter elements can make every gully-climb a real adventure where the prior passage of other climbers is neither of help nor relevance to the experience ...

DEEP GASH GULLY

'Rock of ages, cleft for me,
Let me hide myself in thee.'

14 February, 5.30am, Strathcarron: I'm running down frost-sequinned tarmac, hands outstretched and heart pounding. With a

Plate 10.11 *Deep Gash Gully*

reluctant growl Martin's car cranks into life and we are on the road to Skye.

7.30am, Glen Brittle: it's hardly light but already we can see big cloudbanks encroaching at speed over the tops, harbingers of an occluded front that threatens to break the freeze which has gripped the hills for a fortnight...

At stake was a personal dream nurtured through two wet winters, one of Skye's finest gully lines. Deep Gash Gully is tucked away high on the north-west face of Sgurr a'Mhadaidh, an evil slit 50m deep, 150m high and guarded by giant chockstones bridged over its mouth. Graded Hard Very Severe and invariably wet, the gully can't have seen more than a handful of summer visitors since Nicol and Parker's first ascent in September 1949. To our knowledge it was untouched in winter.

My partner, Martin Welch, is a spare and rangy character, bred in the 'no mean city', forever impecunious and no stranger to hardship.

He soon outpaced me on the two hour approach march, his tracks snaked up into the gully mouth. Overhung by the gathering stormclouds the dark gash gave every impression of the gateway to Hell. I found Martin 20m up, comfortably couched in the mossy depths of a cave. The mischievous twinkle in his eye told me that this was where the real climbing began, and his horizontal posture that I was the man for the job.

Our cave sported an impressive roof arch, but we were baffled as to how to progress until we spotted two ancient threaded slings at its apex. Then the truth dawned that the arch had been surmounted by 'back and footing' techniques – but could we do it wearing crampons, and with spindrift avalanches thundering down through a hole in the roof?

All went well as far as the thread runners, but then two problems became manifest. First, every ounce of spindrift from the upper reaches

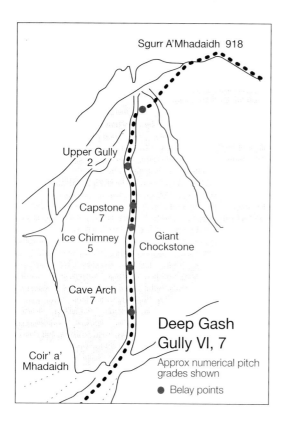

Sgurr A'Mhadaidh 918

Upper Gully
2

Capstone
7

Ice Chimney
5

Giant
Chockstone

Cave Arch
7

**Deep Gash
Gully VI, 7**

Coir' a'
Mhadaidh

Approx numerical pitch
grades shown

● Belay points

of the gully was being channelled on to my head through a well-placed aperture; it was akin to being bridged out at full stretch under the hopper feed of a flour mill, only the flour was icy cold and wetting. Second, I realised that to get down and under the arch I would have to make a 180 degree pirouette at this point. With delays to change into thicker gloves and rewarm my fingers, the manoeuvre took several minutes to execute. Then I chimneyed out to the lip, at which point my feet were so extended that they could barely keep contact with the opposite wall. I cleaned a flat, verglassed hold behind my right buttock; a slip would have deposited me back in Martin's lap in one giant swing. After careful calculation I took all my weight on my right palm and let my feet slip down from the far wall. Holding my breath, I pivoted on the palm until I was facing inwards, and pulled over to easy ground.

Two hours were gone, but surely the worst

of the climb was over. The gully broadened a little, and easy snows led up leftwards and out of sight; we even chanced a lunch break in the shelter of the right wall. While I snacked, Martin snatched ... my sandwiches! His sack contained nothing but a headtorch, and his clothing was as wrecked as his car. Already close to soaked by the spindrift and with a storm raging overhead, we were counting on getting out of the gully in a couple of hours at most.

On leading round the corner such hopes were dashed in one glance. My eyes were drawn upwards through 90 degrees to a towering ice groove topped by a black capstone from which curtains of spindrift tumbled. The pitch looked unbroken for at least fifty metres. I had rarely seen such a challenging nor, at this moment, so depressing a sight on a new winter climb.

A vague recess below the final roof offered the only hope of an intermediate belay. The groove began with a free-standing pillar of ice. Above this the runnel offered uncertain placements, varying from good water ice to honeycombed cavities filled with powder snow. This was not the sort of ground to apply full traction on the axe picks. Instead, I progressed by a combination of squirming and chimneying, buoyed by one decent wired nut runner. Access to the recess was barred by an ice window, but a couple of minutes' work with my adze revealed a tiny cave, lined with moss and totally sheltered from the storm. I squatted awkwardly in its gloom, shivering spasmodically while Martin thrashed his way up to me.

Above us hung a bottomless verglassed chimney and then the capstone roof. Lacking any visible protection, the first five metres appeared desperate. Martin took the first look, stretching sodden salopettes across the cleft with a mass of ice-choked gear sagging from his waist. Five minutes later he was back at my

Plate 10.12 *Martin Welch takes a first look at the crux capstone, 'stretching sodden salopettes across the cleft with a mass of ice-choked gear sagging from his waist'*

niche, his staring eyes betraying a healthy fear of what lay above.

Now four o'clock, there was little over an hour of light left as I squeezed past Martin and took my turn on the sharp end. The chimney was too wide for back and footing, and the only way I could see to gain access was, literally, to fall across it and slap my palms on the far wall. Such a move, whilst not complex, would be totally irreversible. If I missed I would plummet down into the lower groove and straight on to Martin's belay, and the consequences of a smashed leg here did not bear thinking about. Logic said retreat while there was some light left, yet my heart really wanted this route, and a lull in the spindrift gave me just sufficient encouragement to abandon inhibition and let my body go.

After ten minutes spent lying prostrate across the chimney and scraping for cracks in the smooth gabbro, I realised that the next move would also have to be made without protection. The day was fading, and if I didn't move soon there was a real prospect of benightment. Again a lull in the snowfall provided the cue. I let my legs drop and dangle, then mantleshelfed on to a sloping hold on the left wall. Now I could get my axes back into iced cracks and two good runners materialised from cracks in the roof. During a pause between the snowslides I arched my body out from the capstone and swung both axes into the névé snow above; one heave and I was kneeling thankfully on a simple 50 degree slope.

By the time I was belayed ten metres higher it was virtually dark. Martin prusiked the pitch, bombarded throughout by appalling spindrift. Hopes of a quick finish were dashed as steep snows twisted left into another bay. By torchlight I put in a half-hearted peg, no longer attentive to the vital details of security. Martin then led through. His rope snaked steadily upwards and his torch-beam disappeared in the mist, leaving me to fight convulsions of shivering on the stance.

A barely audible yell and the rope drew tight. It led me up an icy step, turned sharp right over a snow ridge and across a rocky bluff where I found Martin bent double against a southerly gale. How he was managing to cheat hypothermia I didn't know, for I was already at that disembodied stage of having to tell my body what to do.

We bundled tangles of gear into our sacks and staggered off through masses of fresh snow in search of the summit of Mhadaidh. A fluted arête of snow had formed on the ridge, erasing all memories of summertime rock features. Lacking map or compass we held a course

Plate 10.13 *Deep Gash Gully: Martin Welch thrashes up the chimney pitch below the crux capstone*

solely by keeping the wind on our left side and, moving one at a time for fear of avalanche, we edged precariously towards the An Dorus gap. Down in Coire a'Ghreadaidh the snow turned into pouring rain. Four kilometres of slippery grass, melting ice and thawing peat took us down to the Glen Brittle road, then it was a further hour's tramp back to Martin's car which we gained at something after ten o'clock, a mere 14½ hours since setting out.

The failure of Martin's starting motor, the heater's stubborn refusal to work and our tendency to aquaplane round every rainwashed bend in the rush to catch the 11pm ferry to Kyle – I could ignore them all. We'd got our route and we were going home.

The dénouement came six weeks later, six weeks of living 'high' on this route which we described as an 'atmospheric and formidable' grade VI. Andy Nisbet, guardian of the Scottish Mountaineering Club's 'new routes' file, came on the phone with more than the usual hint of reserve in his voice: 'You know that route on Skye you reported to me last month?' he began. 'Aye, well I've just got a letter from Mick Fowler. It seems he did it a week before you.' For a while I was stunned. Had we not given our all for the climb? And more particularly, were it the first time I had been beaten to a prize by a gentleman of that name, I might not have minded quite so much!

So our diary of Deep Gash Gully turned into the 'first ascent that never was', although years later, 'first ascent' credits don't matter as much as the memory of the day. Deep Gash in a storm was Scottish gully climbing at its incomparable best, a total adventure where we were forced to surpass ourselves in order to succeed.

11: TEARS AND SMEARS

PURE ICE CLIMBING

'For an hour we flogged up the stalker's path under the glare of the afternoon sun. The snow, sticky and soft, became progressively deeper until the path was obliterated. Now we entered the shade and felt that arctic chill of dry air at −5 degrees. Tension mounted. The source of the rumour was reliable, but he might well have exaggerated what lay over the shoulder. We breasted the ridge, looked across – and our breaths froze at the sight of a stunning series of icefalls. Every watercourse on the hillside had been spray-frozen into eggshell-blue cascades. The central ravine spouted a continuous 150m plunge of frosted glass. It was hard to believe we were standing in an undistinquished corrie only a few miles from home and not in some stupendous amphitheatre of the Canadian Rockies. A degree of self-delusion might be excused. The scene fired the imaginations and induced urgent plans of attack, for every single line was untouched and come next week they might not be there ...'

The ephemeral nature and pristine beauty of pure ice formations ensures their special affection in the hearts of winter climbers. Undeterred by the maritime whims of the climate, Scottish climbers sharpen their tools and, thus prepared, lie in wait for the big freeze which can be expected at some time in each winter season. The traditional gullies no longer bound the ice climber's ambitions: whether climbing low-level water ice, mountain icefalls, hanging icicles or the thinnest smears out on the faces, anything and everything goes so long as it is just frozen!

THE SHIFT FROM THE GULLIES

Pure ice climbing became a pursuit in its own right as a result of the front-point revolution around 1970; up until then there had been only a handful of excursions onto icicles and icefalls, Smith's Route (Gardyloo Buttress) and The Curtain on Ben Nevis being the most notable. These were bold achievements, and must have been extremely precarious routes to climb in the step-cutting style. With the establishment of front-pointing, the era of classic gully exploration came to an early end and a wholesale movement towards the icefalls began. The shift from the gullies took several directions, as dictated by terrain and conditions (Fig 11.1).

Low-level frozen waterfalls: When frozen, cascades and falls such as the Eas Anie on Beinn Chuirn by Tyndrum, Steall Falls in Glen Nevis, and Oui Oui on Creag Dubh, Newtonmore, provide excellent training in grade III ice-craft. They give a rare opportunity to develop and practise personal skills on steep ice, free from the objective problems of mountain crags. The icefalls which we discovered in Glen Carron in 1996 yielded over half-a-dozen climbs between grades III and V at 80 to 150m in length. With time to do three or four routes in a day, we could climb more pure ice there in a single visit than we might in a week of slogging up to mountain cliffs.

Plate 11.1 *Classic frontpoint style on water ice, wholly dependent on a solid platform from the feet (Martin Welch)*

Fig 11.1 *The shift from the gullies*

Watercourses won't freeze without a prolonged cold spell of a week or more in duration when daytime temperatures hover at or below zero degrees, and a sustained spell of polar continental or arctic maritime airflow during the short days of December and January is required. By late February, daytime sunshine can be sufficiently intense to strip low-level ice formations. The rate of freezing is accelerated by strong winds, which spray flowing water onto the adjoining rocks and spread the ice. Where spray has been blown outwards at the lip of a waterfall, weird ice-umbrellas are formed, bristling with horizontal daggers of ice which look like giant sundews ready to clasp and swallow the errant climber.

The rate of flow of water is of equal importance in the freezing process. Thus a total drought may leave the watercourses too dry to form substantial ice, however cold the weather. By contrast, major streams rarely dwindle to the steady trickle that will feed a growing icicle. Despite a week of Siberian temperatures, an attempt on the Falls of Glomach in January 1987 failed after a few feet, with the fallen leader submerged under the ice which covered the plunge pool at the bottom; luckily he was fished to safety by his second man. The flow of the feeder stream, the Abhainn Gaorsaic, is invariably too strong to allow a complete freeze at the falls – though we still live in hope!

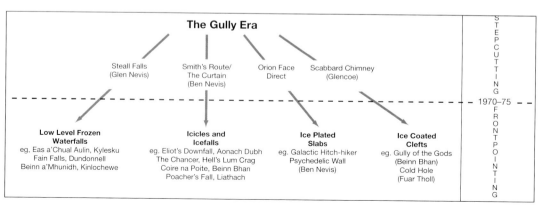

A copious spring-line provides a slow but continuous water supply, and is the ideal source for progressive freezing downstream. The Glen Carron falls on Sgurr na Feartaig all form just below dependable springs. They are likely to form with great regularity and I am sure they would have been climbed many years ago but for their secluded location on an obscure Corbett, hidden from any valley view. In the Southern Highlands the better-known ice venue of Coire Daimh on Beinn Udlaidh benefits from comparable drainage conditions.

Whilst Britain's most impressive major fall at Glomach has so far resisted the designs of ice climbers, our highest cascade – the triple-tiered, 200m spout of the Eas a'Chual Alumn by Kylesku in the far north-west – was conquered in 1986 by Andy Cunningham and Andy Nisbet. Many of these falls have been tackled when an appreciable volume of water is still flowing down the back of the ice. The lowest of Scotland's low-level icefalls was found on the side of Edinburgh Castle in January 1987. Although only grade III in standard, the route's name, 'Breach of the Peace', suggests that the ascent was not without outside interference.

Mountain icicles and icefalls: Wherever rock jointing produces groundwater seepage, pure icefalls and icicles may form on mountain crags. Although they are often augmented in girth by the addition of snowmelt and direct accretion from fresh snowfall, they are essentially formed from water flow. The Cairngorms are not renowned for pure ice climbing, yet they still possess an ice paradise in Hell's Lum Crag: facing south-east, the crag can develop fine runs of ice on its slabs, and overlaps early in the season with the assistance of a daily sunshine-and-freeze cycle; indeed, the icicle epoch was really initiated on Hell's Lum when Cunningham and March climbed The Chancer in 1970. This ascent turned eyes long blink-

ered by gully walls towards similar free-standing monsters all over Scotland. In the eastern Gorms, Creag an Dubh Loch has, on rare occasion, sported superb icefalls, the line of Goliath being the most notable so far climbed at a scary grade VII.

Ben Nevis has its icy spouts, chiefly on and around the Carn Dearg cliffs. The Curtain gives a straightforward grade IV with modern tools, and is undoubtedly Scotland's most hacked and hackneyed piece of ice. Nearby icefalls are considerably steeper. Mega Route X, the 60m icicle which can form down Central Trident Buttress, is now famous thanks to 'Cubby' Cuthbertson's ice-cool lead in front of television cameras for BBC's *The Edge* series. Round on the left side of Waterfall Gully, Shield Direct (VII), Gemini (VI) and more recently the Bewildabeast (VI) are less often on display, but are first-class routes with an 'out there' feel. In January 1993 the hanging ice fang left of Harrison's Climb Direct, for long the conjecture of all who walk up to the CIC hut regularly in winter, finally came within a metre of touching earth. Within days it had been climbed as The Shroud (VII) by Andy Clarke and John Main, their ascent featuring among other things a semi-hanging belay from ice screws.

Some of the most impressive mountain icefalls have been found in the North-west Highlands thanks to the contrasting geology of the Torridonian sandstone and quartzite rocks. The quartzite which forms the cappings of many peaks is permeable and stores a supply of groundwater which flows outwards on meeting the impermeable bands of sandstone underneath. Coire Dubh Mor on Liathach is the most likely place to see the resultant icefalls, of which Poacher's Fall and Salmon Leap are now classics that are often in condition. Even where there is no juxtaposition of different rock types, the horizontal bedding of sandstone produces

good seepage lines. In Applecross, Beinn Bhan's nest of great corries can on occasion harbour what Hamish MacInnes once described as 'some of the finest ice climbing in Europe'. The colossal 300m backwall of the central amphitheatre, Coire na Poite, has exhibited perhaps the largest expanse of icicles in Scotland and was one of the first new places to be investigated with 'terror' axes and front-point crampons in the early 1970s. Even remote outposts such as Creag Urbhard on Foinaven have provided tremendous icicle climbs during prolonged cold spells.

The majority of mountain icefalls lie in the altitude range from 750 to 900m, and will only form well when a continuously cool spell of weather allows a cycle of freeze-thaw to proceed each night and day. A sudden thaw is disastrous, and two consecutive days of tropical maritime air coupled with heavy rain will destroy most of these ice features.

Ice-coated clefts: Some might argue that these features represent the final phase of gully exploration, but only an optimist would use the term 'gully' to describe ice-lined overhanging chimneys of Torridonian sandstone, such as Gully of the Gods and Great Overhanging Gully in Coire an Fhamhair, Beinn Bhan (see Plate 11.7). Both require contortionist bridging tactics, in total contrast to the neater footwork of normal front-pointing, and can be guaranteed to stretch both the mind and hamstrings. The impressive dyke lines on the Black Cuillin appear to offer potential for similarly awesome winter routes. However, the run-off of rainfall from the gabbro rock is so rapid that the gradual seepage of groundwater needed for reliable ice formation is rarely achieved on Skye.

Thin-ice face routes: In contrast to the frozen

Plate 11.3 *Starting the crux pitch of Salmon Leap (VI), a classic icefall on Liathach (Allan Clapperton)*

'tears' of icicles and icefalls, there are now many face routes which depend on thin ice-plating; these are best described as ice smears. These predominate on the upper reaches of the Nevis cliffs, where they form from heavy riming coupled with slow seepage from melting snow, rather than water drainage. The Ben's smooth, slabby rock strata and humid climatic conditions are especially predisposed to surface icing. Most of these routes are bold in character because, by definition, thin ice does not allow placement of ice screws, and even if one can expose some rock, any cracks are likely to be glued with verglas.

The technical difficulty of face routes varies

Plate 11.2 *Andy Nisbet approaching the crux umbrellas of The Stonker (IV), a long water ice line on Sgurr na Feartaig, Glen Carron (Martin Welch)*

Plate 11.4 *Thin face ice — Dave Hesleden on the first ascent of Il Duce (VII) on Fuar Tholl (Simon Richardson)*

greatly with the thickness of the ice. The angle of the routes is not especially steep, being typically in the 65–75 degree range. A liberal coating (ie 8cm or more) gives good, secure placements, and then the actual climbing may be straightforward. In leaner conditions, one dares not swing the axes or crampons with vigour, for they will strike the underlying rock and cause the ice to 'dinner plate'. Instead, one must teeter upwards, hooking the last-most notches of the axe-picks into the surface and kicking the crampon tips with the most gentle precision. One proceeds in the imminent fear that the ice may disappear altogether, leaving the fearful prospect of reversing a pitch.

Yet despite these obvious discourage-

ments, a network of routes has been established across the Minus Buttresses, the upper Orion Face, the Hadrians and Psychedelic Walls and Gardyloo Buttress, most of them at grades VI and VII. The Orion Face Direct was an early precursor of the style, taking iced rocks on its crucial pitches above the Basin. Thin ice-plating is encountered on occasion in other areas, where water seepage flows down a steep slab. Hardest of this genre is Foobarbundee on Liathach, where the slab happens to be 80 degrees in angle! The climbing was so thin and protection so lacking on the first ascent in 1994 by Chris Cartwright and Dave Hesleden that the route was given a grade of VIII.

SLAV ROUTE, BEN NEVIS

The longest face climb on Ben Nevis is Slav Route. Despite a low technical grading of 5 and despite having been soloed at least once, the route is serious enough to be VI overall. In 1992 Paul Potter and I had something of an epic on it, which illustrates how much harder such climbs can be in lean conditions:

'One last chance to do a big route after an indifferent winter had lured us to the Ben. The morning had been fresh and crisp, we had met frost on the tracks below the CIC hut, and all had seemed set fair for an ice romp. We both wanted to do a climb that we hadn't done before, and Slav Route was smeared with ice, albeit thinly. Although it is the longest route on the face, with 450 metres of climbing in nine or ten pitches, we reasoned that if "Cubby" and the "Brat" had soloed it in a hour or so back in 1986, the route should not hold any real horrors.

'Now, a pitch and half up and fully engaged, we were beginning to regret those careless threads of reason. From twenty-five metres up Zero Gully, Slav Route breaks out left up a ramp and surmounts an overlap onto the main sweep of Orion's slabs. With absolute trust in the weather, I hadn't even bothered to put on my jacket at the start. Several sackloads of spindrift from Zero had disabused me of that notion, but my overtrousers remained stowed in the sack. Then came the slight shock of failing to find any anchors for a belay for the first pitch. The rock was totally compact, and the ice was either slushy or honeycombed. Paul had led the pitch without a belay.

'The slab and overlap were my job. Paul belayed me from dubious anchors. Someone had abseiled off from here in the recent past because I found a peg and sling in place on the ramp. At least that gave protection for what lay above. Looking to the overlap, a short hanging icicle seemed the only way over, and was clearly the watershed of the route. I swung onto its stub, changed my feet, and steadied myself ready for the pull up and back into balance. Then the rope jammed in the stalactites beneath my feet. Hanging from one axe I stretched down with the other, unhitched it, and hastened onto the slabs above. A strong sense of bridges burnt tempered my relief.

'Fifteen metres higher I reached a stance in a V-groove, and, belayed solely on two thumbnail-sized spikes of rock plus a bedded axe pick, I brought Paul up with a suitably tight rope. Above, the angle was little more than 55 degrees: a grade III walk if the ice had been thick. Paul weaved among the ice smears seeking a solid line. A gradually thickening mist was slowly obscuring the Orion Face, and climbers there faded from view, their presence evidenced only by discordant shouts and hammerings. As I huddled on my stance a wet snowfall became established. At times like this you realise your trust of your partner: with one runner in thirty metres above my imaginary belay, Paul could not afford to fall.

'I led through, up another pitch of unpre-

dictable slabbiness. Some sections were iced, others were temptingly masked with snow but revealed only the Ben's bare backside an inch or two below. If the technical standard was unexceptional, the psychological demands were growing. Our world was confined to a fifty-metre radius of snowy slabs and shallow grooves, plus the occasional glimpse of a buttress edge to our right where Zero Gully cut the cliff. Lacking visibility or a guidebook, routefinding had boiled down to one simple dictum: if we kept near that edge we would eventually reach the top.

'Paul's next lead was thin and necky, featuring successive mantleshelvings with toe-tips next to fingertips on bare rock edges and fragile ice smears. Seconding, I was shivering so much that I almost shook my axe picks out of their precarious lodgements. "Please say its easier above," I said when I reached Paul, part in hope and part in respect for his efforts. For

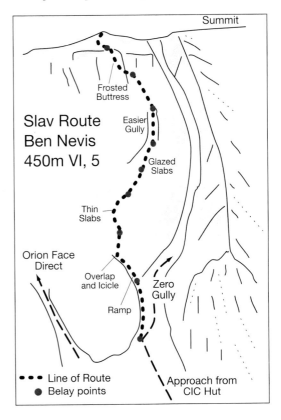

Slav Route
Ben Nevis
450m VI, 5

Summit

Frosted Buttress

Easier Gully

Glazed Slabs

Thin Slabs

Orion Face Direct

Overlap and Icicle

Zero Gully

Ramp

●●● Line of Route
● Belay points

Approach from CIC Hut

one pitch it was, a grade III ice gully overlooking the upper trench of Zero and leading to a Friend belay below rimed steps. Here Paul did more desperate work on a mixture of rock, ice wafers and the odd tuft. I was paying for my earlier neglects: my legs, stiff with cold, began cramping on the strenuous moves, and puddles of water slopped about in my plastic boot shells. Still it snowed with mournful silence.

'A frosted buttress took shape in the evening gloom, dashing hopes of an easier finish. It sported three corners, each beautifully rimed and revealing nothing of its secrets. Which to choose? A bad choice could cost us the daylight. The left-hand and shortest corner was also the steepest, but nonetheless I plumped for it, and scrapings in the crack unearthed two wedged stones for thread runners, the first certain protection in six pitches. With frantic knee and shoulder jams I surmounted the corner and emerged on a short snow ridge which cut through the final cornice.

'Paul hurried through to gain a plateau blessed by thick fog and dead calm. I pulled out my watch for the first time in six hours and was amazed to see 8.40pm on the display. The air was freezing well, and with it our ropes and harnesses. Paul slipped his bowlines in seconds; five minutes later I was still hacking and chewing at my figures-of-eight. But rather than berating me for the delay, Paul shot me a wry grin, knowing that I was well and truly 'sandbagged'. At last freed from the gear, I grabbed my first drink in eleven hours.

'We wandered down open snow wreaths to the Red Burn path and parted with a closing time pint in the Fort. I drove the eighty miles home fighting sleep with the windows open, but at 1.30am I finally stripped off soggy clothes and flung my goosepimpled carcass into a warm duvet. Sheer bliss!'

STEELING THE NERVES: GEAR, GRADES AND ETHICS
Gear

Recent ice activities have been considerably helped by continual improvements in tools and hardware:

Boots: (Plate 10.1) Steep ice requires absolute rigidity in the boot soles, because these must act as a platform for the levered support of the body's whole weight on front-points; this is why most climbers prefer plastic boots, their moulded shell construction offering a lasting stability and the best ankle support, plus the guarantee of dry warm toes. However, there are now a few models of leather boot offering similar rigidity and protective toe-rands, which are given the full B3 boot rating for technical ice.

Crampons: Most of the classic grade V and grade VI ice climbs in Scotland were first accomplished wearing the strap-on Salewa crampons universally popular for all winter mountaineering in the 1970s and early 1980s. Nowadays there is a wide choice of specialist climbing crampons:

- *Classic snow and ice crampons:* These have two front-points and a second set of forward-pointing points, giving a 'lobster's claw' effect. They provide excellent support and stability on snow-ice of up to 80 degrees, and are excellent for ice routes of grades IV and V. The crampon is articulated so it is also suitable for all styles of general mountaineering.

- *Rigid crampons:* Fully rigid crampons offer a better platform to support the feet on steep ice. Salewa Chouinard and Camp 'Footfangs' were the original rigid models, and are still popular, but there are now many alternatives. The front-points protrude further than on classic crampons, and are cut vertically to give better penetration in water ice without the danger of shattering the surface; they sport serrated teeth for maximum grip. The second set of points are also cut vertically and point forward to give extra support on easier angled ground. Rigid crampons are designed specifically for climbing hard ice up to the highest grades, and are unsuitable for walking.

- *Monopoint crampons:* Crampons with a single front-point are proving highly effective on the most technical ice routes. Though the single point of support may appear precarious, it allows the feet to swivel from side to side without risk of the crampon levering off, as is the case with double front-points; it also allows precision placement in tiny pockets or notches of ice. Monopoints are less suited to bashing up long, middle-grade routes – here the support and stability of the 'lobster-claw' designs are needed.

All ice-climbing crampons should have clip-on cable bindings, or a ring strap for the strap and clip-up heel. Needless to say, the fit to the boot must be tight.

Axes and Hammers: (Plate 11.5) Any serious ice climber should choose a modular axe system with interchangeable picks. Reverse curve ('banana'-shaped) picks are used universally for technical winter climbing because they are much easier to extract than curved pick-axes. Some picks are specially designed with a longer and slightly thinner blade for pure ice climbing.

For ice climbing, choose a shaft length of between 45 and 55cm according to personal height and preference. Curved shafts help the placement of the axes and prevent rapping of the knuckles when the axe is swung. However, a straight-shafted axe is perfectly sufficient for all but the very hardest ice climbing and can be used for general mountaineering, which highly specialised tools cannot. Most serious ice climbers will periodically sharpen their ice

Plate 11.5 *Modern ice climbing tools: (top) Grivel hammer: durable all-rounder for ice and mixed climbing; (middle) Simond icefall hammer; (bottom) DMM curved shaft specialist icefall axe*

picks. The teeth on the underside of the pick can also be filed to give a steep hooking angle, although such practice inevitably diminishes the life of the gear. Worn down and blunt tools can ideally be retired from ice climbing and used on mixed routes. Broad wrist-loops with sliders to prevent them pulling through a gloved hand should be fitted to the exact length of the axe shafts to ensure full support when in traction.

The Grading System

The extended grading system now used in Scotland gives an overall grading range from I to VIII for ice climbs, with subsidiary numerical rating for technical difficulties up to 7. Smith's Route on Gardyloo Buttress has a benchmark of grade V,5 which with modern equipment is regarded as a route of average difficulty. The potential seriousness of most pure ice routes is reflected in the overall grading. The numerical technical grade relates directly to the angle of ice encountered: 3=60 degrees, 4=70 degrees, 5=80 degrees or vertical steps,

6=vertical, 7=vertical with overhanging sections. International grades for pure ice are prefixed WI (meaning water ice) and run from WI 1 to WI 7. The international equivalents of Scottish grades are, on average, one full grade lower, so that a Scottish 6 would typically rate WI 5 in North America.

Ethical Practice

The style of climbing ice routes is now subject to close ethical scrutiny, and ice climbers should aim for totally free leads on ice pitches – in other words, they should not take any rests either by clipping in to ice screws, taking tension from the rope, or clipping the axe wrist-loop into their harness. All were admissible sins prior to the 1990s, but with the dwindling stock of unclimbed lines it has quite rightly become important to achieve 'clean' ascents, with any deviations from the ideal being honestly reported.

The greatest difficulty of making an unaided front-point ascent lies not in the actual climbing, but in placing protection. It is technically feasible to free-climb long sections of sheer or even gently overhanging ice – but how on earth does a leader stop to place much-needed ice screws on such ground? There are four options:

1 Don't stop, do without any protection and go for the top on a mixture of ability and adrenalin.
2 Clip a sling from harness to ice-axe for rest and support while hammering the screw. This is the unethical option, but is ostensibly safe, provided one is sure that the embedded axe-pick will support the body's full weight. Catastrophe results if it does not.
3 Carry an 'ice fi-fi hook': this is simply a toothed pick with short sling which can be quickly hammered in, and used for protection or for aid while inserting the ice screw.
4 Insert the screw without aid or protection by

sliding one wrist-loop up to the elbow for support, and using that hand to hold the screw while it is tapped or screwed into place.

Even though the problem has been greatly alleviated with the use of 4-bit tubular screws which can be part-inserted by hand, the placement of protection is undoubtedly the most difficult and hair-raising operation on vertical ground. It is therefore essential to stop and place good protection wherever the angle eases – then one is more readily prepared to take chances on the steep stuff above.

Responsibility for ethical practice on ice lies with the individual's conscience. Not even the second might notice if the leader takes aid when placing protection, but it is wrong to delude either oneself or the bar-room audience that a lead on ice with rests on axes, hooks or screws equates to a clean lead.

A CAUTIONARY TALE

Whilst enjoying those rare spells of good ice conditions, climbers must also realise that such periods do inevitably come to an end sometimes, and it is a good idea not to be halfway up an icicle when they do. The craggy flanks of the Three Sisters of Glencoe develop a myriad of icefalls during a good season, but undoubtedly the most famous is the 30m icicle barring the entrance to No 5 Gully on the West Face of Aonach Dubh, which became known as Elliot's Downfall. When formed, it hangs free of the rock for nearly 15m and offered a tantalising challenge until Dave 'Cubby' Cuthbertson made the first ascent in February 1979. Towards that season's end when the winter's freeze was slowly waning at lower levels, the icicle still winked down at passing travellers. Wisely or not, three rather hung-over climbers, Pete Thexton, John Given and Phil Swainson, in search of a short but exciting day, decided that it would bear a repetition.

Thexton took the lead, leaving his companions standing in a drip of cold meltwater in the cave below. His progress was steady and sure, but he was unhappy with the ice-screw protection and moved left at 12m into a small grotto where he placed a tied-off piton as a back-up runner. His second, Given, watched him move back onto the ice just 5m away from success, when there was a resounding bang – '*I dived into the cave. All I could see was this pillar of ice in the sky, settling for a shattered brittle second on its fang into the slope, like a factory chimney might just before it tilts out and thunders down.*'

When he opened his eyes again, the ice was gone – but Thexton was still there, clinging to his 'terrors' 15m up, inches above the fracture line: 'The fracture had sprung from the tip of Pete's right axe, run down beside him and curved back under his feet.'[1]

Thexton's ice screws had pulled out of the tumbling ice, yet somehow he had stayed on. It was a miraculous escape. Unable to help, Swainson took the opportunity to capture Thexton's horrific position on film (Plates 11.6a and b) – and it was only at this point that his seconds noticed the substantial volume of water that had been draining behind the ice: looking up at the fracture line, they could see that the whole weight of the icicle had been hanging from a sheet of ice just 20cm thick. Their leader meanwhile put his heart in his mouth and abseiled off the piton that had probably saved his life.

Plates 11.6a and b *The collapse of Elliot's Downfall and a hair's-breadth for climber Pete Thexton (Phil Swainson)*

Icicles are fragile beasts, at all times to be treated gently, but strictly to be admired from a safe distance when a thaw sets in.

ICE FANATICS

The French Connection: Climb ice on Ben Nevis at any time in late March or early April and you are just as likely to hear the nasal tones of French voices echoing round the cliffs as the English and Scots vernacular. This is because with unfailing regularity over the last fifteen years, French mountain guide and globe-trotting ice expert Godefroy Perroux has brought his clients over to Ben Nevis for a couple of weeks' courses. Exhibiting the usual British trait for self-deprecation, I wondered how on earth the Ben could hold such appeal for a man who has climbed waterfall ice all over the world, and who could be earning his living just as easily in the sunny climes and icy *goulottes* of the Alps. The inspiration for Perroux's first visit in 1982 came from Scotland's reputation as 'the birthplace of extreme ice': '*With no information except the name of a little town in the Highlands, we covered 2,000km non-stop in our quest. Expecting so much we were not disappointed, and everything we had come for was there in our first route: a little ice, waves of powder snow, bad weather, a hellish wind. What we didn't like was the long approach.*'

Tackling Point Five as his first major ice route on the Ben, he encountered the soft snow-ice which is so special a feature of Scottish climbing: '*Drawn like moths to the flame, we arrived at a run. With so much new snow the climbing was delicate and we progressed with serpent-like movements on what seemed to be vertical snow. There was no ice*

on which to anchor our axes, but improbably, the snow held.'

Godefroy endured considerable privation on his first visits. He was discovered camping outside the CIC hut without fuss or complaint, and impressed the hut guardian of the time so much that he was enlightened as to the booking system. Since then he has stayed at the CIC each year, and by 1998 had amassed some sixty different routes on Nevis, with many repeat ascents of the great classics. There are only a handful of British climbers who could remotely match his tally. And if the length and steepness of the Ben's ice routes fail to match those of his home area in the Dauphiné Alps, then their purity and boldness have continued to impress. Writing in 1988 he reflected: '*I can now understand the British ethics which forbid bolts. I accept the custom of protection as one leads, even if nuts, pitons, 'Friends', deadmen and so on amount to a lot of weight. Each ascent feels like a first ascent and is always an adventure.*'

The injection of Gallic flair and culinary skill has certainly added a new dimension to life at the CIC. A Perroux party will arrive for a week's stay with a selection of fine wines and all the ingredients for piquant *entrées*. One of my clients endured a stay there in open-mouthed envy of the French *haute cuisine*: while he endured boiled and unseasoned vegetables with pasta two nights running courtesy of his Aberdonian chef, the Perroux party were tucking into fish in white wine sauce with peas and *sauté* potatoes, followed by several of Godefroy's legendary *crêpes*.

Many of Godefroy's clients have become regular visitors, likewise addicted to the esoteric appeal of Nevis ice. Keenest and undoubtedly the most prominent among

Plate 11.7 *Gully of the Gods, the great cleft of Beinn Bhan, one of Mick Fowler's finest first ascents (climber: Robin Beadle)*

these is Belgian physiotherapist, Jean-Pierre. Despite weighing something upward of seventeen stones and rocking the CIC to its foundations with his mighty snoring, he has followed his guide up some thirty-eight routes over the years. Godefroy will select a route for the day over breakfast and point Jean-Pierre in its direction. While J-P trudges slowly up to its base Godefroy cleans the hut, prepares the sauce for dinner, and perhaps enjoys a last cup of coffee, before racing up the hill to catch him at the start of the difficulties. Thereafter Jean-Pierre is in his element, marshalling his great strength to overcome grade V ice. His successful passage suggests that those belays on Zero Gully can't be as bad as everybody thought.

There is much to learn from watching Godefroy's style on ice, as well as his cooking. He leads on 60m or even 70m ropes, and by making long pitches can save himself the fruitless game of finding decent belays on Nevis face routes. Even on the Ben there is usually some decent anchorage every 60m. Long leads necessitate a bold style, and Godefroy uses his personal skill and confidence to complete big runouts without fuss or fear, even when guiding clients. Top modern ice performers can only climb as boldly as they do by following the dictum coined by Jeff Lowe, that every placement of an ice tool should be treated as a portable belay. Godefroy's speed enables him to do two routes a day in good conditions plus, occasionally, a quick evening solo before dinner.

Despite lean conditions and poor weather through many of his visits in the 1990s, Godefroy has not been deterred and continues simply to enjoy the Scottish winter experience for what it is, as should we all.

The English Predator: If the name Mick Fowler should arouse painful personal memories, thanks to the aptly named 'Pipped at the Post' on Fuar Tholl and the afore-described Deep Gash Gully, not even I would deny him his place as one of the inspirational ice climbers of the last twenty years. Mick's raiding weekends on the most remote Highland cliffs became as legendary as they were frustrating to Scottish climbers during the 1980s. He combined an unconventional image, cultivated disorganisation and an adventurous style of pioneering on steepest or thinnest ice.

Somehow, on a weekend time-budget, Fowler and friends would often drive up from London, pinch plum ice routes from under the noses of both natives and local residents, and still get back to work for 8am on Monday morning. Prior to his arrival on the scene, Scots climbers had a virtual monopoly of winter pioneering – a game where local knowledge and residence seemed crucial to success. Yet the list of his first ascents comprises a substantial proportion of the finest lines climbed in the last two decades, and some are as yet unrepeated. So how has he done it?

Undoubtedly he has a considerable natural talent. Back in 1977 Mick was frantically rock-climbing at the highest standard throughout Britain, but the stereotyped style and tactics of modern crag-climbing were of limited appeal, and for a man whose mind was infused with a spirit of adventure as well as a sense of the outrageous, there was a much wider world to explore. Thus he turned his energies to sea cliffs of the loosest variety, and of course to ice. After a brief apprenticeship in Wales, a visit to Scotland with Victor Saunders in March 1979 produced the first winter ascent of Shield Direct, the awesome line up the right side of Carn Dearg Buttress on the Ben. The ascent was an eye-opener: *'Realising that such a good line on the most popular cliff had not been climbed really made me wake up to the potential of Scotland. We graded it V, and were very confused when it was reported as VI in the journals and guides, as neither of us ever said this.'* But local opinions, too, were obviously sufficiently impressed at the sight of the route that they made it the first grade VI in the country without having set a foot on it. Moreover the second ascent was not made until 1986, seven years later. Mick, however, long maintained it was a 'good' grade V.

In his grading, as in his whole approach to climbing, Mick is a traditionalist. His only concession to purism is that he will on occasion clip in to his axes while placing protection on vertical ice. Those who consider Point Five a standard grade V were greatly perplexed and a little overawed by many of Mick's routes which he also graded V. With the extension of the grading system in 1991 other climbers had to make an inspired guess as to how these routes truly rated on the new scale.

To achieve such success has required exploratory enthusiasm and dogged persistence. The North-west Highlands satisfy Mick's exploratory instincts to perfection, offering natural ice lines in a wild, remote setting, which must be climbed on sight (ie without any prior inspection). The highly technical mixed climbing of known summer rock routes is less to his taste. It is the lure of the wholly unknown and the appeal of 'the line' that counts. Persistence has been essential. Mick is sometimes suspected of holding some divine communication upon which to predict good conditions, but like the rest of us, he simply watches the forecast on television and hopes. The long drive north therefore often ends '... *at 4.30am slumped across car seats with a force 10 gale and lashing sleet outside rocking us erratically to sleep, the enthusiasm levels distinctly low.'*

In successive attempts on his 1988 route on Aonach Dubh's North Face, his team drove 4,800km and survived several hair-raising car rotations on an icy Loch Lomond road, plus a 200m fall in an avalanche on the ramp beneath

the climb. Prior to the last bid even Fowler was becoming despondent: 'on calculation, we had so far achieved half an inch of climbing for every mile driven – not up to the usual standard at all.' And the final attempt was not without its excitements: Fowler locked outside the Kingshouse Hotel at 4.30am with partner Watts sleeping soundly inside, and the unfortunate failure of Watts to remember his crampons, necessitating a two-hour detour back to the hotel; then forcing the route in worsening weather, knowing that their driver was leaving for London at 8pm prompt. No wonder then that Mick christened the climb 'Against All Odds'.

West Central Gully on the Triple Buttress, Beinn Eighe is with little doubt the hardest gully climb in Britain, the final 80m headwall being vertical or gently overhanging throughout. On the first ascent in April 1987 and close to the top, Mick ran out of steam in the most inopportune position. His means of extrication shows the depths of ingenuity that the hard-pressed ice-climber must display to ensure self-preservation. Protection was a single knife-blade piton a considerable way below: '*A high axe placement over a bulge is good, but all strength is gone. That weak drained feeling comes over me, legs dangling beneath an icicle fringe, axe firmly planted above it. I try and pull up to clip my harness into the axe. Can't do it – no strength. I hang limply from the wrist-loop. It is time for the last resort. My axes have long safety cords attached to the straps of my ten-year-old rucksack. Wriggling my hand out of the wrist-loop, I cross arms to keep my rucksack in place, and lower onto the straps. The stitching strains nastily, but holds. Heart in mouth, I take a rest.'* A second attempt brought the most slender of successes – all good character-building stuff, as Mick would have us believe. Still unrepeated by 1998, modern guidebook writers considered that the route might rate grade VIII. Even Mick conceded

route might rate grade VIII. Even Mick conceded that it was VI!

The proximity of the chalk cliffs of Dover played a major role in training the Londoners to the highest standards of performance on ice, the soft rock being climbed with axes, crampons and ice screws for protection and belays. Only the Scottish cold is absent. After one abortive weekend in Torridon, Mick even found better ice conditions in the middle of his own city. This was the big freeze of January 1987, and St Pancras Station's wall had developed a magnificent spout of ice from a broken drain. With his second belayed to a parking meter, the icicle was duly climbed, but protracted negotiations with British Rail police followed.

Partner quality is another key to Fowler's success. Although Mick is the prime motivator, he has always assembled a team of equal ability who will lead through on hard routes. Victor Saunders, Chris Watts and more lately Steve Sustad have been regular partners. He has no particular affectation with gear as do so many modern climbers. Between 1979 and 1986 he used the same pair of crampons on all routes, a set of 'bent tin' Salewa Classics. His simple style and approach draw their inspiration from the great ice-climbers of the 1950s; he has particular admiration for Tom Patey and Robin Smith, and his own purist spirit links him right back to the days of Naismith and Raeburn.

In 1988 Mick saw plenty of further challenges on Scottish ice, commenting: 'I'll get even older and shrivel up before it is all dealt with.' But conditions in the 1990s have been restrictive, and now that Mick is married and a father, so his visits to the Highlands have become less frequent than of old. However, there is no sign of the flame dying: having beaten me to Deep Gash Gully by ten days in 1991, he was back during the deep freeze of Christmas 1995. With Sustad he nipped up to Skye and climbed two big ice gullies on the massive cliffs behind the Old Man of Storr. This raid had all the hallmarks of the Fowler style – an obscure location known to few, and an inspired guess at conditions. Meanwhile he has maintained his 'other life' as manager of an Inland Revenue tax office with remarkable aplomb, and has amassed a superb record of climbs in foreign parts during his summer vacations.

In an era when regulation, technical intricacy and ethical wrangles were spreading insidiously into the winter scene, Fowler brought a refreshing breeze, reminding us that, above all, climbing is still fun. And indeed, as a means of rebelling against all convention, of defying the arid logic of safety and of knowing the thrill of being alive, ice climbing cannot be surpassed.

12: MIXED FORTUNES

WINTER BUTTRESS CLIMBING

CLASSIC BUTTRESS ROUTES

Winter buttress climbing has a pedigree stretching back to the first days of Scottish mountaineering in the 1890s. The great ridges of Nevis and Glencoe were tackled with style and audacity by the early pioneers, who set levels of technical performance which are still respected today. Using nailed boots for precision placement on icy rock, gloved hands for clearing and preparing holds, and axes for cutting steps on snowy sections, a unique climbing style evolved. There was no direct comparison in the Alps where summer mixed climbing meant a mixture of snow and dry rock. Even today Scottish buttress climbing, with its menu of frozen turf, verglas, powder snow and rime ice, has an atmosphere which is found in very few other mountain ranges of the world.

Having graduated from traverses such as the Aonach Eagach, many winter mountaineers cut their climbing teeth on the classic ridge and buttress routes of grade III and IV standard. Not only are these routes of great stature, but they also offer an education in the full gamut of mixed climbing techniques. Many come away from ascents of the Ben's great ridges either so impressed or so satisfied that their mixed climbing careers are stillborn; and those who have endured prolonged torment in crossing the Tower Gap under thick rime ice or hauling desperately up the Mantrap

late in the Nevis day, might be excused for turning away from buttresses to the easier gratification of ice gullies.

Observatory Ridge on Ben Nevis was undeniably the high point of the early wave of buttress pioneering. Apart from its basic intrinsic difficulty in winter, the ridge is subject to a perplexing variability of condition. Though currently graded IV, 4, I firmly believe it should have a technical grade of 5. Observatory was only the second Scottish route for French expert Godefroy Perroux. Later he recalled his ascent as:

'...my most vivid memory of mixed climbing...Since this was a classic climb we thought there would be fixed pitons, and for our two ropes carrying only three pitons and no nuts, the route was harrowing. We had underestimated the Ben, darkness was falling, the length of the route was astonishing...One must pay homage to the pioneers. Their technical level was fantastic and their courage was beyond belief.'[1]

As well as the four renowned ridges of Nevis, three other great classics at the upper end of grade III are North Buttress on the Buachaille Etive Mor, Black Spout Buttress on Lochnagar and Pinnacle Ridge of Sgurr nan Gillean; all enjoy superb situations. When lean, they can be climbed using traditional 'gloved-hand' techniques; in snowy conditions classic snow-climbing styles suffice for all but the crux moves. Pinnacle Ridge is a personal favourite, giving the most dependable winter conditions on Skye thanks to its relatively high altitude and northerly aspect. Three to four hours are needed from the start of the difficulties at the Third Pinnacle to the summit, and inexperienced parties may take longer. Featuring an exposed abseil and a tricky climb down from Knight's Peak, the route has an alpine atmosphere, and if transhipped to Switzerland would rate at least *assez difficile* in standard. Although I have enjoyed it when thickly plated in névé snow, my best memory was one March day in 1992 when we left drizzle and drab moors at Sligachan and climbed past the freezing level into an ethereal world of mist and rime. The route was in amazing condition.

We moved as vague shrouds in the shifting mist, our breaths forming white clouds of freezing vapour. Each slab and crack of black gabbro was varnished grey by a glaze of ice. Fringes of rime bristled from every windward block and edge, drawing a crystal tracery along the crest. We climbed the ridge with crampon tips biting the icy skin, mittens curled round frozen edges, and axes grating in the deeper slots, in a frozen procession of balance and rhythm. No move was rushed, for every step required thought and precision. Yet neither did we pause, for the way was long and the route so intricate that hours could pass unbidden. Muffled calls to climb echoed eerily between the pinnacles. Above, the frosted mass of Gillean's summit buttress quivered in the cloud. For brief hours we imagined ourselves as lonely voyagers lost to the time or cares of the world below.

Not only do the classic buttress routes offer great positions and climbing, but their ascent provides an essential foundation of skills for the step into what we might call modern mixed climbing. Though founded on the great traditions and ethical purity of the early pioneers, the modern scene requires new definitions, new techniques, and a reappraisal of attitudes.

DEFINING MIXED CLIMBING

In recent times, every winter climbing style that is not dependent on thick ice has tended to be lumped together and labelled as 'mixed'. The term 'mixed' originates from alpine climbing where it refers to a mixture of rock and ice, often broken rocks cemented together by ice as on the North Face of the Matterhorn, and usually climbed with bare hands and crampons. Two features of Scottish conditions complicate this simple definition: rime ice and frozen turf.

Rime: Rime ice is formed by the freezing of cloud droplets directly onto the rocks; it can plaster the faces with bushy cakes of fragile white ice, and gives Scottish winter crags a pristine white appearance whenever moist air has been uplifted over the summits and into the freezing zone. The accumulation of rime is especially rapid when the cloud blows in on a steady wind, but it is quickly disintegrated in severe or turbulent gales; it is rarely encountered in the drier climates of continental mountain ranges. Although classed as a form of ice, it is not sufficiently strong to be climbed as such; however, attempts to clear it away regularly reveal the underlying rock to be verglassed. In such conditions, easy moves between big holds, as found on the old classics, can usually be achieved by much scrattling of crampons and grovelling of arms; but the use of gloved hands for progress on thin holds or vertical ground is somewhere between the ineffectual and impossible, hence the need for a new range of axe techniques applicable to rock.

Frozen Turf: Many of Scotland's mountain crags, and particularly those of granite and schist, are heavily vegetated with only limited areas of steep, clean rock; when frozen, the moss or turf acts as a form of reinforced ice, providing placements as reliable as the best névé. Many buttress climbs rely almost entirely on turf for progress, and even at the highest grades, tiny tufts of vegetation often provide the key holds – indeed, this sort of climbing is sometimes referred to as 'tufting'. The axes are swung in exactly the same manner as would be used on ice, but greater precision in placement may be needed if the available vegetation is sparse.

So, not only is 'Scottish mixed' a different style to 'alpine mixed', but the word itself is sometimes a misnomer, since certain Scottish mixed climbs involve the same style of moves all the way up. However, the term has survived and has been used regularly in a derogatory sense (ie mixed versus pure) by those without the initiative to leave the ice gullies. I prefer, therefore, to use the term 'buttress climbing' to encompass the sport, and within its range two identifiable types of route can be found:

1 Summer rock routes climbed in winter under powder snow or rime ice conditions, which tend to feature little by way of vegetation or ice smears and require axe torquing in cracks and hooking on small edges.

2 'Winter-only' routes taking natural lines up cliffs which are typically too wet or vegetated to appeal to the summer rock climber. These may have substantial sections of thin ice, as well as tufting and rock, so they are genuinely mixed. They usually need to be well frozen to be climbable.

Inevitably there are overlaps between the two categories. In addition there is a blurred distinction between some of the icier mixed routes and the thin-ice face routes as described in Chapter 11. Many climbs can be classed as ice or mixed and climbed as either, depending on the prevailing conditions, particularly some of those on the faces of Ben Nevis. Invariably a route will be considerably easier to climb if liberally iced as opposed to being mixed in condition.

Prior to the 1970s nearly all winter but-tress ascents were summer routes in the range of Difficult to Severe in standard, a route like Lochnagar's Eagle Ridge being the limit of what could be achieved by traditional gloved-hand climbing. However, the introduction of axe-torquing and hooking techniques brought much harder rock-climbs into the domain of winter climbing. A considerable number of Very Severes and Hard Very Severes in the Cairngorms have been climbed under powder snow, and even the odd Extremely Severe (E1 or E2) has been accomplished with co-operative rock features and a lot of effort. But the torquing style has remained something of an obscure cult: it takes a certain nerve to abandon gloved-hand techniques and trust to the twisted pick of the ice-axe instead, and indeed many have remained sceptical that torquing in the underlying rock cracks constitutes winter climbing at all.

This mistrust of both the effectiveness and the ethics of mixed-climbing techniques has dissuaded many people from trying the climbs – yet it is undoubtedly in this sphere that the future development of Scottish winter climbing lies. Those on the pioneering fringe have long realised this, and have enjoyed unpressured freedom in opening up hundreds of new routes in the last two decades. It would be true to say that the greater proportion of these new climbs remained unrepeated by 1998, not because of any especial difficulty, but simply due to the prevailing fashion for ice.

Gradually the tide is turning, however, and a great many climbers are now awakening to the real qualities and advantages which mixed climbing has to offer over pure snow and ice. These are, namely, a greater reliability of suitable conditions; logistical intrigue; technical interest and unfailing variety; the regular availability of good protection; safety from avalanches; and a thankful escape from the crowds which throng the classic ice gullies – in

Plate 12.1 *Ethereal conditions on the Pinnacle Ridge of Sgurr nan Gillean, Skye – a classic grade III mixed ridge*

sum, the opportunity to push to one's physical and technical limit, be it grade III or VII.

TACTICS FOR BUTTRESS CLIMBING

Good planning and organisation are essential to success in buttress climbing, particularly if you choose a big route or a remote venue. To quote one of the most active exponents of the 1990s, Simon Richardson:

'I treat the whole day as part of a well thought out game plan which starts when the alarm clock goes off and doesn't finish till I'm back home again. This includes selecting crag and route, inspiring my partner, agreeing the best approach and descent, selecting gear, travelling to the venue, walking in, climbing the route, walking out and driving back home. Often, climbing the route is the easiest part of the day!

The crux of any winter climb is deciding what to go for on any particular day. The trick is to choose an objective to fit the prevailing weather and conditions, and not to try to fit something the other way around. A measure of a successful day in my book is predicting the conditions correctly and being completely safe when on the hill.'

Planning and tactics therefore add an absorbing dimension to buttress climbing, and one's choice of partner and appraisal of the weather and the conditions prevailing are vital ingredients:

Partners: Buttress climbing cannot be treated as a casual affair, to be undertaken with whoever happens to be available. The time and personal discomfort that you will commit to it makes the choice of a compatible partner absolutely vital, preferably someone who is willing and able to share the leading; a reluctant recruit is likely to turn mutinous after several hours spent shivering on stances while you send a continuous stream of powder snow down his or her neck. Andy Nisbet makes no secret of the fact that the key to the success of many of his most important pioneering climbs has been in his choosing a partner of high calibre, someone with the technical skill to pull off the crux pitches when necessary. With a team of two climbers of similar ability, one or the other is usually in a sufficiently warm or motivated condition to take on the leading. Selfless teamwork not only ensures the best chance of success, but often provides the best memory of the day out.

Having a team of three on some routes is sociable, but seconds must climb simultaneously to save time, and the bigger the team, the less opportunity there is to lead. For me, the real thrill of mixed climbing is in getting a turn out in front, and the real contentment is in sitting alone on a stance watching the play of light on the corrie floor.

Weather and Conditions: As a planned climbing trip approaches, one's anxiety as to the likely conditions can reach fever pitch. Such stress can be unhealthy, however, and may spoil one's enjoyment when the great day arrives; the best advice is to gather all the information you can regarding conditions in the preceding week, and then to plan a series of options in the event of the likely range of weather on the day. To focus on one route alone will only lead to extreme disappointment should it be found to be out of condition, or too far to approach under deep snow cover.

There are certain norms as to when particular cliffs come into condition. For example the Nevis ridges are unlikely to be in good condition until there is a decent cover of stable snow in mid- to late season. However, harder buttress routes are very different from pure ice in that they require no more than frozen conditions and a thin snow-cover or riming to come into condition. Routes which are primarily dependent on rock features can be in prime condition when there is little or no snow accumulation in the gullies – indeed, they can become climbable at two or three days' notice from the start of a cold snap at any time from October to late April.

Mixed routes which are dependent on a deeper freeze or partial icing are less easy to catch in good condition. As an example, both the big routes on the right face of Fuar Tholl's Mainreachan Buttress use commodious ice columns at the cruxes on their first ascents – yet the remainder of each route depends largely on rock, so that a liberal coating of rime or powder is also needed. Given the vertical nature of the rock and the exposure of the face to prevailing westerly winds, it is unlikely that Mainreachan will be in condition for more than a few days each year. Other big mixed cliffs where some icing is essential – such as Creag an Dubh Loch – are similarly elusive, and should not be considered in doubtful conditions.

The frustration of making the wrong choice can be agonising, especially if conditions everywhere else are good. On the last day of the freeze-up at New Year in 1997 Martin Welch and I went to the East Face of Blaven to try a fine chimney line, having eschewed feasible options on the mainland. Having walked all the way in to it, we were dismayed to find that most of the climb lay below a clearly defined snowline at 600m altitude. Lacking any other options we climbed the route anyway, but knew we couldn't record it. By evening, rain and south-westerlies had swept back in and the best spell of the winter was over.

There is now a multitude of information sources on weather and conditions, and these are listed in Appendix V. Having gained a general weather outlook which hints favourably for the coming trip, it is essential to get some idea of conditions on the ground. The written reports from the 'Climbline' mountain weather service give a summary of climbing conditions in each area, and the avalanche bulletins sometimes give an indication of buttress snow-cover. Reference to the 'Winter Climbs Bulletin Board' web-site or similar will often give information on conditions in popular areas. Beyond this, a local informant resident in the climbing areas can confirm your guesses or dash your hopes as to what can and can't be done – though don't trust the local 'expert' to give away all the secrets! Having processed all this information by comparison with your 'wish-list' of climbs, some suitable options should emerge. However, the best-laid plans can still be frustrated by an unannounced change in weather, and the buttresses are the first to be stripped in a thaw, so keep tuned to the immediate forecast for the day of action.

Having sorted both partner and conditions, we must now move on to the choice of hardware and clothing.

EQUIPMENT AND PROTECTION

In mixed climbing, as in all forms of winter climbing, the ability of the climber is more important than the gear used. A quick poll of leading buttress climbers reveals wide variations in their chosen gear, as between leather and plastic boots, from stub-toed Chouinard rigid crampons to state-of-the-art 'monopoints', and fifteen-year-old Grivel axes to the latest curved-shaft 'Quasars' and 'Aliens'! Clearly there is a great deal of individuality in choice of gear, and it would be quite wrong to be prescriptive in recommending any particular types. Different models of kit can perform with similar effectiveness at the highest current standards, and so Aberdonian considerations of economy are as relevant as performance in

picking your buttress-climbing kit. And if there is no concensus among leading activists, those aiming for lower-grade mixed climbs should not feel obliged to purchase a whole new set of kit; thus anything spiky on the feet and an axe in the hand will suffice for the IIs and IIIs.

Boots: As for general snow- and ice-climbing, rigid-soled leather or plastic boots will do the job on the buttresses. A close fit gives a greater edge of control in delicate footwork or foot-jamming, provided the toes do not get pinched and cold. In this regard, leather boots might have an advantage over double-shelled plastics, but the case is open to doubt.

Crampons: Mixed climbing will quickly blunt your sharp-fanged crampons and ruin them for ice climbing. Furthermore, although long front-points and forward-angled second points might be desirable on a pair of snow-and-ice crampons, they are not suitable for buttress routes. Shorter front-points reduce the considerable strain on leg muscles when standing on small rock-holds, and vertical second points allow greater precision of foot placement in mixed climbing. The chisel-cut toe points of the old-style Salewa crampons may have an advantage on intricate edging, but many climbers are perfectly happy with regular points. In short, the pair of blunted crampons you have retired from ice-climbing or else use for winter walking will get you up most types of mixed ground, except perhaps thin ice smears.

Axes: Suitable shaft length depends on height and wrist strength. The extra reach from a longer axe (55cm) can be useful, but it is more tiring to swing than a 50cm shaft. The bent shafts of many technical ice-climbing tools do not seem to be a hindrance on mixed climbs, but nor do they confer any special advantage. Banana picks give better penetration and easier extraction on all grades of

Fig 12.1 *Hardware for mixed climbing*

Recommended racks for a party of two: it will be noted that considerable affluence as well as ability is needed to tackle the harder modern routes. These selections are necessarily generalised, and particular types of route may require more or less of each item. They assume that the party is climbing close to its limit of ability, and therefore needs whatever protection is available. The key is as follows:

Grade	II–III	IV–V	VI–VII–VIII
Wired nuts ('rocks')	1 set from sizes 1–9	1 set from sizes 1–9	2 full sets
Large hexentric chocks	Sizes 7–9	Sizes 7–9	2 in size range 7–9 (in case cracks are glazed)
'Friends'	Useful but not essential	3 or 4 of sizes between 1 and 3	Full set of 7 from size ½ to 3½
Pitons	4–6 of assorted size	6–8 of assorted size	8–12 of assorted size including leepers and blades
Slings	3 or 4 long (2.5m) 2 short (1m) 3 extensions	2 long 3 short 6 extensions 3 tie-offs	2 long 3 short 10 extensions 4 tie-offs
Ice screws	1–2 drive-ins (wart-hog) (for turf)	1 drive-in	Rarely of use on very hard routes
Karabiners	10 –16	15–20	20-35

Extensions: short slings for extending runners
Tie-offs: short thin tape (10–12mm width) for tying off pitons

mixed ground. Picks should be thick and chunky so as to withstand the constant stress of torquing and the abuse of being hammered into unyielding rock cracks. Some slim picks are designed purely for ice and will not withstand the wear and tear of buttress techniques. Modular axe designs with interchangeable picks are essential, because if you climb mixed routes regularly you are likely to wear out at least one set of picks each season. Wrist-loops should be fairly tight-fitting, either knotted or tightened by a rubber slider so that axes can be left dangling safely from the wrists on rock moves. Although advantageous to have sharp axes, it is impracticable since they blunt so quickly on rocky mixed ground, and regular sharpening will quickly wear the picks out.

Gloves: These should be as thin as your circulation will allow. With thinner gloves it is less tiring to grip the axes, 'hand-on-rock' moves are easier, and manipulating hardware is simplified. I use 'sticky' rubber-coated gloves, sold cheaply in hardware stores, for leading hard pitches, because they offer brilliant grip and are highly durable. Many of the fleecy inner gloves sold in dedicated climbing stores wear through with a few days of climbing use. Dachstein mitts are ideal for seconding, belaying and easier leads. For long routes, dry spare pairs of gloves or mittens should be carried. If tempted by really pricey Gore-tex gloves or mitts, remember how easy it is to drop one when tangled up on a buttress route!

Clothing: Buttress climbers alternate between sustained bursts of high energy output and prolonged periods of inactivity on stances, and there is no single clothing system that will handle both situations. By taking a layered system, some adjustments can be made during a climb. A protective outer shell is all-important. Three-layer Gore-tex material gives good friction and durability, but many climbers find overtrousers constricting and dispense with them in all but the worst conditions. In fine, calm weather, one might advantageously avoid wearing a jacket on the route. Sweaters or pile jackets offer more friction for wedging and chimney moves, but ultimately keeping warm is the prime concern, and it is easy to underestimate clothing needs when you first arrive at a cliff, hot and steaming after the walk in. On hard or constricted climbs, all spares and kit can be stowed in one rucksack, which is carried by the second, leaving the leader unencumbered and free to climb to the limit. Many teams leave both their sacks at the bottom of the route. With this system it is a good idea to have one extra fleece or duvet which can be swapped over to keep the belayer from freezing.

Climbing Hardware: Mixed routes require a comprehensive rack of gear, which gets bigger and heavier as you approach harder routes. Fig 12.1 summarises the average needs for routes of different grades. An ample stock of long slings can often supply all the main belays on easier routes up buttress and ridge crests. Drive-in ice screws may prove highly useful on turfy routes, although the holding power of frozen sods of earth has never been formally tested. On harder routes I always take a couple of Hexentric chocks in addition to a set of 'Friends', because of the unreliable grip of camming devices in iced cracks. A stock of pitons is normal on 'winter-only' mixed routes, but the use of pegs on winter ascents of regular summer rock-climbs may cause serious damage to the rock. If the route is already a summer classic, and is merely covered in loose powder so that all rock cracks are accessible then it is best not to carry pitons. However, such tactics could be disastrous on a route like Observatory Ridge where cracks are usually iced up.

In mixed climbing one is relying largely on the underlying rock for progress and security, so the protection tends to be as reassuring as it is when rock climbing. By taking up buttress climbing one can largely forget those scary experiences that enliven an ice-climbing career, of belaying off buried axes and screws in honeycombed mush. As long as the leader is willing to hang around in awkward positions and clear the snow from the cracks, then the protection is normally available. Even if runners are widely spaced they will usually be dependable, and this allows one to try moves of a highly experimental nature without great risk of serious injury.

However, every big buttress route is a battle against time as well as strength, and the search for protection must on occasions be traded off in favour of quick progress, particularly on easier sections near the top of a route. Rab Anderson described a real scare while running out the rope in darkness on grade III/IV terrain on the first ascent of Headfault on Beinn Ime in the Southern Highlands:

'*I put in one runner above the belay as I normally try to do, then ran out a lot of rope quickly, since excavating for gear would have taken time. About thirty metres above the gear I made a short right traverse on a snow shelf which slabbed off. I was spun round to face outwards and slid forwards as if on a surfboard. I remember looking out into this black void before my heels dug in right on the edge. However, my momentum kept my upper body going and I had to windmill my arms to get my weight back from the edge. It was all over in a flash, but it left me feeling sick.*'

A few modern buttress routes have gained a reputation for seriousness, and I would guess that the future trend will be towards ill-protected face routes. Guerdon Grooves on the Buachaille Etive Mor owes its aura of difficulty to the reputed lack of protection. However, in most buttress climbing the degree of seriousness is quantifiable at the outset, and is not imposed by some unforseen change in conditions as can happen on ice routes; the mixed climber can weigh the risks in advance and retain the crucial edge of control. You may frequently have a 'pseudo-epic' – an extended adventure where the party remains just in control of the situation – but rarely a 'genuine epic' where the party is out of control and at the mercy of fate. On almost all Scottish mixed climbs you can push as hard as you dare, yet can decide to call a halt at any time, a series of abseils taking you quickly down to safety.

HOOKS AND TORQUES

The variety of technical moves between different mixed climbs, or even on a single route, is really extraordinary. Any of the rock-climbing contortions may be required, such as jamming, laybacking, mantelshelving and chimneying, and then you may add in the winter peculiarities of thrutching, squirming, wriggling, grovelling, crawling, scratching, scraping, chipping, chopping, and all the torquing and hooking moves, the number depending on the ingenuity of the climber and the design of the axes. Not surprisingly, with all these to choose from, it can take ten minutes to work out each difficult move on a route.

Of all the mixed techniques, hooking and torquing are the most difficult to master pyschologically. Hooking requires total reliance on placing the axe tips on rock edges. Torquing is radically gymnastic by comparison to traditional winter techniques and brings the fear that the axe picks will snap or spring out under the stress of twisting. On the winter ascent of Sting, an HVS on Beinn Eighe, I marvelled how Andy Nisbet coolly hooked his way up a plumb vertical wall on the second pitch. He placed rather than locked his picks on small edges, kept the body straight and tried to take as much weight as he could on the crampon points. Where adjacent hooks were not available for each axe he simply crossed one pick across the other, and pulled with both arms on the same placement (as shown in Plate 12.2). Lacking his trust I found the moves so trying

Plate 12.2 *Crossing axes to improve pulling power on a single axe hook*

when seconding that my head was cooking in my helmet by the time I reached his stance.

In complete contrast, the third pitch, the summer crux, was a thin bulging crack, ideal for torquing. The style was totally different: with perfect locks for the axes but very little by way of footholds, I had to crank my body as high as I could by walking my feet up the walls. Then with one arm locked and the axe twisted sideways, I could remove the other axe and gain a higher placement. Despite the strenuous nature of the climb, the torquing crack seemed more positive and simpler than the hooking wall, not least because of perfect protection in the crack.

Despite being a modern vogue among the avant-garde of winter climbing, torquing is by

Plate 12.3 *Axe torquing in a finger-width crack*

no means new. Prior to World War I, Geoffrey Winthrop-Young had observed:

> 'One or two guides in the Alps have perfected a remarkable trick. When a vertical or sloping crack in a slab gets too small even to admit a finger, and all other holds are lacking, they force the point of the pick into the crack above their heads and give a slight outward and upward twist to the shaft with the wrist so that the point of the pick and its square edges are jammed slantwise and upwards in the crack. Holding the shaft rigid in this position, they then raise their weight by sheer strength inside the bent arm which holds the shaft, at the same time using whatever friction-holds they can find for their feet to help them. A second's cat-like clinging of the feet and of their free hand to the rock gives them just time to thrust the pick further up the crack and twist it firmly in again.'[2]

Modern torquing is just as Winthrop-Young described it, except that, with an axe in each hand, the process is considerably less dynamic because one simply leapfrogs the axes alternately up the crack. In general, the narrower and deeper the crack, the more secure the placement. The exact technique depends on the design of your axe and hammer, though nearly every width of crack can be covered:

1 **Hairline (under 4mm):** Batter the pick into the crack or slot it in above a constriction, and use it for a direct downward pull. This does not involve the twisting action of true torquing.

2 **Thin (4–15mm):** Torque on the inserted pick, maintaining a constant sideways pull to hold it in place (Plate 12.3).

3 **Finger (15–30mm):** Jam the pick further in, including the head-retaining bolts or weights, and torque, albeit more precariously. This facility depends on an appropriate axe design.

4 **Finger to hand (30–40mm):** Slot in the hammer head and pull down to a narrowing, or torque on the inserted hammer head. The success of either ploy depends on the shape of the head: tapered for slotting, square for torquing.

5 **Wrist to clenched hand (40–70mm):** Use the axe adze, slotting or torquing. A straight adze will work in thinner cracks.

6 **Off-width (greater than fist width):** As in rock-climbing, this is by far the most awkward width. Improvise (eg with a pick-to-adze wedge) or abseil off.

If dependent on torquing, the precise line of the modern mixed route will often seek the best cracks rather than the equivalent summer line which may follow flat rock-holds. The Cairngorms are particularly accommodating in the provision of thin cracks. These are often too thin or outward flared to be of use in summer, but are ideal for torquing.

While experimenting with these techniques, one must expect to fall off occasionally, but they all require cracks and the protection should be good – provided that you remember to put it in. Once mastered and taken to its full potential, torquing opens up an exhilarating new world of hard mixed gymnastics.

THE GRADING SYSTEM

The widening gap in style between mixed and pure ice climbing during the 1980s made it increasingly difficult to grade harder routes consistently within the strictures of a single tier system. The relatively greater technical difficulty of many classic mixed routes had been obvious ever since the front-point revolution lowered the technical demands of ice climbing. Furthermore, some of the desperate modern buttress routes seemed to warrant an overall grade VII instead of the existing ceiling of VI. Indeed, the apparent stiffness of mixed gradings had deterred many people from trying the routes. For instance, grade VI held an aura of mystery and difficulty to climbers operating outside the inner circle of Scottish activists – although the type and severity of difficulty encountered on a grade VI could not always be gauged from a verbal description. So in 1991, guidebook writers and editors in the SMC initiated a major revision of the system, introducing two-tier grades: an overall I to VIII grade to denote length, seriousness and overall ambience of a climb; and a numerical grade from 1 to 9 to indicate the technical severity of its crux.

A tentative list of the revised grades was sent to several activists. There were recalcitrant murmurs from a couple of die-hard traditionalists who wished to maintain a sense of the unknown on harder climbs, yet the general consensus was to open up the system for the benefit of newcomers to the sport, and a surprising degree of agreement was achieved on the new grades for particular climbs. Fig 12.2

gives the revised grades for some of the country's more notable winter routes; most climbs below grade IV remain unchanged in standard.

All new guidebooks have adopted this system, and as routes are repeated and reassessed under differing conditions, consensus and consistency will improve even further. The benefits of expanding and detailing the old system are obvious upon scrutiny of Fig 12.2. Serious ice routes now can be fairly compared to safe, hard buttress climbs. A serious but technically straightforward ice route such as Zero Gully at V,4 is now clearly distinguished from a safer but stiffer buttress route such as Mitre Ridge at V,6, whereas both were previously straight grade V's. Similarly, the bold Pointless on Ben Nevis at VII,6 compares fairly with hard, sustained Cairngorm mixed routes such as Citadel on Shelterstone Crag at VII,8. There will, of course, be many climbers who can handle the bold ice of Pointless, yet who will fail on the desperate technical crux of Citadel, and vice-versa. Individual climbers can argue all they like as to which climb is the greater achievement, but at least the two-tier system makes their differences clear.

Having overcome a personal reserve about the elaboration of gradings, my only complaint about the new system is that the technical grades have not yet been applied with sufficient imagination. Looking at Fig 12.2, I am convinced that a classic ice route such as Green Gully, though perhaps worth an overall grade IV on account of its seriousness, is a full two technical grades easier than Observatory Ridge. The one should be IV,3 and the other IV,5.

As with ice climbing, the extension of the mixed-climb gradings in Scotland has led to some divergence with the scales used in North America and the Alps. Thus Jeff Lowe assigned an overall grade IV to Citadel (with the easier variation finish) in his book *Ice World*, com-

Fig 12.2 Comparison of mixed and ice-climbing grades *(showing typical examples of recommended quality)*

Grade	SNOW/ICE Examples	MIXED Examples
I	No 5 Gully, Ben Nevis	Carn Mor Dearg Arête, Ben Nevis
II	Gardyloo Gully, Ben Nevis	Central Buttress, Lochnagar
III	Penguin Gully, Beinn Dearg	Tower Ridge, Ben Nevis
IV,4	Green Gully, Ben Nevis	North East Buttress, Ben Nevis Observatory Ridge, Ben Nevis
IV,5	Route Major, Carn Etchachan	Grooved Arete, Aonach Mor
IV,6	–	Garricks Shelf, Buachaille E.Mor The Message, Coire an t-Sneachda
V,4	Zero Gully, Ben Nevis	–
V,5	Point Five Gully, Ben Nevis	–
V,6	–	Mitre Ridge, Beinn a'Bhuird Savage Slit, Coire an Lochain
VI,5	Psychedelic Wall, Ben Nevis	–
VI,6	Tholl Gate, Fuar Tholl	Eagle Ridge, Lochnagar
VI,7	–	Central Buttress, Beinn Eighe Fall-Out Corner, Coire an Lochain
VI, 8	–	Punster's Crack, The Cobbler
VII,6	Labyrinth Direct, Creag an Dubh Loch	Reach for the Sky, Fuar Tholl
VII,7	Shield Direct, Ben Nevis	Central Grooves, Stob C. nan Lochan White Magic, Coire an t-Sneachda
VII,8	–	Citadel, Shelterstone Crag Salmonella, Aonach Beag
VII,9	–	Cornucopia, Ben Nevis Ventricle, Coire an Lochain
VIII,7	Foobarbundee, Liathach	Raven's Edge, Buachaille E. Mor Viva Glasvegas, The Cobbler
VIII,8	–	The Needle, Shelterstone Crag

pared to its Scottish grade of VI. This reflects the emphasis on length of climb in the American ratings, where the highest overall grade of VI is reserved for routes of super-alpine scale. The international technical ratings for mixed climbing run from M1 to M8, and here there is a closer equivalence with Scottish technical grades: Scottish technical 8 probably equates to M7, Scottish 7 to M6 and so on.

Those who climb on the international stage may think that Scottish routes are now being overgraded. However, the new system is not intended to bear any direct comparison to grades in other countries: it has been designed for Scottish conditions, and so far seems to be serving the needs of Scottish winter climbers well. A full explanation of buttress-climbing grades incorporating the revision is approximately as follows:

Grades I and II The traditional grades for the classic ridge scrambles such as the Aonach Eagach; these are clear and consistent in their usage.

Grade III The standard grade for the classic

ridge climbs, Tower Ridge being the benchmark of the type, ie Moderate to Difficult rock-climbs rather than scrambles under snow, involving sustained pitches and steep moves where commitment of weight to axes is necessary. They can be much harder under deep soft snow.

Grade IV Represents a psychological jump: to climb grade IV requires commitment to the sport. Many IVs involve technical moves in exposed positions, climbing onto open, steep ground and placing protection in strenuous positions. Gloved-hand techniques may no longer be an option on crux moves. On short routes technical difficulties may be as high as 6.

Grade V Under the new system, V applies both to classic long routes such as Scorpion on Carn Etchachan or Mitre Ridge, Beinn a'Bhuird which are Very Difficult and Severe summer rock-climbs; and to short but technically testing modern routes which are typical of the Northern Corries of Cairn Gorm, Savage Slit at V,6 being the best known example of this genre. Technical difficulties may be as high as 7 on short, protected grade V routes.

Grade VI These are usually long and sustained, needing modern techniques and a high standard of fitness, plus good planning; Central Buttress on Beinn Eighe is a good example. Shorter routes of exceptional technical severity, ie 7 or 8, are also given grade VI, such as Fall-Out Corner in Coire an Lochain.

Grade VII Many of these routes have required two or more attempts on their first ascents. To have a good chance of success, all conditions must be right, meaning snow, weather and personal preparation, together with precise planning. The routes will usually be long as well as technically hard (7 or 8).

Grade VIII Routes of this calibre are the challenge for the future. Several climbs of exceptional severity or seriousness have been graded VIII, but only a few have been repeated.

Many people moving into the Scottish mixed scene from a summer climbing background want to know the technical rock-climbing equivalents of winter grades. In terms of overall strenuousness and technical demand, these are the approximate equivalents for an 'on-sight' lead on rock:

Grade IV, 4	Very Severe
Grade IV, 5	Hard Very Severe
Grade V, 6	E1/E2, 5b/c
Grade VI, 7	E3, 5c
Grade VII, 7	E4, 5c/6a
Grade VII, 8	E5, 6a, 6b
Grade VIII, 8	E6, 6b

However, it would be most unwise for an E5 rock climber to make a straight jump into VII,8 mixed climbs! There is a considerable learning curve to master in winter climbing, in particular coping with the elements, practising the new techniques, learning the tricks of getting good protection, and adapting to an 'on-sight' mentality when leading. Equally, climbers who struggle to lead E3 in summer should not be deterred from aiming at grade VII winter routes. On rock, limitations of finger and wrist strength can severely limit one's performance, but, when 'tooling' with axes the wrists are supported by axe loops, and the arms and shoulders can do the work. With a quick technical brain, all-round bodily strength and bags of stamina, the harder buttress climbs are accessible.

THE MODERN SCENE: ETHICS AND ATTITUDES

Not only does Scottish winter provide brilliant technical climbing, it is probably the most ethically pure form of mountaineering in the world.
Simon Richardson, writing in 1998

This proud claim is one which reflects modern attitudes as well as long-held traditions, and

Scottish buttress climbers are perhaps more aware than ever before of their ethical reponsibilities in order to preserve the challenge of the sport. Ethics fall into several categories: first and foremost is defining what constitutes a 'winter' ascent.

Winter Condition

The most specific and widely accepted definition is that a route is in winter condition when it is easier to climb with axes and crampons than with boots and bare hands; in addition the crag should be of 'wintry' appearance, in other words there should be a substantial cover of snow or rime on the route. Experienced buttress climbers quickly sense when a route has a winter ambience. In early spring when snow patches alternate with dry rock the easier buttresses can give highly enjoyable climbing, but this condition doesn't count as winter. Similarly, in late autumn a cold dry snap may freeze the vegetation so as to enable buttress ascents with axes and crampons, but in the absence of some snow or rime ice they cannot be called true 'winter' ascents.

Whilst this definition seems simple enough, it is being complicated by two trends. The first is the international vogue for 'dry-tooling', where hard rock sections, devoid of snow, have been tackled with axes and crampons, first in order to reach hanging icicles but more lately as challenging climbs in their own right. In Canada a few climbers have dispensed with wearing boots and crampons, and have used rock slippers on pure 'dry-tooling' routes; also chalk sea-cliffs in southern England have been developed as summer venues for dry-tooling. As regards this practice, inevitably there is a fear that such styles will confuse the Scottish winter scene. Secondly, buttress routes are now being tackled with overhanging sections that very rarely hold any snow or rime ice. Climbs with such short 'dry' sections may

have to be acknowledged as standards rise – but it is to be hoped that new winter ascents in wholly bare conditions will be discouraged by established convention.

On Sight, Ground Up

The Scottish ethic is for ground-up leads in winter conditions. Pre-placed gear as employed in American mixed climbing is not considered good style.

American Alpine Journal, 1997

There is no more satisfying an experience than to approach a previously unknown piece of cliff and make a new route. Every part of the climb, whether easy or hard, feels like a genuine adventure, and if one succeeds without using any aid, there is lasting pleasure in knowing that the style of the ascent could not have been bettered. This ethical approach has underpinned the history of Scottish winter climbing, it maintains its links to classical mountaineering, and commands international respect.

If anything, the ethical expectations of mixed climbers have risen since the 1980s. Although the essential 'ground-up' ethic prevailed, several of the big routes of that era were 'forced' to some extent with repeated attempts, planned bivouacs, occasional points of aid and rest-points on axes. In the 1990s, however, climbers have put a major effort into making cleaner, faster ascents, 'on sight' in a single one-day push without any aid or resting. The practice of 'yo-yoing' – lowering off from a runner to allow repeated attempts on moves – is now either avoided or specifically declared as a resting point in first-ascent reports.Yet the pursuit of purity has made it far more difficult to raise technical standards on the Scottish cliffs. By contrast, climbers in other countries have employed abseil inspection, pre-fixed gear, and prior top-roping in order to push technical standards on mixed ground a full grade above the current limits in Scotland. Most leading continental and American climbers apply the 'red-point' ethic, whereby the initial tactics are irrelevant provided one eventually makes a clean ascent without falls – most Scottish climbers, on the other hand, would contend that an 'on-sight' ascent with a couple of points of aid is a more worthy achievement than a long-awaited 'red-point'.

In Scotland there is obvious temptation to climb a buttress route in summer with the deliberate intent of inspecting the ground for a prospective winter ascent. Some, such as Andy Nisbet, would regard a summer ascent as an element of good planning and commitment. Other top climbers contend that they have neither the time nor energy for such preparations – although often prior summer inspections occur without specific intent: for instance, one may be climbing a rock route and suddenly the idea comes that it would make a marvellous winter line. No wonder the ethical waters do get somewhat muddied! The practice of summer abseil inspection is more clearly a breach of the 'on sight' ethic and diminishes the subsequent winter achievement.

Such discussion may seem to be of little relevance to the majority of buttress climbers who wish simply to work up through the grades and enjoy some good sport: these might well ask the question, 'Who cares what I do on a winter route?' Well, quite apart from the personal pride in climbing a route by fair means, the adoption of slack ethics can quickly infect the climbing community, whether they spread from those at the cutting edge or from the broader mass of activists. And every climber has an environmental responsibility to the cliffs, not to cause rock-scarring by clumsy technique or over-zealous peg placement and not to destroy precious vegetation by climbing mixed routes when unfrozen. We all have a contribution to make to the future of our sport by the style in which we climb. Scotland's cliffs are so small in relative stature that the winter game must be played by fair rules.

MIXED CLIMBING IN DIFFERENT AREAS OF SCOTLAND

Granite: *Cairngorms, Aonach Mor, Arran*
Granite is particularly suited to mixed climbing. Ledges and lower angled sections are heavily vegetated, as is steeper ground on north-facing crags; moreover the vegetation is usually based on soil, which gives deep and reliable axe placements. Granite joints weather into horizontal and vertical cracks, which offer good protection and torquing possibilities on steep ground. Many of the routes are in remote corries, have had few ascents and they require more general mountaineering skills than climbs elsewhere. By contrast the Northern Corries of Cairn Gorm are an accessible playground with a host of technical test-pieces. Also, Cairngorm buttress routes can be in condition over a longer seasonal span than any other area of the country.

Andesite: *Ben Nevis; Stob Coire nan Lochan (Glencoe)*
The same rock exhibits quite different formations in the two venues. The Nevis faces are slabby, clean and frequently crackless, and so are highly unco-operative to mixed tech-

Plate 12.4 (page 268) *Modern mixed exposure; Andy Clarke following Hangman's Crack (VI, 7) on the Buachaille Etive Mor in late-December gloom (Mark Garthwaite)*

Plate 12.5 (page 269) *Remotest Cairngorm pioneering; Chris Cartwright leading the first ascent of Cherokee Chimney, Garbh Choire Mor, Braeriach (Simon Richardson)*

niques. Of course, the Ben has the magnificent classic ridges – Castle, Tower, Observatory and North-East Buttress – and these routes give many their first taste of mixed climbing. Some of the face routes become mixed in style if the ice is thin or absent (eg Route II on Carn Dearg Buttress). Apart from the notable ascent of Centurion, the big crackline splitting the Carn Dearg Buttress at reputed grade VIII, there were few modern, rock-based buttress climbs on the Ben until 1996 and 1997 when Chris Cartwright and Simon Richardson established a trilogy of impressive lines on the left sidewall of Creag Coire na Ciste. These routes reveal a new potential for buttress climbing on the Ben, but they will be significantly thinner and more serious than those elsewhere.

By contrast, the andesite of Stob Coire nan Lochan is columnar in structure, well cracked and vegetated on its ledges, sporting soaring groove-lines of magnetic appeal, and offering sensationally steep winter climbing. Central Grooves (VII,7) is one of Scotland's finest modern mixed routes.

Rhyolite: *Glencoe, eg Buachaille Etive Mor*
Although clean and poorly cracked, and thus frequently unhelpful to the mixed climber, the rock of the Buachaille Etive Mor has recently yielded several hard routes in addition to the enigmatic Guerdon Grooves (VIII). The Buachaille also has several easier classics to satisfy the mountaineering instinct, most notably Curved Ridge and North Buttress. The great chimney lines on the North Face of the Aonach Dubh are now coming into their winter maturity. Dank, dark and slimy, this forbidding cliff satisfies the modern mixed climber's tastes to perfection.

Gabbro: *Skye*
The potential of Skye has been little explored because conditions are unreliable, and because there is also an obvious want of vegetation on the clean gabbro, and a lack of cracks in the

basalt dyke lines. But whatever deters the present generation should be the challenge for the next, and the Cuillin cliffs will doubtless receive more serious scrutiny in the new millennium.

Schist: *The Cobbler, Beinn an Dothaidh, Aonach Beag, Creag Meagaidh, Kintail, Fannichs*
Many crags in the Central, Western and Southern Highlands are schist, which tends to be very heavily vegetated, thus offering much scope for mixed climbing, particularly in the middle and lower grades. The climbing can be rather repetitive (turf, turf and more turf), but there are dozens of schist crags to be explored on quiet mountains away from the regular winter-climbing trail. Although the buttress routes on Creag Meagaidh are disappointing, Skyscraper Buttress on Sgurr nan Clach Geala (VI,6) is an all-time classic tucked away in the remote Fannaichs, and many fierce routes have more recently been established on the cleaner schist buttresses in the Southern Highlands, notable for thin tufting and boldness.

Torridonian Sandstone: *Beinn Bhan, Fuar Tholl, Liathach, An Teallach*
Sandstone forms extremely steep tiers split by horizontal terraces which are generously vegetated; the rock is alternately blank and compact, and cracked and blocky. Mixed routes are variable in quality. Some are spoilt by their blatant escapability along the terraces, or they are inconsistent in standard, with short, vicious pitches through the tiers linking long meandering sections on the ledges. However, there are many good, turfy lines on the easier buttresses, and excellent harder routes are being found where continuous lines are offered. The 450m Die Riesenwand on the Coire an Fhamair headwall, Beinn Bhan (VII,6) is a *tour de force* of mixed ice and turf climbing, epitomising the bewildering exposure and devious route-finding of the best sandstone routes. As with Ben Nevis, the further potential

for very hard buttress routes has only recently been realised, but sandstone's heathery vegetation is slow to freeze.

Quartzite: *Beinn Eighe*

Quartzite is very steep and blocky, with plentiful square-cut footholds and good cracks, but little vegetation or ice. There is good climbing in the higher grades. The Triple Buttress of Coire Mhic Fhearchair is one of the finest of Scottish cliffs, its three great prows being among the finest Scottish mixed routes, particularly the grade VI Central Buttress. Many hard routes have been established on the intervening walls featuring exciting steepness, generally good protection and thin crack torquing. With an altitude of 900m and northerly aspect, Beinn Eighe is frequently rimed or powdered and makes an excellent venue for those wishing to graduate to longer and harder rock-based routes.

FUTURE DIRECTIONS

Far from being played to exhaustion, conversation with leading activists of the 1990s suggests to me that winter buttress climbing has an exciting future. Can standards significantly improve? For Simon Richardson the answer is unequivocal: 'The sky is the limit – I think we're just scratching the surface. If the new generation of Scottish rock climbers can acquire the necessary mountaineering expertise and combine this with their undoubted greater technical skills, some amazing things will be done.'

But at what price in terms of ethical compromise will these advances be made? Mark Garthwaite, otherwise known as 'Doctor Death' for his bold winter leads, has not so far deviated from a clean on-sight ethic in his winter first ascents, but recognises that to make the jump in standards certain compromises may have to be made: 'We might have to relin-quish ideas about what constitutes an "in-condition route". The way forward in technical terms is pre-inspection, pre-practice and pre-placement of gear, but only on the very hardest routes. Once established, the new routes can be the focus for on-sight ascents.'

Similarly, Rab Anderson regards sport style tactics as a possible way forward: 'If you were to "prepare" a route one day, "work" it and then come back the next, I am sure standards would improve.'

Whether this is feasible or desirable is another matter. Prime winter conditions rarely last long enough to allow repeated attempts on a route over several days, and prolonged engagement on a route is hardly desirable in wild and windy weather; one really big day out on a mountain buttress route leaves me feeling knackered for the best part of a week, and to repeat the walk-in and discomforts on several consecutive days would require Herculean stamina. Simon Richardson realises this and sees a different future: 'My vision is that the cutting-edge routes of the future will be winter-only lines. Such routes do not lend themselves to pre-inspection and depend upon on-sight skills. Bolts, red-points, winter abseil inspections are neither logical or practicable in the Scottish winter – and fortunately the weather is always the final arbiter!'

However the future style unfolds, all activists are unanimous that in order to raise standards, climbers will have to apply specific training towards the winter season and devote much more time to the pursuit of new lines. Andy Nisbet and Colin Maclean were the first team to apply this 'professional' approach, training solely for winter and then giving up employment for full-time winter climbing in 1985. According to Nisbet: 'We were able to go out on any day, could set our sights on a specific route and wait up to two weeks for perfect conditions and weather. Standards will rise again when *a suitably skilled modern climber applies this level of dedication.'*

Perhaps it is more surprising that current standards are as high as they are when most of the leading activists are holding down full-time jobs, are restricted to weekend climbing, have responsibilities to wives and families, and lack any form of sponsorship!

Quite apart from the excitement of pushing out winter routes on ever steeper and more fearsome buttresses, Scottish mixed climbing has the challenge of broadening its appeal to mainstream winter climbers over the coming decades. Buttress climbing has everything going for it, regular conditions, technical intrigue, total engagement and 'relative' safety. And whatever your climbing grade or ambitions, Mark Garthwaite's words sum up the pleasures of pursuing the 'mixed': *'The total experience is what counts – close friends are essential, the feeling that you're doing something that really sets you apart. You're elevated mentally and physically – but more than that, the beer tastes so good when you get down!'*

WALL OF THE OUTCRY

The upper wall of Alligin's incipient 'Cleft' or 'Gash' has all the ingredients for epic mixed climbing. It is a dramatic feature, the architectural apex of the mountain, sheer and intimidating, with occasional vegetated breaks and weeping vertical corners, plus the added spice of a chilling legend. Local folklore tells of a man's voice which could be heard wailing and crying up in the Cleft. Then one day a man fell to his death down the wall and the shouts were never heard again. The gully where he landed is known as the Eag Dubh na h-Eigheadh, 'black cleft of the outcry'. There is no history of summer climbing here, nor any reasonable prospect of doing so – this would be a winter-only cliff, if at all.

Then there is the prospect of a gruelling three-hour approach to its base. Better leave it until later in the season, you say – but the Cleft faces south, and the best chances of finding the face frozen and rimed are in the short days around the solstice. Even so, the first attempt was in the middle of April, a constant storm keeping the face well hidden from the sun – but in the face of a soaring final corner and the inability to stop shivering, we failed. Now I took my second chance with Andy Nisbet in the first week of December, and we went round the ridge in deep snow over Tom na Gruagaich. Despite rising at 5am we were not on the route until 11.15! In an April blizzard the first two pitches had seemed hard, very hard. Even today in clear and freezing weather, they took us all of three hours! A steep technical groove, black and verglassed, was followed by a sequence of scary mantleshelves up the ensuing wall.

But they led at last to the day's big prize, a right-facing thirty metre corner, overhanging at its top, which if followed direct, would complete the mixed climber's dream, a new line straight up the centre of the face. There seemed ample time here for a tussle before sundown; but after twenty minutes trying fruitlessly to get off the belay stance I began to have second thoughts! This is sandstone, a rock that can, without warning, close up and blank out. Lacking decent cracks, tufts or rock edges to overcome the first four metres, I fumed and pondered. As the heat rose, I finally got together a series of shallow placements in blind cracks to reach a tuft. No stopping now: fighting burning forearms, I pulled furiously onto a resting ledge.

Now I could get into the corner, and bridged strenuously up for six metres towards a roof under which sat a lonely spike on a tiny ledge – this offered the sole means of protection or progress. Surmounting the roof would be distinctly gymnastic, the ground above wholly unknown, and I knew all too well that sandstone spillikins are usually loose and detached in summer. Unable to reach up to test its attachment, the best I could manage was to lasso a sling over it, and it was easy to envisage me peeling off at the roof and sending this two-foot rock dagger hurtling towards Andy on the stance below. But how else could I finish? To the left I was faced by desperate bulging rock. I looked right, and scanned a wall that was absolutely blank and vertical save for two tiny grass ledges. Some six metres to their right a broken ramp cut though the final bulges. This was my only hope.

To swing down to the first ledge I had to accept tension from the rope: the mantleshelf up right onto the second ledge would be irreversible! A pivotal move in more ways than one. Placing my axe picks in the tufts of the second ledge at shoulder height I arched my body and pulled through until I was pressing down on the axe handles. Cocking my right toe onto the ledge, I stretched up with the free axe but I could find no rugosity to assist the transfer of weight from arms to foot. If I stood up and toppled out of balance off the ledge, I would swing 5 metres back into the corner. The shadows lengthened. From my tenuous perch the wall swept down past Andy into the gully of the Cleft, which itself fell away for 500 metres into the bouldered depths of the Toll a'Mhadaidh. Such a superb situation, so fine the line of control. Unlike any of a thousand heaves on a regular ice climb, this move would never be forgotten.

I inched up a little more, breathed in – and then, without really willing it, I locked my knee muscles and stood up. I didn't topple,

and reached a slight scoop with my axe to steady myself. Rightward shuffles along the frozen ledge took me ever away from the corner, with the knowledge that any lapse of balance would send me flying. After three metres of blind groping across the wall my gloved hands felt a decent flaky crack. I slotted in two running belays and swung more confidently right, into the final ramp.

Just after sunset I pulled onto the final terrace, and savoured the moment of triumph that puts all the hours of struggle into perspective. Andy followed, first by twilight and then by torchlight. A biting north breeze froze the sweat to my body. Strapped to the prow of Alligin I shivered through the spectacle of the afterglow down Loch Torridon. Over Applecross a multitude of lochans reflected the dying light against chocolate brown moors. The Inner Sound was a silver millpond, the hills of Storr a rolling black silhouette. To the north shone the crescent lights of Gairloch, and beyond it a faint neon glow from Stornaway, forty miles to the north-west. I could not have seen the view as I did, had I not climbed that pitch. Despite freezing down to the soles of my boots, I was freed from desire for that brief night hour.

But later, inevitably, the itch would return. It was a shame about that point of tension. What about the final corner? Perhaps that spike was OK really! Might it not go direct with a bit more strength and poise? And what about that groove line further right? All too soon we find an excuse to go back and recapture the thrill of climbing the winter buttress.

And so the game goes on

13: SKI-TOURING ON SCOTLAND'S HILLS

ALPINE AND TELEMARK SKI-MOUNTAINEERING

THE DEVELOPMENT OF SCOTTISH SKI-TOURING

It was one of those rare windless Nevis days. Away to the west the crenellated crest of the Cuillin Ridge was clearly visible, and all around the snow-crusted Scottish Highlands stood sharp above the valley haze. Far below, the surface of Loch Linnhe silvered the reflected sunshine of a northerly airstream.

To the watcher on the shore of the halfway lochan, the group of figures first appeared on the break of slope at the top of the Red Burn, then began an erratic yet swift descent. Frequently their swooping progress was halted as they cratered into the spring snow – with one exception: a single figure detached himself from the others and swooped from side to side in long arcing turns, pausing from time to time to offer a word of encouragement to his less able companions. As they approached the lochan, the party halted to draw breath and dust the clinging snow from their tweeds – except for one of the ladies who, hampered by the excesses of her long Victorian skirts, was unable to make the last vital turn and careered full tilt into the icy waters ...

The year was 1904; the occasion, the Scottish Mountaineering Club's Easter meet; and the mode of travel was of course skis. The early pioneers of the SMC had quickly developed the notion of using skis for recreational mountain travel in Scotland, and William Naismith was one of the innovators. The account of Nansen's epic ski traverse of the Greenland ice-cap in 1888 had filled Naismith with tremendous excitement, and such was his conviction that after first trials he reported back to his SMC friends: 'Skis might be employed with advantage in winter ascents in Scotland.'[1] And in 1903 that winter mountaineer *par excellence*, Harold Raeburn, bought a set of Norwegian skis and used them effectively on the Pentland hills, even skiing to his home in Edinburgh using the tramway track for his Norwegian-based *langlauf* technique. Yet unlike Naismith, he was sceptical as to the suitability of snow conditions for skiing in Scotland. He wrote in the SMC journal: 'However, as far as my opinion is concerned, the ski will be but seldom used in Scotland with advantage and enjoyment.'[2]

Then in 1904 W. R. Rickmers, a German who was resident in London and married to a Scot, was invited to attend the SMC Easter meet based on Ben Nevis. He introduced the club to the short, rigid, Alpine-type ski with its Lillienfeldt plate binding. This was the system favoured by the German authority of the day, Mathias Zdarsky, who argued that short skis were essential for steep ground as they were easier to manoeuvre. By contrast, the Norwegian technique used a longer ski with more flexible bindings, adapted for mountainous terrain by using two sticks in conjunction with the telemark, christiana and stem turns.

After the 1904 meet, Rickmers presented the SMC with a dozen pairs of skis and Allan Arthur was one of the members who made good use of the gift. At the 1913 SMC Easter meet, Arthur's diary records the following three ski-tours: Glenmore–Cairn Gorm–Ben Macdui–Derry Lodge; Derry Lodge–Carn Ban Mor–Sgoran Dubh Mor–Loch an Eilein; Aviemore–Braeriach–Cairn Toul–Derry Lodge. All three are serious and arduous tours of some 32km (20 miles) over the most isolated country in Scotland. They would be demanding itineraries using modern sophisticated equipment, but in the days of soft leather boots, home-made bindings and without the benefit of steel edges on their skis, it was a considerable accomplishment.

The Scottish Ski Club was founded in 1907 and it is interesting to look at some of its entry requirements in those early days:

- Five different tours of 15 miles each, ascending at least 3,000ft in all, or three different tours of 25 miles each, ascending at least 4,000ft in all.
- Each tour to be completed in the day, and a pack weighing no less than 8lb (3.6kg) must be carried the whole way. Stones may be used to make up the weight if desired, but nothing which may be worn or eaten during the journey will count.[3]

In these early days ski-bindings had lifting heels, and uphill progress was helped by either wax, sealskins or, more simply, by wrapping rope around the skis.

After the 1920s ski-racing became popular on the Continent, and soon a shift towards Alpine downhill skiing began in Scotland. The development of mechanical uplift, plastic boots, heel-hold safety bindings, and metal or glass-fibre composition skis in the 1960s widened the gap between 'downhillers' and traditional ski-tourers. Alpine downhill skiers no longer came from the ranks of the mountaineers and lovers of wild places, and many of its participants had an indifferent regard for the natural mountain environment. In turn, those who did go ski-mountaineering in Scotland were increasingly influenced by the boom in downhill skiing and used Alpine touring bindings and skis with synthetic skins attached on the climbing sections. The downhill techniques could be practised on the prepared pistes and then transferred to the more demanding off-piste conditions, albeit with some loss of style on the way. The graceful telemark of the *langlauf* style became something of a rarity. Until the 1970s, Nordic technique and its associated equipment, as favoured by Raeburn, was the preserve of the armed forces and a relatively small band of enthusiasts.

Then came the arrival of what could be termed the 'Nordic package deal'. Boots, long narrow skis, and sticks for use with Nordic techniques were offered at bargain prices and advertised as 'instant' skiing. Waxing, hitherto a troublesome esoteric chore with traces of the occult, was no longer necessary. The fish-scale ski base that helped the ski grip when climbing was widely marketed for low-level touring: 'Slide one way, stick the other, and away you go,' was the message, and Nordic as an alternative form of skiing was seized upon much as the alternative life-style and diet. However, whilst lightweight 'skinny' skis provided great exercise on forest trails and easy angled terrain, they required considerable expertise on steeper descents and were ill suited to the variable snow conditions typical of the high tops.

Nevertheless, this renewed interest in 'free-heel' skiing stimulated the development of heavier Telemark equipment, which meant skiers could handle steeper descents with much greater ease and enjoyment as well as cope more readily with the severity of mountain conditions and climate. A lack of reliable snow-cover at lower altitudes in the 1990s also encouraged a shift away from the pure Nordic style, and as a result many more 'free-heel' skiers have been taking on serious mountain tours.

So Scottish ski-touring now has three distinct schools of technique: Nordic, Telemark and Alpine, plus a further diversion into steep gully skiing. The fickle winters of the 1990s have hardly curbed the enthusiasm of Scottish skiers. By combining patience with an opportunistic approach, the potential remains for superb mountain days on ski whenever the snows arrive.

NORDIC AND TELEMARK TOURING

LIGHTWEIGHT NORDIC TOURING

The pure Nordic style of skiing is designed for tours on level or easy gradients, and enjoys the benefits of light, simple and relatively cheap equipment coupled with fast movement on gently undulating terrain, without the need for halts when switching from uphill to downhill terrain. The gear is best used for recreational tours on forest tracks at low levels, and for longer journeys on the plateaux on days when the snow-cover is of soft and uniform texture.
Skis: Because Nordic skis tend to be narrower than Alpine skis, the bearing surface area is reduced so they are usually used in longer lengths. As a rule Nordic skis should be about 20–25cm taller than the skier. Typical Nordic skis have widths of around 65, 55 and 60mm at tip, waist and tail, making them considerably lighter than Alpine skis and giving about 10mm of side-cut in the waisted mid-section. The side-cut produces an arc along the edge of the ski and interacts with the ski flex to give

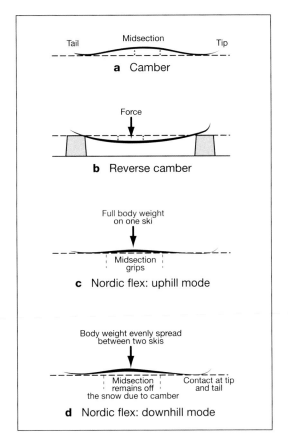

Fig 13.1a-d *Nordic flex and camber*

the ski its turning properties. For any use on the hill-tops where the snow may be icy or crusted the skis must have metal edges.

The ability of Nordic skis to grip on uphill climbs yet glide on the downhills is also due to their unique camber (Fig 13.1). If a Nordic ski is laid flat the mid-section remains off the ground (Fig 13.1a). This camber can be flattened when the skier's weight is all on one foot, so that the mid-section grips when skiing uphill, but when the weight is distributed evenly between the two skis, as when sliding downhill in a *schuss*, the camber keeps the mid-section off the ground (Fig 13.1c and d). This property is known as 'Nordic flex', and a Nordic ski can therefore have its mid-section fish-scaled or waxed for uphill grip without impairing downhill glide.

When turning, the skis not only need to be flattened, but actually forced into reverse camber with the tips raised above the mid-section (Fig 13.1b), and the more flexible the ski, the easier it is to pressure it into reverse camber. When a ski is on its edge and pressed down, it assumes an arced curve, formed by the interaction of the side-cut and the reverse camber. It is this arced curve which allows the ski to turn. However, the stiff centre section of a Nordic-flex ski tends to make a flat spot in the ski when making downhill turns, so a ski with Alpine flex will be easier to turn. Alpine-flex skis are more easily pressed together, the whole base flattening as one, so that in downhill mode, the entire length of the sole is in contact with the snow.

Fish-scale and Waxing: The grip on Nordic skis can be provided either by a manufactured fish-scale base or by grip-waxing the mid-section. A pre-cut fish-scale base provides 'instant' uphill traction without the chore of waxing, but it will only hold on gentle inclines and eventually wears out. Moreover, unless the camber of the ski is finely tuned to the weight of the skier, a portion of the fish-scaled section may come into contact with the snow on downhill runs, reducing speed and impeding smooth turning. Thus fish-scale skis may be regarded as suitable for beginners and for low-level tours, but not for serious mountain excursions.

The option of grip-waxing the mid-section offers a better potential performance. There is a bewildering range of waxes for different snow temperatures, but given the oft-changing textures and temperatures of Scottish snow, sophisticated waxing is not a sensible option and it is far better to stick to a simple two wax system, one for above freezing-point and one for below. These waxes come in blocks or in tubs, and should be crayoned thinly onto the mid-section, then rubbed in with a cork; they

are used for new snow, or snow that has not altered since falling. Klister wax is used for old snow which has melted and refrozen; it comes in tubes, and should be smeared on the mid-section and then spread out thinly using the spreader provided with the tube. Thus waxing is convenient, and even with the addition of a can of wax-removing liquid, some old rags and corks, the Nordic skier is not encumbered with unduly complex kit and should not have the day spoilt by constant stops to change wax. The tip and tail of the ski base should be glide-waxed to improve downhill running.

Waxing is less successful, however, on the coarse icy snow often encountered on Scotland's tops, because wax is quickly stripped off the ski base. On steeper ascents a Nordic-flex ski will not provide enough grip to climb whether it is fish-scaled or waxed, and climbing skins will have to be used to make progress. A Nordic tourer who goes into mountainous terrain without skins will soon be seriously inconvenienced, and once the need for skins is accepted, one is less willing to grip-wax the mid-section, and the idea of using heavier Telemark skis becomes correspondingly more attractive. This line of reasoning has led to the swing towards the Telemark style of touring since the 1980s.

TELEMARK SKI-MOUNTAINEERING

The Telemark combination of wider, heavier, Alpine-flex skis with side-cut and a free-heel binding provides a highly adaptable mode of travel, and the Telemark skier can feel equally at home on steep mountain terrain, long-distance tours and piste skiing. The intricacies of grip-waxing can be happily abandoned, and skins are used for all ascents whilst glide-wax is applied to the full length of the ski base. The heavier weight of Telemark gear is a drawback

Plate 13.1 *Telemark ski-equipment. (left) Dynastar Max-molly ski, Voile pin/cable binding, ScarpaT-2 plastic boots – for steeper terrain. (right) Dynastar Montana Plus ski, Voile 3-pin binding, Alico leather boots – for longer distance general touring (Braemar Nordic Ski Centre)*

from the Nordic ideal, yet the kit is not nearly so heavy as Alpine equipment due to the lighter bindings. Scotland's Nordic ski centres are now basing all their instruction on the Telemark gear and style for serious mountain touring.

Skis: Telemark mountain skis have Alpine style flex and side-cut, but are generally narrower than Alpine skis, particularly at the waist, and slightly lighter and stiffer. They are used at the same lengths as Alpine touring skis. Typical width dimensions of Telemark skis would be 77–57–67mm at tip, waist and tail, giving 15–20mm of side-cut for ease of turning. They must be metal-edged and highly robust. The ski design tends to be a compro-

mise between performance on:

a soft or 'cruddy' snow where a softer camber and even flex allows full contact of the ski base with the snow for easier turning; and

b hard, icy snow where a wide, soft ski will not hold an edge and a stiffer, torsionally rigid and narrower ski with lower side-cut works best.

Specialist advice from a dedicated Telemark gear retailer will ensure that the best choice is made.

Bindings: The *75mm Rottefella Super Telemark binding* or its equivalent is a popular choice for both Nordic and Telemark skiers. This is a traditional three-pin 75mm binding with a flat steel bail and a serrated boot-gripping strip which runs from the binding body about halfway to the heel plate, which is also serrated. The disadvantage of the three-pin system is that it may damage the pin-holes in leather ski boots rendering them ineffective, whilst plastic Telemark boots do not fit snuggly enough in the pins to be fully efficient. *Pinless cable bindings* offer the best all-round performance for telemarking. They act to 'stiffen up' a lighterweight leather boot, adding torsional rigidity, they will not damage the boot pin-holes, are easy to use and adjust, and yet are relatively light. Releasable Telemark bindings are an option for those concerned about injury in a fall. Although they are heavier and more expensive, they are becoming increasingly popular. *The New Nordic Norm system* (NNN) has not proved to be robust enough for Telemark mountain touring. The following binding accessories are also useful:

- ski leashes clipped from binding to boot;
- heel-lifts which flip up or down under the heel of the boot to aid in steep skinning ascents;
- binding shims ('packers') which raise the binding on the ski to enable better edging control on steep descents;

- ski crampons ('harcheisen') which are now available for Telemark skis.

Boots: Boots should match the robustness of the skis, whether for Nordic or Telemark style touring. They should have reinforced 75mm (3in) Nordic Norm pin-holes at the toe, and a heel groove to take cable bindings and vibram soles. Gaiters are as essential as in general mountaineering. Good leather boots also have quick-drying linings, such as Cambrelle. There have been major developments in Telemark boot design and construction since the mid-1980s, and although a good quality lace-up or clip-up leather boot is still effective, plastic-shelled boots have now entered the market, offering the same advantages as they do for climbing: warmth, dryness and stiffness. The features of a good mountain touring boot are:

- a degree of flex across the ball of the foot to allow all the free-heel techniques;
- torsional rigidity (ie it should resist a twist along the sole of the boot so that any skiing control via leg and foot movement is transferred directly onto the ski);
- firm ankle support from adjustment of lacing or clip buckles to assist precise ski control.

Plastic boots are very rigid torsionally, and the clip-up system can be tightened or released at will according to the techniques required. Stiff Telemark boots, whether leather or plastic, will take crampons for walking and have been used successfully on ice climbs up to grade V!

Poles: Adjustable Alpine-style poles with the 'classic Alpine' basket are the most popular for telemarking. The poles may be used at Nordic length (ie at armpit height from the ground) for flats and undulating terrain, and shortened to Alpine length for descents or piste-skiing.

Skins: Telemark skins are identical to those used for Alpine skis, except for their narrower width. The skins must not cover the metal edges of the ski at the waist. They are usually cut to a rounded 'vee' about 10cm short of the tail.

NORDIC AND TELEMARK TECHNIQUES

Pure Nordic ski-touring is an athletic and skilful pursuit, and anyone wanting to Nordic ski in Scotland's winter mountains should first serve an apprenticeship on the lower slopes by tackling Nordic light touring in the forests and on prepared tracks, and preferably by going to a recognised Nordic ski school for a series of lessons with qualified instructors. By contrast, those who approach Telemark touring with trepidation should be assured that the techniques bear a much closer affinity with Alpine skiing than with pure Nordic. So consequently, Alpine skiers convert to Telemarking more easily than pure Nordic skiers. All Alpine-style techniques are appropriate on Telemark gear. The only addition to the repertoire is the famous Telemark turn, which has several variations and takes more time and practice to master. Nevertheless, skiers used to downhill Alpine skiing will have to refine their techniques on a number of fronts in order to enjoy proficiency in Telemark touring. On Alpine skis big forward and backward movements may be made and held securely by the boots and bindings, but the same movement on free heel bindings is likely to end as a head-plant or flying buttocks arrest! So it is important to adopt a good posture and stable stance over the skis.

Those used to Alpine downhilling may imagine that because their heels are free, they will not be able to make turning movements on Nordic and Telemark gear; however, with a good stance and using the right gear there need be no problem because the boot will be held firmly by the binding, and its lateral stiffness means that it will not twist or slip off the plate.

Plate 13.2 *The Telemark turn (Andy Cunningham)*

repertoire of Nordic and Telemark techniques is much enhanced by an intuitive ability to anticipate and adapt to the changing snow conditions, and to pick the best lines of descent.

ALPINE SKI TOURING
ALPINE EQUIPMENT

Skis: Gone are the days when the aspiring ski mountaineer would slap a pair of touring bindings onto any old pair of skis and set off into the white-out. Up until the 1990s there was a limited variety of specialised touring skis available. These were robust enough to cope with the rigours of a ski tour, but sacrificed performance for durability. But with the advent of the so-called 'carving revolution' in down-hill skiing, as well as the introduction of wider skis for off piste and the development of new materials technology, the prospective buyer is faced with a bewildering choice of ski:

1 *Conventional downhill skis:* It is not unusual to see people ski-touring with a pair of perfor-mance downhill skis fitted with touring bindings; this enables them to get the best performance on the descents, which are so often the highlight of a tour. A moderately stiff downhill ski such as a giant slalom (GS) type, will give good control on icy ground, yet be sufficiently responsive in varied snow condi-tions. It can also be used to full advantage for piste skiing. However, the broken snow-cover so often encountered in Scotland inevitably leads to encounters with rocks. So when buy-ing, why invest in a top-of-the-range downhill ski, only to see it chewed up in record time? An old pair of skis is best reserved for use when conditions are marginal.

2 *Conventional touring skis:* Skis marketed

However, as a result of the heels being free, a Telemark skier does not have the leeway for recovering from errors that Alpine equipment affords, so technique must be precise. Secondly, if the skis have Nordic flex, the skier has to make more vigorous movements to get the skis into reverse camber for turning than with an Alpine-flex ski; this means that edging and weighting has to be that bit more exagger-ated than on Alpine skis. So on Nordic-flex skis skiing is made easier by pronounced weight shifts in order to execute a turning movement.

Uphill Nordic and Telemark technique requires a good kick turn in order to execute a zig-zag ascent fluidly, without losing rhythm and wasting energy. On flats and gentle uphills, fast progress is enabled by an efficient 'kick and glide' technique, skating from one ski to the other with double pole plants. The

Plate 13.3 *Telemark skiing on the north-east wall of Coire an Lochain, the Cairngorms (Jas Hepburn)*

Plate 13.4 *Alpine skis: (left) an ordinary piste ski (narrower with little side cut); (right) an all-terrain ski (wider with more pronounced side cut)*

nounced side-cut than conventional Alpine skis, and the waist section is significantly narrower than the tip in order to facilitate turning. 'Carving' means turning the skis on their edges, as opposed to skidding the tails of the skis round in the turn. Such skis are used in mountain Telemark skiing, and a greater side-cut offers some advantage for Alpine ski-tourers operating in difficult snow conditions.

4 *'Fat boys'* and *'Plump boys'*: These are much wider, shorter and more flexible skis specifically designed to aid the skier's flotation on deep soft snow. They are not suitable for Scottish touring where icy snow is as common as powder and edging performance is essential.

5 *All-terrain skis:* Incorporating the principles of both carving skis and 'fat boys' there are now several models of all-terrain skis on the market. These are broader than a piste ski to give some 10 per cent more flotation, yet sufficiently narrow that edge control is not seriously impaired. They have a significant side cut and are used in lengths 10cm shorter than normal. These versatile skis are the best of the new breed for handling the varying snow conditions that can be expected on the Scottish hills. They add an extra sophistication in design and performance to conventional touring skis.

Bindings: The prerequisite of a touring binding is that the heel should lift to permit progress uphill, and clamp down firmly for skiing downhill. A ski-mountaineering binding must function under conditions of extreme cold, even when it is covered in snow and ice and endure constant motion at the toe during skinning uphill. Most of the modern bindings are strong enough to withstand normal abuse, however, and are designed so they will release both forwards or sideways. All bindings have two pieces, a heel and a toe: sideways pressure

specifically for touring now offer a downhill performance approaching that of GS piste skis but have a tough running surface that sacrifices gliding properties for durability on rocks. As a general rule a touring ski will be between 10 and 15cm shorter than the same person's piste ski to enable quick kick turns and to assist turning in a wide variety of snow. The bases are usually brightly coloured so they can be more easily located if they get buried. A single eyehole in each tip allows the skis to be attached to a rope or harness for crevasse rescue or building an emergency stretcher.

3 *Carving skis:* These skis have a more pro-

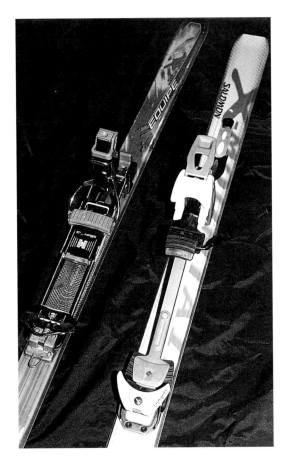

Plate 13.5 *Alpine touring bindings: (left) Silvretta 404 on a piste ski; (right) Frtischi Diamir on an all-terrain ski*

releases the toe, forward pressure the heel. The most up-to-date models are spring-loaded, step-in bindings with up to four height settings at the heel to cater for increasingly steep gradients in ascent. A DIN (Deutsch Industrial Norm) standard setting on both toe- and heel-piece means that the pressure required to effect a release will vary according to the skier's weight and ability, and the skis' intended use.

Touring bindings are all expensive, and the only way to avoid buying them is to purchase adaptors which can be used on ordinary downhill bindings, converting them for the duration of the tour into touring bindings. Binding adaptors are suitable for all designs of ski-boot and most downhill bindings. Leashes are supplied with touring bindings. Ski-brakes can be fitted onto certain makes.

Ski-crampons (also known as *harscheisen* or *couteaux*) are fitted over the binding onto the ski to provide greater traction when ascending or traversing on hard snow surfaces.
Boots: All ski-mountaineering boots are a compromise, and are never going to be as efficient for downhill skiing as a downhill boot, and never as comfortable or flexible for walking around or climbing in as a plastic climbing boot. That said, some of the modern designs come very close to providing us with the ideal touring boot, ie stiff enough to ski in, yet soft enough to walk and climb in. All touring boots are front entry and contain an inner boot. Good ankle support is essential, and the heel should be gripped lightly on either side of the tendon. There will be flex at the ankle when adopting the forward lean position, though some models now incorporate a lockable cant for downhill mode. The boot can be tightened by means of grooved ratchets and wires on clips on the plastic shell. A firm grip on the ankle-bend clip is necessary in order to hold the heel down. The sole of the boot is vibram. It should be possible to fit a step-in crampon to all touring boots.

Although people do use downhill boots for ski-touring in the Alps, this is not recommended in Scotland where sections of walking are often needed in the absence of continuous snow-cover. For those determined to enjoy the best possible downhill performance and who don't mind a few blisters, it is possible to graft a vibram sole onto the base of a downhill ski-boot. The modified boots should not be used with downhill bindings, however, as the sole will interfere with the release procedure.

Virtually all downhill and touring boots will fit into touring bindings. Most plastic climbing boots will also fit, provided they

Plate 13.6 *Ski touring accessories: shovels, avalanche probe, ice axe, crampons, transceiver, skins and harcheisen*

don't have an exaggerated camber on the sole and as long as they possess a well preserved toe groove in order to fit into the binding toe-piece. This means that climbers can ski in to routes in the high Cairngorms, or indeed Aonach Mor, where a climbing day can be combined with some great skiing.

Skins: These are essential for upward progress when ski-touring. They are stuck onto the base of the ski for the uphill slog, and stripped off prior to a descent; on occasions they may be left on if the descent is brief, or on flat ground in between uphill sections. Two main functional aspects need to be considered before purchasing:

1 *Choice of material:* this will be nylon or mohair – nobody actually makes skins out of sealskin any more. Mohair runs faster, but is less durable than nylon; nylon is *very* durable, and provides good grip when going uphill, but does not run so well. A nylon/mohair mix is a bit of a compromise without the real benefits of either material. An American-made glueless skin, akin to that of a snake, has yet to be tested in earnest in Scotland.

2 *Points of attachment:* some skins are hooked over the tip of the ski and then glued flat along the base, the skin being trimmed to a point to fit 2–3cm short of the tail. Alternatively a metal hook goes over the tail of the ski, and the skin is then pulled tight and attached in a similar fashion to the tip. The advantage of the latter arrangement is that there is less dependence on the performance of the glue, since the skin remains attached at the back even if the skin becomes unstuck in between. However, the rubberised extender for stretching the skin over the tip may wear and eventually fail.

The glue on the skins should last for anything up to two years. When not in use, each skin is folded in on itself, sticky side in, and should be easy to pull apart when needed. Skins can be waterproofed periodically with a spray, but this does not last for long. The performance of the glue is improved if skins are kept warm – inside a pocket for instance – when not in use. Skins should always be hung up to dry after use.

Sticks: Normal piste-skiing sticks are the best bet for touring. Length is dependent on height, and can be determined by standing on the flat holding the pole upside down underneath the basket with the handle on the ground: with the correct length of pole the forearm should be parallel with the ground surface. Adjustable poles, especially those in three sections, are inevitably weaker and can collapse unexpectedly, especially when iced up.

Other Equipment:

Rucksack: This should be lightweight, 40–45 litres, and designed to keep the centre of gravity low, eg pear-shaped. Quick, easy access to gear is important eg via a zipped opening as opposed to straps; it should have side straps and/or plastic panels to carry skis on steeper ascents and on the walks to and from the snowline.

Axe and crampons: Use the lightest models that will get you off an icy slope: medium length (55cm) axe and ten-point (with front-points) crampons.

Shovel: Essential for overnight trips (whether snow-holing, camping or excavating bothies) and for digging through avalanche debris. Metal blades have better penetration in hard snow, but polycarbonate blades are equally strong.

Avalanche probes: For locating buried avalanche victims, and for testing snow depth and layering; they should be lightweight, folding, and between 2.5 and 3.5m in length.

Avalanche transceivers: These are *de rigueur* for serious ski-tours on the high hills: a competent searcher, well versed in the grid and induction methods, will find two victims in a 30sq m area within five minutes. All transceivers now operate on a frequency of 457kHz.

Repair kit: This should include spare skins, pliers, wire, glue, strap, binding spare parts, screwdriver, plastic scraper; also sprays for waxing the ski bases and re-glueing skins.

Other items to consider: Snow-saw, snow-study equipment (eg crystal screen, magnifying lens, thermometer, ruler), harness, helmet, rope (eg 30m of 9mm).

ALPINE TECHNIQUES

Once basic skills are mastered, skiing is largely a matter of confidence, although a little bit of practice will not go amiss. Most ski-tourers will have progressed to a reasonable standard of linked parallel turns on the piste before venturing further afield. This is not essential, however, as the novice tourer can make do with good snow-plough turns and a lot of traversing under favourable conditions on a straightforward day out. Nevertheless, before tackling steeper slopes and moving into more remote terrain, it is worth acquiring the confidence to deal with whatever vagaries the Scottish snowpack may have to offer.

Whatever type of snow is being skied, there are certain aspects of technique that remain constant. For example, balance and control are always important; so too is the ability to flex and extend the body, keeping the upper body at an even height while the knees and legs act as shock absorbers. The arms maintain lateral stability. Posture can be adjusted according to slope and terrain. For instance, weight can be moved forwards onto the forebody of the ski to reduce vibration and chattering on hard snow. In general, the skis are kept hip width (about 15cm) apart.

Powder snow: yes, it does occur. It has even been skied off piste at the Lecht in October ... good stuff too! Deeper snow slows you down. Good balance is essential. Stay close to the fall-line and ski smoothly and rhythmically. With ankle-deep powder adopt the classic skiing position, the skis rest on a firm layer of snow beneath the powder and the edges can still be used. Should you be so lucky as to be skiing knee-deep powder, then the ski tips need to be kept up, breaking the surface so that the skis are planing over the snow; do not sit back. One turn should lead rhythmically to the next. Skis should be kept more evenly weighted than on the piste, as excess weight on one ski will cause it to dive. Use the knees to steer the skis round.

Breakable crust: sometimes this breaks con-

Fig 13.2 *Alpine downhill touring techniques*

Technical manoeuvre	Applications
Side-slipping – no turns.	Safest way of losing height on steep slopes.
Traverse with side-slip – kick turn traverse.	The reliable 'get you home' technique; kick turns best done from a platform facing uphill with partner support below if in difficulty.
Traverse with snow-plough or stem turn.	Snow-plough turns are very tiring in deep snow but enable good control of speed; easier if whole party uses the same tracks.
Linked snow-ploughs in the fall-line.	A good technique for narrow descents, but not on steep terrain; of some help in deep snow; readily leads on to parallel technique.
Linked parallel turns in the fall-line.	Best technique for deep snow; less effort and good control ensured; once mastered, a delight to execute, especially in powder.
Edge-to-edge short swing turns.	For steep and/or narrow slopes; athletic; practice needed to maintain rhythm and control.
Jump turns.	For crust or heavy wet snow; very tiring.
Descending with skins on.	For bad visibility; enables a straight downhill course to be held; danger of pitching head-first over tips due to the drag.

sistently, and sometimes it breaks when you least expect it to. It is very difficult to ski stylishly, and has been known to reduce the so-called expert to traversing and kick turns. Power is required if this is to be skied properly, so keep the speed going. The terrain will dictate the radius of the turn, and the skier will need to adapt to changes in the snow.

Wet, heavy snow: this is found during a thaw. A determined approach is required. Again, power is needed in order to drive the skis round.

Hard, wind-packed snow and névé: good edge control is essential (not to mention good edges!). Turns can be carved rather than skidded, using pressure on the inside edge of the lower ski.

Ice: ever tried skating with skates almost 2m in length? Maybe it's time to get the crampons on!

Steeper slopes: the steeper-pisted slopes offer challenging runs up to around 30 degrees in inclination. At this gradient and beyond a well honed technique and complete confidence is required. Snow conditions should be carefully assessed: firm, stable, hard-packed

snow is best, and if you are in any doubt about the conditions or your own ability, then don't do it. The surface quality will vary with the aspect of the slope, depending on whether it has been sun-softened.

Angulation is the body position when edging: the upper body leans out while the hips and knees are pushed into the slope. Up to a point the lower ski can be used as a platform to initiate the turn; beyond a certain angle the skier will want to weight the upper ski in order to facilitate turning of the lower ski early. This is a prelude to the jump turn, whereby the skis are rotated through 180 degrees in mid-air, to land at a right-angle to the fall-line. Progress can be hesitant, but as the angle decreases, turns can be linked, more as short swings, and eventually – as relief surges through – ordinary short-radius parallel turns can be made. The pole plant is both a psychological trigger for the turn, and provides support. The adept will use a double pole plant for increased stability.

The *aficionado* of the steeper couloir should also be a master of the side-slip, including diagonals. Many an awkward passage can be negotiated by judicious use of this technique, albeit with bated breath because it is invariably a last resort to when you are totally committed to a descent and encounter either unfavourable snow, or a steeper-than-anticipated section, or have lost your bottle (or all three).

WHICH IS BEST: NORDIC OR ALPINE?

The long-running debate over which discipline is more effective for Scottish mountain conditions has shifted with the modern development of Telemark ski equipment and style; this has effectively bridged the chasm and blurred the distinction between Nordic and Alpine techniques, so that the lines of argument are no longer so clear cut. With pure Nordic skiing on lightweight 'skinny' skis best adapted to low-level trails and gentle tours, the serious mountain tourer has an effective choice between the Telemark and Alpine modes. Those whose personal preference is for Alpine ski-touring will point out certain benefits, such as being able to handle really steep or icy terrain with the rigid platform of Alpine skis; and the technical difficulty of adapting to free-heel techniques, especially for those weaned on downhill skiing.

Nevertheless, the Telemark skier enjoys faster travel because of the lighter equipment and the kick-and-glide uphill technique. Telemark technique is undoubtedly more precise, but with top quality equipment, some initial instruction and intensive practice, the equipment can handle all Scottish routes and has even proved its worth on descents of grade I gullies.

Ultimately what you choose is likely to be determined by your skiing upbringing. Those who have learnt to ski on piste with Alpine equipment, and who have done some ski-mountaineering in the Alps, are likely to stick to Alpine equipment when they ski-tour in Scotland. Likewise, climbers who want to be able to use their plastic climbing boots on skis tend to make the Alpine choice. By contrast, those who have been taught on cross-country Nordic skis, who are attracted to the Scandinavian ski-touring scene, and who are inspired by long mountain traverses, will be attracted to the Telemark style; and many have been converted to Telemark techniques by following a course of instruction. On balance, Alpine skis are perhaps to be preferred by those who seek the thrill of steeper ground and want to combine shorter day tours with piste skiing, whilst Telemark kit and techniques are slightly more effective for longer distance touring across the high tops.

The argument becomes arid and divisive if prolonged. Both Alpine and Telemark ski-mountaineers are attracted by the same thrills and rewards in their sport. Compare the descriptions of Jonathan Preston on an Alpine tour in the Cairngorms, and Andy Cunningham on Telemark skis on the round of Coire Ardair, Creag Meagaidh, and it will be clear that little, if any difference is discernible between the two experiences. First, Jonathan Preston:

'It was a glorious day, and while racing back across the plateau from Macdui I toyed with the idea of doing something steeper to finish. My new skis and bindings were performing well, giving a good stable platform for hammering into the turns on the descents. The Goat Track into Sneachda was the obvious choice to end the day with, despite the inherent risk of encountering *in situ* snow belays complete with bucket seats. But, hurtling down towards the Feith Buidhe, I picked up enough speed for the momentum to carry me up the other side a little way, and I soon found myself putting skins on again to make the short ascent up to the top of Cairn Lochan.

in the rucksack for the last time that day, because instead of the Goat Track, a descent of The Couloir now beckoned. I walked to the edge and down to the little col where I stepped back into skis. It's strange how something you would quite happily potter up with axe and crampons becomes so daunting when viewed from above on a pair of skis. I started with side-slips and finally made a few turns, only vaguely aware of the impressive surroundings. After one last steep bit, the gully fanned out into the upper reaches of Coire an Lochain. I saw a couple of people I knew climbing Fallout Corner, but otherwise the corrie was deserted. Fantastic skiing on perfect snow followed, and the slope seemed delightfully straightforward after the intensity of The Couloir. Branching off right before the base of the corrie saved valuable height, and a speedy ten-minute jaunt back to the car park, whooshing past returning walkers and climbers alike, brought to an end a superb day.'

And now Andy Cunningham on Telemark skis:

'It had cleared enough to view a daunting line of cornices sweeping up to Point 1051m at the head of Coire a'Chriochairein. At the bealach the cornice petered out into a steepening, and we peered down a perfect run to the Coire Ardair footpath 400m below. The initial section was a wide, steep couloir, bounded on both sides by rocks and with a rocky runout. Our line would quit the couloir with a long traverse out to the right onto wider slopes leading into the bottom of the corrie. From there a perfect line of snow by the outlet burn led down to the path.

'Skins off, boot clips tightened; then I side-slipped over the edge and tested the snow. It was dry soft slab, but safe! Jeni followed and we decided to descend the first part singly. I slid forward to gain a bit of momentum, double-poled into a jump Telemark and traversed to a stop.

With confidence building from the first turn and good telemarking snow, I relaxed into a series of linked short turns, keeping careful control with the long runout in mind.

'Jeni led out across the traverse, and without stopping, swung into some wider, faster Telemark turns, weaving through giant snow-covered boulders which looked like sleeping trolls. The clouds of the next shower chased us out of the corrie. With the fresh snow thinning and older refrozen snow emerging, we adapted our technique to parallel turns and skied to lunch at the footpath.'

EXTREME SKIING: THE CHALLENGE OF THE GULLIES

Gully skiing must be accepted for what it is: highly dangerous. A slip will at best mean a long slide and a big fright; at worst – well, it is only wise to know the score. To assess the suitability of a gully for a ski descent requires the sound judgement born of countless hours of ski-mountaineering experience, and to make a descent in good style requires a high level of skiing ability. The obvious grade Is in the Northern Corries of Cairngorm, such as Aladdin's Couloir and The Couloir in Coire an Lochain, were skied by Harry Jamieson, an instructor at Glenmore Lodge during the 1970s, a period when extreme skiing was taking hold in the Alps. Since then a small but committed band of enthusiasts has exploited the adrenalin potential of Scotland's gullies.

'Some may well doubt the sanity and point of skiing steep and confined ground in an exposed and serious situation, and not infrequently I have shared similar feelings myself. However, speaking personally, the challenge has become addictive and I am constantly searching for the perfect ski descent, hopefully completed in good style and control.'[4] So wrote Martin Burrows-Smith, leading exponent of the art. Extreme skiing would

Plate 13.7 *Martin Burrows-Smith 'at it' in the Coire an t-Sneachda gullies (Richard Mansfield)*

seem to be much akin to solo climbing in terms of its dependence on the adrenalin rush: it can seduce some people completely, while terrifying the majority.

But Martin is no fool, and he is certainly Scotland's most experienced skier of steep ground. He, too, has moments of doubt. Of Forked Gully on Stob Coire nan Lochan, Glencoe, he commented: 'A lot of side-slipping required. Disappointing and worrying.' He is also possessed of the mountaineer's vital survival instinct: 'Ice and fear prevented the link from the summit of Sgurr Fiona into Lord's Gully on An Teallach.' Confidence is all-important when one is faced with that first

committing turn, but it must be the confidence of experience, and not of bravado.

For those who aspire to ski steep slopes, snow assessment is absolutely critical, preferably gained first by climbing the gully. The experienced ski-mountaineer will ideally look for firm wind-pack (although not slab) or coarse-grained spring snow. Equally important is the tight adjustment of ski bindings, for they must not release in mid-flight.

Besides the Cairngorms massif, there are abundant possibilities for steep skiing in grade I gullies, but many involve a lengthy approach. Provided there are no great cornice problems or encounters with ascending mountaineers on foot, Scotland's potential for fine exciting descents is literally endless. With grade Is and some grade IIs now fair game, the stage is set for a move to grade III terrain where an occasional abseil might be necessary in mid-flight, and in this regard the Post Gullies of Creag Meagaidh come first to mind. All that is required is a dedicated local skier who can resist the lure of the Alps and has the patience to wait for the right conditions. If this all sounds rather daunting and inappropriate, there is no compulsion to try the game. Just sit back and let Martin Burrows-Smith take you down Lord's Gully, the great forked cleft splitting the pinnacles on An Teallach:

'A quick coffee, some chocolate, then awkwardly on with the skis, trying to ignore the 300m of couloir ghosting down to the loch. Tighten the sack, grip the poles, warm up the legs, adjust to the two metres of metal edge on the feet; then don't delay, *go*!

'A few bouncing, jumping side-steps, getting into a rhythm for the first turn. Total commitment, double-pole plant for stability and launch into the fall-line. Upper body quiet, skis turn in mid-air, pulse racing. I'd underdone the turn: an instinctive twist of the skis across the line of travel and they bite. Great, the form was there. I could relax and enjoy it. The slope was steep, perhaps 50 degrees, but the snow's smooth texture more than compensated. One turn at a time down the ridge into the narrows. It was tight. A short hop avoided a lump of ice; then I could cruise, linking turns down the lower section with a long, orgasmic, diagonal *schuss* into the brightness on the far side of the corrie.

'The relief that I was still in one piece was tinged with the usual sadness that it was all over. A long, fast run back to the car remained – GS turns, drop-offs and schusses unwound in a carefree cruise to the jungle of trees by the road.'[5]

ROUTE-PLANNING AND LOGISTICS IN SKI-TOURING

Because skiers can travel faster and further than pedestrian mountaineers, they can venture into positions of great commitment on the mountains, where otherwise a broken item of equipment, an adverse change in snow conditions or a sudden storm might have particularly serious consequences. Alan Hunt remembers having to terminate a tour of the Cairngorm tops just below Braeriach summit as storm-force winds arrived earlier than predicted:

'We side-slipped and slithered into the depths of Gleann Einich, down the only safe slope our spindrift-confused navigation could locate. Exposed skin was agonised by the shot blast of driven ice, and from our knees downwards a tormented mass of whirling snow and ice articles concealed boots and skis from view. The down-draught impelled us valleywards, ski edges grating over rocks and ice patches, the sudden snatch of a soft drift threatening to pitchpole us into oblivion.

'With relief we finally reached the comparative shelter of the glen and began the long, easy, angled glide to the main road, hoping the thinning snow-cover would hold all the way. It was past midnight when aching limbs and rock-scratched skis delivered us to the Coylumbridge phone-box. The cars were in the ski-ground car park, and the access road was now closed by drifted snow.'

Route-planning strategy prior to a trip and decision-making on the hill can help avoid such fraught situations, and should take several factors into account:

1 Gauging the length of the touring day is difficult, and only experience will indicate the time that a trip might take. In good snow, a fit skier may achieve a steady 6kmph on Nordic gear, and 5kmph on the heavier

Alpine kit over level ground, plus for either technique a climbing rate of ten minutes per 100m of vertical ascent. A steep 300m descent might take no more than ten minutes, and gentle inclines can be cruised at 8–12kmph. All this changes if the snow becomes patchy or difficult, and once visibility is reduced in any way, be it by nightfall, spindrift, falling snow or mist, the skier's speed of travel falls far more dramatically than that of the walker.

2 Safe escape routes must take easy terrain on skis. Escapes are often considerably longer in distance for the skier than the climber and may greatly extend the finish to an outing. An early decision to escape in deteriorating conditions is especially critical to the tourer, allowing swift downhill travel on skis while good visibility lasts.

3 Bad visibility coupled with a featureless snow-cover dramatically impairs balance and orientation on skis. Relative momentum with the ground cannot be sensed, and prior judgement of slope is, of course, impossible. For descents in mist, it is a good idea is to keep the skins on to ensure that you can control your speed and maintain your direction.

4 Strong winds, especially if gusty, disturb skiing balance and control.

5 Slope angles need careful interpretation by skiers when formulating a route plan. A range from 10 to 30 degrees in slope angles is of little significance to the foot traveller, but for the skier, 10 degrees is an easy glide, while 30 degrees is a steep, serious slope, equivalent to a 'black' piste run and requiring favourable snow coupled with expertise. All slope angles must be safely within one's margins of ability. Angles can be calculated from contour spacing. On the OS 1:50000 maps, the approximate conversions from the spacings between the thick 50m con-

tours are: 2mm spacing = 27 degrees; 4mm spacing = 14 degrees; 6mm spacing = 9 degrees; 8mm spacing = 7 degrees. For comparative reference, the White Lady piste run on Cairn Gorm averages 21 degrees, and a grade I snow gully is around 45 degrees.

6 Snow conditions may change as suddenly as the weather. For instance, thawing spring snow can turn into bone-hard névé within an hour of the onset of a sharp frost. Ski-edge control becomes difficult, and what would earlier have been a harmless slip may now commence a bone-rattling plunge valleywards. Breaking crust, the *bête noire* of all tourers, can be encountered on descents without any prior warning, and can be too exhausting for anything other than easy-angled traverses linked by kick turns.

7 The distribution of snow-cover greatly influences the tourer's choice of route, in particular the linking of major snowfields and the use of sheltered gullies and hollows which hold the deepest and longest drifts for descents.

8 Avalanche hazard can be encountered with little or no warning when gliding on skis. Ski tracks themselves can cause a windslab fracture far more easily than the walker's boots on an open convex slope. When forced to descend or traverse a suspect slope, the skier should take several precautions to minimise the risk:

a Ski slowly and carefully under control. Descend by diagonal traverses linked by easy turns. Undue vibration, as might be caused by a fall, for instance, can trigger the slope.

b Ski well away from convexities at slope tops or on shallow gully side-walls, which are zones of tension in an unstable snowpack.

c Descend one at a time across the danger area.

d Remove your hands from the ski-pole loops ready to cast them away if you find yourself engulfed, and untie safety straps on bindings. Attachment to skis and poles much increases the risk of injury or burial in an avalanche.

e The idea that it is advisable to ski down and away from an avalanche is an old wives' tale and should be disregarded: all this is likely to achieve is burial in the deepest part of the debris cone. It is far better to try to ski across and off a moving windslab.

9 Navigation on skis is far more difficult than on foot because it is impossible to judge the distance travelled when one's speed is so variable; the use of an altimeter and possibly a GPS receiver is therefore recommended. Compass work is also difficult on skis because both hands are holding the poles, so for ease of reading it is a good idea to carry the compass strapped to the wrist. In a total white-out, reverting to foot travel should be considered as the safest option – though that walking in deep, loose snow will be far slower and more exhausting.

A ROUTE TO SAVOUR: THE CAIRNGORM FOUR TOPS

Let us now put all these variables into practical use with a look at Scotland's most famous, and arguably its finest ski-tour. The traverse of Cairn Gorm, Ben Macdui, Cairn Toul and Braeriach, the four 4,000ft tops, is a very long outing, but it has a circular route and can be abbreviated at several places, while it takes the skier over some of the most remote terrain and reliable snow-cover that the Highlands can offer (Fig 13.3, page 294).

Once Cairn Gorm's northern corries are left behind, and especially after the Lairig Ghru is crossed, you are likely to enjoy near-total solitude. Because of the tour's remoteness, its

exposure to the elements, and the difficulties of navigation on the plateaux, it should only be attempted in settled weather. Although the slopes are never excessively steep, a high level of competence is required to avoid unnecessary energy expenditure. A tired skier on the Braeriach plateau is a long way from home by any route.

The guidebook time for this tour is 12–15 hours. This can be derived by personal calculation for each section using the suggested rates of travel for Alpine or Nordic techniques (see 'Route-planning') to give a total skiing time from the Cairn Gorm car park of about 10 hours. If an additional 10 minutes per hour of travel is added for rests and gear adjustments, a total time of 12 hours results. Then if the skiing conditions are not optimal, the tour could easily stretch to the 15 hours' guidebook limit.

Clearly there are insufficient daylight hours for this length of outing until very late in March, and thereafter a lack of snow-cover may necessitate slower foot travel on the lower ground. Thus only the fit skier favoured by conditions will make the route without a pre-dawn start or twilight finish. If time is pressing, section B on its own can make a fine day tour, especially for the Nordic enthusiast, taking in the tops of the northern corries' rim and returning from Ben Macdui down the spur to the west of Cairn Lochan, with a fine run down to Lurcher's Gully to finish. A time of 5–6 hours should suffice for this. Skiers intent on the complete round will probably contour south of the northern corrie tops to save time.

Section C provides the finest descent of the tour down the Tailors' Burn from Macdui summit, a drop of 600m to the River Dee; however, this slope has a reputation for being avalanche-prone, so a careful prior assessment of the

Plate 13.8 *Exiting Jacob's Ladder gully in Coire an t-Sneachda (Mungo Ross)*

snow's state should be made before a final commitment. Furthermore once the descent is made, there are no convenient homeward escape routes: escape to the north through the Lairig Ghru defile is long and very prone to strong winds due to funnelling in the pass; otherwise one is forced to descend to Braemar, which is 110km by road from your start. It is a prospect to weigh most carefully before pressing on from Macdui in worsening weather.

An alternative descent from Macdui is the Allt a'Choire Mhoir: this is slightly steeper, but leads straight across to Coire an t-Sabhail, which provides a good direct approach to Cairn Toul summit provided there is no cornice at the exit. The normal ascent route is to follow the summer path route west from Corrour Bothy. Either way involves a foot section on the final steepening.

The most challenging way onto the Cairn Toul plateau is to go up to the Garbh Choire Bothy, then climb the ice-fall (with axe and crampons) to reach the North-East Ridge of Angel's Peak, which gives a route of true alpine character to the summit. Although never very difficult, the ascent requires winter climbing experience, particularly if it is to be tackled unroped (as it should for speed).

Section D is the most rewarding part of the journey as you cross the undulating plateau from Cairn Toul to Braeriach summit. This is as near to true arctic terrain as one will encounter in Britain, and its wilderness atmosphere should be savoured to the full. It is also the most committed section of the journey. There is no easy way back into the Lairig Ghru, and the only escape route leads down into Gleann Einich and a 12km ski or walk back to the main road at Coylumbridge; undoubtedly an 'emergency exit' only.

After the exhilarating descent from Braeriach down the Sron na Lairige, the correct route back to the car park south of the Chalamain Gap is straightforward, and it can be negotiated by torchlight if necessary. However, this is still inhospitable country and people have been overcome by storms here so close to safety. So aim to finish in daylight, and enjoy contouring round from the Gap back to the car park. The downhill skiers will have long since gone home.

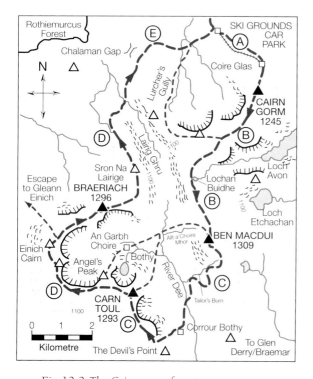

Fig 13.3 *The Cairngorms four tops tour*

WHEN AND WHERE TO SKI TOUR

The aspirant ski-mountaineer has a mouth-watering choice of hill country in Scotland for touring. Given unlimited time, the observant opportunist can take advantage of snow and weather conditions to make fine ski-tours almost anywhere in the Highlands. Unfortunately, most people have to plan their time off some way in advance, or they are confined to weekend trips, so it is just as well to know the areas that offer the most reliable conditions, when these are most likely to be found, and the most representative routes in each.

The period from early February through to mid-April gives the most reliable snow-cover. The later you go, the more likely are there to be foot sections because of the receding snowline, and the more frequently is the dreaded breaking crust encountered; but the early spring can offer glorious sun-tanning conditions, while the longer days allow for extended tours or at least a greater margin for error. Earlier in the season the snowline will be lower, but skiing conditions are more variable, from iron-hard névé through to powder, with frequent windslab forming after winter storms. Days are also shorter, the onset of blizzards more likely and minor access roads may be impassable. However, when it is good, a February tour can be an absolute joy with deep snow-cover and startlingly clear atmospheric conditions. Prior to February, touring opportunities are dependent on the chance of major individual snowstorms, for a good snow base rarely develops early in the winter.

The Eastern and Central Highlands and the Cairngorms offer the most reliable snow-cover, the touring season lasting sometimes into May on the higher plateaux. Further west, the thawing maritime air can work with the efficiency of a giant blow-lamp at times, and strip the cover from slopes and summits exposed to its hot breath in a few days; also the more rugged terrain of the western and northern mountain blocks holds less snow and requires a thicker cover for good skiing. Favourable touring conditions are, therefore, a matter of good fortune.

For a detailed and very well illustrated guide to the individual tours throughout the Highlands, see *Ski Mountaineering in Scotland*, published by the SMC in 1987.

GREAT DEEDS ON SKI: LONG DISTANCE TOURS

The Easter meet of the SMC in 1913, when the Cairngorms massif was crossed three times, ranks as an early landmark in Scottish ski-touring achievement. Then for forty years thereafter little was recorded of note. Competition downhill skiing provided an outlet for the record-breaking mentality, while ski-mountaineering spirits of the day such as Willie Speirs were content to plough their own lonely furrow and simply enjoy the hills.

In January 1953, Speyside was enjoying heavy snowfalls with temperatures down to –8 degrees C. Conditions on the hills were ideal for ski-touring, and before daybreak one morning Norman Clark set off from Glenmore to make the first traverse of the Cairngorm Four Tops. His route was anticlockwise, first traversing Braeriach and Cairn Toul, then swooping back into the Lairig by Soldier's Corrie (Coire an t-Saighdeir). What a superb final descent it must have been off Cairn Gorm back to Glenmore without the inelegant teeming confusion of the modern pistes, which were not established until the early 1960s.

Then in April 1962, Adam Watson junior, the great naturalist and current advocate for the protection of the fragile Cairngorm environment, added the summits of Ben Avon and Beinn a'Bhuird to cover the Cairngorm Six Tops in a sixteen-hour day starting from Invercauld by Braemar and finishing in Glen Derry, a total distance of 61km with 2,650m of climbing. He used fairly primitive Nordic equipment, and his main sustenance was six tins of fruit, all of which were, of course, carried in his sack in addition to clothing and sleeping-bag. Most remarkably, this great feat was done on a pure impulse occasioned by good snow and weather. Adam Watson had done no skiing at all over the previous six weeks. Twenty years later he

Plate 13.9 *Ski touring in early April on the Ladder Hills above Strathdon (Diana Woodman)*

looked back to that wonderful day and commented pertinently:

'The weather can be too settled. A breeze does wonders for the body and the snow, and even a fairly strong wind drifting the snow can be good as long as it's not in your face most of the time ... Equipment is relatively unimportant, but what constitutes the best is a topic for endless argument. Basically, whatever makes you feel better will be less tiring for psychological reasons. And on a long day it's how your mind feels that is crucial ... I could have taken less time by not taking photographs, looking at views and wildlife, and talking to people ...'[6]

In February 1986, the Six Tops were completed in a round trip of 63km plus 3,750m of ascent from the Cairn Gorm ski grounds by Blyth Wright and Roger Wild in 23hr 25min;

they used Nordic gear. So complete was the snow-cover that they wore skis all the way. Blyth Wright was also involved in a marathon 80km coast-to-coast crossing on Nordic skis in 1982, starting from Shiel Bridge in the west to Beauly on the east coast, accomplished with Sam Crymble, Keith Geddes and Tim Walker. However, this was essentially a low-level crossing. They left at 7am and travelled by way of the Lichd-Affric watershed to Cannich, reaching Beauly at around midnight.

These efforts using Nordic techniques served to illustrate the speed of travel with lightweight equipment, but it was Alpine techniques that were used on the more demanding terrain of the 'Scottish Haute Route'. The concept of a high-level route across the Highlands linking the Cairngorms and Ben Nevis had been germinating for many years, and various attempts were made. This was to be Scotland's answer to the famous Alpine Haute Route from Chamonix to Zermatt. It was first travelled in seven days starting on 26 February 1978 by David Grieve and Mike Taylor, their route of 160km beginning on Deeside at Crathie (Fig 13.4). The serious nature of this trip and the variance of Scottish touring conditions is well illustrated by David Grieve's account:

'The conditions experienced on this section (Glen Feshie to Dalwhinnie) were arguably the most dangerous we encountered. The chilling effect of gale and rain must not be underestimated. Once wet, stops to rest and eat became inadequate because of rapid chilling. The tendency to press on quickly in order to keep warm increased fatigue and exhaustion/exposure was perhaps already taking effect.'[7]
And later, in Lochaber, *'the slope leading over*

the Carn Mor Dearg col was unskiable – in fact, it was quite poisonous with soft new snow lying on old, and numerous patches of green ice.'

Conversely there were pleasant and rewarding moments, for example on their first night at Corndavon Lodge bothy when *'... abundant firewood was to hand and a fine steak supper was shortly washed down by a bottle of claret in front of a roaring fire;'* and there was some great skiing, too. On the summit (Beinn na Lap) the cold was very severe with considerable spindrift. *'Westward, the Mamores and our ultimate goal of Nevis looked magnificent. Conditions for the descent were the best yet – soft powder on a frozen base, extending right down to the Loch Treig railway line.'*

The descent from Nevis in the grey light of evening was a fitting climax to the trip, 500m of perfect powder snow, followed by a further 400m of variable packed snow, frozen crust and Easter snow.

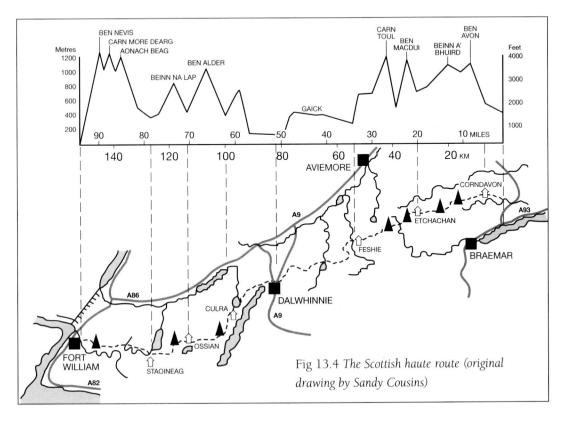

Fig 13.4 *The Scottish haute route (original drawing by Sandy Cousins)*

But like so many Scottish finishes, 'The final mud slide to the Youth Hostel in Glen Nevis was accomplished by torchlight.'

But it is V. A. Firsoff in his seminal work *On Ski in the Cairngorms* who takes us back to the atmosphere of earlier touring and who draws on the natural environment of the Cairngorms to enrich his encounters:

'It was calm on the Great Moss, the air just stirring at the edge of the snows, which were much more patchy than usual at this time of year, so that I had to choose my way carefully to avoid uncovered ribs. Mossy cyptel and club mosses were preening themselves in the warm sun. Golden plovers were invisibly voicing the solitude of the melting snows to the pale sky, and some small birds, which may have been snow buntings, darted along the obtuse crest in the direction of Meall Dubhag.

'Having crossed the snowless tops of Carn Ban Mor, I started down at a fairly good speed towards Loch nan Cnapan. Ptarmigan, all paired off, the cocks speckled with black, but the hens still pure white, fluttered up at my passage like huge butterflies. The burns were rumbling ominously underfoot, with here and there a dark "pocket" gaping open or a miniature crevasse marking the danger zone. On the way back, the snow actually collapsed under me and landed me in a narrow chest of moss-grown rocks some 3m deep with swirling water rushing furiously underneath. Not without difficulty did I lever myself up on my arms, and my hands were shaking when I had re-emerged on the surface.'[8]

Mountaineering – and that includes travel on skis – should give time to take photographs, to talk to people and to look at the views and the wildlife. If we don't notice the mosses, the small birds and the smell of the sun-dried grass between the thawing snow patches, we will be missing an essential aspect of the mountain experience. And if in our haste to break records we miss the scars left by our own and others' intrusions into the wilderness, we will find ourselves sliding into the gaping crevasse of indifference. The great beauty of being on ski in the mountains is the accentuated experience created by combining the thrill of a gliding descent with the rewards of physical effort. Break records by all means, but as Adam Watson said: 'the best days on the hill are the ones you snatch unexpectedly without much planning.'

APPENDICES

APPENDIX I:
A HISTORICAL REVIEW

Although there were isolated explorations earlier in the nineteenth century, Scottish winter mountaineering was only truly established as a recreational and adventure pursuit with the formation of the Scottish Mountaineering Club in 1889. However now that the sport is over a century old, it is surely timely to review its progress and development since there is such a rich and exciting catalogue of achievements, events and epics contained within this one-hundred-year span. However, because space within these pages is limited, this chronology must be selective in its content – the definitive history of the winter game would fill a large volume in itself. So only the major ascents and most influential developments are picked out and set against their natural backcloth of weather and conditions. It is inevitable that in a subjective selection, many great climbs and tours are excluded from the list, and for these omissions, I apologise in advance.

Key to categories:
NAT: Major natural events (weather, snowfall, conditions)
GEN: Events common to all aspects of winter mountaineering, and points of general interest
SKI: Ski-touring
CLI: Important snow, ice and mixed climbs. All climbing grades are quoted under the modern revised grading system, created in 1991

1812	GEN	12 November: Col Hawker climbs Ben Lomond and is obliged to cut steps with a knife on the icy snow of the final slopes; the first recorded piece of winter mountaineering.
1870	CLI	No 3 Gully of Coire na Ciste (I), Ben Nevis, climbed under snow; the first known ascent of a graded snow climb.
1883	GEN	Ben Nevis summit observatory commences operation.
1884	GEN	Ben More, Crianlarich, climbed by William Naismith in March using an alpenstock. The inadequacy of alpenstocks on hard snow was soon realised, and they were replaced by ice-axes for winter use in the 1890s.
1887	GEN	Cairngorm Club formed; growing recreational interest in summer hill walking, which soon spread to winter mountaineering; other local clubs, such as the Dundee Ramblers, also sprang up at this time.
1889	GEN	Scottish Mountaineering Club formed under the initiative of Naismith. One of its avowed aims at inception was the encouragement of winter ascents. At the first annual dinner the president, Prof. G. G. Ramsay, admitted that in mountain pioneering the Scots had lagged behind members of the English Alpine Club, who had achieved so much in the Alps over the previous thirty years.
	GEN	First recorded winter ascent in the Cuillin of Skye, Bruach na Frithe climbed by Swan.
1890	GEN	The first volume of the *SMC Journal* appears with articles by Hugh Munro and A. I. McConnochie strongly encouraging winter-mountain expeditions. The *Journal*'s 'Notes and Climbs' section provides a record and inspiration for the new and growing winter activism, eg Munro's 110km three-day round in the Eastern Grampians in January 1890.
1891	GEN	New Year's Day: A. I. McConnochie crosses the Cairngorms from Coylumbridge to Braemar via Braeriach and Cairn Toul in thirteen hours.
	GEN	Munro's Tables published, giving a major impetus to Scottish mountain exploration.
	CLI	Exploration of gullies and snow faces in the Southern Highlands – notably Ben Lui and the Cruachan group.

1892	SKI	Naismith writes enthusiastically on Scotland's skiing potential in the SMCJ.
1893	GEN	'Snowcraft in Scotland' by Naismith appears in the SMCJ, the first instructional treatise on the Scottish winter sport which was dubbed by Naismith 'one of the noblest forms of recreation'.
	CLI	Inaccessible Pinnacle, Skye, climbed by J. H. Gibson in April with snow on the rocks; other semi-winter climbs made on the Cuillin.
1894	NAT	Climbing activities thwarted by 'dreary months of rain' in the early winter but redeemed by late snows.
	CLI	**29 March**: First winter ascent of Tower Ridge (III) Ben Nevis by Collie Collier and Solly in a remarkable five hours – a major landmark and still Scotland's most famous winter climb.
	CLI	Several climbs recorded on the Buachaille Etive Mor at Easter, eg Great Gully (II).
1895	GEN	Extension of West Highland Railway to Fort William opens potential for further exploration of Ben Nevis and Lochaber. First SMC Easter meet to be held at Fort William.
	CLI	Castle Ridge (II) Ben Nevis (Collie Naismith Thomson Travers) and NE Ridge (III) Aonach Beag (Maclay, Naismith Thomson) climbed – classic mountaineering routes.
1896	NAT	First recorded avalanche incident on a Scottish climb during attempt on Centre Post, Creag Meagaidh: cornice collapse in thaw conditions; a narrow escape for Douglas, Raeburn and Tough.
	GEN	Highly favourable snow and weather conditions at Easter. Tower Ridge repeated five times during SMC Fort William meet.
	CLI	**3 April**: N-E Buttress (IV) Ben Nevis; first winter ascent in seven hours by Naismith and party.
1897	CLI	Two notable gully climbs: the Upper Couloir (II) Stob Ghabhar giving A. E. Maylard and party a genuine ice pitch, and Gardyloo Gully (II), Ben Nevis (Hastings and Haskett-Smith).
1900	GEN	Easter mountaineering on the Torridon Hills: six-man ascent of Northern Pinnacles (II) and Main Ridge of Liathach in wintry conditions.
1902	NAT	Windslab avalanche witnessed on Ben More, Crianlarich and its cause correctly diagnosed as 'superimposed dry snow' on a windswept ice-slope.
1903	GEN	Further semi-winter exploration of the Cuillin during SMC Easter meet, eg the Dubhs Ridge and T-D Gap.
1904	SKI	Skiing in Scotland given impetus by W. R. Rickmers in an illustrated SMCJ article.
	CLI	North Trident Buttress (III), Ben Nevis (Maclay, Raeburn, C. Walker and H. Walker) Central Trident Gully (III), Ben Nevis, (Raeburn, W. and Mrs Inglis-Clark): Harold Raeburn now the leading winter activist.
1905	SKI	Raeburn is sceptical of Scotland's ski-touring potential in his article 'Scottish Snow' and discusses the Norwegian *langlauf* technique.
1906	CLI	April Green Gully (IV), Ben Nevis, climbed by Raeburn and Phildius; the hardest pre-1914 ice-gully: 'two of the pitches were what is usually known as perpendicular' (HR). Although recorded, this ascent was not established and acknowledged by guidebook writers until c1970.
1907	GEN	**28–9 December**: Protracted all-night epic on Tower Ridge (Goodeve, C. Inglis-Clark, McIntyre) – the first of many. The party extricated themselves from the cliffs by courageous climbing on uncharted ground, reaching the summit at 2am.
	CLI	Central Buttress (IV) Stob Coire nan Lochan, Glencoe, climbed by Raeburn, Ling, Glover and W. Inglis-Clark.
	SKI	Scottish Ski Club founded.
1909	CLI	**Easter**: Crowberry Gully (IV) Buachaille Etive Mor climbed by Raeburn, Brigg and Tucker in $4\frac{1}{2}$ hours – another ascent that was not acknowledged until c1970; now the epitome of Scottish winter-gully climbing.
1910	GEN	First of a series of mild, wet and snowless winters which held up winter pioneering.
1913	SKI	Great trans-Cairngorms tours achieved during SMC Easter meet at Aviemore: thus contrary to Raeburn's view, a potential for ski-touring on the high tops is fully realised.
1914–18	GEN	World War I imposes a near-complete interruption on mountaineering activity, and extinguishes the enthusiasm for bolder pioneering – a legacy which continued for the subsequent twenty years, during which recreation and enjoyment replaced exploration and adventure as the criteria of winter mountaineering.
1920	GEN	*Mountaineering Art* by Harold Raeburn published, the first textbook to devote a substantial portion of its content to the Scottish winter sport.

1920	CLI	**April**: The last of the great Nevis ridges falls in winter; Observatory Ridge (IV) climbed by Raeburn, F. Goggs and W. Mounsey – Raeburn's last major Scottish winter ascent, and the sole winter advance during the 1920s.
1925	GEN	Junior Mountaineering Club of Scotland (JMCS) formed, providing a channel for youthful climbing energies, which bore fruit in winter during the 1930s.
1929	GEN	**1 April**: Charles Inglis-Clark Memorial Hut (CIC) on Ben Nevis opened; the ideal base for future winter pioneering on the mountain.
1932	SKI	Scottish Ski Club hut erected on the slopes of Ben Lawers.
1933	GEN	**January**: Tragedy on Cairn Gorm: Ferrier and Mackenzie, both young and ill-equipped, perish in storm. The incident was one of the first winter fatalities and attracted much general publicity, which cast doubt on the sense and purpose of winter mountaineering.
1934	CLI	**March**: SC Gully (III), Stob Coire nan Lochan, Glencoe, climbed by P. Baird, E. Leslie and H. Fynes-Clinton, a Cambridge University party.
1935	CLI	**17 March**: Glover's Chimney (III), Ben Nevis, climbed by G. Macphee, G. Williams and D. Henderson. This climb, together with SC Gully, heralded a renaissance in Scottish winter climbing that was cut short by World War II.
1936	CLI	Despite Macphee's lament in the SMCJ that 'Munrovitis' was sapping the SMC's younger talents and energies, this was a year of new activity and equipment modifications – longer ropes 36m (120ft) per man, and short slater's picks for stepcutting.
	CLI	**April**: Semi-winter ascent of Slav Route/Zero Gully by J. H. B. Bell and C. Allen gives clear evidence of new enthusiasm to explore intimidating winter terrain. Willingness to climb through the winter season; Crowberry Gully repeated in February. All-night retreat from Garrick's Shelf on the Buachaille in December by Dunn MacAlpine, Mackenzie and Murray emphasises the seriousness of climbing in the darkest month.
1937	CLI	**March**: Garrick's Shelf (IV), Buachaille Etive Mor, climbed by W. Mackenzie and W. H. Murray; probably the hardest pre-war ascent on mixed ground.
1938	CLI	Comb Gully (IV), Ben Nevis, climbed by F. Stangle, R. Morsley and P. Small.
1939–45	SKI	While the war interrupted serious mountaineering activity, skis were used extensively on the Scottish hills for armed services mountain training.
1945–7	GEN	RAF Mountain Rescue service commenced; it continued after the war in service of mountaineering accidents. Rescue equipment now in place in major climbing centres. Local men carrying out rescue work on an *ad hoc* basis. Donald Duff, surgeon at Fort William's Belford Hospital, developing rescue equipment and techniques. Henceforth winter mountaineers in distress could take comfort that an organised rescue effort would be mounted.
	GEN	Flood of ex-WD equipment available to mountaineers. Nylon ropes and vibram-soled boots appear in the UK, together with pitons and karabiners. Improved gear lays a foundation for an advance in winter climbing over the next decade.
1947	GEN	*Mountaineering in Scotland* by W. H. Murray published, a literary landmark which provided an historical tradition for the inspiration of future winter mountaineers.
1950	GEN	*A Progress in Mountaineering* by J. H. B. Bell gives an instructional update to Raeburn on Scottish winter climbing.
	CLI	**29 January**: Giant's Head Chimney (IV), Lochnagar, by W. Brooker and J. Morgan. **28 December**: Douglas-Gibson Gully (V), Lochnagar, by T. Patey and G. Leslie (Patey was eighteen years old). A new advance begins in the Cairngorms.
1951	NAT	1950/1 is the snowiest winter of the century to date at high altitudes; snow lies for 102 days at Dalwhinnie (300m).
	GEN	**30 December**: The Corrour tragedy: four perish in a severe blizzard en route from Corrour to Ben Alder Cottage.
	SKI	Scotland's first ski-tow is operated at Glen Shee, beginning the progressive divorce of downhill skiing from mountain-touring.
	CLI	Zero Gully, Ben Nevis, spectacularly repulses H. Nicol and A. Rawlinson, who fell from the last pitch to the foot of the climb; both survived.
1952	GEN	Three avalanche fatalities in Cairn Gorm's northern corries; two died on Nevis in the following year. These accidents created a new awareness of Scotland's avalanche hazard, especially the windslab.

1952	CLI	**6 December**: Scorpion (V), Cairn Etchachan, climbed by Patey, M. Taylor, G. Nicol and K. Grassick – a bold ascent on a major face. Remarkably, Patey forgot to bring gloves for the climb, yet the party somehow won through.
1953	SKI	**January**: Norman Clark makes the first continuous traverse of the Cairngorm 4,000ft summits in a one-day round trip from Glen More.
	CLI	**14 February**: Raven's Gully (V), Buachaille Etive Mor, gets its first winter ascent from Hamish MacInnes and a young Chris Bonington, after several epic attempts by MacInnes and members of the Creagh Dhu Club; Glencoe's first grade V. Crampons worn by MacInnes, and soon to be generally adopted on steep ice in preference to nails.
		25 January: Eagle Ridge (VI), the queen of Lochnagar's winter routes, and the epitome of the 1950s tricounied mixed-climbing technique, yields in an astounding 4½hours to Patey, Brooker and Taylor.
		2 April: Mitre Ridge (V), Beinn a'Bhuird: another classic buttress route climbed by Patey and Brooker.
1956	GEN	Winter climbing courses run by the Mountaineering Association in Glencoe, the first practical instructional training in the winter skills.
	CLI	**4 March**: Parallel Buttress (VI) Lochnagar, climbed by Patey, J. Smith and Brooker with four aid points in severe conditions of high wind and blown powder.
		25 January: The great Joe Brown is violently rejected by Point Five Gully, falling 45m (150ft) to the foot of the route when the ice gave way. Point Five and Zero Gullies now the prime objectives for several competing teams.
1957	CLI	**18 February**: First winter ascent of Zero Gully (V), Ben Nevis, by MacInnes, Patey and G. Nicol in five hours, MacInnes using front-point crampons and ice pitons placed for protection and tension.
		27 December: Sticil Face (V) on Shelter Stone Crag climbed by Ken Grassick and Graeme Nicol, an impressive face route snatched from Patey – one of the hardest 1950s routes and still respected.
1958	CLI	**22 February**: Parallel Gully B (V) Lochnagar, climbed by the Edinburgh raiding party of Jimmy Marshall and Graham Tiso; a major ice-line solved in crampons, and a significant pointer to the coming surge of ice pioneering by the Edinburgh-based group.
	CLI	Tragedy in Zero Gully: three English climbers killed when wooden axe broke under load in a fall. MacInnes stimulated to produce metal-shafted axes, as this accident forcibly demonstrated the lack of security on the new steep ice-routes. Waist belays now the norm, and rock piton anchors used whenever available in preference to direct axe belays.
1959	CLI	A golden year in winter pioneering. Point Five Gully (V) was sieged into submission over five days in January by Ian Clough and party but more significant ascents in purist style were: • Orion Face/Epsilon Chimney (V), Ben Nevis, by Robin Smith and R. Holt. • Minus Two Gully (V), Ben Nevis, by Marshall, J. Stenhouse and Dougal Haston. • Tower Face of the Comb (VI), Ben Nevis, by Smith and Holt. • Smith's Gully (VI), Creag Meagaidh, by Marshall and Tiso. • Aladdin's Buttress (IV), Coire an t Sneachda, Cairn Gorm; boldly soloed by Tom Patey.
1960	GEN	In the early 1960s, Glenmore Lodge began winter survival and skills training courses largely under the initiative of Eric Langmuir, setting a standard of excellence that has been maintained to the present and has greatly improved the knowledge and safety of the winter-climbing fraternity.
	CLI	**February**: Jimmy Marshall and Robin Smith repeat Point Five Gully in good style and climb six new routes, including Orion Face Direct (V) and Gardyloo Buttress (V), in an eight-day campaign on Ben Nevis. This was the pinnacle of achievement of the stepcutting era, and their routes cast an aura of difficulty which was not dispelled until the adoption of front-pointing in the 1970s.
1961	SKI	Cairn Gorm chair-lift opened, and downhill skiing developed in Coire Cas. The ski access road also opened up the Northern Cairngorms, giving quick access to ski-tourers and winter climbers that has rarely been spurned, despite ethical misgivings.
	CLI	Winter grading system (I–V) introduced in Malcolm Smith's Cairngorm Guides.

1962	SKI	**April**: Adam Watson skis the Cairngorm Six Tops (ie those tops over 4,000ft, plus Ben Avon and Beinn a'Bhuird), starting from Invercauld and finishing at Derry Lodge, in sixteen hours. Wooden Nordic skis used.
1964–5	GEN	Hamish MacInnes markets short metal-shafted ice-axes and hammers. Salewa ice-screws and front-point crampons imported and used for the first time in Scotland.
1964	GEN	Avalanche accident on Beinn a'Bhuird: one victim, Robert Burnett, found alive after twenty-two hours' burial – one of the longest survival times under snow debris recorded anywhere and certainly the longest in Scotland.
1965	GEN	**31 January–1 February**: Cuillin Main Ridge is traversed for the first time in winter by Patey, MacInnes, B. Robertson and D. Crabb – north to south with one bivouac – closely followed by Tiso and J. Moriarty. Thus the greatest mountaineering expedition in the British Isles was established after many conjectures and attempts.
	GEN	Search and Rescue Dogs Association (SARDA) formed under the initiative of Hamish MacInnes. The use of dogs enabled much greater speed and efficiency in avalanche rescue.
	CLI	Two notable first winter ascents on iced slabs: The Curtain (IV), Ben Nevis, by D. Bathgate and J. Knight; and Djibangi (V) on Creagan a'Choire Etchachan, Cairngorms, by J. MacArtney and W. Barclay. Explorations in the Northern Highlands (Fannichs, Beinn Dearg) by members of the Corriemulzie Club.
	SKI	*On Ski in the Cairngorms* by V. A. Firsoff published: the first commentary and guide to ski-touring in the area.
1969	CLI	Excellent conditions and a highly productive winter. Forays in the Northern Highlands by Patey produce classic routes such as March Hare's Gully (IV), Beinn Bhan. Over twenty-five middle-grade new routes produced by Glencoe Winter School of Mountaineering parties largely led by MacInnes and Clough. Patey soloes the 2,450m (8,000ft) Crab Crawl across the cliffs of Coire Ardair, Creag Meagaidh, at IV. 'Deadmen' snow-anchors manufactured and widely adopted in Scotland.
	CLI	Winter climbs guide *Ben Nevis and Glencoe* by Ian Clough published. Mountain magazine begins regular reporting of winter climbing developments.
1970	GEN	The front-point revolution is initiated by Chouinard's visit to Scotland and his discussions with MacInnes and John Cunningham; MacInnes produced the drop-picked 'terrordactyl' axes and Cunningham adopted the curved-pick style.
	CLI	Patey, Clough and Jim McArtney – three of the greatest winter pioneers – killed in separate accidents. Cunningham and Bill March demonstrate the potential of front-point methods with their icicle climb, The Chancer (V) on Hell's Lum Crag, although their ascent was partially aided.
	SKI	*Scottish Mountains on Ski* by Malcolm Slesser, a touring guidebook, published.
1971	GEN	**November**: 'The Cairngorm Tragedy': five children and one teacher perish in a blizzard after failing to locate the Lochan Buidhe refuge on the Macdui-Cairn Lochan plateau – the worst winter tragedy to the present. Sparked an intensive debate on training methods and the hazards of high-mountain shelters.
	CLI	Astronomy (VI), Ben Nevis, climbed by A. Fyffe, K. Spence and MacInnes using 'terrors'– a hard, open-face route. Repeats of the 1950s routes using front-point techniques, including an ascent of Point Five in less than three hours by Cunningham and March. The new style proves its worth and lays the seeds for a new wave of pioneering.
1972	CLI	**11 March**: Labyrinth Direct (VII), Creag an Dubh Loch, front-pointed by James Bolton without runners or wrist-loops from a belay of axes and useless ice-screws: Scotland's hardest and boldest ice-route at that date.
1973	SKI	Harry Jamieson, a local ski instructor, skies several grade I gullies in the Northern Cairngorms, including Aladdin's Couloir.
	CLI	Ian Nicolson soloes Zero and Point Five Gullies in a combined time of three hours, a myth-shattering feat which opened these and comparable routes to wholesale attack from front-pointers.
1974	CLI	**February**: Minus One Gully (VI), the last of Nevis's unclimbed gully lines falls to Ken Crocket and Colin Stead.
1977	GEN	Cairngorm Automatic Weather Station comes into operation – a new source for winter weather data and forecasting.
1978	GEN	Equipment advances: banana-picked Chacal axes appear and further facilitate the ascent of steep ice; Gore-tex material greatly improves the performance of shell garments in winter.

1978	SKI	The Scottish 'Haute Route', a continuous traverse from Ben Avon to Ben Nevis of 160km established by Mike Taylor and David Grieve using Alpine techniques in seven days starting **26 February**.

1978   SKI   The Scottish 'Haute Route', a continuous traverse from Ben Avon to Ben Nevis of 160km established by Mike Taylor and David Grieve using Alpine techniques in seven days starting **26 February**.

    CLI   Major developments in the north-west and on Ben Nevis, and a renewed interest in Cairngorm mixed climbing. Poacher's Fall (V), Liathach (Andrew Nisbet and Richard MacHardy), and Central Buttress (VI), Beinn Eighe (first complete ascent by Alex MacIntyre and Alan Rouse), demonstrate the north-west's ice- and mixed-climbing potential respectively. Several major thin-ice face routes climbed on Ben Nevis, notably Galactic Hitch-hiker (VI) (Mike Geddes and Con Higgins), Pointless (VII) (Gordon Smith and Nick Banks), Psychedelic Wall (VI) (Arthur Paul and Norrie Muir), and Route 2 on Carn Dearg Buttress (VI) (Geddes and Rouse).

1979   NAT   An abnormally cold, snowy and prolonged winter in which the lowest temperatures for two hundred years were recorded in many places in Northern Europe.

    CLI   Sustained activity in all areas. Significant routes included: **27 January**: Link Face (VI), Lochnagar, by John Anderson and Andy Nisbet – a venture into the technical unknown, VS summer ground – and harbinger of 1980s grade VI mixed climbing. **15 March**: Shield Direct, Ben Nevis, by Mick Fowler and Victor Saunders, a staggering line that prompted its unilateral declaration as Scotland's first grade VI (now VII) by the usually conservative *SMC Journal*; Fowler's first Scottish winter coup, though he long maintained the grade was only 'good V'.

1980   CLI   Another memorable season with several major advances, notably: **5–6 January**: Postern (VI), Shelter Stone Crag, climbed free with a bivouac by Murray Hamilton, Kenny Spence and Alan Taylor. **16 January**: Goliath (VII), Creag an Dubh Loch, by Neil Morrison and Andy Nisbet; a summer HVS climbed mainly on thin ice – bold and exposed; one point of aid. **26–7 January**: Die Riesenwand (VII) Beinn Bhan, by Andy Nisbet and Brian Sprunt, tackling the stupendous 400m (1,312ft) headwall of Coire an Fhamair. Climbed with a bivouac. **23 February**: Citadel (VII), Shelter Stone Crag, by Hamilton and Spence – the first complete ascent with one aid point after many epic attempts and partial successes. A touchstone of modern mixed climbing. **8 March**: Epitome (VI) Lochnagar – a short, desperate route led by visiting Polish climber Jan Fijalkowski with rests on axes, showing the high standards of mixed/ice-climbing attained in other countries since the front-pointing revolution. No longer could the Scots claim a monopoly of winter expertise.

1981   CLI   Updated winter climbs guide to Ben Nevis and Glencoe by Ed Grindley makes a liberal use of grade VI. Cairngorms winter climbs guide by John Cunningham and Allen Fyffe published.

1982   NAT   Exceptional cold spell in early January. Braemar registers Britain's equal lowest recorded temperature of –27.2 degrees C.

    GEN   **15 February**: A 'black day' for avalanches: four separate accidents, three on Ben Nevis and one on Creag Meagaidh, with three fatalities, demonstrating how the same deadly conditions may prevail across the country in certain conditions of snow and weather.

    SKI   The Lurcher's Gully affair ends with rejection of the planning application to extend Cairn Gorm's ski area westwards; a temporary victory for conservationists over the growing downhill-ski interests.

    SKI   **13 January**: A Glenmore Lodge team of Sam Crymble, Keith Geddes, Tim Walker and Blyth Wright ski coast-to-coast from Loch Duich to Beauly on Nordic gear – c100km (60 miles) in seventeen hours.

1983   CLI   **20 February**: Fly Direct (VII), Creag Meagaidh's major outstanding line, gets a clean ascent from Fowler and Saunders. February: Central Grooves (VII), Stob Coire nan Lochan, climbed after several attempts by Kenny Spence and John Mackenzie. **3 April**: Gully of the Gods (VI), Beinn Bhan – the great cleft cleaving the Coire an Fhamair headwall climbed by Fowler and Fenwick.

1984   NAT   **21 January**: The day of the 'great storm', a blizzard unmatched in severity in modern times. Cairn Gorm's anemometer unfortunately malfunctioned when the windspeed was rising above 160kmph. Hundreds of skiers, climbers and travellers trapped, and five lives were lost in the Cairngorms. Remarkably, a new route was climbed by Rick Allen and Brian Sprunt during the storm – Raven's Edge on Buachaille Etive More.

    CLI   **28 January**: Guerdon Grooves (VIII), Buachaille Etive Mor, climbed by Cuthbertson and Paul – hard and serious, HVS in summer. **16–17 March**: Fowler and Butler pick two Torridonian plums – Tholl Gate (VI) on Fuar Tholl, and Great Overhanging Gully (VI) on Beinn Bhan.

1985	GEN	Martin Moran ascends all the Munros within the calendar winter season taking eighty-three days for the 277 summits which involved 126,000m of climbing. Motorised support and transport between the mountains used. Helped by a particularly dry and cold winter.
	SKI	Martin Burrows-Smith skis down Hell's Lum in the Cairngorms, a grade II/III winter climb, and one of the hardest 'extreme' descents yet achieved.
	CLI	A lean year with one major exception: Colin MacLean and Andy Nisbet's ascent of The Needle on Shelter Stone Crag, EI in summer, grade VIII in winter; climbed over two days, **13–14 February**.
1986	NAT	Britain's highest-yet recorded windspeed, a gust of 275kmph (171mph), registered by the Cairn Gorm AWS at 00.30 on **20 March**.
	CLI	A remarkable year, giving superb conditions in all areas and at all levels – over one hundred new winter routes produced between November and the end of April including **8–9 February**: Centurion, Carn Dearg Buttress's great central corner line, Ben Nevis, climbed as far as Route 2 with a bivouac by Mackenzie and Spence at grade VIII. **21 February**: Eas Coul Aulinn, Britain's highest waterfall ascended at V by Andy Cunningham and Andy Nisbet. **30 March**: Dierdre of the Sorrows (VIII) on Lochnagar by Doug Dinwoodie with Nisbet, probably the hardest mixed route yet achieved, E2 5c in summer. The crux pitch only yielded after eleven hours of effort spread over three attempts.
	CLI	With the ascents of White Magic (VII), The Migrant (VI) and Fall Out Corner (VI), Cunningham and Nisbet instigate the sustained development of the Northern Corries of Cairn Gorm for modern mixed climbing
	CLI	**April**: A soloing *tour de force* on Ben Nevis by Dave Cuthbertson and Grahame Livingston, climbing in tandem on two separate days – several of the harder modern routes included, and a testimony to the skill of modern climbers as well as the effectiveness of ice-climbing tools.
1987	NAT	**12–17 January**: A big freeze-up, during which the Cairn Gorm AWS registered its lowest temperature, −16.5 degrees C, in ten years of recordings
	SKI	*Ski Mountaineering in Scotland,* edited by D. Bennett and W. Wallace, published, an updated touring guide produced in response to the growing popularity of the sport in both the Nordic and Alpine camps.
	CLI	Despite more variable conditions, another good year for new routes. Several fine ice and mixed lines added in the north-west, notably Fowler's West Central Gully (VII) on Beinn Eighe, climbed as late as 11 April. Controversial new route, Torquing Corpse on Lochnagar, by Grahame Livingston and M. Lawrence in January, after several attempts and a top-rope rescue. First route to be claimed as grade VII before the 1991 extension of the system. Extremely serious, but the required tactics raised the spectre of 'engineered' winter climbing in contrast to the truly adventurous spirit of pioneering to date.
1988	CLI	Despite variable conditions, an active year with new grade VI routes as far-ranging as Beinn Dorain in the Southern Highlands and Beinn Dearg in the north-west. Roger Everett and Simon Richardson commence a systematic exploration of the cliffs of Aonach Beag and Aonach Mor, soon to become highly accessible from the new ski development
1989	NAT	The windiest and warmest winter season in a decade of Cairngorm summit recordings, with a 43mph mean windspeed and −1.6 degrees C mean temperature between November and March. No snow accumulation until early February. Gusts up to 200kmph (124mph) on **13/14 February**.
	GEN	Scottish Avalanche Project (later to become the Scottish Avalanche Information Service) started in Northern Cairngorms and Glencoe. Lochaber added in 1990. Daily reports on avalanche hazard and snow conditions now available.
	CLI	Icy spells in late February and March enable new lines to be established on The Cobbler in the Southern Highlands and major new lines in the north-west, in particular Mainreachan Buttress of Fuar Tholl and a girdle traverse of the central corries of Beinn Bhan.
	SKI	Lurcher's Gully again a bone of contention with a second application made for ski development, but again ending in rejection after a prolonged environmental battle.
	SKI	Descent of The Alley reported, a grade II on An Teallach, abseil required at the ice pitch.

1990	NAT	A second exceptionally wet and windy season, the wettest since records began in the 1880s. Sixty-one consecutive days with rain, and a 1.7m rainfall total recorded at Fort William for January, February and March. Rainfall at 400 per cent of its average, and sunshine hours at only 40 per cent of their normal in February over the West Central Highlands. Sequence of heavy snowfalls and rapid thaws on the hills throughout the season.
1991	NAT	Excellent snow conditions and weather from New Year to mid-February breaking the sequence of three poor seasons.
	GEN	A dreadful year for accidents, with eighteen fatalities to winter walkers, skiers and climbers in the first three months of the year; slips on ice-hard snow during the fine spell being a major cause also reflects the increased numbers on the hills in winter, especially after two bad years.
	CLI	Some excellent climbs done consolidating the advances of the mid-1980s, notably: **12 January**: free ascent of The Nose Direct on Sgurr an Fhidleir in the north–west at VII by Everett and Richardson. **2 February**: Deep Gash Gully (VI) on Sgurr a'Mhadaidh, Skye by Mick Fowler and John Lincoln. **14 February**: West Central Wall (VII) on Beinn Eighe by Brian Davison and Andy Nisbet, Nisbet continuing to find excellent mixed routes on the steep sidewalls of the Triple Buttresses.
	CLI	Revised guide to Ben Nevis and Glencoe by Alan Kimber published.
	CLI	An expanded grading system is discussed and finally agreed by activists within the SMC, upgrading many routes to VII and even VIII, and introducing a numerical technical grade from 1 to 9 to denote the crux difficulties of climbs; this system was to be adopted in future guidebooks.
	SKI	The new downhill development at Aonach Mor is opened and allows climbers easy access to the summit cliffs; this immediately becomes a highly popular alternative to the Northern Corries of Cairngorm.
1993	NAT	January is the second windiest month yet recorded on Cairn Gorm summit, with a mean for the month of 83 kmph (52mph) and a record-ever gust on the 3rd of 282kmph.
	NAT	Christopher Nicholls survives a six-night open bivouac on the summit of Slioch.
	CLI	Ascent of the Ben's major outstanding icefall left of Harrison's Climb Direct by Andy Clarke and John Main, The Shroud (VII).
1994	CLI	Filming of *The Edge* series for BBC television, with a classic ascent of Tower Ridge plus modern ice- and mixed-climbing sequences; a great advertisement for Scottish winter climbing.
	CLI	Sustained climbing activity throughout a very snowy season including the first ascent of the thin icefall right of Poacher's Fall on Liathach by Chris Cartwright and Dave Hesleden, Foobarbundee (VIII), and new routes on the walls of the Buachaille Etive Mor.
1995	NAT	Worst-ever year for avalanche fatalities: twelve killed and eighteen injured; national media publicity over the rising tide of accidents.
1996	NAT	Remarkably dry winter with some sustained cold spells, especially at Christmas 1995 when the record low temperature of –27.2 deg C was equalled at Altnaharra and new ice routes were found on the cliffs of The Storr, Skye.
	CLI	New phase of hard mixed climbing on Ben Nevis initiated with Chris Cartwright and Simon Richardson's ascent of Cornucopia (VII).
	CLI	*Scottish Winter Climbs* selective guidebook by Rab Anderson and Andy Nisbet published by the SMC.
1998	NAT	Warmest February on record over Scotland, and one of the wettest ever in the West Highlands; temperatures 5.5 degrees C above average in Eastern Highlands; no snow anywhere in the country by middle of month.

APPENDIX II

GLOSSARY AND TECHNICAL TERMS

Gaelic Names

To help the reader's geographical understanding of the Scottish mountains, translations of the most commonly occurring topographical names are given below: With this list, nearly all of the Scottish mountain names in the text can be understood.

ALLT	Stream, burn
AONACH	Mountain ridge, hill, moor
BAN	White, light-coloured
BEAG	Small
BEALACH	Pass
BEINN/BHEINN (BEN)	Mountain
BIDEAN/BIDEIN	Peak, summit
BINNEIN	Pointed peak
BUIDHE	Yellow
CAORANN/ CHAORAINN	Rowan tree
CARN/CAIRN	Heap of stones, cairn-shaped hill
CLACH	Stone
COILLE	Wood
COIRE/CHOIRE	Corrie, glaciated valley bowl
CREAG	Rock, crag
CRUACH	Stack-shaped hill
DEARG	Red
DUBH	Black
EAS	Waterfall
FIONN	White, pale-coloured
GABHAR/GHABHAR	Goat
GARBH	Rough
GEAL	White
GLAS/GHLAS	Grey, grey-green
GORM	Blue, (of grass) green
LAIRIG	Pass
LIATH	Grey, bluish-grey
LOCHAN	Small lake
MAM	Large rounded hill
MAOL	Bald, bare
MEADHOIN/ MHEADHOIN	Middle
MEALL	Rounded hill
MONADH	Moor, hill-range
MOR/MHOR (MORE)	Big
MULLACH	Summit, top
ODHAR/ODHAIR	Fawnish-brown
RIABHACH (RIACH)	Brindled, greyish
RUADH	Red, red-brown
SAIL	Rounded hill
SGURR/SGORR	Rocky hill or peak
SPIDEAN	Peak, summit
SRON	Jutting ridge
STAC/STUC	Steep conical hill
STOB	Pointed hill
TARSUINN	Transverse, cross
TOLL	Hole, hollow
TOM	Small rounded hill
UISGE	Water

Technical terms

Nearly all technical terminology is explained in the text. Meteorological terms are explained in Appendix IV. Some basic climbing terms require translation for the benefit of non-climbers:

Abseil
Method of descent on a cliff face by sliding down a doubled rope anchored above, using a friction device attached to the climber's harness. The ropes are then retrieved by pulling on one end. Used in the event of retreat or escape.

Anchor
The climber's means of attachment to the cliff, whether by sling, inserted chockstone, piton or ice-screw.

Belay
Encompasses the climber's anchorage, the attachment of rope to anchors, and the method by which the rope is paid out to, or taken in from, those who are climbing.

Crux
Hardest section of a climb.

Karabiner
Metal snaplink for clipping the rope into anchors.

Pitch
Individual stage of a climb between belay points. Normal pitch length is between 20 and 45m.

Piton
Metal blade or peg hammered into cracks in the rock as an anchor.

Runner
Anchor placed by the leader while climbing, and clipped into the rope with a karabiner to provide a running belay.

Stance
Ledge occupied by a climber while belaying.

APPENDIX III

BIBLIOGRAPHY

Apart from the specific books detailed below, the Scottish Mountaineering Club's *Journal* and its *District and Climbing Guides* form essential reading for any devotee of the Scottish mountains. Indeed, the *Journals* have provided a comprehensive and authoritative history of a century of winter mountaineering in Scotland. The growth of a Scottish winter tradition owes much to its records, and it is to be hoped that the SMCJ retains its role by carrying the history onwards into the next century.

The sources listed devote either the whole or a significant part of their content to matters directly relevant to Scottish winter mountaineering. Most are currently available in print.

CLIMATE, WEATHER, SNOW AND AVALANCHE

Barton, R., and Wright, B., *A Chance in a Million?* (Scottish Mountaineering Trust, 1985) The only definitive textbook on the Scottish avalanche phenomenon; clearly written with many case studies.

British Mountain Guides, *Avalanche Manual* (published by BMG 1998) Clear and concise treatment of hazard and risk avoidance – covers both alpine and Scottish environments; apply to the BMG for copies.

Burroughs, W.J., *Weather Cycles – Real or Imaginary* (Univ of Cambridge Press, 1992) Investigation of climatic change and weather patterns; for climate enthusiasts.

Burroughs, W.J., *Mountain Weather* (Crowood, 1995) Worldwide coverage and technical analysis.

Daffern, Tony, *Avalanche Safety for Skiers and Climbers* (hardback Diadem, 1983; paperback Baton Wicks, 1992) Well illustrated with some Scottish examples.

Kilgour, W. T., *Twenty Years on Ben Nevis* (A. Gardner, 1905 (reprinted Anglesey Books, 1985)) An entertaining history of the Ben Nevis observatory.

Lamb, H. H., *Climate History and the Modern World* (Methuen, 1982) Gives a global view of climatic change, and its natural and human consequences.

Langmuir, E., *Mountaincraft and Leadership* (MLTB/Scottish Sports Council, 1995) Contains chapters on British mountain weather and avalanches.

Pedgely, D., *Mountain Weather* (Cicerone, 1997) Standard textbook for beginners.

Seligman, G., *Snow Structures and Ski Fields* (MacMillan, London, 1936) A classic exposition on snow in all its wonderful forms; beautifully written; now slightly outdated and out of print but worth seeking in the libraries.

Thomas, M., *Weather for Hillwalkers and Climbers* (Alan Sutton publ) Basic textbook on meteorology and mountain weather; aimed at Mountain Leader Award syllabus.

WINTER MOUNTAINEERING
Textbooks

Barry, J., *Snow Ice Climbing* (Crowood Press, 1987) Entertainingly written textbook, British based.

Cliff, P., *Mountain Navigation* (Bookmay, 1991) Clear and concise coverage of the navigation skills.

Fyffe, A. and Peter, I., *The Handbook of Climbing* (Pelham Books, 1990, revised in 1997) Excellent section on winter climbing techniques.

Langmuir, E., *Mountaincraft and Leadership* (MLTB/Scottish Sports Council, 1995) Covers the Winter Mountain Leadership Certificate syllabus; written by former principal of Glenmore Lodge; the standard text for general mountaineering.

Lowe, J., *Ice World – techniques and experiences of modern ice climbing* (The Mountaineers, 1996) Glossy and glamorous text book on pure ice climbing with excellent pictures of techniques; short extracts of Scottish experiences.

March, W. (revised by W. Birkett), *Modern Snow and Ice Techniques* (Cicerone, 1997) Updated version of March's original pocket textbook.

Walker, K., *Mountain Navigation Techniques* (Constable, 1986).

Narratives

Alcock, D., Barry, J., Wilson, K., *Cold Climbs* (Diadem, 1983) Compilation of essays and illustrations of Britain's classic winter climbs; some excellent writing, first ascent accounts and fine photos; essential reading for the budding winter climber.

Borthwick, A., *Always a Little Further* (Faber, 1939 (reprinted Diadem, 1983)) A gem of a book, capturing the hardship and spirit of 1930s Scottish climbing; chapters on howffing and an epic ice climb on Stob Ghabhar.

Crocket, K. V., *Ben Nevis* (Scottish Mountaineering Trust, 1986) The definitive history of climbing on the Ben; excellently researched and written; traces the winter story of Britain's greatest snow and ice arena.

McNeish, C., and Else, R., *The Edge – One Hundred Years of Scottish Mountaineering* (BBC 1994) The book of the TV series; plenty of winter mountaineering history and pictures.

Moran, M. E., *The Munros in Winter* (David & Charles, 1986) The account of the first completion of all the Munros within a single calendar winter season, with much general information on the mountains in winter.

Murray, W. H., *Mountaineering in Scotland* (J. M. Dent, 1947).

—, *Undiscovered Scotland* (J. M. Dent, 1951) Compilation volume published by Baton Wicks, 1997. These two books, especially the former, are still acknowledged as containing the finest essays on Scottish winter mountaineering ever written; highly influential when first published; they continue to inspire the modern generation.

Patey, T. W., *One Man's Mountains* (hardback Gollancz, 1971; paperback Cannongate, 1997)) A collection of Patey's essays; classic accounts of Scorpion, Zero Gully, the Cuillin Traverse and Creag Meagaidh Crab Crawl, plus historical reviews of climbing in the 1950s; highly satirical and entertaining.

SELECTIVE GUIDEBOOKS

NOTE: The SMC's area climbing guides fully cover the winter routes in each region.

Fyffe, A., *Cairngorms Winter Climbs* (Cicerone Press, 1987) Updated version of original guide by John Cunningham; covers Cairngorms, Lochnagar and Creag Meagaidh.

Kimber, A., *Winter Climbs on Ben Nevis and Glencoe* (Cicerone Press, 1994) Much revised version of Ian Clough's original guide; includes new developments on Aonach Mor and Aonach Beag.

Anderson, R. and Nisbet, A., *Scottish Winter Climbs* (SMC, 1996) A selection of the best and most popular

climbs from each area of the country with modern gradings, excellent diagrams and colour photos: the visiting climber's indispensable guidebook

CLOTHING, DIET, FITNESS

Langmuir, F., *Mountaincraft and Leadership* (ibid) Sections on hypothermia and windchill.

Wilkerson, J. A., et al, *Hypothermia, Frostbite and other Cold Injuries* (The Mountaineers, 1986) Good coverage of clothing and hypothermia.

SKI-TOURING AND MOUNTAINEERING

Bennett, D. and Wallace, W., *Ski Mountaineering in Scotland* (Scottish Mountaineering Trust, 1987) Guidebook to all the major Scottish ski tours; superb photographs.

Cliff, P., *Ski Mountaineering* (Unwin Hyman London, 1987) Excellent, well illustrated manual to Alpine ski-touring.

Firsoff, V. A., *On Ski in the Cairngorms* (W. & K. Chambers, 1965) A classic account of Scottish hill-touring, but not currently in print.

Foxon, F. (ed), *BASI Alpine Manual* (British Asscoiation of Ski Instructors, 1996) Alpine skiing techniques manual, available by mail order from BASI office (address on page 316).

Gillette and Dostal, *Cross-country Skiing* (Diadem) A thorough and highly entertaining instruction in pure Nordic skiing.

Oakley, *Ski Touring in Scotland* (Cicerone, 1991) The standard planning book for highland and lowland tours.

Parker, P., *Free Heel Skiing* (Diadem 1988, revised c.1996) The 'bible' on Telemark skiing.

Townsend, C., *Wilderness Skiing and Winter Camping* Textbook from a leading British exponent of Nordic touring.

APPENDIX IV
METEOROLOGY: THEORY AND TERMS
by Jim Barton

To study winter mountain weather, the first requirement is a sound background in general meteorology, which can be put to good use in understanding weather maps, in getting the best out of forecasts and in interpreting our own experience on the hills. This appendix introduces these background ideas and concepts in non-mathematical terms. For further information consult the Bibliography and cultivate the habit of daily weather observation, however casual.

THE ATMOSPHERIC SKIN
On the large scale, the atmosphere is surprisingly thin: compared to the globe, it is about as thick as the skin of an apple. The weather systems that affect us directly are confined to the lowest layer or troposphere (Fig IV.1) in which the air is well stirred up. By contrast, the air in the next layer, the stratosphere, experiences little overall vertical motion.

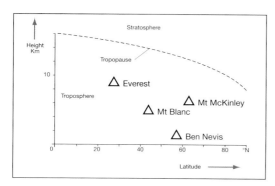

Fig IV.1 *Idealised cross-section through the northern hemisphere*

Weather systems clearly represent energy. Where does this energy originate? The earth's surface receives more energy from sunlight in the equatorial regions than in high latitudes and this imbalance is particularly marked in winter. The atmospheric skin responds by exporting heat from the tropics towards the arctic regions and weather systems are the result. Given warm air to the south and cold air to the north (a northern hemisphere viewpoint), a

zone of lukewarm air in the middle latitudes might be expected, but in practice the division between air-masses is quite distinct (see Air-masses and Fronts, below).

ISOBARS: DRAWING AIR-PRESSURE MAPS
There is a strong connection between the type of weather and both the barometer reading, ie air pressure, and its change over a short time (1–3 hours), the pressure tendency. This connection suggests that air pressure may be a useful variable in constructing a weather map, and this is indeed so. Pressure is the weight of air in a vertical column of unit area cross-section above the point of interest. Air pressure is measured in units of millibars. The average sea-level pressure is always around 1,000mb. Variations of a few per cent above or below occur, depending on the thickness of the air above and its density, which is the amount of air in a given volume. Cold air is denser than warm air, so a cold part of the atmosphere will exert a higher pressure at the surface than the same depth of warm air.

Air pressure over a region at any given time can be represented by plotting barometer readings on a map of the area (Fig IV.2). Then the pattern of air pressure is revealed by drawing lines, known as isobars, which are contours of equal air pressure, just as contour lines on a conventional map reveal the shape of the land surface. This is a simple example of a surface chart, in which the pressure readings are those on a hypothetical sea-level surface. Because air pressure falls with height, barometer readings from weather stations are corrected to sea level before being plotted on the chart.

Fig IV.2 shows a series of closed isobars defining a low-pressure area, a familiar feature on British weather maps. The isobars are drawn at the conventional 4mb interval. If such a low moves across the country, the barometer at any one place would show pressure falling at first, and then rising as the low moves away. The surface chart, or synoptic chart, therefore displays an overall view of the weather at any one instant.

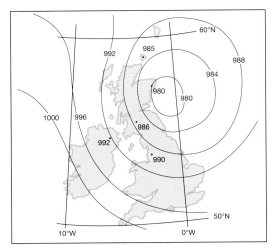

Fig IV.2 *Barometer readings at selected sites (marked o) and corresponding isobars drawn at 4mb intervals*

ISOBARS AND WIND

The presence of several isobars implies the existence of a pressure gradient or change of surface pressure over a horizontal distance. Air at higher pressure experiences a net force, tending to move it towards lower pressure. In other words, unequal pressure gives rise to wind, but because of the intervention of a second force (caused by the earth's rotation), winds on the large scale blow not directly from high to low pressure, but along the isobars. In the low of Fig IV.2, the corresponding winds would circulate anticlockwise around the low centre. One can calculate the windspeed expected from a given pressure gradient. For example, a gradient of 2mb pressure change over 100km distance gives a wind speed of about 48kmph. This calculated geostrophic wind relates to wind 500m or so above ground level in freely moving air away from obstructions near the surface.

This relationship between pressure patterns and winds is very important in interpreting weather maps. Deep lows with large pressure gradients (isobars closely spaced) mean strong winds. Conversely, surface charts with few isobars mean calm weather.

AIR-MASSES AND FRONTS

The contrast between cold polar air and warm tropical air brings in another important idea: that of air-masses. These are regions of air of large hori-zontal extent, perhaps 2,000km or more across, in which the air properties such as temperature and humidity are fairly uniform and characteristic of the source region of the air-mass. For example, continental air-masses are less humid than maritime air-masses that originate over the oceans. Polar continental air is cold and dry, tropical maritime air is warm and moist.

The boundary between two air-masses is known as a front, by analogy with the line of battle between two opposing armies. The frontal zone may be quite sharp in relation to the size of the air-masses – about 100km wide. Looking at the earth as a whole, the cold-to-warm air transition in mid-latitudes is often sharply defined as the polar front, lying roughly east/west across the Atlantic. If a warm air-mass is moving into cold, a warm front results, while a cold front is the boundary of an advancing cold air-mass. Fronts have their own symbols on the surface chart (see Fig IV.3) and the symbols are always placed on the side towards which the front is advancing.

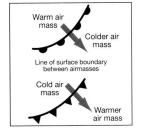
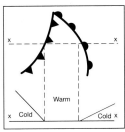

Fig IV.3 *Warm and cold fronts on the weather map*
Fig IV.4 *Vertical cross-section (X–X) across warm and cold fronts*

Vertical cross-sections of warm and cold fronts are shown in Fig IV.4. In both cases the frontal surface is sloping at a shallow angle in such a way that the cold air undercuts the warm air. Warm frontal surfaces slope at about 1 in 150, cold frontal surfaces are steeper at 1 in 60.

WEATHER SYSTEMS: DEPRESSIONS OR LOWS

Despite the apparently random patterns of isobars and fronts on surface charts for the British Isles, there is a kind of order in the chaos, and particular weather systems appear so often that we must pay them due attention.

The frontal depression is one type of low-pres-

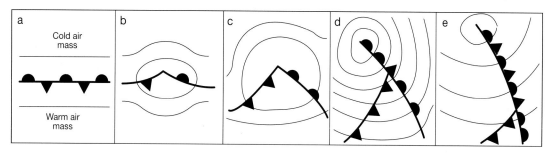

Fig IV.5 *Life cycle of a typical depression:*
a Polar front **b** Wave formation **c** Deepening depression **d** Mature stage occlusion **e** Depression now filling

sure area. This begins as a small kink or wave on the polar front (Fig IV.5a), representing a slight northward extension of the warm air-mass into territory previously held by the cold air. The warm-cold temperature contrast means that heat energy is available to allow the frontal wave to grow in size and for the associated low to deepen, as in the sequence of Fig IV.5. The wedge-shaped area of warm air is the warm sector, lying between warm and cold fronts. As the low deepens, the depression develops, evolving a new type of front known as an occluded front, in which the warm sector is raised clear of the surface. Eventually, the low begins to fill and to lose its identity as a weather system. This life cycle might take four to five days, during which the depression could travel several thousand kilometres. Frontal depressions commonly form off the eastern seaboard of the USA, travel eastwards and reach Britain in various stages of their development, which is a major reason for the variable nature of our weather.

It is important to grasp that a low is not simply a large whirlpool of air moving bodily – the speed of the moving low-pressure structure is not the same as the speed of the winds blowing within it. A very slow-moving but deep low could bring storm-force winds. Air moves into a depression circulation and out again at a higher level. The depression is a complicated three-dimensional wave caused by the warm and cold air mixing process on a large scale.

Depressions are far from abstractions of meteorological theory – they bring vigorous weather. Air is moving upwards in the frontal regions and this upward motion leads to cooling and formation of clouds over a large area, usually giving rain or snow as the front passes. Precipitation areas for a typical low are indicated in Fig IV.6. The air behind the cold front is likely to generate cumulus clouds, with rain or snow showers.

Depressions need not necessarily be formed by the warm and cold front process. In winter, polar lows are non-frontal depressions sometimes forming in the air-stream behind the cold front of a conventional low by heating of the cold air over a relatively warm sea, and give rise to rain or snow showers. Fig IV.7a shows a polar low west of Scotland.

Another non-frontal feature which can give cloud, rain or snow is the trough of low pressure, as shown in Fig IV.7b, often occurring to the south of a frontal depression.

WEATHER SYSTEMS: ANTICYCLONES OR HIGHS

As their name suggests, high-pressure areas, or anticyclones, are the meteorological opposite of the low (Fig IV.7c). Fronts are not usually associated with highs, nor are they necessary for their formation. Air has a clockwise motion around a high and is generally slowly sinking or subsiding, leading to an overall warming and therefore dissipation of cloud. So highs can bring clear skies and sunshine with little wind near their central areas. Complications can arise if fog forms near the ground, a common occurrence in autumn anticyclones. Very large and persistent highs can become established in such a way that the advancing depressions are steered around them away from their normal tracks, a situation known as blocking. Highs tend to be anchored over continental landmasses such as Russia, particularly during winter.

A ridge of high pressure (Fig IV.7d) is analogous to the trough of low pressure. Ridges are often found between lows, giving a short respite from wet weather until the next front arrives.

THE ATMOSPHERE IN THE VERTICAL

The surface chart shows the atmosphere in the horizontal. Obviously, mountaineers are interested in weather changes in the vertical dimension also.

Pressure falls with height, because if there is less atmosphere above, it exerts less weight. Change of pressure with height is not linear but follows an exponential curve. Fig IV.8 shows this curve for the 'standard atmosphere' in which the surface pressure is deemed to be 1,013mb and temperature +15 degrees C. In this example, pressure falls initially at the rate of 8.3m per mb. Pressure at 1,000m is close to 900mb, just over 10 per cent down on its surface value.

Temperature is the second feature of Fig IV.8, which shows that it falls linearly with height as far as the tropopause. This is approximately true in practice and is caused by air that is rising, experiencing lower pressure. Equilibrium demands that the air expands, which leads to cooling. Conversely, air that has been caused to sink experiences compression and warming. The rate of fall of temperature with height is called the lapse rate, and is 6.5 degrees C per kilometre in the standard atmosphere, a value close to the average actually observed. It follows from such a lapse rate that there must be some height at which air temperature equals freezing point, 0 degrees C, ie the freezing level. In Fig IV/8 the freezing level is at 2,300m; if sea-level temperatures were 6 degrees C then freezing level would be at around 1,000m. This is clearly important in assessing snow level and snow condition.

A further property, known as stability, is also related to temperature and height. A localised parcel of air will cool if it is forced to rise. The lapse rate prevailing in the surrounding air-mass dictates whether or not this air will continue rising, like a balloon, or will sink back down. The first case is an unstable atmosphere, where the parcel remains warmer than the surrounding air, with positive buoyancy tending to keep the air bubbling upwards once it starts rising. The opposite extreme is a stable atmosphere, with air in layers, such that the parcel meets a layer of air warmer than itself and therefore subsides. Stability has a strong influence on the formation and growth of clouds. Extremely stable air often occurs during anticyclones, producing valley temperature inversions, which may reveal themselves as layers of haze, valley fog or a low-level cloud 'sea', above which the hill-tops rise into clear and slightly warmer air.

WATER: VAPOUR, CLOUDS AND PRECIPITATION

Water vapour is a term that sometimes causes confusion: water in the atmosphere occurs in all three forms as solid, liquid and gas. Water vapour is the latter – a dry, invisible gas, the amount being expressed in millibars as its share in the atmos-

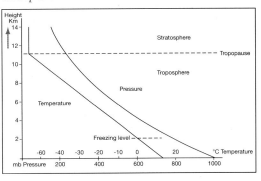

Fig IV.8 *Pressure and temperature in the 'standard atmosphere'*

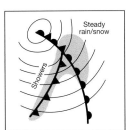

Fig IV.6 *Precipitation areas in a mature depression*
Fig IV.7 *Types of pressure system:*
a   A polar low (P) in a cold northerly air-stream
b   A trough of low pressure
c   High pressure or anticyclone over Britain
d   A ridge of high pressure

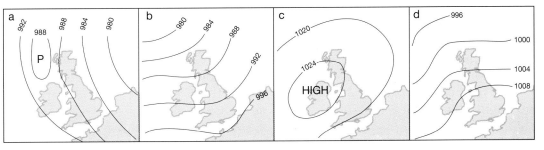

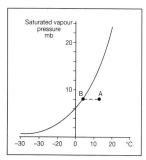

Fig IV.9 *Water vapour pressure at different temperatures. Cooling a sample of vapour from A to B would reduce condensation*

pheric pressure. Fig IV.9 shows water-vapour pressure at different temperatures. The curve is the maximum pressure allowable, as adding more water vapour causes condensation to take place and liquid water begins to appear in droplet form. At this point, the water vapour is saturated and the curve's value is saturated vapour pressure (SVP). Air containing less water vapour than SVP (eg point A in Fig IV.9) would reach SVP if it were cooled (to point B), where condensation would occur. Relative humidity is the actual vapour pressure in the air as a percentage of the SVP at that temperature, so saturation means 100 per cent RH. To take an example, tropical maritime air, warm and humid, at +15 degrees C and 80 per cent RH contains 8.5g of water (as vapour) per kilogram of air. If this were cooled to +5 degrees C, then saturation would be reached: +5 degrees C and 100 per cent RH corresponds to 5.4g water, so the excess, 3.1g, would appear in liquid-droplet form as condensation.

Here we have a strong clue to cloud formation: unless the air is completely dry, there must be a condensation level at which SVP is reached and excess water appears either as liquid-cloud droplets or ice crystals. Forecasters can use the RH and lapse rate observations for a given air-mass to estimate condensation level and hence cloud haze.

Cloud droplets are tiny – around 1/100mm across. Especially in such small volumes, water has the surprising property of remaining liquid well below freezing point. It is not until –40 degrees C is reached that all such supercooled droplets become ice particles. Clouds encountered on Scottish winter mountains are often in the range 0 to –10 degrees C, in which the droplets are supercooled liquid. On impact with any solid object, the droplets freeze and build up an icy crystalline deposit to windward known as rime.

Cloud heights can be classified as low (height of base 0–2,000m), medium (2,000–6,000m) or high (6,000–12,000m). All of these types are seen in the clouds associated with a frontal depression. Firstly, upper-level cirrus gives warning of the approaching warm front, especially when it thickens and changes to medium-level altostratus, through which a 'watery sun' might still shine palely. The widespread lifting of the warm air-mass produces an unbroken sheet of grey stratus at low level, with cloud base below the hill-tops. Thinning cloud and a lifting of its base might occur in the warm sector. As the cold front passes, the change in air-mass tends to lead to unstable air, which is easily triggered off into large cumulus or shower clouds, giving locally heavy falls of rain, hail or snow with bright intervals between. This classic sequence of clouds, wind and weather associated with a frontal depression is very common in westerly weather, usually taking one to three days to unfold, depending on the speed of movement of the fronts.

Precipitation describes drizzle, rain, hail, sleet and snow. It is not usually seen from shallow clouds, requiring a reasonable depth of cloud in which to grow. In winter over Britain, condensed water in clouds produces snowflakes above freezing level by the Bergeron process, in which ice crystals grow at the expense of supercooled water.

Once the flakes are large enough, they fall through the cloud and begin to melt as they pass below the freezing level, forming raindrops once the temperature is around 2 degrees C. Thus, the familiar sequence of rain, sleet then snow occurs when a hill is climbed on a wet day in winter. Rainfall is enhanced in mountainous areas as the air that has been forced to rise over the hills cools and produces local cloud.

To sum up, the weather map, if it is read properly, is as valuable as the ordinary map. If the right questions are asked the forecaster can be met halfway and our own on-the-spot judgement can be used. Weather type, air-mass, fronts, wind, stability, cloud, freezing level – all these elements are linked together and it is always a fascinating exercise to assess what weather awaits us up on the hill.

APPENDIX V

INFORMATION AND CONTACTS

Winter Mountaineering Courses, Guides and Instructors

Association of Mountaineering Instructors
Siabod Cottage, Capel Curig, Gwynedd LL24 0ET
Tel: (01690) 720314
Office for professional body representing
Mountaineering Instructors (MIC), trained through the
Mountain Leader Training Board, many of whom run
winter courses in Scotland

British Mountain Guides (BMG)
Siabod Cottage, Capel Curig, Gwynedd LL24 0ET
Tel: (01690) 720386 Fax: (01690) 720248
E-mail: futurmedia@infinet.u-net.com or
ml.tb@virgin.net
Web site: http://www.bmg.org.uk
Training and assessment of qualified international
mountain Guides – highest and broadest level of
technical mountaineering qualification. 140 members.
Many individual Guides offer private
instruction/guiding in Scotland, or else run winter
courses (see below).

Glenmore Lodge – The National Mountaineering
Centre
Aviemore, Inverness-shire PH22 1QU
Tel: (01479) 861256
Courses in all aspects of winter mountaineering and ski-
touring. Training and assessment for Winter Mountain
Leader award and Mountaineering Instructors (MIC)
qualification.

Individual Guides (BMG) and Instructors (MIC) who
currently run Scottish winter course programmes on a
regular basis are:
Celtic Horizons, (Andy Cunningham MIC),
Fraser Ho, West Shore St, Ullapool IV26 2UR
Tel/Fax: (01854) 612429
Alba Mountaineering, (Andy Ravenhill MIC),
24, Lundavra Rd, Fort William PH33 6LA
Tel: (01397) 704964
E-mail: andy@alba-mtnguides.demon.co.uk
Web site:
http://www.alba-mtnguides.demon.co.uk/alba.htm
Climbwise, (Roger Wild BMG), Tarradale, Argyll Rd,
Fort William PH33 6LD
Tel: (01397) 700684
E-mail: rwild@climbwise.demon.co.uk
Web site: http://www.climbwise.demon.co.uk

Hadrian Mountaineering, (Mark Tennent MIC),
19b, Carnoch, Glencoe, Argyll PA39 4HS
Tel/Fax: (01855) 811472
Web site: http://www.glencoe-mountain-sport.co.uk
Highlander Mountaineering, (Pete Hill, MIC),
3, Highlea, Auchnarrow, Glenlivet AB37 9JN
Tel/Fax: (01807) 590250 E-mail: highlander@sol.co.uk
Web site: http://www.highlander.vnetuk.com
Simon Jenkins Mountaineering, (Simon Jenkins
BMG), 43, Croila Rd, Kingussie PH21 1PB
Tel/Fax: (01540) 661224
Alan Kimber (BMG), 'Calluna', Heathercroft,
Fort William PH33 6RE
Tel: (01397) 700451 *Fax:* (01397) 700489
E-mail: mountain@guide.u-net.com
Web site: http://www.guide.u-net.com
Martin Moran Mountaineering, (Martin Moran BMG),
Park Cottage, Achintee, Strathcarron,
Ross-shire IV54 8YX
Tel/Fax: (01520) 722361
E-mail: martin.moran@btinternet.com
Web site: http://www.w-o-w.com/clients/moran-mtrng
Mountaincraft, (Nigel Gregory MIC), Glenfinnan, Fort
William PH37 4LT
Tel: (01397) 722213 *Fax:* (01397) 722300
E-mail: mountaincraft@zetnet.co.uk
Web site: http://www.users.zetnet.co.ukmountaincraft/
Nevis Guides, (Mick Tighe BMG), Bohuntin,
Roybridge, Inverness-shire PH31 4AH
Tel: (01397) 712356
Outdoor Odyssey, ('Smiler' Cuthbertson BMG),
Strone Cottages, Dores, Inverness-shire IV1 2TR
Tel/Fax: (01463) 751230
Snowgoose Mountain Centre, (John Cuthbertson,
MIC), The Old Smiddy, Station Rd, Corpach, Fort
William PH33 7JA
Tel/Fax: (01397) 772467

Weather Forecasts, Climbing Reports, Avalanche Reports

Climb Line: West Highlands *Tel:* (0891) 654 669
East Highlands *Tel:* (0891) 654 668
Mountain weather and climbing conditions reports
available on recorded message or Fax. Updated twice
daily. Two-day forecast with predicted summit temperatures, windspeeds and cloud levels plus a three day
general outlook. The service is operated by Ski Hotline
with weather data supplied by Oceanroutes UK Ltd.

Mountaincall: West Highlands Tel: (0891) 500 441
East Highlands Tel: (01891) 500 442
Specialist mountain weather reports similar to Climb
Line

Five Day Scottish Weather Forecast
Web site: http://www.impactweather.co.uk/regional/
Forecast/NOSC.html

Cairn Gorm Weather Station Data
Web site:
http://www.phy.hw.ac.uk/resrev/aws/new_aws_data.html
Read-out of current day's data

Internet Weather Sites: there are several weather sites
with a wealth of information for weather enthusiasts,
including synoptic charts and many links. Two of the
best currently are:
UK Weather Directory
Web site: http://homepages.enterprise.net/meo/weather/
UK Weather Links
Web site:
http://www.greasby.demon.co.uk/weather/pages

Avalanche Forecasts (as issued by the Scottish
Avalanche Information Service)
Free Tel/Fax service: (0800) 987988
Web site: http://www.sais.gov.uk/latest_forecast
Also published daily in Scottish broadsheet newspapers

Avalanche Reporting: details of avalanches witnessed
should be sent to:
Scottish Avalanche Information Service (SAIS)
(Co-ordinator: Blyth Wright), Glenmore Lodge,
Aviemore, Inverness-shire PH22 1BR
Tel: (01479) 861264
Accuracy of avalanche forecasting can be significantly
increased if mountaineers report incidents to the SAIS

Winter Climbs Bulletin Board
Web site:
http://194.164.52.83/ukclimb/reports/winter.shtml
Recent reports on conditions, climbs completed or
attempted, new routes submitted by activists who also
like playing on the web

New winter climbs can be reported to:
Andy Nisbet (SMC Journal): 20, Craigie Ave,
Boat of Garten, Inverness-shire PH24 3BL
E-mail: anisbe@globalnet.co.uk
Simon Richardson (High Magazine), 22, Earlswell Rd,
Cults, Aberdeen AB15 9NY
E-mail: simrich@wintermute.co.uk

Mountaineering Organisations, Clubs and Training Board

British Mountaineering Council (BMC)
177–179, Burton Road, Manchester M20 2BB
Tel: (0161) 445 4747 *Fax:* (0161) 445 4500
E-mail: office@thebmc.co.uk
Web site: http://www.thebmc.co.uk
Unifying body for all climbing clubs in England and
Wales.

Mountaineering Council of Scotland (MCS)
4A, St Catherine's Road, Perth PH1 5SE
Tel: (01738) 638229 *Fax:* (01738) 442095
Co-ordinating body for all Scottish climbing clubs;
access and environmental matters.

Scottish Mountaineering Club (SMC)
The Secretary, 4 Doune Terrace, Edinburgh EH3 6DY
Tel: (0131) 226 4055
Scotland's senior climbing club; now a century old, and
intimately associated with the birth and progress of
winter mountaineering to the modern day.

Scottish Mountain Leader Training Board (SMLTB)
c/o Glenmore Lodge, Aviemore PH22 1QU
Tel: (01479) 861248
Administration of Winter Mountain Leadership and
Mountaineering Instructor's Certificates (WMLC and MIC).

Ski Touring Organisations, Training and Courses

Scottish National Ski Council
Caledonia House, South Gyle, Edinburgh EH12 9DQ
Tel: (0131) 317 7280
E-mail: admin@snsc.demon.co.uk
Web site: http://www.snsc.demon.co.uk/
National governing body for skiing in Scotland; initial
contact for skiing clubs and courses.

British Association of Ski Instructors (BASI)
c/o Glenmore Lodge, Aviemore,
Inverness-shire PH22 1QL
Tel: (01479) 861717 *Fax:* (01479) 861718
Training and assessment courses for ski instructors in
both the Alpine and Nordic skills.

Highland Guides
Rothiemurchus, Aviemore, Inverness-shire PH22 IQH
Tel: (01479) 810729
Courses in Nordic and Telemark skiing; privately run.

Braemar Nordic Ski Centre,
Invercauld Rd, Braemar AB35 5YP
Tel: (013397) 41242
Courses in Nordic/Telemark skiing; Nordic, Telemark
and Alpine ski equipment sales

REFERENCES

SMCJ: Scottish Mountaineering Club Journal
CCJ: Cairngorm Club Journal

CHAPTER 1

1   Dutton, G. J. F. *Lament for the Highland Glaciers*, SMCJ, Vol 28, No 158, (1967).
2   Sissons, J. B. *The Evolution of Scotland's Scenery* (Oliver and Boyd, 1967).
3   Manley, G. *SMCJ*, Vol 30, No 163 (1972) p14.
4   Kilgour, W.,T. *Twenty Years on Ben Nevis* (1905), reprinted Anglesey Books (1985), pp82–84.
5   Begg, J. S. *SMCJ*, Vol 33, No 175 (1984) p49.
6   Baird, P. D. *CCJ*, Vol 17, No 91 (1957), p148.
7   Gillon, S. A. *SMCJ*, Vol 8, No 47, (1905) p233.
8   Tabony, R. 'Changes in Weather in the Scottish Highlands, 1708–present', paper presented to seminar: *The Effects of Global Warming on the Highlands of Scotland*, Kingussie (1993).
9   Lawrence, E .N. *New Scientist* 24 Aug 1996 p46.
10 Hurrell, J. W. *Science*, Vol 269, 4 Aug 1995, pp676–679.
11 Rahmstorf, S. 'Ice Cold in Paris', *New Scientist*, 8 Feb 1997, pp26–30.

CHAPTER 2

1   Brown, W. *SMCJ*, Vol 2, No 2 (1892), pp59–60.
2   Douglas ,W. *SMCJ*, Vol 2, No 2 (1892), p73.
3   Inglis Clark, W. *SMCJ*, Vol 16, No 95 (1923), p266.
4   Broadhead, D. J. *SMCJ*, Vol 33, No 176 (1985), pp170–2.

CHAPTER 3

1   Seligman, G. *Snow Structures and Ski Fields* (Macmillan, London, 1936).
2   Naismith, W. *SMCJ*, Vol 1, No 2, (1890), p57.
3   Patey, T.W. *SMCJ*, Vol 27, No 153 (1962), p282.

CHAPTER 4

1   SMC District Guide, *The Southern Highlands* (1949 edition), p45.
2   Munro, H. T. *SMCJ*, Vol 1, No 1 (1890), p21.
3   Almond, H. H. *SMCJ*, Vol 2, No 5 (1893), p236.
4   McConnochie, A. I. *SMCJ*, Vol 1, No 1 (1890), p12.
5   Raeburn, H. *Mountaineering Art* (Unwin, 1920), p154.
6   Raeburn, H. *SMCJ*, Vol 8, No 48 (1905), p291.

CHAPTER 6

1   Naismith, W. *SMCJ*, Vol 1, No 5 (1891).
2   Geddes, M. *Cold Climbs* (Diadem, 1983), p132.
3   Bonington, C.J.S. *The Next Horizon* (Gollancz, 1973), pp108–9.

CHAPTER 7

1   Bell, J. H. B. *A Progress in Mountaineering* (Oliver & Boyd, 1950).
2   Borthwick, A. *Always a Little Further* (Faber, 1939, reprinted Diadem, 1983), p149.
3   Hodkin, Dr P., et al 'Hypothermia', Report for Lake District Search and Mountain Rescue Association (1994).
4   Munro, H. T. *SMCJ*, Vol 2, No 2 (1892), p50.
5   Lawson, H. G. S. *SMCJ*, Vol 6, No 35 (1901), p154.

6   Nimlin, J. B. *SMCJ*, Vol 24, No 139 (1948), p6.
7   Humble, B. H. *SMCJ*, Vol 25, No 143 (1952), p18.
8   Inglis-Clark, W. *SMCJ*, Vol 18, No 108 (1929), pp333–4.
9   Speirs, G. B. *SMCJ*, Vol 19, No 109 (1930), p12.
10 Murray, W. H. *Mountaineering in Scotland* (J.M.Dent 1947, reprinted Baton Wicks, 1997), p168.
11 Murray, W. H. *ibid*, p180.
12 Murray, W. H. *ibid*, p186.
13 Inglis-Clark, C. *SMCJ* Vol 10, No 56 (1908), p74.
14 March, W. *SMCJ* Vol 29, No 162 (1971), pp364–8.

CHAPTER 9

1   Raeburn, H. *SMCJ*, Vol 9, No 50 (1906), p60.
2   Campbell, R.. N. *SMCJ*, Vol 30, No 163 (1972), p48.
3   Robertson, R. A. *SMCJ*, Vol 1, No 5 (1891), p238.
4   Raeburn, H. *SMCJ*, Vol 8, No 48 (1905), pp297-8.
5   Goggs, F. S. *SMCJ*, Vol 15, No 90 (1920), p316.
6   Williams, G. C. *SMCJ*, Vol 20, No 120 (1935), p396.
7   Murray, W. H. *SMCJ*, Vol 28, No 155 (1964), p2.
8   Raeburn, H. *Mountaineering Art* (Unwin, 1920), p160.
9   Murray, W. H. *SMCJ*, Vol 30, No 166 (1975), p321.
10 *SMCJ*, Vol 25, No 145 (1954), p240.
11 Patey, T. W. *One Man's Mountains* (Gollancz, 1971), p40.
12 Patey, T. W. *ibid*, p86.
13 Patey, T. W. *ibid*, p35.
14 Marshall, J. R. *In correspondence* (1988).
15 Bathgate, D. *SMCJ*, Vol 28, No 156 (1965), p110.
16 Cunningham, J. & March, W. *Alpine Journal* (1972), p79.
17 *SMCJ*, Vol 30, No 164 (1973), p186.

CHAPTER 10

1   Smith, R. *SMCJ*, Vol 28, No 155 (1964), pp29–30.
2   Inglis Clark, W. *SMCJ*, Vol 5, No 26 (1898), p50.
3   Raeburn, H. *SMCJ*, Vol 8, No 48 (1905), p291.
4   Raeburn, H. *SMCJ*, Vol 6, No 36 (1901), p252.

CHAPTER 11

1   Given, J. 'Peter and the Icicle', *Mountain* No 71 (1980), pp22–3.

CHAPTER 12

1   Perroux, G. *SMCJ*, Vol 34, No179 (1988) pp1–3.
2   Winthrop-Young, G. *Mountaincraft* (Methuen, 1920).

CHAPTER 13

1   Naismith, W. *SMCJ*, Vol 2, No 2 (1892).
2   Raeburn, H. *SMCJ*, Vol 8, No 48 (1905).
3   Simpson, M. 'Skisters'. *The Story of Scottish Skiing* (Landmark Press, 1982), p30.
4   Burrows-Smith, M. *SMCJ*, Vol 33, No 177 (1986), p301.
5   Burrows-Smith, M. *'Cruising the Corries Climber'* (February 1988).
6   Watson, A. *SMCJ*, Vol 32, No 174 (1983), p388.
7   Grieve, D. *SMCJ*, Vol 31, No 169 (1978), pp227–36.
8   Firsoff, V. A. *On Ski in the Cairngorms* (W. & R. Chambers, 1965), p85.

GENERAL INDEX

North-East Buttress (B.Nevis) 195
Number 4 Gully (Ben Nevis)
    135, 215, 230

Observatory Gully (B.Nevis) 16,
    17, 180
Observatory Ridge (B.Nevis) 200,
    253, 260 263
Orion Face (B.Nevis) 206, 207,
    208, 209, 214, 227, 242

Parallel Gully B (Lochnagar) 212
Pinnacle Ridge (Sgurr nan
    Gillean) 111, 253–4, 256
Point Five Gully (B.Nevis) 204,
    205, 206, 208, 224, 230–1, 248
Post Face (C.Meagaidh) 79, 219

Rannoch Moor 90
Raven's Gully (B.E.Mor) 176,
    203, 230
Ring of Steall (Mamores) 112,
    114–6

SC Gully (S.C.n.Lochan) 200,
    224
Saddle, The (Glen Shiel) 70, 71,
    112, 118, 174, 181, 192–3
Scorpion (Carn Etchachan) 203,
    265
Sgurr a'Mhaim 114–5
Sgurr na Feartaig (Glen Carron)
    86–7, 238, 239
Sgurr nan Gillean 83, 111, 113,
    121, 122, 253–4, 256

Shelter Stone, The 167
Shelter Stone Crag 177, 211
Shield Direct (B.Nevis) 209,
    250
Slioch 174–5
Slav Route (B.Nevis) 209, 211,
    232, 242–4
Smith's Gully (C.Meagaidh) 205,
    228
South Post (C.Meagaidh) 219
Sron na Lairig (Glencoe) 112,
    121
Stac Polly 113
Stob Coire nan Lochan (Glencoe)
    200, 211, 224, 267–70, 289
Stob Ghabhar (Blackmount)
    108–9, 146, 159, 195

Torridon 113, 135, 143–4,
    215–16, 239, 251–2, 270–1
Tower Gully (B.Nevis) 232
Tower Ridge (B.Nevis) 21, 22,
    175–6, 195, 199, 265
Triple Buttress (Beinn Eighe) 209,
    212, 251, 271

West Central Gully (B.Eighe)
    251
Window, The (C.Meagaidh) 79,
    136–7, 138–40

Zero Gully (B.Nevis) 177, 205,
    231, 242–3, 250, 263

PEOPLE, CLUBS AND GROUPS